The Arms Control, Disarmament, and Military Security Dictionary

Every gun that is made, every warship launched, every rocket fired signifies, in the final sense, a theft from those who hunger and are not fed, those who are cold and not clothed. The world in arms is not spending money alone. It is spending the sweat of its laborers, the genius of its scientists, the hopes of its children.

—DWIGHT D. EISENHOWER

THE
ARMS CONTROL, DISARMAMENT, AND MILITARY SECURITY DICTIONARY

Jeffrey M. Elliot
North Carolina Central University

Robert Reginald
California State University, San Bernardino

ABC-CLIO

Santa Barbara, California
Oxford, England

Library of Congress Cataloging-in-Publication Data

Elliott, Jeffrey M.
    The arms control, disarmament, and military security dictionary /
Jeffrey M. Elliott, Robert Reginald; with the assistance of Austin
J. Lee and Mary Burgess.
    (Clio dictionaries in political science)
    Bibliography: p.
    Includes index.
    1. Arms control—Dictionaries. 2. Disarmament—Dictionaries.
3. Security, International—Dictionaries. I. Reginald, R.
II. Title. III. Series.
JX1974.E45 1989   327.1′74′0321—dc19   88-37151

ISBN 0-87436-430-2 (alk. paper)
ISBN 0-87436-532-5 (pbk.: alk. paper)

96 95 94 93 92 91 90 89   10 9 8 7 6 5 4 3 2 1 (cloth)
96 95 94 93 92 91 90 89   10 9 8 7 6 5 4 3 2 1 (paper)

ABC-CLIO, Inc.
130 Cremona, P.O. Box 1911
Santa Barbara, California 93116-1911

Clio Press Ltd.
55 St. Thomas' Street
Oxford, OX1 1JG, England

This book is Smyth-sewn and printed on acid-free paper ∞ .
Manufactured in the United States of America

To Drs. Susan Pease and Craig Love, for their
friendship, support, and encouragement, this book,
with affection and admiration.
—Dr. Jeffrey M. Elliott

For my wife and collaborator, Mary Burgess,
whose contributions to this book, as with so many others,
have been as numerous and as significant
as they have gone unheralded.
—Robert Reginald

Clio Dictionaries in Political Science

The African Political Dictionary
Claude S. Phillips

The Arms Control, Disarmament, and Military Security Dictionary
Jeffrey M. Elliot and Robert Reginald

The Asian Political Dictionary
Lawrence Ziring and C. I. Eugene Kim

The Constitutional Law Dictionary, Volume 1: *Individual Rights*
Ralph C. Chandler, Richard A. Enslen, and Peter G. Renstrom

The Constitutional Law Dictionary, Volume 1: *Individual Rights*
Supplement 1
Ralph C. Chandler, Richard A. Enslen, and Peter G. Renstrom

The Constitutional Law Dictionary, Volume 2: *Governmental Powers*
Ralph C. Chandler, Richard A. Enslen, and Peter G. Renstrom

The Dictionary of Political Analysis, Second Edition
Jack C. Plano, Robert E. Riggs, and Helenan S. Robin

The Electoral Politics Dictionary
Peter G. Renstrom and Chester B. Rogers

The European Political Dictionary
Ernest E. Rossi and Barbara P. McCrea

The International Law Dictionary
Robert L. Bledsoe and Boleslaw A. Boczek

The International Relations Dictionary, Fourth Edition
Jack C. Plano and Roy Olton

The Latin American Political Dictionary
Ernest E. Rossi and Jack C. Plano

The Middle East Political Dictionary
Lawrence Ziring

The Presidential-Congressional Political Dictionary
Jeffrey M. Elliot and Sheikh R. Ali

The Public Administration Dictionary, Second Edition
Ralph C. Chandler and Jack C. Plano

The Public Policy Dictionary
Earl R. Kruschke and Byron M. Jackson

The Soviet and East European Political Dictionary
Barbara P. McCrea, Jack C. Plano, and George Klein

The State and Local Government Political Dictionary
Jeffrey M. Elliot and Sheikh R. Ali

Forthcoming

The International Development Dictionary, 1991
Gerald W. Fry and Galen R. Martin

The Judicial Political Dictionary, 1991
Peter G. Renstrom

The Peace and Nuclear War Dictionary, 1989
Sheikh R. Ali

The Urban Politics Dictionary, 1990
John W. Smith and John S. Klemanski

SERIES STATEMENT

Language precision is the primary tool of every scientific discipline. That aphorism serves as the guideline for this series of political dictionaries. Although each book in the series relates to a specific topical or regional area in the discipline of political science, entries in the dictionaries also emphasize history, geography, economics, sociology, philosophy, and religion.

This dictionary series incorporates special features designed to help the reader overcome any language barriers that may impede a full understanding of the subject matter. For example, the concepts included in each volume were selected to complement the subject matter found in existing texts and other books. All but one volume utilize a subject matter chapter arrangement that is most useful for classroom and study purposes.

Entries in all volumes include an up-to-date definition plus a paragraph of *Significance* in which the authors discuss and analyze the term's historical and current relevance. Most entries are also cross-referenced, providing the reader an opportunity to seek additional information related to the subject of inquiry. A comprehensive index, found in both hardcover and paperback editions, allows the reader to locate major entries and other concepts, events, and institutions discussed within these entries.

The political and social sciences suffer more than most disciplines from semantic confusion. This is attributable, *inter alia,* to the popularization of the language, and to the focus on many diverse foreign political and social systems. This dictionary series is dedicated to overcoming some of this confusion through careful writing of thorough, accurate definitions for the central concepts, institutions, and events that comprise the basic knowledge of each of the subject fields. New titles in the series will be issued periodically, including some in related social science disciplines.

—Jack C. Plano
Series Editor

CONTENTS

A NOTE ON HOW TO USE THIS BOOK

The Arms Control, Disarmament, and Military Security Dictionary is organized so that entries and supplementary data can be located easily and quickly. Items are arranged alphabetically within subject-matter chapters. For example, terms like *Limited War* or *Peaceful Coexistence* can be found in the chapter titled "War and Peace." When doubtful about which chapter to refer to, consult the general index. Numbers for entries where terms are defined appear in the index in heavy black type; subsidiary concepts discussed within entries can be found in the index identified by entry numbers in regular type. For study purposes, numerous entries have also been subsumed under major topical headings in the index, affording the reader access to broad classes of related information.

The reader can also more fully explore a topic by employing the extensive cross-references included in most entries. These may lead to materials included in the same chapter or may refer the reader to the subject matter of other chapters. Entry numbers have been included in all cross-references for the convenience of the reader. A few entries can be found as subsidiary concepts in more than one chapter, but in each case the term is related to the subject of that chapter in which the entry appears.

The authors have adopted the format of this book to provide the reader a variety of useful applications. These include its use as: (1) a *dictionary* and *reference guide* to the language of arms control, disarmament, and military security; (2) a *study guide* for the introductory course in international relations, or for more specialized courses in the area; (3) a *supplement to a textbook* or a group of paperback monographs adopted for these courses; (4) a *source of review material* for the political science major enrolled in advanced courses; and (5) a *social science aid* for use in history, education, government, and journalism.

PREFACE

Americans believe themselves to be a moral people. Our history is spangled with the stories of conflicts entered—and won—not in pursuit of mere wealth or power, but in defense of a just cause. Still, when it comes to international relations, many Americans disagree about whether the United States should employ military force in defense of a particular regime, or movement, or nation. Some Americans claim that war is wrong, no matter what the reason; others insist that the United States has a moral obligation to intervene wherever freedom is threatened; and still others contend that while the United States cannot assume the role of world policeman, it cannot stand idly by in the face of armed aggression.

This volume is predicated on the belief that survival in today's world is a race between awareness and catastrophe. Our aim in writing this book is to be accurate, objective, and concise in explaining the lexicon of arms control, disarmament, and military security. In the process, we have tried to simplify, clarify, and express ourselves in a readable way. Realizing that students most often become involved in and learn something if the material can sustain their interest, we have attempted to organize the contents in a manner that will maintain interest and, at the same time, encourage in-depth discussion of some of the core questions in the study of peace and war.

Like most authors, we have found other texts on the subject lacking in one or more ways. Some books present issues from only one point of view, whereas others present a potpourri of ideas without drawing conclusions about the adequacy of the points of view they present. In this regard, we have tried to include discussions of the major arguments in the area while still arriving at some conclusions about the correctness of each.

Although this volume employs a dictionary format, it includes several important variations. Entries are categorized into subject-matter chapters that parallel chapter topics in most leading books in the field. In addition to a brief definition, each entry features a paragraph of *Significance* to assist the reader to better understand the historical roots and contemporary meaning of the concept. Furthermore, an extensive cross-reference system is used throughout the volume, enabling the reader to seek additional information on desired topics.

The 268 entries have been systematically selected and organized to complement most standard works on the subject. Thus, the instructor or student can employ this dictionary as a teaching/learning supplement to the core text or as a tool for unifying courses developed around individual readings. Finally, please remember that, in selecting these entries, we have chosen to be discriminating rather than exhaustive; we included only those terms that we deem essential to a basic understanding of arms control, disarmament, and military security. Since we have drawn on the work of so many other scholars in writing this book, we hope they—and any reader—will feel free to write to us with suggestions on how it can be improved.

Several people have been especially encouraging and supportive in this project. We owe a special debt to Jack C. Plano, series editor, who reviewed and critiqued the manuscript in its entirety, and whose intelligent advice, insightful observations, and editorial improvements have clearly enhanced the volume. Special thanks are also due Austin J. Lee, for his invaluable assistance in the preparation of the manuscript. In addition, we are indebted to the professional staff of ABC-CLIO—specifically, Ronald J. Boehm, Heather Cameron, Marie S. Ensign, Ann L. Hartman, and Terri Wright. Finally, thanks and much more are due to Cecelia A. Albert, our former editor at ABC-CLIO, who inspired the project and suggested many ways to make the presentation of the materials more coherent and useful.

—Jeffrey M. Elliot
North Carolina Central University

—Robert Reginald
California State University, San Bernardino

The Arms Control, Disarmament, and Military Security Dictionary

1. War and Peace

Accidental War (1)

An unintended armed clash caused by human miscalculation or by mechanical or electronic error. Accidental war is easy to conceive, but difficult to document. Dr. Herman Kahn, an expert on international conflict, has discovered few such examples. According to Kahn, the last accidental war occurred in the battle of Camlan, during the reign of King Arthur, in which a knight slew a snake. This incident triggered a bitter clash between two rival armies that had gathered to settle their differences.[1] Today, many scholars and laypersons are concerned that, with the advent of the nuclear age, there exists the frightening possibility that an all-out nuclear exchange could be sparked by a misinterpretation of intentions or by the accidental deployment of a nuclear weapon. Still, the fact that there has been no accidental nuclear war suggests that humankind has made genuine progress in its quest for peace. Several arms control agreements have been ratified over the past 25 years, which have served to decrease the likelihood of accidental war (e.g., Limited Nuclear Test Ban Treaty (LTBT), Hot Line Agreements, the Prevention of Nuclear War Agreement). *See also* CAUSES OF WAR, 8; HOT LINE, 17; HOT LINE AGREEMENTS, 240; NUCLEAR ACCIDENTS AGREEMENT (NAA), 254; WAR, 33.

Significance   Accidental war is, in spite of the above-mentioned initiatives, a distinct possibility, what with the proliferation of nuclear weapons. For instance, the development of intercontinental missiles, armed with nuclear warheads, has dramatically escalated the possibility of accidental destruction of a major city and massive civilian casualties. Of greater concern, however, is the possibility of war through misunderstanding or war by miscalculation. In the case of the former,

3

a war may occur when one nation misperceives the intent or actions of the other, as perhaps occurred in Korea, in 1950, when the U.S. Secretary of State Dean Acheson sent unclear signals to the North Koreans, as to the likely response of the United States to an armed attack against South Korea. Experts believe that Secretary Acheson's speech may have encouraged the North Koreans to misinterpret U.S. policy. As for war by miscalculation, there are occasions where one party understands the goals and motives of the other party, but attacks anyway because it is convinced that it will win. In 1971, for example, the Pakistanis precipitated a war with India, believing that they would prevail. Obviously, the Pakistanis miscalculated Indian military superiority, as they suffered a devastating defeat. In recent years, the superpowers have become ever aware of the dangers of accidental war, particularly with the increasing number of new nations which possess nuclear weapons, but which lack the experience and security systems necessary to guard against human miscalculation and mechanical error. To reduce the possibility of accidental war, the United States and Soviet Union, in 1963, established a "hot-line" Teletype communication link between Washington and Moscow, so as to resolve possible conflicts before they could develop into full-scale confrontations. Similar links were established in 1966 between Moscow and Paris and, in 1967, between London and Moscow. In addition, in 1968, superpower negotiations were launched to ratify the Treaty on the Non-Proliferation of Nuclear Weapons. Today, sundry agreements have been signed or are under consideration to decrease the possibility of accidental war.

Alliance (2)

A pact formed by states to assist each other militarily in the event of an attack by other states, in order to fortify the state's own power or to maintain the existing balance of power. Alliances have long characterized interstate relations; they were prevalent in ancient China and India, in Greece during the days of the city-states, and in Renaissance Italy. Indeed, they have held sway since the advent of the modern nation-state in the 1650s. Although alliances have existed throughout history, recent alliances have been marked by increased longevity. For example, the North Atlantic Treaty Organization (NATO), which was founded in 1949, has continued to function on a day-to-day basis as a defense against aggression. In the past, alliances were often short-lived. Born of crisis, they served to coordinate the individual members' military plans and actions. In most cases, alliances are formed for defensive purposes. This is not always the case, however, as some alliances (e.g., the pact between Nazi Germany and

4

the Soviet Union in 1939, which resulted in the dismemberment of Poland) serve far more aggressive aims. *See also* CONFLICT, 10; INTERNATIONAL LAW, 18; POWER, 27; WAR, 33.

Significance   Alliances are frequently formed by states that share a common ideology, similar economic and political objectives, or a compatible cultural identity. Again, this is not always true, as witnessed by the bond between the Soviet Union and the People's Republic of China, or between Nazi Germany and Communist Russia, which boasted radically different ideologies. These alliances are explained, in part, by the old adage: "My enemy's enemy is my friend."[2] Alliances may take one of two forms: bipolar or multipolar. In the bipolar system, superpower alliances are inherently unequal, owing to the disparity in power between the superpower and its allies. In exchange for support, the superpower furnishes its allies with security. For example, in NATO, the superpowers provide the strategic nuclear capacity to deter possible aggression, as well as vital conventional support. With multipolar alliances, friends and foes can shift—that is, all states view each other as potential adversaries and allies. When two or more members grow too powerful, or are perceived as a potential threat, members may form alliances, to counter the specific threat. Ultimately, multipolar alliances depend on loyalty; mutual defense obligations play a vital role. Defections or dealignments threaten multipolar alliances, as they undermine its collective strength and weaken its deterrent capacity. Despite their perceived importance, alliances boast mixed results. In one major study, political scientists Randolph M. Siverson and Michael R. Tennefoss examined the "peace-producing" effects of alliances. They analyzed 256 interstate conflicts (which involved one or more major powers) between 1815 and 1965, concluding that "whether or not a major power has allies does not make much difference with respect to its war proneness . . . while having allies has made a definite difference in the war proneness of minor parties."[3] In other words, "for minor powers, a major power ally was evidently able to provide the augmentation of national strength necessary to achieve deterrence."[4]

Appeasement   (3)
The granting of concessions to an adversary to maintain peace or prevent aggression. Appeasement derives from weakness or confusion, an inability to assess a nation's vital or secondary interests. Clearly, most nations wish to avoid the carnage of war. As a result, leaders may be tempted to listen sympathetically to conciliatory demands, even if they entail the sacrifice of national principles or self-

interest. Appeasement reached its zenith at the Munich Conference of 1938, where British Prime Minister Neville Chamberlain and French Premier Edouard Daladier acquiesced to Adolf Hitler's demand for the Sudetenland in Czechoslovakia in exchange for an empty promise of peace. In this case, appeasement resulted, in the view of many experts, in a loss of security and war. In their view, World War II could have been averted if Great Britain and France had forcefully opposed German violations of national sovereignty and self-determination. *See also* BALANCE OF POWER, 4; CAUSES OF WAR, 8; WAR, 33.

Significance   Appeasement has not always boasted negative connotations. Indeed, at the time of the Munich Conference, it was perceived quite favorably, particularly where it involved justifiable demands. As political scientist David W. Ziegler notes: "To be against appeasement was to be rigid, inflexible, in favor of the policies that had led to World War I."[5] In this case, appeasement failed. Within six months, Hitler abrogated his pledge and seized the rest of Czechoslovakia. The British succumbed to appeasement, argues political scientist John Spanier, because of a variety of domestic and international factors. According to Spanier, Great Britain was "essentially an inward-looking nation.... The need to concentrate on domestic problems and to do something about the economy—an economy that even before the depression was suffering large-scale unemployment—was bound to make foreign policy a secondary matter."[6] Clearly, memories of World War I fortified this view. British policy only changed when its leaders and the public concluded that further German expansion would seriously jeopardize Britain's security and threaten its vital interests. Shortly thereafter, Great Britain and France recognized the folly of appeasement, as Hitler sought not only Czechoslovakia, but world domination, a fact made clear by Germany's subsequent invasion of Poland. In the end, appeasement symbolized the failure of the nation-state system, in that the fear of war and threat of loss of security—both of which were legitimate concerns—served to create the conditions that made war inevitable. On the other hand, another theory holds that the Munich Agreement worked to Britain's advantage by giving that nation time to build some of its military defenses, especially in strengthening the Royal Air Force.

Balance of Power (4)

A relationship in which countries attempt to achieve national security in an environment of shifting alignments and alliances by maintaining an approximate power equilibrium in the state system. The term *balance of power* is a venerable one with multiple meanings. It has been used to describe both equilibrium and disequilibrium among states, the prerequisites for national survival, the distribution of power, and the rules, limitations, and standards that govern acceptable state conduct. Part of the definitional problem lies in the term "power," which has long been the subject of scholarly dispute. According to Karl Deutsch, an authority on international relations, a state's power is dictated by five main factors: geography, population, economic base, military capability, and national character.[7] Despite attempts to define and measure the balance of power, "it may be enough," argues political scientist James Dull, "to know that a balance of power is what leaders think it is and that it exists when they perceive that it does."[8] Thus, if a country succeeds in preventing its enemies from initiating hostile actions, then it can be assumed that the balance of power, however imprecise and incalculable, is sufficiently strong. *See also* ARMS RACE, 65; BALANCE OF TERROR, 5; BIPOLARITY, 6; CAUSES OF WAR, 8; PEACEFUL COEXISTENCE, 26.

Significance   The concept of balance of power, both as a heuristic device in understanding the distribution of power and as a rational and prudent instrument in foreign policy formulation, exercises enormous influence on the decisions and actions of top policymakers. Its impact is particularly evident in U.S. foreign policy, with the establishment of the Truman Doctrine, the Marshall Plan, and the North Atlantic Treaty Organization. A leading advocate of the balance of power system, former Secretary of State Henry A. Kissinger, has written:

> . . . the management of a balance of power is a permanent undertaking, not an exertion that has a forseeable end. To a great extent it is a psychological phenomenon; if an equality of power is perceived, it will not be tested. Calculations must include potential as well as actual power, not only the possession of power but the will to bring it to bear. Management of the balance requires perseverance, subtlety, not a little courage, and above all understanding of its requirements.[9]

Clearly, from 1946 to the present time, the concept of balance of power has exerted considerable influence on the policies of U.S. presidents, as well as on the thinking of the general public. Although it is only one of several key foreign policy concepts, it is certainly uppermost in the minds of those officials who establish policy and define the terms for foreign relations.

Balance of Terror (5)

The equality of power among nuclear nations deriving from a shared fear of annihilation in a nuclear confrontation. The balance of terror reflects the adage, "If you want peace, prepare for war." Simply put, hostile states will eschew war where the possibility of defeat looms large. Likewise, aggressor nations will be more likely to seek peace if the consequences of defeat ensure total destruction. This thought was best expressed by Alfred Nobel, the illustrious inventor of dynamite, when he observed: "Perhaps my factories will put an end to war even sooner than your Congresses; on the day that two army corps may mutually annihilate each other in a second, probably all civilized nations will recoil with horror and disband their troops."[10] The balance of terror between the United States and the Soviet Union stems from their conviction that each side possesses sufficient destructive power to obliterate the other side, should one nation choose to unleash a nuclear attack. This mutual understanding is reflected in the efforts of both nations to develop deadlier weapons and more effective delivery systems. *See also* ARMS RACE, 65; BALANCE OF POWER, 4; POWER, 27; WAR, 33.

Significance   The balance of terror has, for all intents and purposes, served to render nuclear war impossible—that is, if rationality predominates in such calculations. However, many experts believe that the nuclear arms race has exacerbated the dangers of accidental war. Following World War II, the superpowers adopted the balance of terror, which led to the proliferation of atomic weapons. This commitment has intensified with the development of thermonuclear devices and warheads, far more destructive than the bombs dropped on Nagasaki and Hiroshima. Clearly, the creation of nuclear weapons has changed the face of international relations and, with it, the nature of modern warfare. As a result, military analysts have been forced to rethink basic strategic nuclear doctrine. The old guidelines have become outmoded. In the past, conventional weapons served to deter aggressive actions prior to the outbreak of war. Where they failed, these weapons were used to foil enemy actions. Today, the superpowers—and an increasing number of other states—boast a nuclear capability. In some ways, the balance of terror can be viewed as a positive force, which is maintained by deterrent weapons. If these weapons fail to deter potential aggressors, they are rendered obsolete, as they are irrelevant for defensive purposes. In the end, nuclear superiority and parity in numbers of weapons are of little importance. What is important, however, is the ability of nations to produce sufficient weapons to deter enemy attacks. This requires, in the case of the United States, the ability to inflict "unacceptable damage" on the Soviet Union to prevent it from initiating a war.

8

Bipolarity (6)

A balance system, dominated by two superpowers, each with its own political ideology, bloc of supporters, and client states. Bipolarity describes the post–World War II international system, which has been dominated by the United States and the Soviet Union. The term is often used interchangeably with such descriptive phrases as East versus West, communism versus democracy, and dictatorship versus the free world. It reflects the long-standing rivalry between the United States and the Soviet Union, each of which has acted as a "pole" around which most other nations have aligned themselves—thus, the concept "bipolarity." In this system, each superpower and its allies are known as a "bloc" (e.g., the Western bloc and the Eastern bloc). A bipolar system may be distinguished from a "multipolar" system, which is composed of at least five nuclear powers, and a "tripolar" system, which describes (generally, but not totally) the balance of power among the United States, the Soviet Union, and the People's Republic of China. *See also* ALLIANCE, 2; BALANCE OF POWER, 4; BALANCE OF TERROR, 5; PEACEFUL COEXISTENCE, 26.

Significance   Bipolarity attempts to explain the ideal distribution of power. According to political scientist John Spanier, it consists of two superior states, a simple and rigid system, and a cohesive alliance relationship, which encourages confrontation, crisis, arms competition, preoccupation with the adversary's preemptive or first-strike capability, and the search for allies.[11] By contrast, multipolarity comprises many (five to ten) approximately equal states, a complex and flexible system, and a rapidly changing alliance relationship, which promotes self-restraint and an emphasis on negotiating major political differences. Tripolarity encompasses three fairly equal states, a stable system marked by self-restraint, and a durable alliance relationship; it furthers nonintervention in one another's sphere of influence, moderation in each pole's demands and behavior, and abstention from large-scale confrontations and lower-level military encounters. Among most scholars, the debate over the optimum distribution of power centers around bipolarity and multipolarity. Kenneth N. Waltz, a well-known proponent of bipolarity, contends that this system enhances international stability for four main reasons: (1) The absence of peripheries, in which the two world powers involve themselves in events throughout the globe, results in a solid and determinate balance. (2) Competition is both intensive, as well as extensive, as each power is concerned about even small changes in the balance. (3) It encourages the development of alternative schemes for coping with recurrent crises. (4) With preponderant power, minor shifts in the power balance will not prove decisive.[12] On the other hand, political scientist Richard N. Rosecrance maintains that multipolarity is far more desirable, arguing that it: (1) provides increased opportunities for interaction; (2) encourages crosscutting loyalties; (3) minimizes the attention paid to other states and conflict situations; (4) stabilizes the arms race; and (5) provides mediators who can positively diffuse potential clashes.[13]

Brinkmanship (7)

The strategy of deliberately provoking a crisis to the brink of conflict to force the other side to withdraw. Brinkmanship was initially popularized by U.S. Secretary of State John Foster Dulles, who believed that peace could be realized by exploiting the risks of war to expose a potential foe's lack of resolve or ineptness. Brinkmanship assumes that a state can prevent aggression by intentionally pressuring an adversary to retreat from its commitment by demonstrating its political and economic clout. Obviously, the success of brinkmanship is dependent on the initiating nation realizing its objectives without precipitating a war. Thus, many analysts have likened brinkmanship to a game of "chicken." Examples of brinkmanship include: Fashoda, 1898; First Morocco, 1905–1906; Bosnia, 1908–1909; Rhineland, 1936; Berlin, 1948; Korea, 1950; Sino-Indian, 1962; Cuba, 1962; and Arab-Israeli, 1967. Brinkmanship is motivated by three main objectives: (1) to deter an adversary's commitment (e.g., Sino-Indian border dispute); (2) to force a concession (e.g., Berlin conflict); and (3) to humiliate a foe (e.g., Cuban missile crisis). Obviously, these three goals are not mutually exclusive—an act of brinkmanship may involve all three. *See also* ACCIDENTAL WAR, 1; CAUSES OF WAR, 8; ESCALATION OF WAR, 15; PREVENTIVE WAR, 28.

Significance Brinkmanship is usually employed where one nation believes that it can upend an adversary's commitment by capitalizing on a serious internal or external threat, or where one nation concludes that it possesses sufficient strength to force a foe to abandon a commitment when challenged. Political scientist Richard Ned Lebow, an authority on the subject, believes that brinkmanship is motivated by five main factors: (1) a dramatic impending shift in the balance of power of an adversary; (2) the weakness of the initiator's political system; (3) the political vulnerability of a leader of a government; or (4) an intraelite competition for power.[14] Historically, most brinkmanship crises have resulted from domestic or strategic problems which either emboldened or obliged one country to challenge the commitments of the other. Frequently, brinkmanship is inspired by a combination of incentives, each of which reinforces the others. To prevent a brinkmanship crisis, argues Lebow, a state must: (1) define its commitment clearly; (2) communicate its existence to possible adversaries; (3) develop the means to defend it, or punish adversaries who challenge it; and (4) demonstrate its resolve to carry out the actions this entails. Ultimately, brinkmanship results from perceptions—both accurate and inaccurate. Its likelihood is enhanced by the appearance of weakness, vulnerability, discord, and instability. If these conditions prevail, brinkmanship can be a potent political strategy. If the initiator misjudges the situation—and its perceptions prove incorrect—the consequences can be devastating. For these reasons, brinkmanship is a dangerous strategy, one that must be utilized with extreme caution. Failure to accurately gauge the situation can spell defeat or even extinction.

Causes of War (8)

The causal explanations of global conflict. The causes of war are many and varied, not to mention complex and enigmatic. In 1925, the Conference on the Cause and Cure of War posited over 250 reasons for war, grouped under four main categories: political, economic, social, and psychological. In his seminal study of international conflict, Quincy Wright concluded that "war has politico-technological, juro-ideological, socio-religious, and psycho-economic causes."[15] Specifically, major explanations include: (1) war is inherent in the nation-state system; (2) war is caused by conflicting beliefs and values; (3) war is innate in human nature; and (4) war is a natural by-product of a turbulent social environment. Other explanations are equally compelling. For example, political scientist John Spanier contends that war derives from the failure of nations to bridge the gap between their search for peace and preparations for war; states' inability to maintain order and security; and war's effectiveness for achieving national and international objectives.[16] Despite popular folklore, a case can be made that war is neither irrational, immoral, nor impractical—that is, that it is a viable instrument of state policy, which is why many nations are willing to forego the benefits of peace in favor of armed confrontation. *See also* APPEASEMENT, 3; BALANCE OF POWER, 4; INTERVENTION, 19; POWER, 27.

Significance The causes of war depend, in part, on one's perspective. Ethnologist Konrad Lorenz, in his landmark 1962 study, *On Aggression,* argues that war cannot be explained by aggression—that human beings fight.[17] Rather, the problem is that "human beings fight to the death. They kill members of their own species, whereas wolves do not. It is not our lack of humanity, but our lack of animality

11

that causes our troubles."[18] In this regard, as victors, human beings possess the ability to kill their defenseless victims. As losers, they possess the ability to fight even when defeated. Moreover, human beings are prepared to die for abstract causes. In recent years, studies of animal behavior have tainted Lorenz's findings—that is, there is ample evidence of intraspecies killing (e.g., subordinate elephant seals, gangs of chimpanzees, and others). More persuasive are those explanations that point to the failures of the international system. Simply stated, wars occur because nations are often powerless to prevent them. Some experts maintain that wars are initiated by "troublemakers" (e.g., Adolf Hitler, Benito Mussolini, Ayatollah Khomeini, and Muammar Qaddafi). According to psychologist Theodore Abel, "throughout recorded human history, the initiators of war were individuals and groups who held power."[19] This theory, too, is fraught with contradictions. For instance, history suggests that the frequency with which one "troublemaker" is replaced by another calls this theory into question. Ultimately, wars occur because: (1) nations possess instruments of violence; (2) leaders eschew alternative means to resolve their differences; (3) states believe that war promises a reasonable chance of victory; and (4) nations choose to employ force, while their victims choose to resist.

Cold War (9)

The state of fierce rivalry and tension that has characterized U.S.-Soviet relations since the conclusion of World War II. A "cold war" differs from a "hot war" or a "shooting war," in that the latter involves an actual state of war between two nations. The origins of the cold war have been the subject of bitter dispute. Some scholars believe that it began in 1917, with the Bolshevik Revolution, while others contend that it developed following World War II. Although the United States and the Soviet Union were wartime allies, the Soviets became increasingly suspicious of the West, owing, in part, to Western intervention in the Soviet civil war, attempts to reduce Soviet influence in Central Europe, and Western appeasement of Adolf Hitler (specifically, the Munich Agreement), all of which led the Soviets to conclude that the West sought to "open the gates to the East." On the other hand, President Franklin D. Roosevelt felt that U.S.-Soviet cooperation during World War II had diminished Soviet mistrust of Western motives and had created a new atmosphere based on mutual understanding and respect that would ensure that future disputes could be settled in an amicable manner. The cold war, contend most orthodox political scientists and historians, was the inevitable result of a precipitous confrontation in Central Europe, which was intensified by two diametrically opposed economic and political systems, each competing to establish its own sphere of influence. These experts blame the Soviets for the cold war, claiming that Soviet belligerence and aggression were responsible for destroying superpower relations. In recent years, however, revisionist scholars such as William Appleman Williams, D. F. Fleming, Gar Alperovitz, and Gabriel Kolko have argued that the cold war could have been prevented if the United States had adopted an alternative course of action. Although the revisionists disagree among themselves, many attribute the cold war to the actions of President Harry S Truman and his advisers, whom they criticize for abandoning President Franklin D. Roosevelt's attempts to understand and maintain friendly relations with the Soviet Union. Other revisionists fault U.S. capitalism, the decision of the United States to drop the atomic bomb on Japan, and the absence of strong U.S. diplomatic initiatives aimed at influencing Soviet behavior. *See also* ALLIANCE, 2; BALANCE OF POWER, 4; BALANCE OF TERROR, 5; BIPOLARITY, 6; DÉTENTE, 73; PEACEFUL COEXISTENCE, 26.

Significance   The cold war, for sundry reasons, has continued to dominate U.S.-Soviet relations for the past four decades. Clearly, both nations represent different cultural, historical, political, and economic backgrounds, are geographically situated at opposite ends of the world, and are motivated by divergent national and international objectives. Inevitably, this clash of interests was certain to produce hostile relations. Moreover, both the United States and the Soviet Union are driven by totally opposite ideological goals, possess vast human and material resources, and are determined to pursue their objectives with dedication and resolve. Increasingly, however, many Americans have become disillusioned with the cold war policies of the past 40 years. This dissatisfaction has been fueled by a burgeoning arms race and the possibility of a disastrous nuclear war. Likewise, the Soviets have become increasingly cognizant of the enormous political and economic costs of the cold war, which can be seen in their ever-deteriorating economy. Like the Americans, they fear the consequences of a suicidal war and have, under General Secretary Mikhail S. Gorbachev, proposed a series of measures to improve relations and reduce tensions between the two superpowers. Despite these initiatives, the United States remains wary of Soviet aims and military power, as evidenced by their active involvement in Central America and the Caribbean, the Middle East, and the Third World. Still, the two superpowers—despite their long-standing rivalry—share a common interest in avoiding a nuclear confrontation. Recent arms control proposals by both sides attest to their mutual concern. More specifically, both nations share a common interest in stabilizing the strategic balance, preventing nuclear proliferation, strengthening crisis management, and, where appropriate, cooperating in areas of mutual interest. Hopefully, these concerns will produce a major thaw in cold war relations and lead to a new superpower consensus.

Conflict (10)

A struggle, clash, dispute, or controversy between two or more states. Conflict is an inherent feature of life, a salient aspect of interstate relations. Despite its importance, there is no single theory of conflict which is acceptable to both theorists and practitioners of international relations. As a result, most of the discussion about conflict focuses on moralistic or pragmatic explanations of human nature or national self-interest. Forest L. Grieves, an authority on world affairs, posits four propositions about the nature of conflict: First, human conflict is a fact of modern social life and is likely to remain so for the indefinite future. Second, the abolition of war is a dream. Third, theories of Armageddon are likely to be not only empty but even dangerous. Fourth, wars may be inevitable but nuclear war is unthinkable.[20] There are two major kinds of conflicts: those that are justiciable and those that are not. Justiciable conflicts are subject to legal remedies— that is, they are solvable by international organizations and tribunals. Nonjusticiable conflicts are typically political in nature, involving vital national interests. Many of these conflicts can be resolved peacefully through negotiation and compromise. Some conflicts, however, defy simple categorization; whether a conflict is a legal or a political problem depends upon a nation's attitude toward the conflict. *See also* DÉTENTE, 73; DIPLOMACY, 13; WAR, 33.

Significance Conflict plays a central role in international relations. Despite popular thought, conflict may serve several positive purposes, argues social scientist Lewis Coser.[21] These include: enhancing social solidarity, clarifying values, stimulating growth, and promoting learning. Interestingly, notes Coser, "Close contact leads to both friendship and enmity, for cooperation may produce conflict, and that conflict, paradoxically, may promote cooperation."[22] In many cases, however, conflict is mismanaged. When this occurs, the result may be violence or war. Ultimately, interstate conflict is not so much the product of misperception, but the fact that nations boast conflicting objectives. John Spanier, an astute analyst of world affairs, echoes this view, stating: "Human beings may well be alike, in spite of their different languages, clothing, and manner. But politics starts where the commonalities of humanity stop, and it starts here because of the different interests, values, ideologies, and histories of the many nation-states. All want peace—but only on their terms."[23] Obviously, peace is attainable if one state accedes to the demands of the other. However, few nations have adopted this course. Thus, conflict cannot be explained simply as a failure in communication. By itself, communication is not necessarily a potent antidote to conflict. In the end, the problem is not conflict—which is inevitable—but how to manage conflict, so as to avoid the carnage of war.

Coup d'État (11)

A sudden forcible internal uprising by a military or political group to wrest power from the established regime. Coups d'état are precipitated by religious, ethnic, and tribal rivalries, as well as social, political, and economic dissatisfaction with the government in power. Since World War II, over 200 coups d'état have occurred, over 100 of which have proved successful. Coups d'état are particularly common in the Third World, where conditions are often ripe for such upheavals. Possible explanations include: (1) the concentration of power in an isolated elite (frequently the military); (2) the absence of democratic traditions; (3) widespread public apathy; and (4) the lack of any institutionalized mechanisms for succession. Typically, the leaders of a coup d'état attempt to seize or murder top-level political and military leaders, capture control of government buildings and public utilities, and lay hold of the communications apparatus to stem the fears of the masses and win their acceptance of the new regime. *See also* GUERRILLA WAR, 16; POWER, 27; REVOLUTION, 29; TERRORISM, 31.

Significance Coups d'état pose a formidable threat to totalitarian governments, military oligarchies, and even democratic regimes, particularly in those nations that are plagued by widespread poverty and social injustice. Since these governments often rely on terror and coercion to control the people, they face a precarious future, in which dissidents or revolutionary groups may seek to topple them from power. Once a coup d'état begins, these governments are quick to declare a national emergency, suspend the constitution, and impose martial law. In such cases, the government may attempt to place the military under civilian control or, at the very least, to curb its power once the crisis subsides. In many instances, military governments tend to be rather conservative and reluctant to play a major role in the international arena. According to Claude E. Welch, Jr., an authority on civilian control of the military, many Latin American military coups d'état may have resulted from a "fairly benign international environment in which the military is confined to dull, repetitious garrison duty."[24] Welch contends that military involvement in foreign conflicts might have succeeded in reducing their participation in domestic affairs, whereas excessive idleness may have encouraged internal plotting. At times, governments that view themselves as prime targets of potential coups d'état will solicit aid from a superpower nation, hoping that such assistance will reduce the likelihood of potential insurrection. Many Third World leaders depend on the United States and Soviet Union to guarantee their personal safety, as well as maintain their rule. For example, if a coup d'état were to arise in Saudi Arabia or other Persian Gulf nations, it is highly likely that the leaders of these nations would turn to the United States to help suppress the uprising. Obviously, the likelihood of a coup d'état increases when local conflicts and instability exist. These regimes must endeavor to promote order and stability, as well as economic and social progress if they hope to minimize the possibilities of future coups d'état.

Declaration of War (12)

An official pronouncement issued by a nation to proclaim that a legal state of hostilities exists with another nation. The declaration of war requirement, as an international obligation, originated with the 1907 Hague Convention Relative to the Opening of Hostilities. Despite this stricture, many ratifying nations have ignored the requirement, as have most of the over 100 new countries created since 1907. Declarations of war serve several purposes, among them: (1) to serve appropriate legal notice to enemy nations; (2) to inform neutral states of impending hostilities; and (3) to authorize sundry domestic measures, including the use of the government's emergency powers. In the United States, the authority to declare war rests with Congress and is potentially that branch's most awesome power, in spite of the fact that it has not invoked it since 1941. In recent years, some U.S. presidents have claimed the almost unlimited right to commit troops abroad under a broad interpretation of their powers as commander in chief, and have ignored Congress's constitutional authority to declare war. *See also* INTERNATIONAL LAW, 18; PEACE, 24; WAR POWERS ACT OF 1973, 34.

Significance Declarations of war have become relatively uncommon since World War II. Although the United States Constitution clearly grants Congress the authority to declare war, the Congress chose, for a variety of reasons, to vest the president with additional war-making powers. However, the Vietnam War precipitated a new era in congressional assertiveness. Beginning in 1973, Congress approved legislation designed to limit presidential authority in such areas as the commitment of U.S. forces abroad, the spending of funds appropriated by Congress, weapon sales and military aid to other nations, and the international shipment of nuclear materials. These actions reflect Congress's concern over the growth of presidential power, which led some presidents to define the United States as the "world's policeman," often in defiance of the will of Congress. This view was ably expressed by Senator J. William Fulbright, who, as chairman of the Senate Foreign Relations Committee in the 1960s, observed: "Out of a well-intentioned but misconceived notion of what patriotism and responsibility require in a time of world crisis, Congress has permitted the president to take over the two vital foreign policy powers which the Constitution vested in Congress: the power to initiate war and the Senate's power to consent or withhold consent from significant commitments."[25] According to Fulbright, "it is not an exaggeration to say that . . . the United States has . . . become a . . . presidential dictatorship."[26] This concern led to the enactment of the War Powers Act of 1973, which sought to limit the president's ability to commit U.S. troops abroad without prior approval by Congress. Although doubts persist about its constitutionality and effectiveness, the War Powers Act has served to redefine the war-making power of the executive branch. Many experts contend, for example, were it not for the War Powers Act, President Ronald W. Reagan would have adopted a more aggressive military posture in El Salvador and Nicaragua.

Diplomacy (13)

The practice of conducting international relations between nations through official representatives. Diplomacy seeks to eliminate the disputes that lead to war by resolving differences, clarifying objectives, and exploring alternatives. The diplomatic process is carried out by special agents, called diplomats, who strive to promote: (1) respect for sovereignty; (2) nonuse of force; (3) inviolability of frontiers; (4) territorial integrity; (5) peaceful settlement of conflicts; (6) nonintervention; (7) respect for human rights and fundamental freedoms; (8) equal rights and self-determination; (9) interstate cooperation; and (10) fulfillment of international obligations. Diplomatic success depends on myriad factors, chief of which is personal contact. To discharge their duties, diplomats follow codified procedure, known as diplomatic protocol. Protocol places strong emphasis on ceremony, formality, precision, and communication. Diplomacy may be open or secret, bilateral or multilateral, ministerial or summit. Diplomatic initiatives may take many forms: political, military, economic, scientific, technical, cultural, or environmental. *See also* DÉTENTE, 73; INTERNATIONAL LAW, 18; PEACEFUL COEXISTENCE, 26; WAR, 33.

Significance   Diplomacy plays a vital role in interstate relations. Diplomats attempt to achieve international cooperation through the use of negotiation, inquiry, mediation, conciliation, arbitration, and judicial settlement. Obviously, success is by no means assured. Although diplomats work diligently to settle disputes peacefully, wars still occur. Some analysts, such as Hans J. Morganthau, believe that the realities of modern life preclude the success of diplomatic overtures.[27] In the nineteenth century, argues Morganthau, diplomats shared certain common values, among them: discretion, face-saving, compromise, and civility. The "new" diplomacy, however, is markedly different. Today, diplomats no longer come from similar backgrounds or communicate in the same language. Moreover, the new diplomacy is marked by the loss of confidentiality, which is the result of various technological and political changes, including television and government leaks. In addition, increased participation by politicians has complicated the role of diplomats, as has the expanded importance of domestic constituents, who are both vocal and, at times, powerful. For these reasons, Gilbert R. Winham, an authority on international relations, maintains that "diplomats are losing their unique status as agents of a unified and coherent state and are becoming instead political operators."[28] Despite its limitations, diplomacy is fundamental to the maintenance of peace. Clearly, diplomacy has, on numerous occasions, prevented minor disputes from erupting into wars. On the other hand, diplomacy, in and of itself, is not always sufficient to prevent war. Still, whatever its limitations, asserts political scientist Forest L. Grieves, "diplomacy will surely continue to be what it has been in the past, a primary vehicle of international intercourse."[29]

Embargo (14)

A device to prevent the shipment of specific products or all products to a targeted nation. An embargo is an instrument of economic warfare—a method of denying an adversary the consumer products and military hardware it requires to wage a successful war effort. For example, during the zenith of the cold war, the United States imposed an embargo on the Soviet Union, hoping that it could deny the Soviets badly needed supplies and equipment. An embargo is most likely to prove effective when the state initiating the action can persuade its allies to join suit. This is difficult to accomplish, as moral suasion is rarely sufficient to compel compliance, particularly where a nation's economic interests are at stake. At the apex of the cold war, for example, the United States attempted to convince its allies in the North Atlantic Treaty Organization (NATO) to support its embargo against the Soviet Union. However, many NATO countries were less restrictive in the items they embargoed than the United States. Still, in spite of the embargo, the Soviets were undeterred, with the result that the cold war continued to intensify until the early 1960s. *See also* ALLIANCE, 2; POWER, 27; WAR, 33.

Significance   An embargo, although potentially effective, is difficult to organize and maintain. With the election of President Richard M. Nixon in 1968, the United States, as part of its policy of détente, sought to make the Soviet economy more dependent on U.S. assistance. The United States hoped that by offering the Soviets "carrots," in the form of U.S. industrial and agricultural assistance, it could reduce the escalating tensions that had marked U.S.-Soviet relations. In some cases, an embargo can be a potent political weapon. Clearly, the economic strength of the United States—and its ability to extend or withhold essential goods and services to its adversaries—provides the United States with increased political leverage when dealing with hostile nations. For example, in the case of Cuba, the U.S. embargo has exacted a heavy toll. According to Cuban President Fidel Castro, President Ronald Reagan has "incessantly and tenaciously endeavored to place obstacles in the way of Cuba's economic and trade operations . . . to keep us from selling our products, to block our nickel sales to Western nations, to try to prevent loans to Cuba, and to even rescheduling our debt. . . . Not only does the U.S. blockade ban all trade between the United States and Cuba . . . it has also expanded its boycott throughout the world, as part of its unceasing harassment . . . against Cuba's economic operations."[30] Obviously, political concerns frequently dictate economic policy, as with Cuba, and the embargo has been used—frequently, with mixed results—to promote the strategic and security interests of the United States.

Escalation of War (15)

Increasing, enlarging, or intensifying the nature, magnitude, or parameters of a war. Escalation may entail an increase in troops, additional third party involvement, the use of deadlier weapons, or a change in political or military objectives. Escalation may be likened to a ladder, in that the level of coercion and force tends to increase as the war becomes more costly and uncertain. In a limited war, states can employ sundry military measures to challenge one another's resolve and capabilities. In such conflicts, the goal of escalation may be to defeat or force the surrender of an adversary, or to mete out increased punishment to pressure a foe to negotiate or terminate the action that originally precipitated the conflict. In a limited war, military objectives tend to escalate rapidly. In a nuclear confrontation, however, the stakes are far greater—rapid escalation must be avoided, as it could spell instant disaster or extinction. In a nuclear age, most experts believe there is no such thing as a "limited" nuclear war. For example, if one side initiated a war in Europe, even with conventional weapons, it is highly likely that it would escalate inevitably to a global strategic nuclear war, since neither side would be willing to accept defeat in such a critical arena. *See also* BALANCE OF POWER, 4; CONFLICT, 10; ESCALATION, 74; LIMITED WAR, 20; TOTAL WAR, 32.

Significance   Escalation usually occurs as a result of combat decisions by one side, which are prompted by the actions of the other. In Vietnam, for example, decisions by the United States to increase troop strength, expand the war effort, enlarge the bombing, and augment the bombing sites clearly inspired the North Vietnamese and the Viet Cong to escalate their own war effort to resist what they viewed as an escalating military presence and intensification of hostilities. Obviously, escalation is far more dangerous in the nuclear age, as it can result in the total destruction of the planet. In this regard, Paul Warnke, former Assistant Secretary of Defense for International Security Affairs and Director of the Arms Control and Disarmament Agency, contends: "I think that any use of nuclear weapons has inherent risks of escalation to an all-out nuclear exchange. The entire concept of a 'limited' nuclear war makes no sense at all. To contemplate a nuclear war limited to Europe would be adopting a policy analogous to the famous statement made during the Vietnam War— that we had to destroy Europe in order to save it."[31] Indeed, in a confrontation with the Soviet Union—be it conventional or nuclear— it is highly unlikely that the United States (or, if the situation were reversed, the Soviet Union) would permit the Soviets to achieve the upper hand in battle, thus making escalation inevitable. On the other hand, some authorities, like Norman R. Augustine, Chairman of the Defense Science Board, maintain that it would be preferable for the United States to risk the dangers associated with a nuclear war escalation than to allow its allies to be overrun in a conventional war.[32] His views are strongly endorsed by other policymakers, including Charles Kupperman, Executive Director of the Advisory Committee of the Arms Control Agency, who recently observed: "Nuclear war is a destructive thing but still in large part a physics problem. . . . It is possible to survive and prevail over the enemy."[33] Kupperman's position is extremely controversial, as most experts believe that it is impossible to survive a nuclear confrontation.

Guerrilla War **(16)**

Irregular warfare often instigated by political dissidents who seek to win power in order to transform the social, political, and economic institutions of the nation. Guerrilla war differs from most conventional conflicts, in that it is less costly and requires fewer materiel resources. At the outset of a guerrilla war, the revolutionaries are usually far weaker than the government they seek to overthrow. Faced with myriad disadvantages, a guerrilla movement is most likely to succeed if it is able to exploit popular discontent and garner the loyalty of the people. This is essential if the revolutionaries hope not to be betrayed by the people, which could cripple the revolution before it achieves momentum. Thus, it is critical for the guerrillas to win the political loyalty of the people. Typically, this requires occupying a physical area, creating an alternative governmental structure, and providing services superior to those the government is able to deliver. Once the guerrillas win widespread support, argues political scientist Donald M. Snow, the revolutionaries will benefit in three important ways: (1) the people will protect the guerrillas from government authorities, thereby creating a sanctuary in which the revolution can be waged; (2) the people will provide the guerrillas with food and supplies; and (3) the people will be a major source of recruits for the guerrillas' army.[34] Ultimately, the revolutionaries must succeed in winning "the minds and hearts of the people"; if so, the government will find it difficult, if not impossible, to reverse the transfer of loyalties. *See also* CONFLICT, 10; CONVENTIONAL WEAPONS, 120; COUP D'ÉTAT, 11; REVOLUTION, 29; TERRORISM, 31.

Significance   Guerrilla wars are extremely problematical. Rarely can they be won by outside nations, which are often unfamiliar with the terrain and unable to cope with the tropical climates of many Third World countries. In addition, most guerrilla wars are fought in what were once colonial areas, where there is a deep-seated aversion to imperialism. To succeed militarily, the guerrillas must deploy their forces wisely and safeguard their resources. Strategically, they must avoid major clashes with government forces, except where they enjoy a clear advantage. Otherwise, they must retreat or disappear when faced with defeat. Ultimately, the advantage will shift to the guerrillas if they are able to frustrate government forces, who will be unable to locate and destroy the insurgents. This strategy boasts several major virtues. First, it casts the revolutionaries in the role of victors—that is, when the guerrillas engage government forces, they usually win. This, in turn, serves to spur recruitment. Second, government forces frequently become demoralized, as their initiatives inevitably result in failure. This produces desertion, with an increasing number of government troops joining the insurgents. Third, defeated government forces frequently leave their arms behind, which serves to bolster the guerrillas' lack of weapons. The longer the war continues, the more likely the balance of power will shift to the revolutionaries, until they ultimately enjoy clear superiority. With that accomplished, the guerrillas—who have been joined by ex-government forces—will employ conventional means to destroy what remains of the government's forces and to bring about the eventual overthrow of the government.

Hot Line (17)

A set of Teletype machines, linked by communications satellites, designed to expedite the flow of information to U.S. and Soviet leaders to diffuse crises and avert potential conflicts. The hot line was established by a U.S.-Soviet memorandum of understanding, signed at Geneva in 1963, six months after the Cuban missile crisis. Prompted by the slowness of the traditional diplomatic means of exchanging notes (often six to seven hours), both sides recognized the critical importance of instant communications. Interestingly, a missile can travel the same distance in 40 minutes. Despite public misconceptions, the hot line is not a telephone. It consists of two Teletype machines—one in the Cyrillic alphabet, the other in the Latin alphabet. Originally, the hot line was connected by sea and land cable. Today, however, it is linked by communications satellites, and is reasonably secure and immune to disruption. Since its establishment, the hot line has been used several times, most notably during the 1967 Arab-Israeli war, during which period more than 20 messages were exchanged between U.S. and Soviet leaders. *See also* ACCIDENTAL WAR, 1; COLD WAR, 9; DIPLOMACY, 13; HOT LINE AGREEMENTS, 240; WAR, 33.

Significance   The hot line was further improved in 1971, when Washington and Moscow signed the Nuclear Accidents Agreement, which requires its use by each country in the event of a nuclear accident or the discovery of unidentified objects on early warning systems. In addition, each nation is obligated to inform the other of missile tests that will extend beyond its own borders and are aimed in the direction of the other. Still, the hot line is an imperfect system. For example, if one side decided to initiate a first strike, it would most likely use the hot line to mislead the other side into believing that it was only a test. For this and other reasons, the United States and the Soviet Union have developed other means to improve their information-gathering capabilities, one of which is espionage. Simply put, espionage is synonymous with spying—that is, one nation uses agents to obtain secret military or political information from the other government. Many governments, if not most, practice espionage. The danger, of course, is that such activities will be discovered, which has occurred on a number of well-publicized occasions. In 1960, for example, a U.S. spy plane, the U-2, was shot down over the Soviet Union just prior to an important summit conference in Paris. The Russians exploited the incident, as a justification for canceling the summit. In recent years, both sides have advanced a number of proposals to minimize the dangers of a nuclear confrontation, among them: ground observation posts, notification of major military movements, and aerial observation of military installations. To date, these proposals have not been adopted, as one side or the other has objected that they will lead to espionage or result in an unfair advantage in the arms race.

International Law (18)

Global principles and practices which sovereign states regard as legally binding upon interstate relations. Most international law originated in customary law—that is, it derived from standard norms of conduct that have evolved over time and which states automatically accept as legally valid. Along with customary law, international law also includes treaty law, which, unlike the former, covers only those nations that are signatories to the treaties. Article 38 of the Statute of the International Court of Justice recognizes five main sources of international law, among them: (1) treaties (legal obligations between or among states); (2) custom (laws arising from accepted international practices); (3) court decisions (rulings by national and international tribunals, without binding force); (4) general principles (rules that become law because of international acceptance); and (5) writers and publicists (principles that emerge from the works of modern international legal literature). In addition, international law incorporates laws based on common sense and fairness, as well as such other sources as draft conventions, policy decisions by United Nations organs, and resolutions of the United Nations General Assembly. *See also* DIPLOMACY, 13; PEACE, 24; UNITED NATIONS: INTERNATIONAL COURT OF JUSTICE (ICJ), 104; WAR, 33.

Significance   International law is, in a sense, an amorphous term—that is, the word *law* itself is a misnomer. In fact, there is no international government with the authority to impose legal sanctions against those countries that defy international law. International law boasts numerous strengths and weaknesses. Although most states obey international law and honor their commitments, they do so not because they are required to do so, but because of logic, fear, self-interest, and morality. Ultimately, it is the states themselves that decide whether or not international law applies in a specific situation. Unfortunately, international law is often violated in the name of self-interest and self-defense. To function effectively, international law depends on self-restraint, which is, at best, undependable. Where international law threatens a state's vital interests, it is likely that that state will choose to ignore its obligations. Still, most countries follow international law, particularly in such areas as shipping, extradition, fisheries, airline traffic, public health, and telecommunications. Major violations are few in number and tend to be widely publicized. For example, in 1979, Iran seized the U.S. embassy in Tehran, even though, according to international law, embassies are viewed as extensions of the nations they represent and diplomats are immune to seizure and captivity. In this case, Iran argued that the United States had abrogated international law by illegally interfering in its internal affairs. In response to the Iranian action, the United States took the case to the International Court of Justice, which ruled in its favor. Iran, however, chose to ignore the court's decision. In the end, international law rests on common agreement and voluntary compliance. Fortunately, most states respect international law, as it promotes world order and stability.

Intervention (19)

Forced interference in the affairs of a state by another state(s) to affect the domestic or foreign policies of that state. Interventions are usually implemented by the military or by intelligence organizations. These actions may either be overt (open) or covert (secret). In the case of the United States, recent overt military interventions include: Korea, 1950–1952; Lebanon, 1958; Vietnam (plus Laos and Cambodia), 1965–1973; Dominican Republic, 1965–1966; and Grenada, 1983. Major covert operations include: Iran, 1953; Guatemala, 1954; Cuba, 1961; Chile, 1970–1973; and Nicaragua, 1981–present. Other interventions involve the use of military advisers, as was true in the late 1940s, when the United States sent advisers to Greece, and in the early 1960s, when the United States dispatched advisers to Vietnam prior to full-scale military involvement. Like the United States, the Soviet Union also engages in intervention, frequently through the use of proxy forces, as it did in Cuba, Angola, Ethiopia, and South Yemen. Proxy interventions can be quite effective, as they reduce the risks of the nation that initiates such actions. *See also* ALLIANCE, 2; CONFLICT, 10; INTERNATIONAL LAW, 18; NEUTRALITY, 22; POWER, 27.

Significance   Intervention is a salient aspect of interstate relations. Not all interventions, however, are illegal. Under international law, intervention may be permissible if: (1) the intervenor is authorized to do so by treaty; (2) a state abrogates an agreement requiring joint determination by unilateral action; (3) intervention is essential to safeguard a country's citizenry; (4) it is critical for self-defense; or (5) a nation violates international law. The United Nations Charter also legitimizes intervention when it is sanctioned by a collective action by the international community against a state that threatens or violates the peace or initiates an act of aggression. Intervention has predominated since the demise of isolationism, which dates back to the early missionary movements in China and continued with the Open Door policy toward China. However, U.S. intervention has been particularly pronounced in Latin America, following the proclaiming of the Monroe Doctrine in 1823, which opposes outside intervention in the Western Hemisphere. This doctrine has been invoked to justify U.S. intervention in numerous Latin American states, including Nicaragua, Dominican Republic, Haiti, and El Salvador. In fact, U.S. troops have been deployed abroad without a declaration of war in over 100 nations, in the alleged defense of representative government. In many cases, U.S. political leaders have adopted legalistic and moral arguments to justify intervention—often as a pretext to support friendly governments, which may or may not have enjoyed the support of the people. On the other hand, many political analysts contend that the United States has erred in not actively opposing Soviet intervention in various parts of the world. These critics maintain that U.S. policy has become overly reactive—that instead of initiating policy, the United States tends to react to Soviet policy. In this regard, former Secretary of State Henry A. Kissinger maintains that U.S. reluctance to intervene in international crises has enabled the Soviets to extend their sphere of influence and expand their satellites. In Kissinger's view, U.S. policy is essentially reactive—that is, "it improvises a counter to every Soviet move, while the Soviet emphasis gives them the certainty to act, to maneuver, to run risks."[35]

Limited War (20)

An armed conflict, fought for specific political purposes, in which restrictions are imposed on weapons employed and objectives attacked. Limited war, as opposed to total war (a military confrontation in which one side seeks the complete destruction of the other side's armed forces and the elimination of its government), attempts to achieve finite military objectives short of an all-out nuclear contest.

25

Limited wars, argues political scientist Jack C. Plano, may take one of several forms: (1) clashes between nuclear powers in which neither side deploys such weapons nor attacks major population centers; (2) conflicts between small states with no direct participation by the great superpowers; (3) battles between small states assisted directly or indirectly by nuclear powers, waged within a defined geographical area and without wielding nuclear or atomic weapons; (4) military actions initiated by a nuclear power against a small state without intervention by other great powers; (5) internal uprisings aimed at a colonial power or established government in which both parties employ conventional weapons and receive tactical or manpower support, or both, from rival nuclear powers; (6) collective actions instigated by police units of an international organization to forestall territorial conquest or to realize political objectives; and (7) theoretically limited nuclear wars in which the major powers only utilize tactical atomic weapons against strictly military targets.[36] *See also* CONVENTIONAL WEAPONS, 120; NUCLEAR WAR, 23; TOTAL WAR, 32.

Significance   Limited wars, however infrequent, have been waged in recent decades (e.g., in Korea and Vietnam), in which military operations have spanned from two to three years to over a decade, necessitating a major commitment of troops, arms, and money. Limited wars of the post–World War II era differ markedly from those of earlier times. For example, most European wars waged between 1648 and 1914, with the exception of the French Revolution, were fought for limited political aims. However, they were restrained by the lack of large-scale industrial might, and were waged with a technology that lacked the destructive capabilities of modern times. Today, however, notes Professor Bernard Brodie, "We speak of limited war in a sense that connotes a deliberate hobbling of a tremendous power that is already mobilized that must in any case be maintained at a very high pitch of effectiveness for the sake only of inducing the enemy to hobble himself to like degree."[37] In today's world, a nation's political objectives are dictated, in large part, by the benefits and costs of nuclear technology.

Living Room War   (21)

An armed conflict, covered by television, in which on-the-scene, graphic battle reports are beamed into viewers' homes on the network evening news. Living room wars are a relatively new phenomenon, originating, in their present form, with the Vietnam experience. Beginning with the American Revolution, the media have played a prominent role in reporting wartime adventures. Daily war reportage dates back to the Civil War, with the use of telegraphy, and in World War II journalists were escorted by the military to key combat zones. The Vietnam conflict—which was reported nightly by the three major television networks—dramatically changed the nature of wartime coverage. Not only did the networks present daily reports, but their broadcasts served to galvanize public opposition to the war. Since the Vietnam era, the networks have covered numerous other international conflicts, including the Iran hostage crisis, which was reported as the lead story for 445 consecutive days by the three networks. Indeed, nearly two-thirds of each network's newscasts focused on the hostage crisis, not to mention such national news programs as ABC's "Good Morning America," NBC's "Today," and CBS's "Morning." *See also* CONFLICT, 10; VIETNAM SYNDROME, 62; WAR, 33.

Significance   Living room wars have influenced, and will continue to influence, the public's perceptions of future international crises. In many ways, living room wars, such as Vietnam, can either increase or undermine citizen support for important presidential initiatives. By highlighting various international troublespots, television can either reinforce the wisdom of government policy or stimulate a reappraisal of current actions. Some media analysts, such as Doris A. Graber, contend that living room wars have forever changed the nature of modern combat. In Graber's view, "There is a growing belief among politicians and other political observers that fighting lengthy wars has become nearly impossible for democratic societies in the age of full-color, battle-front television. When battle scenes are broadcast nightly in gruesome color in the nation's living rooms, public support for wars is quickly lost."[38] Clearly, television coverage of the Israeli invasion of Lebanon and the accompanying human carnage cost Israel enormous support, even among its staunchest allies. Ultimately, network coverage of international conflicts will depend, in large part, on the political and human drama of the stories. The Iran hostage crisis, like the Vietnam War, contained the crucial elements of which living room wars are made. As media watchers Dan Nimmo and James E. Combs note, "The seizure of the American embassy was tailormade for the American networks: drama, conflict, international tension rising and falling, open and behind-the-scenes negotiations, American hostages, foreign mobs, oil production, hostage families, a stark and simple confrontation between two sides."[39]

Neutrality   (22)
The state or policy wherein a nation refuses to take sides in a war and which stipulates certain rights and duties vis-à-vis the belligerents.

Neutrality permits states to eschew participation in hostilities that could jeopardize their interests or threaten their survival. Under international law, neutral states are entitled to: (1) freedom from territorial encroachment; (2) acceptance of the nation's claim of impartiality; and (3) freedom from interference with its commerce, except where otherwise permitted. In terms of obligations, neutral states must: (1) act in an impartial manner; (2) refrain from assisting one side; (3) deny the use of neutral territory to any party; and (4) allow disputants to interfere with commerce, where permitted by international law. Throughout history, neutral states have steered clear of superpower rifts and wars, preferring to develop their own countries, and perhaps to offer moral leadership to the belligerents as a means of solving the conflict. *See also* ALLIANCE, 2; APPEASEMENT, 3; BALANCE OF POWER, 4; WAR, 33.

Significance   Neutral states are, in most cases, motivated by social, political, or economic self-interest. Despite their desire to provide moral leadership, they are rarely able to offer more than moral advice. In most instances, they lack the military power necessary to influence the actions and decisions of the superpowers. Moreover, the neutrals rarely constitute a unified bloc, which mitigates their impact. Neutrality reached its apex in the prenuclear era; since the advent of nuclear weapons, neutrality has become increasingly ineffectual. Clearly, nuclear war precludes the legal restraints which protected neutral nations in the past. Obviously, nuclear warheads are blind to international law, imperiling neutrals and nonneutrals alike. Like nuclear war, total war reduces the efficacy of neutrality, as commerce between a third party and a belligerent can be construed as aiding the enemy. When commerce is stopped, the neutral nation has only one of two options: it can capitulate or it can take sides. Neutrality, argue its critics, encourages immorality—that is, it refuses to draw distinctions between the aggressor and the victims of the aggression. In this sense, they contend, neutrality emboldens hostile states by refusing to support innocent nations. Moreover, it increases the likelihood of further aggression, as it reassures the aggressor that its actions will either be ignored or condoned. In the end, neutrality may well threaten the interests of third-party states, as the belligerent may conclude that it has little to fear by violating the sovereign rights of innocent nations. These fears are recognized by international law—specifically, the United Nations Charter, which obligates member-states to oppose aggression. Still, permanent neutrality, as practiced by such nations as Switzerland and Austria, is recognized by the world community. Finally, legal neutrality differs from political neutralism, in that the latter refers to political nonalignment in the cold war between the United States and the Soviet Union.

Nuclear War (23)

A hostile conflict waged with atomic and/or hydrogen bombs, in which one or more nations stand vulnerable to destruction. The specter of nuclear war was first raised on August 6, 1945, when the United States dropped an atomic bomb on Hiroshima, Japan, to bring World War II to a swift conclusion. The bomb itself—a fission weapon—was pioneered by German scientists, who, by 1938, had theoretically concluded how to produce an atomic explosion. Today, the nuclear powers possess over 50,000 nuclear weapons, equal in destructive power to one million Hiroshima bombs. Together, the United States and the Soviet Union account for a majority of these weapons, constituting nearly 54 percent of the world's military expenditures. Nuclear weapons have revolutionized modern warfare. Still, some people believe, rightly or wrongly, that a country may be capable of "winning" a nuclear war. Despite their dangers, many nations seek to develop or acquire nuclear weapons for several reasons, among them: (1) national security; (2) prestige; and (3) domestic advantage. At the same time, the pursuit of nuclear weapons is not without costs. Indeed, nuclear weapons may undermine superpower support for a newly nuclearized state; intensify regional conflicts; escalate the arms race; weaken scientific and technological progress in other vital areas; and precipitate severe cutbacks in social spending. Ultimately, nuclear weapons are of limited value, in that they raise the possibility of mutual extinction. Since both the United States and the Soviet Union possess sufficient power to destroy the other side many times over, the use of nuclear weapons has become virtually unthinkable. *See also* ARMS RACE, 65; BALANCE OF POWER, 4; BALANCE OF TERROR, 5; TOTAL WAR, 32.

Significance   The shade of nuclear war has contributed enormously to the balance of terror. The primary value of nuclear weapons lies not so much in their utility as an instrument of war, but in their ability to prevent war. In this regard, some analysts argue that the relative peace that has prevailed since World War II may be due, in part, to the deterrent capability of atomic weapons. Still, in spite of the nuclear argument—which is based on deterrence—proponents of this view assume a degree of rationality that many experts refuse to concede. In fact, the existence of atomic weapons raises the possibility of a nuclear war unleashed by accident, miscalculation, or fear. This danger is further compounded by nuclear proliferation. Clearly, the acquisition of nuclear weapons by thirty or more nations would dramatically increase the statistical odds of nuclear war, as it is impossible to predict what an Ayatollah Khomeini or a Muammar Qaddafi would do with such weapons. As a result, the nuclear nations have endorsed a variety of legal and technological strategies to prevent further proliferation. For example, the United States, Soviet Union, Great Britain, West Germany, France, Japan, and Canada have endorsed a series of principles for regulating their own nuclear exports. In addition, the nearly 130 signatories to the Treaty on the Non-Proliferation of Nuclear Weapons, have agreed not to provide nuclear weapons to other nations and that, if they lack a nuclear capability, they will refrain, to the extent possible, from manufacturing nuclear devices.

Peace (24)

The absence of war or other strife. Peace is, for most states, a prized goal—one that inspires words and deeds that reflect humankind's ongoing search for cooperation and understanding. Yet, in most parts of the world, peace remains an elusive goal. The dictates of national self-interest and power politics have shaped the international agenda. Throughout recorded history, man has repeatedly voiced the utopian aspiration of peace. Indeed, the evils of war have produced a widespread abhorrence of violence and a desire to avoid future conflict. Many early observers viewed war as a disease, one that threatened to engulf the body politic. Humankind could not survive, they reasoned, unless peace was attained. For example, President Woodrow Wilson, in response to a question about whether his plan for a League of Nations would succeed in keeping the peace, observed: "If it won't work, it must be made to work."[40] Clearly, most leaders share a desire for peace. The problem, however, is not peace; it is the means to achieve it. In this regard, there is a noticeable lack of consensus. Today, most international observers subscribe to one of two views: first, that peace can best be achieved through its enforcement and, second, that peace can best be realized through public education and citizen action. Obviously, neither view is sufficient, by itself, to eliminate war. *See also* CAUSES OF WAR, 8; CONFLICT, 10; INTERNATIONAL LAW, 18; PEACE STUDIES, 25; PEACEFUL COEXISTENCE, 26; WAR, 33.

Significance For most persons, peace is a desired end in itself—a goal to be approached directly and forcefully. In the past, however, little emphasis has been placed on establishing the conditions in which peace can take root and grow. To achieve peace, contend many experts, it is necessary to wage a frontal assault on those social and economic evils that give rise to war—namely, hunger, poverty, racism, illiteracy, disease, and inequality. In this sense, peace bears a direct relationship to other human values. Moreover, some critics contend that history and technology have fundamentally altered the nature of interstate relations; that human ingenuity has empowered man with the instruments to either eliminate war or to seal his own destruction. In many ways, the advent of nuclear weapons has led many people to call for peace at any price—even at the expense of freedom. Few persons would disagree with Albert Schweitzer, when he urged the world's leaders "to consider not only our own personal well-being but . . . human society as a whole."[41] Despite such sentiments, it is clear that evil persists in the world, be it greed, exploitation, or oppression. To pretend differently is to invite disaster. In the end, peace will depend on practical idealism or enlightened realism. Platitudes will not eliminate war; neither will human indifference. If peace is to be achieved, the world community must strive to eliminate suffering, hopelessness, and tyranny. This is no simple feat. Its success will rest, in large part, on a renewed commitment to preventive diplomacy, international peacekeeping, and multilateral action. These actions, in turn, will necessitate a reaffirmation of such traditional political virtues as negotiation, compromise, and flexibility. Nothing less will produce a durable peace.

Peace Studies (25)

An academic discipline that promotes rigorous interdisciplinary research, education, and training to facilitate conflict resolution and peacemaking. Peace studies is a relatively new phenomenon that derives its modern impetus from the scholarly contributions of Quincy Wright and Lewis F. Richardson, the first of whom analyzed the study of war, the second, the quest for peace. Peace studies encompasses three main areas: (1) peace as absence of war; (2) peace as social justice; and (3) peacemaking techniques and methods. Peace studies has produced a large corpus of literature in the area of conflict resolution, and has established itself as an interdisciplinary program in over eighty colleges and universities throughout the United States. Most peace studies programs are affiliated with the Consortium on Peace Research, Education, and Development (COPRED), an affiliate of the American Association for the Advancement of Science. According to Kenneth E. Boulding, an authority on peace studies, "There is a vigorous and exciting group of scholars around the world coming from many different disciplines and many different commitments, some out of the peace movement, some out of the defense establishments, who are creating an increasingly significant and cumulative

31

body of theoretical insights . . . and increasingly well organized data collections of practical knowledge in this field."[42] Today, peace studies is dominated by three major currents: (1) a commitment to interdisciplinary research; (2) a focus on ethics and values; and (3) an emphasis on practicality and application. *See also* CONFLICT, 10; INTERNATIONAL LAW, 18; PEACE, 24; PEACEFUL COEXISTENCE, 26.

Significance   Peace studies has become a worldwide discipline. Although it is a loosely knit field, peace researchers meet regularly under the aegis of various international organizations, which sponsor conferences, symposiums, and forums on topics of special interest. Although some researchers are affiliated with the peace movement, most are interested in such questions as disarmament and conflict resolution, regardless of their personal philosophies. Presently, peace studies is characterized by theoretical and methodological diversity, free of any shared paradigm. In recent years, it has demonstrated increasing conceptual and methodological sophistication, yielding valuable insights that are both systematic and reliable. Few issues are more critical in today's world than the constant threats to international peace and security. Clearly, peace theory, scholarship, and education can play a vital role in the management of world conflict. Throughout history, nations have devoted enormous energy and resources to the study of war. Peace studies reflects the view that global peace requires an enlightened understanding of the root causes of conflict, as well as the development of those cross-cultural insights and skills so essential to effective peacemaking. Ultimately, peacemaking requires knowledge, judgment, and dedication no less complex than that required for war.

Peaceful Coexistence (26)

A reinterpretation of Marxist-Leninist doctrine, enunciated by Soviet Premier Nikita Khrushchev before the Twentieth Party Congress in 1956, that rejects the inevitability of war between the socialist and capitalist worlds. Peaceful coexistence reflected the Soviet Union's confidence in its defensive capabilities, a recognition of the dangers to both sides of a nuclear confrontation, and a realization that capitalism could be defeated peacefully by the development of a superior social and economic system. Prior to this time, orthodox Communist ideology prophesied an armed showdown between the two systems, from which socialism would emerge victorious. Khrushchev, however, challenged this view, proclaiming: "There are only two ways: either peaceful coexistence or the most destructive war in history. There is no third way. We believe that countries with differing social systems can do more than exist side by side. It is necessary to proceed further to improve relations, strengthen confidence among countries and cooperate."[43] *See also* BALANCE OF POWER, 4; BIPOLARITY, 6; DIPLOMACY, 13; PEACE, 24; PEACE STUDIES, 25.

Significance   The doctrine of peaceful coexistence did not, however, signal an end to all wars, as the Soviet Union took the position that Third World peoples retained the right to wage "just wars" of national liberation. The Soviets also retained the right to "export" aid to revolutionary groups to counteract capitalist support of reactionary regimes that opposed fundamental reform. Many tenets of peaceful coexistence were restatements of Vladimir Lenin's and Joseph Stalin's analysis of Karl Marx, but recognized the danger of a nuclear face-off as an unacceptable risk to world peace and the spread of international communism. Khrushchev's rejection of pure Marxist-Leninist thought was viewed by many Soviet leaders as "revisionism" at its worst, a heretical transgression. If adopted, they argued, it would seriously undermine the Soviet goal of worldwide revolution. In the 1950s and 1960s, the Chinese attacked peaceful coexistence as a betrayal of Marxist ideology, which would seriously undermine Communist influence throughout the world. This led to a major Sino-Soviet split, in which the Chinese argued that the Soviets had abandoned their historical mandate and, thus, had forfeited their right to lead the Communist world. In the 1970s, however, the Chinese articulated their own doctrine of peaceful coexistence as a basis for a new U.S.-Chinese détente.

Power   **(27)**
The ability of one nation to influence or control the behavior of others. Power is a salient aspect of interstate politics. Generally, the term "power" is used to describe a nation's military capacity. However, power is an elusive concept, as it means different things to different people. In this regard, one must draw a distinction between actual power and perceived power. In most cases, a country's power is unknowable—that is, until or unless it wins a decisive military victory. With the advent of nuclear weapons, and their enormous destructive potential, the power of most nations remains untested. As a result, a country's "perceived power" will often confer power, whether or not that nation has actually demonstrated its strength on the battlefield. According to Hans J. Morgenthau, an authority on international relations, global politics is best defined as a struggle for power. In his view, "political power is a psychological relation between those exercising it and those over whom it is exercised. Further, the

struggle for power is universal in time and space."[44] Thus, international politics is a contest over power, and power is a relationship between states. Typically, power relations exist, argues Spanier, when the following factors are raised: (1) There must be a conflict of values or interests. (2) For a power relationship to exist, one nation must comply, however unwillingly, with another country's demands. (3) One of the parties invokes sanctions that the other regards as likely to inflict "severe deprivations" or pain upon itself. (4) When the differences between states are extreme, force is most likely to be employed.[45] *See also* BALANCE OF POWER, 4; BIPOLARITY, 6; COLD WAR, 9; INTERVENTION, 19; WAR, 33.

Significance   Power derives from such tangible assets as a solid industrial base, a sizable population, sophisticated technology, and exploitable resources, as well as such intangible factors as mass support, effective leadership, and widespread literacy. Despite these advantages, a nation may not be able to translate these assets into actual influence. Political scientist Lloyd Jensen, for example, suggests that: (1) power is a perceptual relationship; (2) power is a relative and reciprocal relationship; (3) power tends to be issue oriented; (4) power is affected by one's expectations in relation to another state; and (5) power is dictated by the tendency of both decision makers and analysts to ascribe high rankings to nations that are perceived as more aggressive.[46] Conversely, nations that lack several of the above advantages may actually wield greater power than might be expected, given their limited resources. Therefore, power is a product of a nation's perceived capabilities, as well as its willingness to utilize its resources. Still, every country is concerned with power—how to get it, how to keep it, and how to use it. Indeed, its decisions and actions must reflect its own power position within the international community. Ultimately, a nation has few policy options—all of which depend on its power position. It may choose to maintain its power (status quo), increase its power (imperialism), or demonstrate its power (prestige). Obviously, power is not the clear, sharp, simple concept that it may at first appear. In many ways, it is an extremely complicated term, one that is subject to sundry interpretations, depending on one's goals, motivations, and assumptions.

Preventive War   (28)
A military strike by one state that enjoys a temporary advantage over another state. Preventive wars, however dangerous, have become an increasing concern in the nuclear age, as hitting first may be believed to be tantamount to victory. If a powerful offense is the best defense,

then a preventive war poses particular dangers in periods of crisis. A preventive war differs from a preemptive strike. In a preemptive war, the aggressor plans the strike beforehand with the expectation that it will destroy the enemy; the aggressor selects a specific date and then deploys its forces, regardless of any possible provocation. By contrast, in a preventive war, the attack is launched to avert a potential strike by the other side; the aggressor strikes first to destroy the enemy's forces before they can be mobilized. Preventive wars are inspired by actions by the other side that are interpreted as belligerent or threatening. They assume that the enemy is planning a future attack, that the time is ripe, and that a decisive strike could eliminate a possible future threat. *See also* BALANCE OF POWER, 4; ESCALATION OF WAR, 15; FIRST STRIKE, 194; NUCLEAR WAR, 23.

Significance   Preventive wars are more conceivable during a conventional arms race between states of limited military and economic power. In the Middle East in 1967, for instance, the Israelis launched a preventive war against hostile Arab forces. The Israelis surmised that superior Arab manpower resources and potential Soviet aid could seriously imperil the existence of the state of Israel. As far as the superpowers are concerned, the United States has, for all intents and purposes, concluded that nuclear technology all but precludes a preventive war, as the retaliatory power of both sides is sufficient to produce a major conflagration, in which there would be no winners. Still, the uncertainty created by a diminishing military advantage, coupled with aggressive saber rattling by a potential adversary eager to narrow the military gap enhances the likelihood of a preventive war. The danger is that a perceived crisis could encourage one side to conclude that a preventive attack is its best chance to wage a victorious war. Hopefully, these states will recognize the risks implicit in such a strategy. Clearly, thermonuclear war promises no victors and, in fact, may well encourage nations to seek improved relations as an alternative to a potentially suicidal preventive war. Obviously, preparations for war, as well as attempts to rationalize one's reasons for initiating a preventive war, can critically jeopardize whatever chances exist to avoid a calamitous military confrontation.

Revolution (29)

A radical transformation of a state's social, political, and economic institutions, resulting from a major upheaval or the overthrow of an established government. Revolutions usually occur as a result of popular dissatisfaction with the regime in power and the policies of the governing elite. Once the revolutionary leaders seize control of government, they may, if they choose, institute the promised reforms that initially inspired their struggle. Many nations owe their existence to revolutionary movements, among them the United States, France, the Soviet Union, and the People's Republic of China. Several years ago, Henry A. Kissinger, former secretary of state, coined the term "revolutionary state," which, according to Kissinger, poses a major challenge to world order. Revolutionary states are not new, nor are they always totalitarian. Indeed, in the late eighteenth century, France could be classified as a revolutionary state in aristocratic Europe. Typically, revolutionary leaders challenge the injustices of the day, be they poverty, illiteracy, disease, or war. Their argument is relatively simple—that is, the poor are poor because they have been systematically exploited by the ruling class. Wars are waged, they contend, to enhance national prestige, acquire additional territories, or secure financial gains. Ultimately, only the privileged class benefits, while the masses die in defense of a corrupt order. Their answer is equally simple: peace, freedom, and justice require the destruction of the established order in favor of a revolutionary regime. By definition, the revolutionary regime is dedicated to "permanent revolution"— that is, the elimination of all vestiges of the old order. *See also* COUP D'ÉTAT, 11; GUERRILLA WAR, 16; RULES OF WARFARE, 30; TERRORISM, 31.

Significance   Revolutions are generally motivated by ideological, cultural, and religious principles. According to Marxist ideology, revolution is the inevitable consequence of class conflict. In Marxist-Leninist thought, history is sequential—that is, states move from feudalism to capitalism to socialism and, ultimately, to communism. In the past, revolutions have been rationalized as instruments of social justice and attacked as vehicles of violence and immorality. In truth, they contain both elements. In recent decades, the world has witnessed the rise of "revolutionary liberators"—states that seek to free others or act as catalysts or supporters of revolutionary movements. As Charles W. Kegley, Jr., and Eugene R. Wittkopf point out, this role conception is particularly common among those nations which themselves developed out of revolutionary circumstances.[47] For instance, phases of China's and Algeria's post–World War II involvements are apt examples of revolutionary liberators. Revolutions are laden with dangers, as well as opportunities. As often as not, they fail to produce many of the changes desired by the masses. Indeed, one order is simply replaced by another order, only to ignore its promises or to institute equally corrupt or far worse practices. Many experts would contend, for example, that the revolutionary movement that precipitated the fall of the Shah of Iran merely substituted one form of oppression for another.

Rules of Warfare **(30)**

Principles and practices embodied in international law to regulate the actions of states involved in conflicts. The rules of warfare, which initially derived from customary law, have since been codified (beginning in the late 1800s) in major international conventions. Some laws govern warfare itself, others limit the weapons of war, and still others oversee the treatment of prisoners of war. The principal international conventions include, among others: (1) the Declaration of Paris of 1856, which restricted maritime conflict by forbidding privateering and maintaining that a blockade had to be effective to be legally enforceable; (2) the Geneva Convention of 1864 (modified in 1906), which guaranteed humane treatment for wounded troops; (3) the Hague Convention of 1899, which codified various standard practices of land combat; (4) the Hague Convention of 1907, which revised the 1899 Convention stipulating the rights and obligations of adversaries, neutrals, and persons, and articulated rules limiting such new weapons as poisonous gas, dumdum bullets, and balloons for bombing; (5) the Geneva Conventions of 1929, which safeguarded the treatment of prisoners of war and the sick and wounded; (6) the London Protocol of 1936, which curtailed the activities of submarines against merchant ships; and (7) the Geneva Convention of 1949, which updated the protections of prisoners of war, the sick and wounded, and civilians. The rules of warfare also encompass a variety of other minor conventions and treaties, ensuring that the victims of war are adequately covered by international law and the "law of humanity." *See also* INTERNATIONAL LAW, 18; PRISONER OF WAR (POW), 60; WAR, 33.

Significance The rules of warfare have continued to expand in recent decades, especially in the area of arms competition. Recent treaties include: (1) the Partial Test Ban Treaty of 1963, which outlawed nuclear tests in the atmosphere, above the atmosphere, or under water; (2) the Non-Proliferation Treaty of 1968, which prohibits nations already possessing nuclear weapons from sharing them and nations not in possession of such weapons from acquiring them; (3) the Seabed Treaty of 1971, which outlawed military emplacements on the ocean floor; and (4) the Biological Weapons Treaty of 1972, which banned the use or production of germ weapons. Obviously, the mere existence of these and other laws is no guarantee of international compliance. Indeed, no legal strictures are sufficient to prevent erring states from ignoring or breaking these rules. Thus, it is a mistake to expect that any rule or set of rules will be universally obeyed. The rules of warfare recognize the impossibility of eliminating interstate conflicts. As a result, they serve as a sanction against the breaking of acceptable standards, such that violators can be held accountable and punished, if necessary. Although it is difficult to regulate the actions of sovereign states in their pursuit of national self-interest, the rules of warfare have succeeded in limiting, restraining, and regulating the conduct of war and the treatment of both combatants and innocent civilians. With the advent of nuclear weapons and ever-more sophisticated conventional weapons, it is highly likely that new rules will have to be promulgated to protect humankind from itself.

Terrorism (31)

A form of state or nonstate violent action that seeks to achieve a political purpose. Terrorism, unlike other kinds of violence, is primarily psychological—that is, it attempts to draw international attention to a perceived injustice, whether real or imagined. Terrorists employ a variety of methods, including airliner hijackings, bombings, hostage taking, assassination, bank robberies, and sabotage, among others. There are three categories of nonstate terrorists, including: (1) national liberation groups (e.g., Palestine Liberation Organization); (2) revolutionary groups (e.g., Italian Red Brigades); and (3) ethnic and/or religious groups (e.g., Sikhs in India). In the 1980s, the world witnessed the rise of a new phenomenon—namely, state terrorism. Increasingly, some states, such as Iran, Syria, and Libya, have viewed terrorism as an attractive political weapon. Brian Jenkins, an expert on state terrorism, has described this phenomenon as "surrogate warfare."[48] According to Jenkins, these nations recognize the limits of conventional war, preferring instead to exploit the possibilities of terrorist organizations, which they may either subsidize or create, in order to disrupt, threaten, or create political and economic instability in an enemy nation. This form of terrorism, maintains Jenkins, "requires only a small investment, certainly far less than what it costs to wage a conventional war, is debilitating to the enemy, and is deniable."[49] *See also* GUERRILLA WAR, 16; INTERNATIONAL LAW, 18; REVOLUTION, 29; RULES OF WARFARE, 30.

Significance Terrorism is on the rise worldwide. Although it is difficult, if not impossible, to obtain accurate statistics on nonstate and state terrorism, the United States government reports that between 1975 and 1985, there were over 5,000 international terrorist incidents. Moreover, terrorist attacks have become far more heinous and more apt to be aimed at innocent bystanders, perhaps because of increased media coverage and protected government facilities. To curb this trend, many Western nations have called for stronger measures to counter the threat of such activities. Still, few terrorists have been apprehended and prosecuted for their crimes. For example, a report by the Jaffee Center for Strategic Studies found that only 10 percent of terrorists were either captured or killed in action in 1984. An international consensus is developing, however, about how best to deal with the problem. Most authorities believe that international cooperation is the single most effective deterrent. In 1986, for example, the heads of seven industrial nations, meeting in Tokyo, issued a six-point statement in which the leaders agreed to ban arms sales to terrorist-sponsoring nations; deny entry to suspected terrorists; improve extradition procedures; upgrade immigration and visa requirements; strengthen cooperation among security organizations; and approve size limits on diplomatic staffs from offending nations. Additionally, these experts have proposed myriad other measures, among them: improved intelligence, stronger security measures, increased public awareness, more effective military and police actions, greater media self-regulation, tightened control of arms and explosives, and heightened public composure.

Total War (32)

An armed conflict fought for unconditional objectives, with unconditional weapons, to achieve complete victory. Total war, which is based on a no-holds-barred strategy, would, in all likelihood, involve the superpowers and their allies. Unlike "limited war," which places restrictions on weapons and objectives, total war requires the: (1) involvement of entire populations in the war effort; (2) terrorization of civilians to undermine their will to fight; (3) deployment of a wide range of modern weapons capable of vast destructive power; (4) participation of countless nations, with warfare conducted on a global scale; (5) blatant violations of human rights and international law; (6) invocation of mass appeals to nationalism, which transform the conflict into a moral crusade; (7) calls for unconditional surrender; and (8) massive reconstruction and reparations of the defeated states as dictated by the victors. In recent years, many experts have argued that total war is the only acceptable war that democracies can wage if they hope to avoid domestic uncertainty and citizen opposition. *See also* ARMS RACE, 65; LIMITED WAR, 20; NUCLEAR WAR, 23.

Significance   Total war constituted a viable alternative in the prenuclear age. Today, however, with the development of nuclear weapons, most nations recognize the suicidal consequences of an all-out nuclear confrontation. While total war may have been possible with conventional weapons, it has been rendered obsolete by nuclear weapons, which promise the assured destruction of society. Thus, most states have eschewed total war in favor of a strategy based on deterrence and retaliation. Increasingly, nations have sought to bolster their security, rather than to rely on defensive measures once attacked. Instead, they hope that massive retaliation will deter potential foes, who likewise share the recognition that nuclear war will inflict unacceptable costs on aggressor states. The age-old goal of vanquishing the enemy on the battlefield is no longer possible in a nuclear age. Nuclear weapons have dramatically changed the nature of warfare. In the past, states could afford to commit strategic errors—given the destructive potential of conventional weapons—and still prevail. Today, there is no room for error, as nuclear weapons promise certain extinction. Although the superpowers today possess unprecedented destructive power, they are helpless to prevent attack and destruction, should one side choose to launch a first strike. In this sense, total war is clearly irrational; the costs of victory are simply too high. As political scientist John Spanier suggests, "Nuclear technology has so vastly augmented the scope of violence and destruction that total war can destroy the very nation that wages it and can do so in a matter of hours, not years."[50] Clearly, peace and security cannot be achieved with nuclear weapons, which is why most nations realize that they ultimately depend on the avoidance of total war.

War (33)

Belligerent actions within or among states or territories conducted by military force. War is legally said to exist when two or more nations declare officially that a condition of hostility exists between them. Despite the above definition, there is no consensus as to the precise definition of war. Moreover, in spite of the serious nature of war, and its impact on the world community, few scholars have produced major works on international conflict. Most of what does exist—which is of relatively recent vintage—has been written by military analysts, philosophers, and historians. Few social scientists have conducted empirical studies of the root causes of war. In recent years, however, an increasing number of social scientists, such as Quincy Wright, in his 1942 two-volume work entitled *A Study of War,* have examined this important phenomenon. In addition, several universities have established institutes, degree programs, and symposia to analyze the dynamics of war and peace. *See also* CAUSES OF WAR, 8; CONFLICT, 10; DECLARATION OF WAR, 12; INTERNATIONAL LAW, 18; PEACE, 24; RULES OF WARFARE, 30; WAR POWERS ACT OF 1973, 34.

Significance War defies a simple dictionary definition, as it is often difficult to explain or laden with contradictions, encompassing a wide variety of political, ideological, economic, religious, cultural, ethnic, historical, and psychological factors. Despite recent attempts by political scientists, diplomats, sociologists, and psychologists to produce a commonly accepted definition of war, these efforts have proven unsuccessful. Part of the difficulty stems from the fact that the varying definitions reflect very different perspectives—that is, some experts focus on war as a condition, others on the techniques of war, still others on the assumptions underlying aggressive behavior, and still others on the causes of war. Despite these definitional difficulties, the history of war is as old as human history. Most experts would agree that war is aberrational—at best a grievous error, at worst a criminal action. Still, war is only one form of conflict that occurs among nations. Unfortunately, global relations—and the struggle for power— are often resolved through bloodshed. In theory, peace should be the natural order of things; in reality, war is a widely practiced method of settling disputes. In the past, many nations have viewed war as imaginable, controllable, and profitable. Today, with the ever-present threat of nuclear weapons and the destructiveness they represent, a growing number of states have been forced to rethink their position. Nuclear states recognize, all too well, the dangers that such weapons pose, which is why their concern has shifted to deterrence and retaliation. In this regard, most leaders would agree with former British Prime Minister Winston S. Churchill, who, at the conclusion of World War I, wrote: "Mankind has got into its hands for the first time the tools by which it can unfailingly accomplish its own extermination."[51] This is why, perhaps, war has become increasingly unacceptable as a means of resolving international conflicts.

War Powers Act of 1973 (34)

A measure to restrict the war-making power of the U.S. president and to hold the chief executive more accountable to the Congress. The War Powers Act, which was approved in the wake of the Vietnam War, requires the president, wherever possible, to consult with Congress prior to the deployment of U.S. combat forces. The act stipulates three emergency situations in which the president is authorized to commit U.S. troops without a formal congressional declaration of war: (1) to resist or discourage an attack on the United States; (2) to defeat or deter an attack on U.S. forces abroad; and (3) to rescue U.S. citizens in specifically defined circumstances. If the president chooses to invoke his emergency powers, he must still, under the act, issue a full report to the Congress and secure formal authorization for any action beyond 60 days. The Congress may, if it so desires, extend the commitment for an additional 30 days (if the troops are endangered) without approving a declaration of war. If the Congress opposes the extension, the president must withdraw all troops. The Congress may, however, terminate the action prior to the 60-day period through a concurrent resolution (a special measure passed by one house of Congress, with the agreement of the other), which is not subject to a presidential veto. *See also* COMMANDER IN CHIEF, 39; DECLARATION OF WAR, 12; INTERVENTION, 19; WAR, 33.

Significance   The War Powers Act of 1973 reflected Congress's desire to play a more active role in the foreign policy process. At the time it was approved, the measure was hailed as a landmark achievement. Indeed, Senator Jacob K. Javits (R-N.Y.) proclaimed: "Never in the history of this country has any effort been made to restrain the war powers in the hands of the President. . . . [This bill] will make history in this country as has never been made before."[52] However, congressional critics, such as Senator Barry M. Goldwater (R-Ariz.), argued that under the language of the act, "the President is no longer prohibited from initiating original actions. He needs only to report during the first sixty days. . . . This language puts into law language that is not contained in the Constitution."[53] Interestingly, Senator Thomas F. Eagleton (D-Mo.), an author of the act, agreed, in part, with Senator Goldwater's analysis, declaring: "If this becomes law we have given a predated declaration of war to the president . . . courtesy of the U.S. Congress. . . . [This] is not what the Constitution . . . envisaged when we were given the authority to declare war. We were to decide *ab initio*, at the outset, and not *post facto*. . . . This is an historic tragedy."[54] Clearly, Congress hoped to require executive consultation and codetermination of the use of armed force by the United States. In reality, neither Senators Eagleton nor Javits proved correct, as the act presaged a redefinition of the chief executive's war-making power. Although the War Powers Act has been invoked, but not constitutionally tested, many experts maintain that it is not likely to produce Congress's hoped-for codetermination of policy.

2. Military Security

Air Force (35)

The branch of the armed forces responsible for military operations in air and in space. The air force maintains aircraft and missiles on constant alert in the event of a surprise air or missile assault. To deter such an attack, the air force possesses the might to immediately strike back with nuclear and conventional weapons. It also assists ground forces in combat and shields them from air attack. Transport planes distribute troops and supplies wherever required, and reconnaissance aircraft monitor the movements of the enemy. In addition, the air force is actively engaged in scientific and technological research. The youngest branch of the United States armed forces, the air force became independent in 1947. Prior to that, it had been part of the army. The air branch was created in 1907, when the Army Signal Corps established an Aeronautical Division. The primary functions of the air force are to: (1) protect the nation against air attack; (2) achieve and maintain air superiority; (3) engage and defeat enemy air forces; (4) control vital air spaces; (5) establish joint doctrines, in conjunction with the other services, for the country's defense against air attack; (6) conduct strategic air warfare; (7) assist the other military arms in combined amphibious and airborne missions; (8) provide close combat and logistical air support to the army; (9) furnish air transport for the armed forces; and (10) conduct aerial photography. The air force, which operates under the Department of the Air Force, comprises 600,000 men and women on active duty throughout the world. Its reserves total more than 235,000. It also employs approximately 250,000 civilians. In addition to over 7,000 aircraft on active duty, the air force has about 2,000 airplanes in reserve and Air National Guard units. Located in Washington, D.C., the Department of the Air Force is one of three military departments within the Department of Defense. The department provides support for national and international policy by organizing, training, and equipping the air force. It is headed by the secretary of the air force, who is a civilian. The secretary operates under the direction of the secretary of defense, and enjoys a rank equal to the secretaries of the army and navy. *See also* ALL-VOLUNTEER FORCE (AVF), 36; MILITARY FORCES, 47; MILITARY LEADERSHIP, 49; MILITARY MANPOWER, 50.

Significance   The air force performs a variety of missions. Defensively, the air force helps to defend the nation against enemy air and missile attack. This task is the responsibility of the North American Aerospace Defense Command (NORAD), which is located near Colorado Springs, Colorado. Offensively, the primary goal of the air force is to attack and defeat the enemy. Air attack can occur unexpectedly, at long range, and with devastating power. The air force engages in two main types of air attacks: tactical and strategic. Tactical air attacks involve the direct help given to ground or sea units in battle, while strategic air attacks hit far behind the battle lines. As a deterrent force, the strategic air force seeks to deter war. In peacetime, the air force attempts to abate emergencies short of war (e.g., the Berlin airlift). The air force uses numerous aircraft, most of which are driven by jet engines. Many carry only a pilot; others have a full crew; still others are guided only by electronic devices. Air force weapons include bombers (e.g., B-52), fighters (e.g., F-15), and missiles (e.g., surface-to-surface, air-to-surface, air interceptor). Air force recruits—which include both men and women—spend about six weeks as basic trainees. They study air force organization, citizenship, military customs, and mathematics. In addition, they exercise and drill to improve their physical stamina. The air force has more than 40 career fields from which to choose. The air force offers several programs for training officers, among them: the Air Force Academy, Air Force Reserve Officers Training Corps (AFROTC), and the Officers Training School (OTS). Most new recruits are trained in the AFROTC and OTS programs. The air force has long played a critical role in the contemporary world of destructive power. Following World War II, for example, the air force implemented the Berlin airlift, in which it transported food, fuel, and sundry other supplies to the over two million people of West Berlin, who were blockaded by the Soviet Union. In the Korean War (1950–1953), jet aircraft battled for the first time. During the Vietnam War in the 1960s and 1970s, the air force employed heavy bombardment to defeat the enemy's jungle guerrilla warfare. Although almost three times the tonnage of bombs dropped during all of World War II were dropped on North

Vietnam and other targets in that region, they failed to produce the expected results. In 1986, the air force struck targets in Tripoli and Benghazi, Libya, in retaliation against the alleged Libyan bombing of a West Berlin discotheque in which two civilians died and 200 others were wounded. This attack was justified, argued President Ronald W. Reagan, due to Libya's long-standing support of state-sponsored terrorism in the Middle East and Western Europe.

All-Volunteer Force (AVF) (36)

A system of military manpower recruitment, in which young men and women willingly enlist in the armed forces for personal career motives and to serve their country. The all-volunteer force (AVF) was instituted in 1973, in response to the abolition of the draft. In its infancy, the AVF engendered considerable skepticism. Many experts—both civilian and military—publicly doubted whether voluntary enlistments would provide the necessary manpower. Born in the post–Vietnam War era, at the height of the "me generation," the AVF found it extremely difficult to attract sufficient recruits. In addition, a strong national economy, marked by low teenage unemployment, served to undercut first-term enlistments. Moreover, increased competition in the civilian sector for skilled manpower also hampered reenlistment rates. For these reasons, the AVF faced innumerable qualitative and quantitative problems. Qualitatively, the armed forces experienced myriad problems in attracting young people with the requisite intelligence and education. The problem was compounded by the unwillingness of veteran personnel, especially noncommissioned officers, to reenlist. In the latter case, many NCOs, who were frustrated by the low quality of new recruits, were attracted by higher salaries for equivalent work in the civilian sector. Quantitatively, virtually all of the services faced countless obstacles in securing the enlistments and reenlistments necessary to meet their manpower quotas. The problem was especially severe for the army—and, more specifically, its combat sector (the actual fighting force). However, the situation improved markedly in 1980, and continued to improve during President Ronald W. Reagan's first term. Donald M. Snow, a national defense expert, notes that "the administration moved vigorously to improve salaries to make military service financially equivalent to civilian jobs and initiated an aggressive advertising campaign to attract recruits."[1] *See also* MANPOWER PROCUREMENT, 45; MILITARY FORCES, 47; MILITARY MANPOWER, 50; SELECTIVE SERVICE, 61.

Significance　　The all-volunteer force has continued to prove its critics wrong. Although the Reagan administration has claimed credit for the turnaround, several other factors have contributed to its success. First, the turnaround coincided with a major surge in the pool of new eighteen-year-olds. Indeed the "baby boom" generation peaked in 1980, with a record 2.1 million eighteen-year-old males in the population. Second, the early 1980s were marked by an economic recession, accompanied by a rise in unemployment, a development which served to increase the number of new recruits. The unemployment rate soared among minority teenagers—to over 40 percent—many of whom enlisted in the armed forces in search of economic opportunity. Third, the period witnessed a resurgence in traditional patriotism, inspired in large part by President Reagan, which clearly served to spur recruitment rates. For these reasons, former Secretary of Defense Caspar W. Weinberger, in his 1984 *Annual Report to the Congress*, was able to state "that all services had met their manpower goals for the preceding year, that the navy and air force had set records for reenlistment in 1983, and that fully 91 percent of the first-term enlistees were high school graduates (compared with 68 percent in 1980)."[2] Despite this "rosy" assessment, several potential problems loom on the horizon. First, demographically, the number of eighteen-year-olds will continue to decline until the end of the decade. This will produce increased competition for the best-qualified young people. Second, from an economic perspective, it is questionable whether the government will be able to continue to make military service attractive to this group. Indeed, "many critics wonder . . . how far equalization can be carried [making military compensation equivalent to pay for similar work outside the military] and whether one can ever make the discipline of military life essentially like that outside the military."[3] Third, there are questions whether today's AVF—given the sophistication of existing weapons systems—can be efficiently operated.

Army (37)

The branch of the armed forces that is charged with military land operations. The army must stand ready to employ immediate decisive action to deter any foe that might threaten the United States or its interests in other parts of the world. Approximately half of the army's combat-ready troops are stationed at overseas bases. The army assists U.S. allies and provides them with the equipment and know-how they need to defend themselves. In addition to its military-related activities, the army often assists in disasters (e.g., epidemics, forest fires, storms, and floods). In this regard, the army coordinates the disaster-relief efforts of the armed services. The oldest branch of the armed services, its history can be traced back to 1775, when the Continental

Congress established the Continental Army, under the command of George Washington. Since its inception, the army has continued to expand its capabilities and strength. Its weapons have grown in power, sophistication, and accuracy, going from muzzle-loading muskets to atomic bursts delivered by guns and missiles. Similarly, army transport has grown from horses and wagons to trucks and aircraft. Battlefield strength has been enhanced by the use of aircraft and airborne troops, while the radio, telegraph, and television have dramatically transformed military communications. Presently, the army includes about 780,000 men and women on active duty throughout the world. Nearly one million men and women serve in the U.S. Army Reserve and National Guard. In addition, the army employs over 410,000 civilians. Located in Washington, D.C., the army is headed by the secretary of the army, a civilian appointed by the president. *See also* MANPOWER PROCUREMENT, 45; MILITARY FORCES, 47; MILITARY MANPOWER, 50; SELECTIVE SERVICE, 61.

Significance   Army combat forces consist of soldiers trained and equipped to fight enemy forces. Major combat arms (units) include the infantry, artillery, air defense artillery, and armored units. In addition, other army units, called the "combat support" and "combat service support," assist the combat arms. The infantry is the army's largest arm; its role is to capture, hold, and defend land areas. Typical weapons include grenades, fire rifles, machine guns, mortars, pistols, flame throwers, and sundry types of rockets and missiles. Artillery provides the firepower required for a successful attack by infantry or armored units. In the case of the army, armor includes tanks and other armored vehicles. Army armored units can move rapidly and penetrate deep into enemy territory. They also possess strong firepower. The army's battlefield mobility is bolstered by army aviation, whose aircraft can identify enemy targets for artillery units. They also provide rapid transportation to and from the front lines, as well as transport troops and supplies and carry wounded soldiers to hospitals located in the rear areas. The army's missile arsenal includes both free rockets and guided missiles. Rockets provide fire support for troops in the field, while guided missiles may be fired from ground to ground in support of troops. Army enlistees attend basic training at an army training center, during which time they learn marksmanship, drill, first aid, and land navigation. In addition, they undergo intensive physical training and are taught to act as part of a disciplined team. After basic training, most soldiers attend a school to learn the special techniques of the branch of the army in which they will serve. These schools are located on military posts throughout the nation. Prospective army officers must follow one of several paths: (1) the

United States Military Academy at West Point; (2) Reserve Officers Training Corps (ROTC) at many colleges and universities; (3) officer candidate schools conducted by the U.S. Army and by state national guards; and (4) direct commissions to civilians with such specialized skills as law and medicine. Officers may receive further training and education by completing courses in branch schools or by correspondence. Additional education may be received in the U.S. Army Command and General Staff College at Fort Leavenworth, Kansas.

Coast Guard (38)

The main federal agency for maritime law enforcement and military safety in peacetime and in war. The Coast Guard falls under the United States Navy in wartime and the Department of Transportation in peacetime. Founded in 1790, the Coast Guard has undergone several name changes; it was officially dubbed the United States Coast Guard in 1915. Since 1790, it has expanded from a fleet of ten cutters (ships) to an effective force of ships and airplanes. The Coast Guard has fought in every war in which the United States has been involved. Under the direction of the navy in wartime, it maintains a port-security program, provides air-sea rescue services, escorts convoys, and staffs troop transports. It boasts a peacetime strength of 39,000 active and 12,000 reserve members. The Coast Guard, which is directed by a commandant, is headquartered in Washington, D.C. It is charged with five main responsibilities: (1) enforcing or assisting in enforcing all pertinent federal laws; (2) administering laws and establishing and enforcing regulations for the promotion of safety of life and property; (3) developing, establishing, maintaining, and operating aids to maritime navigation, rescue services, and icebreaking facilities; (4) conducting oceanographic research; and (5) maintaining its readiness at all times to operate as a service of the navy. The Coast Guard is unique among nations, owing to its military character and broad range of functions. *See also* MANPOWER PROCUREMENT, 45; MILITARY FORCES, 47; MILITARY MANPOWER, 50; NAVY, 57.

Significance The Coast Guard operates a fleet of several hundred ships and boats that can perform various missions. These vessels include cutters, fireboats, icebreakers, lifeboats, motorboats, surfboats, tenders, and tugs. Aircraft play a salient role in Coast Guard operations. It uses numerous types of aircraft for patrol, search, and rescue missions. Helicopters are particularly important, both in air-sea rescues and in inland areas that could not otherwise be reached. In World War II, Coast Guard aircraft bombed enemy submarines. They were also used to rescue many survivors of torpedoed ships. Coast

Guard vessels are armed with at least small arms, which range from .45-caliber pistols, M-16 rifles, and machine guns on small patrol vessels to five-inch guns on large cutters. Some Coast Guard ships also carry sonar and antisubmarine weapons. Coast Guard cadets and recruits receive small-arms training. It also offers a special training program for crews of small-armed vessels. The Coast Guard's military structure is similar to that of the other armed forces. The majority of its commissioned officers are graduates of the United States Coast Guard Academy; others enter by direct commission from the merchant marine; and still others come from the Coast Guard Officer Candidate School at Yorktown, Virginia. The Coast Guard has played a key role in several major conflicts. During World War II, for example, the Coast Guard performed polar icebreaking. When the Korean War broke out in 1950, the Coast Guard initiated an extensive port-security program and built stations to provide navigational facilities to aircraft and surface vessels that might become involved in the conflict. From 1965 to 1972, during the Vietnam War, a Coast Guard squadron patrolled the coastal waters of South Vietnam; 52 cutters were assigned to prevent the flow of enemy troops and equipment from North Vietnam to South Vietnam. Today, the Coast Guard is actively involved in fighting drug smuggling. Charged with responsibility for drug interdiction, the Coast Guard has proven moderately successful in stemming the flow of drugs into the United States.

Commander in Chief (39)

The role of the president as supreme leader of the armed forces of the United States. The commander in chief's authority is defined in Article II, Section 2 of the Constitution. As commander in chief, the president has the ultimate responsibility for the conduct of the armed forces, which guarantees civilian supremacy. Although presidents exercise civilian control, they may delegate certain powers to the secretary of defense, national security advisers, and Joint Chiefs of Staff. During the Whiskey Rebellion in 1794, for example, President George Washington led the troops into Pennsylvania. In the Civil War in the 1860s, President Abraham Lincoln often visited army camps to instruct the officers. Today, presidents do not personally lead the troops in wartime, but they make major decisions on the deployment of the armed forces, as well as the strategy to be followed. Presidents Woodrow Wilson, Franklin D. Roosevelt, Harry S Truman, Lyndon B. Johnson, Richard M. Nixon, and Ronald W. Reagan all authorized the use of U.S. combat forces abroad without a congressional declaration of war. Presidential authority over the armed forces is dramatically illustrated by President Truman's removal of General

Douglas MacArthur as U.S. and United Nations commander in Korea in 1951 for publicly disobeying orders. In war, as well as in peace, the president is the commander in chief. This role is made clear by the locked briefcase stuffed with nuclear codes, sometimes called the "football" or "black box," which is kept near the president, in the event that he must order a nuclear retaliation. *See also* DECLA-RATION OF WAR, 12; MILITARY FORCES, 47; WAR POWERS ACT, 34; WHITE HOUSE SITUATION ROOM, 209.

Significance   The commander in chief may not only deploy the armed forces in support of U.S. foreign policy, but may also take the nation into war. The authority of the commander in chief is an important instrument of the president's foreign and military power, with control over a defense establishment of over two million people. U.S. bases and fleets are scattered all over the world and stand as a constant reminder of presidential supremacy in world affairs. Although the Constitution clearly establishes the principle of civilian control over the military, it is debatable whether the president is empowered to order troops into battle without congressional authorization. Of the nearly 200 wars and military actions undertaken by the United States in its history, only five wars have been formally declared. These include the War of 1812, the Mexican War (1846), the Spanish-American War (1898), World War I (1914–1918), and World War II (1939–1945). Since Japan's surprise attack on Pearl Harbor in 1941, presidents have ordered large-scale combat forces into Korea (1950–1953), Vietnam (1962–1973), Cambodia (1975), and many small-scale incursions. The United States suffered 137,000 military casualties in Korea and 200,000 in Southeast Asia. These costly presidential military actions underscore the primacy of the president's role as commander in chief. To curb the expansion of presidential power in this area, Congress passed the War Powers Act of 1973. This act limits presidentially ordered foreign combat to 60 days and requires the president to report to Congress within 48 hours of the decision to deploy U.S. troops abroad. The president and Congress frequently clash over authorizing and funding wars and weapons systems, although the president prevails in most cases. These battles with Congress, however, are not always easily won by the commander in chief.

Counterintelligence   (40)

That branch of offensive intelligence which specializes in destroying the ability of enemy foreign agents to collect vital security information. Counterintelligence agents employ various physical safeguards and deception to identify and deter enemy saboteurs, subversives, and espionage agents. Despite popular misconceptions, contends Andrew Wilson, an authority on military technology and organization, counterintelligence does not involve the apprehension of enemy agents, which is the province of security. Counterintelligence agents will typically plant "sleepers" (sometimes called "moles") or "turn" enemy agents and allow them to continue to work in an enemy organization as a "defector in place." "Sleepers" live more or less ordinary lives in enemy areas until they are "activated" by intelligence authorities. These individuals often infiltrate openly in peacetime, particularly on commercial transportation. Because well-trained false defectors pose a serious danger, their "bona fides" are carefully checked. These investigations can take one to three years to complete. "The real fear," argues Bob Burton, an expert in clandestine operations, "is not so much what a mole can glean from one's system as what false information, or disinformation, he can plant."[4] *See also* CENTRAL INTELLIGENCE AGENCY (CIA), 86; INTELLIGENCE COMMUNITY, 42; INTELLIGENCE CYCLE, 43; NATIONAL SECURITY, 56; SPECIAL FORCES WARFARE, 137.

Significance   Counterintelligence is a critical intelligence function. It is essential that a nation be able to destroy the ability of enemy foreign agents to collect secret information. Enemy agents typically engage in espionage, sabotage, and subversion. Espionage—which is akin to spying—is commonplace. Indeed, it is widely practiced by the major powers. For this reason, the superpowers usually exchange rather than execute captured spies. This practice gained acceptance when James Donovan, a New York attorney, defended Soviet spy Rudolph Abel. Both the United States and the Soviet Union concluded that a reciprocal agents trade policy was in their mutual interest. Sabotage refers to any act that seeks to damage, interfere, or impede a country's defense by deliberately injuring or destroying (or attempting to do so) any national defense utilities, premises, or material. This act is viewed as extremely serious, and is dealt with accordingly. Subversion describes any action designed to weaken the political, military, economic, psychological, or moral strength of a nation. Subversives seek to lend support, aid, or comfort to individuals, groups, or organizations that advocate the violent overthrow of a government or that are judged injurious to national security.

Force (41)

The exertion of power or strength to achieve an objective. Force is a potent social, political, economic, and military weapon. Clearly, nations must retain the right to use force to protect their interests.

Because one country can employ violence to achieve its aims, all nations must be prepared to do so. A nation that fails to assess the military consequences of its foreign policy or, conversely, that allows military planning to ignore its foreign policy assumptions, is inviting catastrophe. Military "requirements" cannot be realized without a systematic analysis of the country's interests, of the circumstances that would precipitate a war, and of possible alliances. To succeed, a country must also weigh the military strength of its adversaries, how quickly they can be subdued, and the extent to which they can be augmented. Clearly, the use of force is not always required, but it must remain an option. In many ways, resort to force represents the partial failure of policy, except where fighting is prized for its own sake. In most cases, however, armed conflict is viewed as the last alternative. Threats are a second option to diplomatc maneuvers; actual use of force only occurs if the threats fail. *See also* CONFLICT, 10; POWER, 27; POWER POTENTIAL, 59; WAR, 33.

Significance   Force inevitably involves violence, which entails high costs. This is why most nations temper its use by restraints and bargaining. Although most wars entail considerable bloodshed, the consequences could be bloodier. Violence is limited, in part, by the adversaries' shared interests. Still, it is far easier to destroy than to create. If a nation wishes to, it need not negotiate with its enemy. For example, a country may use force to seize disputed territory. However, force will not necessarily accomplish its other objectives. That is, the winner must also maintain and govern the territory. Brute force alone cannot achieve this goal. In most cases, a nation that seeks territory does not wish to destroy it in the process. A country that wants others to embrace its values cannot impose them solely through brute conquest. For this reason, cooperation is best achieved through compromise. The bargain may be unequal or unfair, but it is still a bargain. Each side gains in the process. The mutual avoidance of future problems explains why past conflicts have not been as violent as they could have been, though this should not mask their destructive nature. According to political scientists Robert J. Art and Robert Jervis, three main factors account for the increasing destructiveness of recent wars: (1) the steady technological improvements in weapons; (2) the growth in the capacity and thus the need of states to field ever larger numbers of forces; and (3) the expansion of the battlefield and hence the resort to indiscriminate mass killing of noncombatants.[5] These developments have both increased and decreased the use of force. Furthermore, the advent of nuclear weapons has altered the military equation. In the past, nations believed that the first strike, if skillfully executed, could prove decisive. They also knew that the winner's military forces could protect its own population. In a nuclear confrontation, neither side can save itself—that is, nuclear weapons have brought not overkill, but mutual kill. Because each side can destroy the other, regardless of who attacks first, each has an interest in avoiding a nuclear confrontation. For this reason, the military planning of the superpowers has shifted from victory to deterrence.

Intelligence Community (42)

Those executive branch agencies and organizations that conduct the intelligence activities that comprise the overall U.S. intelligence effort. The intelligence community includes:

1. The Central Intelligence Agency (CIA), which gathers political, economic, and military information and carries out undercover activities around the world

2. The National Security Agency (NSA), which is engaged in coding and decoding operations and electronic surveillance

3. The Defense Intelligence Agency (DIA) of the Department of Defense, which assesses the capabilities of allies and potential adversaries

4. The Bureau of Intelligence and Research (I&R) in the Department of State, which collects scientific, economic, sociological, and political information and forecasts trends

5. Army Intelligence (G2), which assembles data on ground forces and new weapons

6. Air Force Intelligence (A2), which covers air and space affairs

7. The Office of Naval Intelligence (ONI), which accumulates data on foreign navies and fleet movements

8. The Department of Energy, which obtains and disseminates information about foreign energy supplies, production, intentions, and policies

9. The Federal Bureau of Investigation (FBI), which amasses intelligence on internal threats to security

10. The Treasury Department, which collects foreign investment, monetary, and general economic intelligence

11. The Drug Enforcement Administration (DEA), which marshals data on foreign and domestic production and drug trafficking

The United States Intelligence Board, chaired by the director of the Central Intelligence Agency, convenes regularly to review information collected by the intelligence agencies and to present the "national intelligence estimate" to the president. *See also* CENTRAL INTELLIGENCE AGENCY (CIA), 86; COUNTERINTELLIGENCE, 40; INTELLIGENCE CYCLE, 43; NATIONAL SECURITY, 56; SPECIAL FORCES WARFARE, 137.

Significance   The intelligence community advises the director of the Central Intelligence Agency through their members of the various specialized committees that deal with intelligence matters of mutual concern. The evaluation of intelligence includes the verification and accuracy of the information, the reliability of the source, and the agency which obtained the data. Bob Burton, an expert on clandestine operations, argues that pertinence is judged by the following criteria: (1) How does the information relate to the enemy or to the characteristics of the area of operations? (2) Is the information needed immediately, and, if so, by whom? (3) Does the information have present or future value, and if so, to whom?[6] Accuracy is based on the following: (1) Is it possible for the reported fact or event to have taken place? (2) Is the report consistent within itself? (3) Is the report confirmed or corroborated by information from different sources or agencies? (4) Does the report agree or disagree in any way with other available information? (5) If the report does not agree with information from other sources or agencies, which one is more likely to be true? The reliability of a source or collection agency is judged by a rating system: A—Completely reliable; B—Usually reliable; C—Fairly reliable; D—Not usually reliable; E—Unreliable; and F—Reliability cannot be determined. Agency evaluation is based on a system of numerals: 1—Confirmed by other sources; 2—Probably true; 3—Possibly true; 4—Doubtfully true; 5—Improbable; and 6—Truth cannot be judged.

Intelligence Cycle (43)

The process by which information is collected, converted into intelligence, and distributed to policymakers. The intelligence cycle consists of five steps: (1) planning and direction; (2) collection; (3) processing; (4) production and analysis; and (5) dissemination. Step 1 involves the coordination of the entire process, ranging from the request for the information to the final presentation of the data to the interested individual or agency. Step 2 concerns the collection of the raw information from which the final intelligence will be produced. Step 3 includes the the conversion of the mass of information that is compiled to a form suitable to the production of completed intelligence. Step 4 refers to the translation of raw information into finished intelligence. Step 5 involves the distribution and handling of finished intelligence to government officials. *See also* CENTRAL INTELLIGENCE AGENCY (CIA), 86; COUNTERINTELLIGENCE, 40; INTELLIGENCE COMMUNITY, 42; NATIONAL SECURITY, 56; SPECIAL FORCES WARFARE, 137.

Significance   The intelligence cycle, contends Bob Burton, an authority on the Central Intelligence Agency, is designed to systematize the intelligence process.[7] The system is triggered by requests or requirements for needed intelligence. These are determined by the policy objectives of top decision makers, including the president, the National Security Council, and other high-level government agencies and departments. Intelligence derives from many sources, among them: newspapers, magazines, documents, radio broadcasts, and official government personnel. There are, of course, various secret sources (e.g., agents and defectors). In recent years, technical collection—photography and electronics—has become increasingly important. Obviously, the intelligence community collects a vast amount of information, which often necessitates translation, decryption, and sorting by category. Not all information goes to the intelligence analysts; some is sorted and readied for rapid computer retrieval. To produce finished intelligence, the information is subject to integration, evaluation, and analysis, which is presented in the form of briefings, short reports, or in-depth studies. Raw intelligence is often fragmentary and, at times, contradictory. Thus, it is necessary for analysts—who are subject-matter specialists—to interpret and weigh its relevance. Intelligence is collected on important regions, problems, and personalities—political, economic, military, scientific, or biographic. Frequently, current affairs, military capabilities, or possible future developments are also fertile subjects. In the end, informed policy decisions demand accurate information, which is, in short, the goal of intelligence.

Logistics   (44)

That aspect of military activity providing for the movement and maintenance of soldiers, equipment, and supplies. Logistics embodies those planning and operational activities necessary to accomplish a military task. These include the design, procurement, and maintenance of military materiel; the movement, evacuation, and hospitalization of military personnel; the transportation and storage of military supplies and equipment; and the design, construction, maintenance, and operation of military facilities and installations. Today, modern combat forces are armed with sophisticated weapons and equipment that require enormous logistical support. For example, in World War II about half of the U.S. Army had to render logistical support to the other half, which was engaged in direct combat. Twenty-five percent of the troops in a combat division performed logistics-related activities. Logistic requirements have experienced considerable changes occasioned by the complexity and variety of modern weapons, coupled with recent innovations in communication and transportation. These changes have exacerbated logistical problems and increased the proportion of noncombatants in military forces. In earlier eras, for example, weapons were relatively simple and troops, to a large extent, lived off the country. By World War II, the initial requirement was ten tons (40 cubic feet per ton) of supplies and equipment per troop, with an additional two tons per troop per month required for maintenance. As the number of combatants increased, so did the distance from the combat zone to the supply production bases. Today, it is necessary to transport not only supplies but also personnel, replacement personnel, allied equipment, and maintenance materials. *See also* MILITARY FORCES, 47; MILITARY PLANNING, 51; MILITARY STRATEGY, 54; MOBILIZATION, 55.

Significance   Logistics plays a vital military function. In the area of land and air operations, chemical, engineer, medical, ordnance, quartermaster, signal, and transportation units provide logistical support for combat units. At sea, cargo ships, hospital ships, icebreakers, minelayers, oilers, repair ships, transports, and tugs provide this support to warships. The United States has established the world's largest and most extensive logistic system. With its highly developed economic-industrial base, the United States has served as a major supplier for many Western nations. This vast logistic system was created to support U.S. foreign policy and military strategy in order to protect the vital interests of the United States and to promote world order and stability. For these reasons, America's logistic system has been structured to maintain sea, air, and land forces so as to discourage military aggression against the United States and its allies. In addition, the system provides logistic support—military supplies, equipment, instruction, and secure lines of communication—to friendly Western nations. U.S. logistic support is directed by the executive office of the president, in the Office of Emergency Planning.

This office determines the types and amounts of materials to be stock-piled and drafts plans for operation of the nonmilitary industrial plant and transportation system. Responsibility for the development and procurement of weapons, facilities, supplies, and equipment for U.S. military forces lies with the Department of Defense and ulti-mately with the president, subject to congressional authorization and appropriation. The actual movement of troops and the securing of lines of communication rest with the president and his military and civilian advisers.

Manpower Procurement (45)

The process employed by the armed forces to recruit qualified vol-unteers to meet a country's national security commitments. Man-power procurement is a perennial concern within the defense establishment. In the United States, the problem was particularly pro-nounced in the 1970s, when the qualifications of post–Vietnam War recruits dropped to dangerously low levels. Moreover, the services found it exceedingly difficult to keep skilled specialists and techni-cians, who left the services to seek comparable jobs at higher salaries in the public sector. These developments caused many political and military leaders to question the efficacy of the all-volunteer force. By the early 1980s, the situation had reversed itself, leading foreign-policy expert Martin Binkin to conclude that the services presently enjoy both "a bountiful harvest of high-caliber recruits and a substan-tial improvement in the proportion of troops seeking a military career."[8] Still, many critics remain skeptical, wondering whether the current progress might have been accomplished at the expense of quantity—that is, that "today's armed forces have been sized to fit the military's ability to recruit volunteers and are too small to meet na-tional security commitments."[9] In addition, other critics contend that the abolition of the draft and the introduction of the all-volunteer force have led to an unwise—and dangerous—reliance on reserve forces, which are inadequately equipped and, in some cases, are un-dermanned for specific tasks. Other critics challenge the wisdom of the all-volunteer force, arguing that it has undermined the traditional belief that every American has a moral obligation to serve his country. *See also* ALL-VOLUNTEER FORCE (AVF), 36; MILITARY FORCES, 47; MILITARY MANPOWER, 50; SELECTIVE SERVICE, 61.

Significance   The future of manpower procurement depends, in a real sense, on several major societal trends. Clearly, the 1990s will witness a decline in recruits from the "baby boom" generation, as that group slips into middle age. Moreover, if the economy continues to show marked improvement, it is likely that the pool of potential recruits will shrink. On the other hand, projected increases in the size of the armed forces, coupled with anticipated advances in weapons technology, could increase the military's demand for volunteers and perhaps for more highly-qualified ones as well. If these developments occur, notes Binkin, "the armed forces will be squeezed between a diminished supply of prospective high-quality volunteers and an increased demand for better recruits, thus driving up the price of military manpower."[10] Ultimately, the severity of the problem will depend on the number of new recruits that will be required to fill the expanded force structure, as well as the ability of the military to attract better-trained recruits to operate the increasingly sophisticated weaponry. If the demand exceeds the supply, the nation might be forced to choose between reduced forces, less complex weapons, or the reinstatement of the draft.

Marine Corps (46)

The combined armed force of both air and ground contingents that is especially trained and organized for amphibious assault operations. The marine corps plays a strategic role in many parts of the globe, alert to any potential trouble spots. One of the nation's two naval services, it is a partner, but not a part, of the navy. With 185,000 forces and over 1,000 aircraft, the marine corps is larger than most of the world's armies and flies more aircraft than most of the world's air forces. Established in 1775, the United States Marine Corps emulated many of the traditions and rules of the British Royal Marines in its early development. The marine corps was established as a separate service in 1798 by Act of Congress. The National Security Act of 1947, as amended, provides that the marine corps shall: (1) be organized into not fewer than three combat divisions and three air wings; (2) supply fleet marine forces of combined arms, together with supporting air components, for service with the fleet; (3) develop tactics, techniques, and equipment for use by landing forces; and (4) perform such other duties as the president may direct. Headquartered in Washington, D.C., the marine corps is led by a commandant appointed by the president. The commandant, who holds the rank of general, serves on the Joint Chiefs of Staff and is directly responsible to the secretary of the navy. *See also* ALL-VOLUNTEER FORCE (AVF), 36; JOINT CHIEFS OF STAFF, 197; MILITARY FORCES, 47; MILITARY LEADERSHIP, 49; MILITARY MANPOWER, 50.

Significance   The marine corps, which has been called "soldiers of the sea," enjoys the reputation of having been the first to fight in almost every major war of the United States. Indeed, the marine corps has made more than 300 landings on foreign shores, and has served in various areas, ranging from the polar regions to the tropics. The M-16 rifle is the main infantry weapon of the marine corps. In addition, it uses pistols, grenades, and machine guns. Marine corps infantry are backed up by several types of artillery, including guns, mortars, and howitzers. Armored units possess tanks with heavy guns. Major anti-aircraft weapons include HAWK guided missiles and shoulder-fired Red-eye and Stinger missiles. Marine corps aviation provides essential air support for fleet marine and other troops, and reinforces naval operations. Because it attacks enemy forces so close to marine land operations, careful coordination between air and ground units is required. The marine corps, which has aviators with ground units at the front lines to direct and control air support, flies many of the same kinds of aircraft as the navy. The marine corps also flies the Harrier, a type of V/STOL (Vertical/Short Take-Off and Landing) aircraft. In addition, it operates assault helicopters, to land men from naval helicopter carriers. Marine corps recruits spend basic training in "boot camp." Male recruits receive approximately ten weeks of basic training at one of two recruit depots—in Paris Island, South Carolina, or in San Diego, California, where they undergo physical conditioning, as well as learn how to shoot, drill, obey orders, and follow the traditions of the marine corps. Women recruits receive eight weeks of basic training in Paris Island, South Carolina. Although their fitness program differs from that of their male counterparts, they are trained in most of the same areas. Marine corps officers are recruited from four major sources: (1) the U.S. Naval Academy; (2) the Naval Reserve Officers Training Corps; (3) civilian universities; and (4) the enlisted ranks of the marine corps. Officers receive five or more months of preliminary training at the Marine Corps Basic School, in Quantico, Virginia. The training regime consists of field tactics, leadership, marksmanship, infantry weapons and supporting arms, drill, military law, and physical fitness. Throughout the years, the marines have served in virtually every major conflict. A marine regiment fought in the Philippine Insurrection (1899–1904); a regiment marched to Peking during the Boxer Rebellion (1900); and marine forces were employed in China (1905–1941) and for interventions in the Caribbean (e.g., Panama, Cuba, Nicaragua, Haiti, and the Dominican Republic). In addition, the 4th Marine Brigade, dispatched to France in World War I (1917–1918), won worldwide acclaim at Belleau Wood. In World War II (1941–1945), the marines served well in such battles at Guadalcanal, Bougainville, Eniwetok, Saipan, Guam, Iwo Jima, and Okinawa. In 1950, during the Korean War, a marine brigade helped to defend the Pusan perimeter and the

1st Marine Division, assisted by the 1st Marine Aircraft Wing, landed at Inchon and recaptured Seoul. Marines were the first U.S. ground troops employed in Vietnam. Indeed, the 3rd Marine Amphibious Force engaged in continuous combat from 1965 to 1971, notably in the battles of Khe Sanh and Hue. In 1983, the marines and rangers and a small force from six Caribbean countries invaded the island of Grenada, in response to a request from the Organization of Eastern Caribbean States. After a few days, Grenadan militia and Cuban "construction workers" were overwhelmed, hundreds of U.S. citizens evacuated safely, and the Communist regime deposed.

Military Forces (47)

The regular land, sea, and aerospace armed forces of a country, active and reserve, whose main goals are to prevent, defeat, or otherwise engage in military combat against an adversary, as directed, wherever required. Military forces also assist law enforcement or internal security forces when instructed. There are two major types of forces: regular and irregular. Regular forces consist of active and reserve units that are organized, trained, and equipped for conventional or nuclear/biological/chemical combat. They also may engage in irregular activities. Irregular forces consist of individuals and groups—not tied to any official military or law enforcement apparatus—who engage primarily in insurgency, resistance, and/or transnational terrorism. Military service is unlike any other profession. Like most institutions, the military is governed by the managerial ethic. This ethic shapes the way officers and enlistees view their roles. In other ways, however, the military differs markedly from civilian life. Dandridge Malone, a colonel in the infantry, states it best: "The qualities that count in military leadership will always be fundamentally different from those that are rewarded elsewhere. . . . The officer corps is characterized by a 'careerist' emphasis on getting ahead, no matter what the cost. . . . The soldier's task is different—he is asked to kill and to expose himself to death—and the motivations of men who do so are based on requirements that do not exist in most other 'jobs.'"[11] *See also* MILITARY LEADERSHIP, 49; MILITARY MANPOWER, 50; MILITARY PLANNING, 51; MILITARY POWER, 52; MILITARY STRATEGY, 54.

Significance   Military force effectiveness depends, in large measure, on the establishment of strong human bonds. As James Fallows, an authority on national defense, opines: "These are the bonds among the enlisted men in a fighting force; between the enlisted men and the officers who lead them; among the officers; and between the military as a whole and the nation it represents."[12] These bonds are rare in the private sector, which rewards profit, competition, and initiative. Among the military forces there is no room for economic calculations or labor-market models. In this environment, a premium is placed on shared experience and mutual sacrifice, which in turn promotes mutual respect and trust. These bonds are vital if the military is to function effectively. According to Fallows: "Soldiers will risk death only when they feel a bond of trust and responsibility with their fellow soldiers. Units will only follow leaders who have earned their trust through demonstrations of honor and of willingness to sacrifice for the good of their men. A nation's military, especially in a democracy, can endure the hardships of war only if it feels tied to the nation by a sense of common purpose and respect."[13] Although several elements of the civilian world are based on similar principles (e.g., churches, basketball teams, political organizations), they do so in a peacetime environment—one free of death and destruction. In this sense, the military forces differ dramatically from their civilian counterparts.

Military-Industrial Complex (MIC) (48)

An alleged informal alliance among the professional military, defense-corporation executives, and prodefense members of Congress, whereby these groups use their power and influence to win support of increased defense spending, which, in turn, serves their economic and political objectives. The term, "military-industrial complex," was coined by President Dwight D. Eisenhower in his Farewell Address in 1961. According to Eisenhower:

> We have been compelled to create a permanent armaments
> industry of vast proportions. . . . This conjunction of an
> immense military establishment and a large arms industry is
> new in the American experience. The total influence—
> economic, political, even spiritual—is felt in every city, every
> Statehouse, every office of the Federal government . . . . In the
> councils of government, we must guard against the acquisition
> of unwarranted influence, whether sought or unsought, by the
> military-industrial complex. The potential for the disastrous
> rise of misplaced power exists and will persist.[14]

In brief, the theory posits that as new weapons go through a predictable sequence—research, development, testing, selection, production, and deployment—an interested constituency tends to emerge. This consists of the civilian contractors and their employees, the military leaders associated with the specific weapon, and the politicians in whose districts the weapon or its components will be produced or deployed. These parties exert enormous pressures for producing the weapon by rallying their constituencies. Once this process gains momentum, it is extremely difficult to stop the project. *See also*

AEROSPACE AND DEFENSE INDUSTRY, 63; ARMS RACE, 65; MILITARY SPENDING, 53; NATIONAL SECURITY, 56; PERCEPTION THEORY, 58.

Significance   The military-industrial complex plays a salient role in the development and deployment of new weapons systems. Proponents of this view contend that the phrase should, in fact, read, the "military-industrial-governmental-scientific-labor complex." The theory is not without its critics. For example, political scientist John Spanier argues that the MIC explanation is riddled with contradictions. "On the one hand," notes Spanier, "it is suggested that American foreign policy is too interventionist, too involved, and too expensive, and that it distorts national priorities. The emotional appeal of the MIC explanation lies in the belief that the United States' allegedly overextended and dangerous policy is contrary to the interests of the vast majority of Americans, who would benefit from a cutback in external commitments and concentration on domestic affairs. . . . On the other hand, almost every group in the United States seems to have a cash interest in international tension, including the growers who supply flowers for battlefield monuments; if so, the nation must have an interest in the continuation of cold war policies."[15] Spanier's critics disagree, insisting that the military-industrial complex undermines democratic institutions (e.g., political parties and legislatures) and civilian control of the military. Moreover, the MIC serves as an instrument of coercion, disguising its true motives with patriotic rhetoric, while impugning the motives of its opponents. By raising false fears, and railroading their critics, the beneficiaries of the MIC distort national objectives and lure the American people into a false sense of security, not realizing that they have been deceived into supporting costly weapons systems, in order to benefit the economic and political interests of the military-industrial complex.

Military Leadership   (49)

A person who heads or guides a military command. Military leadership varies in style and substance from authoritarian to democratic, its effectiveness depending in part upon the skill, maturity, experience, training, and dedication of his or her troops or support staff. To a considerable degree, military leaders must conform to the expectations of those they command. Although military leaders may be more eccentric than their troops, such characteristics are acceptable only up to a point. According to C. A. Gibb, an eminent psychologist, what a leader does depends on the situation and the group's needs and goals. Major leadership functions include: (1) performing professional and technical specialty; (2) knowing subordinates and showing consideration for them; (3) keeping channels of communication open; (4) accepting personal responsibility; (5) setting an example for others; (6) initiating and directing action; (7) training subordinates to function as a team; and (8) making decisions.[16] What makes a leader? This depends, in part, on how one views leadership. Some experts would say "charisma." Social psychologists, for example, seek specific, measurable qualities. Most studies show little relationship between leadership status and height, weight, energy, health, and physique. Intelligence, on the other hand, has been found to be characteristic of leaders, though it must not exceed that of followers by too much. Self-confidence and self-assurance, often acquired by previous success in meeting challenges, are associated with leadership, as are perseverance, willpower, hard work, dedication, and human-relations skills. *See also* COMMANDER IN CHIEF, 39; MANPOWER PROCUREMENT, 45; MILITARY FORCES, 47; MILITARY MANPOWER, 50.

Significance   Military leadership, like all leadership, requires several specific skills and attributes. Brilliance, for example, is not essential to military leadership. According to Napoléon Bonaparte: "Too much intellect is not necessary in war."[17] What is essential, notes Napoléon, is precision, a strong personality, and the ability to keep things in a clear perspective. Most important, argues Napoléon, "is that a man's judgment should be . . . above the common level."[18] Success in war depends, to a marked degree, on caution, decisiveness, good conduct, and experience. As for boldness, this appears to be a desirable attribute. Carl von Clausewitz, perhaps the world's best-known military strategist, asserts that "a distinguished commander without boldness is unthinkable."[19] However, as Clausewitz notes, "boldness grows less common in the higher ranks. . . . Nearly every general known to us from history as mediocre, even vacillating, was noted for dash and determination as a junior officer."[20] Military leaders are expected to be brave, but, as Napoléon reminds us, this must be tempered by good judgment. This must also include moral courage. Firmness, another requisite for effective leadership, is equally necessary. In the view of many military historians, the most critical quality is firmness of character and personal resolve. In the end, military leaders possess several common characteristics, but vary considerably in ability and style. Some are particularly well suited for some kinds of assignments, but are ill suited for others. In addition, many believe that leadership is situational—that is, that "the emergence of a leader is contingent not only upon his abilities, but also upon his being in the right place at the right time."[21]

Military Manpower (50)

The use of human capital to fight wars and defend the nation. Military manpower plays a salient role in contemporary strategic planning. Although the human element once dominated the military equation, the role of manpower is less clear today. For example, Gregory D. Foster, an authority on international security affairs, opines: "Contemporary strategic planning—and, more broadly speaking, strategic discourse in general—evinces at best only a casual concern with the seemingly pedestrian domain of manpower."[22] In this regard, manpower analysts are partly responsible for the devaluation of human capital, by emphasizing obscure and esoteric considerations. For the past four decades, manpower analysis has fallen victim to such major concerns as nuclear deterrence, escalation control, and arms control, to which manpower issues pale in importance. In addition, the preoccupation with technological advances in modern weaponry has rendered the human element in warfare obsolete. *See also* ALL-VOLUNTEER FORCE (AVF), 36; MANPOWER PROCUREMENT, 45; MILITARY FORCES, 47; MILITARY LEADERSHIP, 49.

Significance Military manpower has made and will continue to make a vital contribution to modern warfare. Despite the failures of manpower analysts, military manpower possesses several distinct characteristics that will continue to make its role both indispensable and unique. As Foster notes: (1) manpower makes decisions; (2) manpower operates equipment; (3) manpower moves from place to place; (4) manpower controls territory; (5) manpower occupies space; (6) manpower presents targets; (7) manpower consumes resources; and (8) manpower is the ultimate manifestation of national commitment.[23] These eight attributes highlight the special importance of military manpower and constitute the basic rationale for its inclusion in strategic planning. Still, these factors are often ignored at many high-level manpower debates. Despite recent technological advances, strategic interaction will demand manpower participation, especially in cases involving the unexpected and unforeseeable. Although machines possess many advantages, they are ill-equipped to make critical strategic decisions. Clearly, the marriage between man and machine will continue to play an essential role in the decision-making process. Moreover, communications-and-control technologies are plagued by myriad shortcomings, which make necessary physical interaction and presence. Furthermore, war makes essential the geostrategic imperative that is part and parcel of military manpower. Coupled with the existence of spacial occupancy limits, the critical nature of targets, and the consumption of resources, it is clear that military manpower cannot help but figure prominently in strategic planning.

Military Planning (51)

The formulation of a military scheme or program for the accomplishment of a specific goal or objective. Military planning is an indispensable element of national security. Indeed, no nation can expect to achieve its military aims unless it practices systematic planning. Given the rapidity with which balances of military power can shift, military planners must hedge against uncertainty by devising a wide range of strategies. In most cases, military planners will seek to hedge against this uncertainty by overarming. Clearly, they do not wish to run the risk of being blamed for jeopardizing the nation's security. For this reason, military planners are more likely to advocate military superiority than to request less than is actually required. Military planning reflects a wide variety of specialized concerns. Moreover, planning decisions about the quantitative and qualitative characteristics of a nation's military arsenal are determined, to a large extent, by the nature of prevailing military doctrine. In the United States, for example, the strategic nuclear arsenal has been shaped by certain doctrinal predilections (i.e., the principle of mutual assured destruction). *See also* LOGISTICS, 44; MILITARY POWER, 52; MILITARY SPENDING, 53; MILITARY STRATEGY, 54.

Significance   Military planning is an imprecise science—that is, there are fierce disagreements over goals, assumptions, strategies, and outcomes. Ultimately, the character, scope, and consequences of the potential threat will determine the kinds of contingencies for which one plans. At the same time, the threat will also suggest the kinds of measures necessary to deter it. Despite this fact, disagreements are likely to arise. In addition, two other major factors complicate the problem: First, it is difficult to determine in advance what policies and weapons will best accomplish the intended objectives. Second, given the limits on defense spending, how resources should best be spent to deal with the problem. Unfortunately, it is difficult to judge definitively which answers are correct. As national security expert Donald M. Snow points out, "The only way to demonstrate effectiveness is in a future conflict, for which one hopes one has guessed correctly. What makes the problem all the more difficult is that that future may be different than the future for which one is planning."[24] Furthermore, what military planners may propose to deal with one threat might prove inappropriate for other threats. Thus, military planners must anticipate the most and least likely scenarios and what weapons and strategies they should and should not recommend to cope with those alternate contingencies. For example, a battle involving the United States in, say, a Middle East nation would be almost totally dissimilar to that in a Latin American country. Thus, military planners must attempt to assess the relative importance of such diverse factors as doctrine, terrain, weapons, manpower, weather, training, resources, and morale.

Military Power (52)

A nation's ability to safeguard its homeland, protect its interests, aid its allies, and achieve its objectives. Military power, argues Michael I. Handel, a specialist in military security, can be schematically defined as Total Military Power = Quantity × Material Quality × Nonmaterial Quality.[25] According to military analysts, wars can be won by various combinations of quantitative and qualitative factors, depending on the adversaries' historical experiences, political values, military resources, manpower pool, and economic and budgetary limitations. The quantitative aspects of military power are relatively easy to identify and measure—for example, the number of aircraft, ships, tanks, artillery, and ammunition. It is far more difficult, however, to assess the qualitative elements that contribute to military power. In this regard, it is necessary to distinguish between two main aspects— namely, the material aspects and the nonmaterial aspects. Material quality refers to the capability and performance of weapons, which is typically measured by their firepower, speed, range, and durability. Although many of these elements can be quantified, it is far more difficult to weigh their respective trade-offs. The nonmaterial qualitative component includes the quality of manpower, level of training, morale and motivation, military organization, staff expertise, military doctrine, and political leadership. Thus, the nonmaterial aspect defies easy definition and measurement. *See also* FORCE, 41; MILITARY FORCES, 47; NATIONAL SECURITY, 56; POWER, 27; POWER POTENTIAL, 59.

Significance Military power depends, to a large extent, on striking the correct balance between the quantitative and qualitative components. Ideally, this balance will enable a nation to realize its security requirements, as well as its political objectives. Clearly, this balance is not easy to achieve, in that it is difficult to determine the effectiveness of the various combinations. Moreover, each new war presents its own challenges, which entail different adversaries, philosophies, and weapons. In this sense, it is often impossible to determine whether a war was won because of quantitative superiority or was decided by a qualitative advantage. Such an assessment is only easy where one side enjoyed a decisive advantage. For example, given the Arabs' overwhelming quantitative superiority and the roughly comparable material quality of weapons enjoyed by the Israelis and the Arabs, a persuasive argument could be made that the superior quality of the Israeli Army proved to be the determining factor in the five main wars that have ensued. On the other hand, Nazi Germany, which did not suffer from qualitative inferiority, ultimately fell victim to the overwhelming quantitative superiority of the allies. Similarly, Finland, which initially proved capable of defending itself and in demonstrating its qualitative superiority, was quickly subdued by the Soviet Union's quantitative superiority. Despite these examples, argues Handel, two main lessons emerge: (1) In those cases where quality proved the key factor, it was the nonmaterial elements of quality (e.g., superior planning, staff work, leadership, and morale) which prevailed. (2) Qualitative elements (particularly the nonmaterial ones) appear to be the most important in quick and short wars, while quantitative superiority prevails only in a protracted conflict.[26] Thus, "the two most important factors are nonmaterial quality in short wars, and superior quantities in prolonged wars."[27]

Military Spending (53)

The total defense expenditure for personnel costs, weapons procurement, maintenance and operations, research and development, and military construction. Military spending is difficult to define and varies depending upon the definition that is used. For example, the Department of Defense (DOD) calculation only includes spending by that agency. The "national defense function"—the most widely used budget formula—includes not only DOD expenditures, but spending figures from other related departments and agencies, among them: civil defense planning (FEMA), the Selective Service System, and military expenditures of the Department of Energy (e.g., the design and production of nuclear warheads and bombs, the production and maintenance of naval reactors, and the maintenance of the strategic stockpile). This estimate is often used synonymously with "the military budget," "military spending," or "military expenditure." The Department of Commerce publishes annual figures on military purchases of goods and services, which are included in the "National Income and Product Accounts" (NIPA). Its figures exclude military retirement pay, but include military assistance. In addition, NIPA calculations do not count military purchases until the final products are received. Official government projections fail to include retirement pay for civil service DOD employees, the costs of previous military activities, the budget for the National Aeronautics and Space Administration, and interest payments on the federal deficit. *See also* AEROSPACE AND DEFENSE INDUSTRY, 63; ARMS RACE, 65; MILITARY-INDUSTRIAL COMPLEX (MIC), 48; NATIONAL SECURITY, 56; PERCEPTION THEORY, 58.

Significance   Military spending, according to the U.S. Constitution, is the prerogative of the Congress, which controls the federal purse strings. The budget process consists of three main steps: (1) The first budget resolution (March or April) sets target levels for spending. (2) The defense authorization bill (June or July) is prepared by the House and Senate Armed Services committees. This bill designates how much may be spent on specific programs, as well as any special conditions. (3) The defense appropriations bill is considered by the Defense subcommittees of the House and the Appropriations Committee of the Senate prior to submission to the full House and Senate (September or October). The appropriations bill actually approves federal spending for military programs. If the House and Senate pass different versions of the spending bill, the measure is sent to a joint committee—comprised of senior members of both bodies—who attempt to resolve the differences. Once a compromise is reached, the bill is returned to the House and Senate for their approval. Upon passage, the bill is forwarded to the president for his signature. If the president vetoes the bill, the Congress may override the veto by a two-thirds vote of both houses. Military spending for Fiscal Year 1988 amounted to $303.3 billion (excluding strategic systems development in the research and development category and research and development in other program areas on systems approved for production). Increasingly, Congress has attempted to assert its role in this area. For example, it tried to substantially reduce appropriations for the Strategic Defense Initiative, leading to a veto by President Ronald W. Reagan and a new approach by the Congress so as to placate the Reagan administration.

Military Strategy (54)

The art or science of military command as applied to the overall planning and conduct of combat operations. Military strategy, as it concerns the U.S. experience, reflects the Clausewitzian notion that "strategy is the employment of the battle to gain the end of War; it must therefore give an aim to the whole military action, which must be in accordance with the object of the War."[28] Another military expert, General Bruce Palmer, Jr., contends that "the term 'strategy,' derived from the ancient Greek, originally pertained to the art of generalship or high command. In modern times, 'grand strategy' has come into use to describe the overall defense plans of a nation or coalition of nations. Since the mid-twentieth century, 'national strategy' has attained wide usage, meaning the coordinated employment of the total resources of a nation to achieve its national objectives."[29] Despite its apparent simplicity, British historian Michael Howard is correct in asserting that the term "strategy" is an evolving one—that it requires constant redefinition.[30] Clearly, Clausewitz's formulation is simple enough—that is, military strategy can be defined as the deployment of the armed forces to achieve a specific political objective. In this regard, military strategy inevitably embodies both military and political considerations. This is especially true of U.S. society, with its emphasis on civilian control of the military. *See also* LOGISTICS, 44; MILITARY FORCES, 47; MILITARY PLANNING, 51; MILITARY POWER, 52.

Significance Military strategy, by definition, must reflect the unique circumstances of each conflict. No single set of rules is universally applicable to every war. Nonetheless, given the realities of today's world, most military experts stress the primacy of nuclear weapons and superpower competition as the centerpiece of U.S. military strategy. Indeed, the Joint Chiefs of Staff have consistently argued that "the fundamental ingredients of U.S. military strategy are nuclear deterrence with arms control, strong alliances, forward-deployed forces, central reserves, force mobility, freedom of the seas and space, command and control, and intelligence."[31] On the other hand, many military experts continue to emphasize the challenge of unconventional conflicts, which explains the creation in recent years of a Special Operations Command, which has been the recipient of a huge increase in resources. In addition, the U.S. Army has initiated a series of new special operations career patterns. Still, the financial resources allocated to special operations forces remains small, in spite of the fact that these resources have grown geometrically in recent years. In short, military analysts continue to stress the salience of nuclear strategy and global confrontations. Although renewed attention has been devoted to limited wars, they tend to be viewed merely as conventional conflicts in special settings.

Mobilization (55)

Measures adopted by a country to prepare itself for war. Mobilization may encompass a variety of actions, among them: placing the armed forces on alert, closing frontiers, calling up the reserves, expelling or monitoring enemy aliens, protecting against sabotage, establishing curfews, and invoking emergency powers for managing the nation's economy. Beginning with the American Revolution, the United States instituted the practice of maintaining a small standing army during peacetime, to mobilize only when the nation was compelled to go to war, and then to demobilize its forces as quickly as possible once the conflict ended. This strategy has, for several reasons, served the United States well. First, the nation's geography provides a shield for the continental United States, making an armed attack difficult. The country could prepare for war at leisure, with no immediate threat while mobilizing. Second, the United States is deeply wedded to the principle of civilian control of the military. In addition, military service, for many Americans, is viewed as a threat to freedom and one's ability to pursue life as one wishes. Third, there have been few times when a professional standing army was required, leading many Americans to conclude that a peacetime army was unnecessary. Fourth, a professional peacetime army was relatively inexpensive. For example, it only consisted of 10,000–20,000 men throughout most of the nineteenth century. This tradition persisted until the Korean War in the 1950s and the decision by President John F. Kennedy to place a renewed emphasis on military preparedness. *See also* CIVIL DEFENSE, 183; LOGISTICS, 44; MILITARY PLANNING, 51; MILITARY SPENDING, 53; MILITARY STRATEGY, 54.

Significance   Mobilization is a vital element in any effective defense strategy. It is critical for a modern nation to develop mobilization plans and standby measures in the event of war. In this sense, mobilization is a sign that diplomatic efforts have failed and that actual fighting may be imminent. On the other hand, mobilization will inevitably produce countermobilizations by other nations and may itself encourage a potential adversary into initiating an armed attack. For example, once Germany discovered that Russia was mobilizing its resources on the eve of World War I, it suspended negotiations and launched a full-scale assault. In today's nuclear age, mobilization can be accomplished within minutes by placing a nation's delivery systems on instant alert. Clearly, the United States cannot afford the luxury of returning to its pre–Korean War stance. To protect itself, as well as its allies, the United States must be prepared should war break out. For these reasons, the old realities no longer apply. First, the United States was rarely if ever (with the exception of the Vietnam War) prepared to fight. Thus, it took the United States considerable time to mobilize and train its army. This explains why, argues political scientist Donald M. Snow, "Americans have entered wars late, and have not begun to fight for some time after being technically at war, with the probable result of making the wars last longer than they would have."[32] Second, the previous mobilization-demobilization tradition made it difficult for U.S. presidents to win support for large peacetime defense budgets—a problem that has plagued several recent administrations. Third, many people believe that the United States faces a real threat, one that requires vigilance and action. Despite these facts, a large number of Americans continue to question the wisdom of what they view as a "radical" departure in the country's defense posture, which adds to their opposition to increased military budgets. This has also led to increased governmental and media scrutiny of defense expenditures, which has unearthed instances of fraud, waste, and mismanagement in recent years.

National Security (56)

The freedom—relative and absolute—of a country from possible armed attack or political or economic sabotage, along with the nation's ability to strike back with deadly effectiveness if attacked. National security is a fundamental federal responsibility. Indeed, the preamble to the U.S. Constitution requires the federal government to "provide for the common defense." At the nation's founding, the framers were motivated by the need to protect the country from conquest or political domination by hostile European powers that retained strongholds in North America. Clearly, they saw little relationship between national security and economic independence. Nor could they have envisaged such twentieth century dangers as large-scale guerrilla warfare, international terrorism, and nuclear annihilation, which threaten not only the security of the United States, but that of the entire world. Today, the United States faces a host of actual and potential threats, both short-term and long-term. Some of these are domestic: static growth, declining productivity, environmental degradation, racial conflict, family disintegration, educational decline, political apathy, urban neglect, and a national economy heavily dependent on the military budget. A wide variety of external threats to U.S. national security exist as well, among them: regional instability, international terrorism, economic competition, worldwide starvation, local wars, debt crisis, and nuclear war. *See also* MILITARY FORCES, 47; MILITARY STRATEGY, 54; POWER, 27; POWER POTENTIAL, 59.

Significance   National security is an elusive concept—its meaning defies simple definition. Still, few experts would disagree that the development and deployment of nuclear weapons pose an ominous threat to the future of humankind. Fortunately, these weapons have been used only twice in the past 44 years, both times at the dawn of the nuclear age. To that extent, the "balance of terror" has probably prevented World War III. On the other hand, one can take little solace in this fact, as it has precipitated a dangerous arms race, in

71

which nuclear stockpiles of the two superpowers have steadily increased in numbers and devastation. Although total megatonnage has declined, the flight time, for many of the weapons of the strategic arsenals of both sides, has been reduced from hours to minutes. Clearly, a conventional confrontation between the United States and the Soviet Union could well escalate into a strategic nuclear war. Given the distrust and hostility that prevails, there always exists the possibility of a miscalculation. Nuclear proliferation continues unabated. More likely than nuclear war, however, is the possibility of a conventional confrontation—one directed at U.S. allies and friends. Although such an attack would not prove immediately catastrophic to the industrialized world, it would certainly undermine their situation in the long run. Of immediate concern is the predicament of the Third World, which is plagued by a litany of problems. Internal instability, coupled with regional interstate conflicts, pose a serious threat to world peace and international order. In the end, the United States must develop a national security policy that realistically reflects Soviet goals and behavior. In addition, it must also come to grips with the realities of the U.S. economy and devise means to reduce U.S. dependence on other nations (e.g., energy requirements). It must carefully reassess its nuclear doctrine, as well as its political and military strategy for dealing with regional conflicts. As national defense expert Harold Brown maintains, the government must "foster a national security policy that is directed at assuring, insofar as possible, that the United States will be free to evolve internally in the direction of its own ideals."[33]

Navy (57)

A country's combat fleet and supporting vessels, their personnel, and land bases. The United States Navy originated in the period of the American Revolution (1775–1783), producing such well-known naval figures as John Paul Jones and John Barry. The Department of the Navy, along with the office of the secretary of the navy, was approved by Congress in 1798. The navy's jurisdiction is defined in the National Security Act of 1947, which, as amended, set forth four major responsibilities: (1) the control of naval policy; (2) naval command; (3) logistics administration and control; and (4) business administration. Although most maritime nations maintain a navy, they vary considerably in terms of size and fighting strength. The United States and the Soviet Union boast the world's largest navies. The purpose of the navy is to maintain command of the sea. In wartime, the navy seeks out and destroys the enemy on, under, or above the sea. If attacked, it can return the fire virtually anywhere in the world from its warships. Navy task forces can transport naval aircraft to any crisis situation. Naval amphibious forces can support troop landings against heavy enemy resistance. Nuclear-powered submarines that carry missiles can navigate around the globe under water. In peacetime, the navy often serves as a vehicle of international relations, whose mere presence may serve to prevent a crisis from erupting into war. Navy ships also conduct errands of mercy, such as delivering food and medical supplies to disaster areas. The navy, which is located in Washington, D.C., is headed by the secretary of the navy. Today, the navy has a strength of about 515,000 men and over 109,000 women. The United States Naval Reserve numbers 109,000. *See also* ALL-VOLUNTEER FORCE (AVF), 36; MILITARY FORCES, 47; MILITARY LEADERSHIP, 49; MILITARY MANPOWER, 50.

Significance   The navy possesses sundry types of ships, including aircraft carriers, battleships, cruisers, destroyers, submarines, and amphibious vessels. The success of these fighting ships depends on such support services as ammunition ships, minesweepers, oilers, repair ships, and tugs. These vessels rely on a well-organized shore organization, which includes naval bases, shipyards, docks, naval air stations, and myriad other stations for supplies, repairs, and training. Major naval combat ships include warships, amphibious warfare ships, and mine warfare ships. The navy possesses aircraft carriers, battleships, guided missile cruisers, destroyers, frigates, submarines, and command ships. Auxiliary ships provide maintenance, fuel, supplies, towing, and other services to warships. Naval ordnance weapons include bombs, guns, mines, missiles, and torpedoes. The navy employs several types of missiles, including surface-to-air (e.g., Terrier) and air-to-air (e.g., Sidewinder). The regular navy, which is the permanent professional naval force, consists of men and women who join the navy as a career. The Naval Reserve provides additional forces in case of an emergency. Navy recruits study discipline and seamanship at a naval training center ("boot camp"). They may attend a trade school (e.g., for enginemen) or be assigned directly to a ship where they learn their duties and practice their trades. To advance, sailors must take competitive examinations. Naval officers train at the U.S. Naval Academy or in one of several naval programs: (1) the Naval Reserve Officers Training Corps (NROTC) for college and university students; (2) officer candidate training for enlisted personnel and college graduates; (3) aviation-officer candidate programs for men and women with college degrees; and (4) programs to appoint warrant officers and limited-duty officers from the enlisted ranks. Doctors, dentists, and ministers may be commissioned with scant military training. Officer candidates train at the Naval Officer Candidate

School, at Newport, Rhode Island. Like the other service branches, the permanent navy has played a prominent role in most major military conflicts, dating back to the Barbary pirates of North Africa (1785). It served with distinction in the War of 1812, the Civil War (1861–1865), the Spanish-American War (1898–1899), World War I (1914–1918), World War II (1939–1945), the Korean War (1950–1953), and the Vietnam War (1945–1975). The navy occupies a central role in the triad, the tripartite U.S. strategic deterrent force, comprised of land-based intercontinental ballistic missiles, submarine-launched ballistic missiles, and strategic bombers.

Perception Theory (58)

When people attribute to others an intention or motive based on their own beliefs and values. According to perception theory, individuals tend to project their own subjective feelings, be they positive or negative, to situations, objects, groups, and nations. Since this process is not a rational one, argument or persuasion is far less effective than one might conclude. It takes considerable critical effort, for example, to recognize that many of the motives we believe another nation possesses are attributed to it through perceptions already present in us. In addition, this theory shapes public perceptions of wars and weapons. For instance, some people believe that nuclear weapons do not differ markedly from conventional ones if used against a nonnuclear enemy. In this case, reality matters little; what matters is the way people perceive reality. Perception theory serves to explain, in part, why people support building weapons beyond those actually required for deterrence. As psychology and zoology expert David Barash notes, this view serves an important psychological purpose: "Large, threatening, ground-based missiles . . . are especially important, not so much for their alleged counterforce capability, but for their visibility and the degree to which they contribute to an image of power that might be intimidating."[34] It is vital to appreciate the distinction between reality and perception; failure to do so can produce frightening conclusions. This point is underscored by former Defense Secretary Harold Brown, who, in his 1979 report to Congress, states: "The United States and its allies must be free from any coercion and intimidation that could result from perceptions of an overall imbalance of particular asymmetries in nuclear forces. . . . Insistence on essential equivalence guards against any danger that the Soviets might be seen as superior—even if the perception is not technically justified."[35] *See also* BALANCE OF POWER, 4; BIPOLARITY, 6; COLD WAR, 9; PEACE, 24; POWER, 27; WAR, 33.

Significance   Perception theory is believed by those who utilize it to be most helpful in understanding the nature of global conflict. In this regard, most proponents of perception theory recognize, for instance, that neither nation possesses a conclusive first-strike capability and that neither side is decisively ahead in any major area. Still, perception-theory advocates continue to argue that the United States must tailor its nuclear weapons programs not to reality, but to public perceptions of reality, because these are, in effect, the real realities. In short, perceptions tend to create reality; hence nations are required to treat perceptions—even wrong ones—as though they were real. Failure to do so could, they contend, erode the confidence of U.S. allies or invite external aggression. For example, consider the Scowcroft Commission, which was appointed by President Ronald W. Reagan to make recommendations on the status of U.S. strategic nuclear weapons. The commission advocated the deployment of the MX missile, despite testimony that it lacked technical, strategic, or military merit. Why? In Barash's view: "Failure to deploy the MX would result in a perception that the United States was unwilling to compete militarily with the USSR."[36] Indeed, the commission concluded that the MX was needed as a "demonstration of national resolve. . . .The overall perception of strategic imbalance . . . has been reasonably regarded as destabilizing and as a weakness in the overall fabric of deterrence."[37] Perception theory is not without its weaknesses. First, the perceived need to exaggerate the U.S.'s military position, vis-à-vis the Soviet Union, has encouraged Congress, on occasion, to appropriate billions of dollars for questionable weapons systems, which add little to the nation's security. In addition, this view has prevented its adherents from attempting to educate its allies, their adversaries, and their own people regarding the dangers of misperception in the nuclear age. In this regard, newspaper writer and commentator Walter Lippmann once commented that in international affairs what counts is not what is true, but what people believe to be true, because that is what determines policy decisions.

Power Potential   (59)

Those internal and external sources and activities that contribute to national and international strength. A country's power potential derives from three main sources: natural and environmental circumstances, social and psychological attitudes, and human and industrial resources. These sources vary in importance, depending on national and international goals. Among natural power resources, geographic position plays a salient role. Indeed, in the past, geography was considered the most important component of national power. Today, most experts view geography and territorial position as major but not decisive determinants of national power. For example, the size and length of borders either increases or decreases the likelihood of armed conflict. In some instances, vast expanses can multiply a country's defense capabilities (e.g., Napoléon's defeat in 1812) or render it vulnerable to enemy attack (e.g., the People's Republic of China's and the Soviet Union's lengthy border). Interestingly, studies reveal that "the frequency of wars correlates with the number of borders a nation shares."[38] A country's images, attitudes, and expectations also affect its power potential. For instance, ideas, however wise, influence a nation's foreign policy. These include such slogans as "manifest destiny" and "world policeman." Images also play an important part in the formulation of foreign policy. Friendly nations are viewed with understanding, trust, and tolerance; unfriendly countries engender hatred, fear, and suspicion. Such images are the result of political socialization, the process by which an individual acquires political attitudes, beliefs, and values. Finally, a nation's human and other resources also contribute to its power potential. The adroit use of such resources contributes to the development, coordination, and execution of national power. This is especially true in war, which places a high premium on industrial capability and resource potential. In this regard, numerous studies confirm the importance of industrial capacity as a primary source of power. *See also* FORCE, 41; MILITARY FORCES, 47; NATIONAL SECURITY, 56; POWER, 27; VIETNAM SYNDROME, 62.

Significance   Power potential is difficult to quantify. In war, for example, how can one determine which of two sides is the more powerful? There are myriad factors which complicate such calculations, particularly in advance of actual hostilities. For instance, it is virtually impossible to measure such psychological elements as the "cost tolerance factor" (the willingness of a nation to endure negative sanctions), or even purely physical capabilities, such as the quantitative and qualitative contributions of specific weapons systems. In most cases, nations even find it impossible to calculate gross defense expenditures. The computer revolution has given rise to repeated efforts to measure social and political phenomena, usually with mixed results. Clearly, the starting point in any such calculations is the relative gross national products of the respective parties. The results suggest the economic capacity of nations to wage war successfully. However, economic data is not sufficient in and of itself. Most experts maintain that such equations must also reflect a country's political development, in that the two do not necessarily occur simultaneously.

Walter S. Jones, a prominent political scientist, contends that a country's internal power potential can be calculated by the following formula:

$$\text{internal component of power} = \frac{\text{gross national product}}{\text{population}} \times \text{(population)}$$

$$\times \text{ (tax effort),}$$

where the tax effort is the computed relation of the tax capacity of the economy (based on gross national product) and the willingness of government to apply pressure to extract enough to wage war effectively.[39] The external component of power can be expressed as: (foreign aid accumulated) × (tax effort of the recipient). Like most such formulas, this one possesses certain inherent limitations. At best, it is an interesting but imprecise tool for assessing a nation's power potential for war.

Prisoner of War (POW) (60)

A person who is captured by the enemy in time of war who is either a member of a military force or a civilian. Prisoners of war, under the 1949 Geneva Convention, are subject to the disciplines and are entitled to the rights and privileges that are defined in the articles of the Convention. Unfortunately, not all countries have signed the Convention. According to Patrick Robert Reid, a former prisoner of war and military historian: "The regulations concerning the conditions under which POWs are to be kept and their treatment generally set out in the convention are the ideal, possible to provide in times of peace but often quite impracticable in wartime with all its shortages and logistic difficulties, the same in every war, problems that will not go away."[40] The spirit and intent of the convention is skillfully articulated by Vattel, the famous French humanitarian and lawmaker who, in 1758, opined: "As soon as your enemy has laid down his arms and surrendered his body, you no longer have any right over his life."[41] Not until 1907 (Hague Regulations) did the POW acquire a status in international law. Prior to that, prisoners of war could be impressed into slavery or sold. They enjoyed no rights and could be disposed of according to the wishes of their owners or captors. They were often killed, imprisoned, tortured, brainwashed, disciplined, or degraded. In modern times, POWs have often been subjected to fierce indoctrination, whose object is to persuade the prisoner of the rightness of the captor's philosophy and then to repatriate the POW at the end of hostilities to serve as an active protagonist in the prisoner's home country. Several countries, including the United States and France, hold the view that once captured, prisoners of war are obligated not to give up the struggle, but are duty bound to attempt to escape and rejoin their forces. *See also* CENTRAL INTELLIGENCE AGENCY (CIA), 86; COUNTERINTELLIGENCE, 40; GENEVA PROTOCOL, 247.

Significance   Prisoners of war did not win international status in law until 1907, with the approval of the Hague Regulations, a set of international regulations governing the treatment of POWs, including the prohibition against cruel and inhuman treatment. These regulations were in force during World War I. Up to the mid-1600s, prisoners of war were viewed as chattel property—to be enslaved, ransomed, exchanged, or killed according to whims of the captor. After the seventeenth century, most agreed that POWs came under the power of the nation that captured them—not their individual captors. Thus, their treatment became the responsibility of the state; this served to lay the foundation for the various international conventions of the nineteenth and twentieth centuries. In subsequent years, numerous other regulations were adopted. For example, in 1920, the International Law Association recommended that laying down of arms be viewed as "an offer of peace."[42] The Geneva Convention in 1929 amplified and amended the Hague Regulations. In 1945, worldwide acceptance of the War Crimes Trials, and the concept of war crimes, held that a soldier is duty bound to disobey an illegal order and cannot use such a defense to justify the commission of an atrocity. The United Nations Command, in 1952, recognized that a POW can still be "an active soldier determined to fight on," suggesting that surrender not necessarily be an offer of peace.[43] In 1953, U.S. Order 207 restated the position that a captured U.S. soldier is obligated to attempt to escape. Despite the widespread acceptance of these and other regulations, many countries fail to honor their provisions. Specifically, POWs must not be subjected to coercion to induce combat information; must be allowed to retain their personal effects; must be given food, water, and shelter; must be allowed to write their families and the Central Prisoners of War Agency; must be grouped according to nationality, language, and customs; must be quartered outside the combat zone; must be properly clothed and given access to a canteen and an infirmary; and must be protected against torture, corporal punishment, imprisonment in premises without daylight, collective punishment, and humiliating and degrading treatment. In recent years, many Americans have lobbied Washington to apply greater pressure on Vietnam to release information on the status of any POWs who are presently in captivity, a fact that is denied by the Vietnamese government.

Selective Service (61)
The conscription system under which the federal government has drafted qualified males for service in the armed forces. Selective service is based on the constitutional provisions which empower Congress to "raise and support" armies and "provide and maintain" a navy. The system, which was created by Congress in 1948 and later revised by the Military Selective Service Act (1967), coordinated the selection and registration of males for the U.S. Army. An independent agency within the executive branch, the Selective Service System administered the draft. The draft required that all male citizens and alien permanent residents register for a two-year term until age 26. Under the system, exemptions and deferments were granted for specific types of study, personal hardship and dependency cases, mental or physical limitations, conscientious objection, or employment in certain jobs or service organizations. Under the system, educational deferments were granted generally through the baccalaureate degree. Students enrolled in medical and dental schools were allowed to complete their postgraduate study, but required to serve at a future time in either the U.S. armed forces or the U.S. Public Health Service. Also exempt were members of the diplomatic corps, while conscientious objectors were required to perform civilian service work. Although many people received deferments, they remained eligible until age 35. In 1973, the induction of qualified males was terminated. Two years later, the registration process for the draft was suspended and was replaced by an all-volunteer army. By 1980, owing to increased international tensions, compulsory registration was reinstituted. This present system, which only applies to males, was held to be constitutional in *Rostker v. Goldberg* (453 U.S. 57: 1981). *See also* ALL-VOLUNTEER FORCE (AVF), 36; MANPOWER PROCUREMENT, 45; MILITARY FORCES, 47; MILITARY MANPOWER, 50.

Significance The Selective Service System has long been the subject of bitter debate. Despite widespread criticism, the U.S. Supreme Court, in *Selective Draft Law Cases* (245 U.S. 366: 1918), held that conscription is not "involuntary service" in violation of the Thirteenth Amendment, ruling that such service by the citizen was "his supreme and noble duty." Although this decision dealt with wartime service, the constitutionality of a peacetime draft is also predicated on this decision. Throughout its existence, the draft was challenged on three main grounds: (1) that it is compulsory; (2) that it discriminates; and (3) that even if it is "representative," it is, by nature, inherently unfair. Clearly, the draft is compulsory. In this regard, it is no different from other laws (e.g., tax laws). Equally true, it was administered in a discriminatory manner. This was especially so in the Vietnam War, in which numerous exemptions were granted. Less obvious, but perhaps equally true, is the charge that it often appeared capricious and unfair—that is, only a small proportion of those eligible were actually drafted. The question of equity raises the most serious problem associated with any involuntary manpower system. In this regard, two key questions must be addressed—that is, the process by which selections are made (whether everyone has an equal chance of being selected) and, second, whether the criteria are fair. Regardless of the answers, the reinstatement of the draft would generate myriad objections, as well as political pressures to permit certain segments of the population to avoid service. In the end, defense expert Donald M. Snow is correct when he opines: "Regardless of how fairly one chooses people to service, the simple fact of a selective system is that some people must serve while others are not required to do so. Thus, the sacrifice that service entails is not equally shared but is shouldered by those forced into service. This form of inequity is simply unavoidable in any selective process."[44]

Vietnam Syndrome (62)

The reluctance of U.S. leaders and the American public to intervene militarily in any foreign country for any reason in any way as a result of the U.S. defeat in Vietnam. The Vietnam syndrome was particularly pronounced in the 1970s, following the U.S. withdrawal in 1973. Clearly, the Vietnam War revealed the limitations, if not the outright futility, of employing force in the face of insurmountable political circumstances. The failure of the nation to achieve its objectives, compounded by the loss of human life and unprecedented domestic opposition, dramatically affected the course of U.S. foreign policy. Indeed, the mood of the country shifted from interventionism to neo-isolationism. Although the Vietnam War is usually blamed for this shift, international developments in Latin America, Southwest Asia, and the Middle East also affected America's conception of its proper foreign policy role. A disillusioned nation turned inward, determined to avoid similar pitfalls in the future. This mood persisted until the early 1980s, with the election of President Ronald W. Reagan, who helped to create a climate receptive to increased defense spending and a large-scale military buildup. *See also* HAWKS V. DOVES, 75; LIVING ROOM WAR, 21; VIETNAM WAR, 143; WAR POWERS ACT, 34.

Significance The Vietnam syndrome produced a fierce national debate. Indeed, the entire post–World War II thrust of U.S. foreign policy came under sharp attack. This led to a major reappraisal of U.S. foreign policy. The debate was dominated by two main viewpoints. On the one hand, many Americans strongly supported the nation's foreign policy initiatives, which they saw as a logical extension of the Truman Doctrine. For example, in 1975, former Secretary of State Dean Rusk was questioned whether the Kennedy or Johnson administration had started the war, to which he replied: "Neither one of them started the war and neither one of them escalated it. Ho Chi Minh started it, and Ho Chi Minh escalated it. . . . I do not apologize for saying that the primary object of American foreign policy is to create a situation in the world in which the great experiment in freedom can survive and flourish."[45] On the other hand, many other Americans, although they would not necessarily disagree with Rusk's observation, "accept the idea that the modern world, particularly the Third World, is in a tremendous state of flux, and that neither the United States nor the Soviet Union has guaranteed control over the course of international relations."[46] In their view, the United States could no longer play the role of "world policeman," and certainly could not automatically endorse the ringing promise of President John F. Kennedy's 1961 Inaugural Address: "Let every nation know that we shall pay any price, bear any burden, meet any hardship, support any friend, oppose any foe to assure the survival and success of liberty." The Vietnam War, whatever one concludes is its ultimate meaning, profoundly affected the U.S. psyche. By 1981, however, the nation responded to President Reagan's call for increased defense spending and a renewed commitment to rolling back the spread of communism (e.g., Grenada, Nicaragua, Angola, and Afghanistan). Despite the president's popularity, large numbers of Americans strongly opposed many of President Reagan's interventionist policies.

3. The Arms Race

Aerospace and Defense Industry (63)
That element of business with a dedicated financial interest in the awarding of defense contracts to the private sector, or in the producing of arms commercially for export to other countries. The defense industry operates under the assumption that the demand for weapons and support equipment will remain fairly constant,[1] both domestically and worldwide. A major segment of the U.S. economy has come not only to expect these lucrative contracts, but to rely on them for their financial survival. In addition to purchasing arms, the U.S. government funds considerable research and development into the production of new weapons systems, and supports its overseas allies by sponsoring arms sales and transfers to foreign clients. The Soviet Union, whose defense industry is controlled by the government, similarly sells or transfers arms overseas on a regular basis. The European, Israeli, and South African defense industries rely heavily on arms sales to Third World countries for their survival. *See also* ARMS EMBARGO, 64; ARMS SALE, 66; ARMS TRANSFER, 67; RESEARCH AND DEVELOPMENT (R&D), 83.

Significance   The defense industry is an essential component of the U.S. military structure, and it contributes greatly to the U.S. economy. The enormous size of defense contracts, combined with a relatively small number of vendors selling proprietary systems at enormous potential profit, have lead to abuses, however. Projects are often funded for five or ten years of development costs, plus another five or ten years of production, with very little competition. During World War II, for example, $26 billion was invested in new plants and equipment (about two-thirds provided by the government).[2] The post–

World War II era has seen major scandals in the American defense industry, involving cost overruns, bribes, influence peddling, and other "sweetheart" deals, while available facilities and contractors have continued to decline, thereby reducing viable competition. This trend has been exacerbated in recent decades through intense congressional lobbying by defense contractors; in addition, many recently retired, high-ranking military officers have found lucrative posts with industries whose contracts they formerly regulated. The few efforts by these businesses to originate weapons systems of their own (e.g., Northrop's F-20 fighter) have had disastrous results, leaving many of them increasingly reluctant to work in isolation. The industry as a whole remains highly profitable, however, particularly in Europe, where the defense contractors have heavily promoted their wares to a large number of Third World clients and conflicts in the 1970s and 1980s. France, Czechoslovakia, Israel, and South Africa are particularly notorious for selling their weapons to any bidders willing to pay their price. The People's Republic of China has also moved into this arena in the last decade, supplying small arms to the Cambodian rebels, and shipping Silkworm missiles to Iran.

Arms Embargo (64)

The interdiction of weapons shipments and sales to a particular nation or group. Arms embargoes are usually imposed as a response to some supposed threat by the offending country, or as part of a total trade embargo designed to weaken the economic, political, or military structures of a perceived enemy.[3] The U.S. economic and military embargo of Cuba is a typical example. Unless the country imposing the embargo has the will and the means to enforce it totally (e.g., the closing of all Southern ports during the U.S. Civil War), such strictures are usually ineffective. A partial embargo may limit the export of certain types of military or related technology, either generally or to specific countries or groups of states; this type of embargo has been used in recent decades to stop the export of sophisticated computers from the United States to the Soviet Union and its allies. *See also* AEROSPACE AND DEFENSE INDUSTRY, 63; ARMS RACE, 65; ARMS SALE, 66.

Significance   The arms embargo can be a powerful weapon if used sparingly and against specific targets for well-defined purposes. Such embargoes were more effective in the days when naval blockades could be imposed around offending states; now, most embargoed nations need only find new suppliers or make new political alliances to have their arms pipeline restored. Iran is an example of both the problems and successes of modern arms embargoes. The accession of the Ayatollah Khomeini in 1979 resulted in the United States banning arms sales to Iran; this has successfully prevented Iran from using its fleet of U.S. fighter-bombers, now largely grounded for lack of spare parts. Advisers to the president then secretly violated the embargo to secure the release of U.S. hostages in Lebanon, directly contravening U.S. stated policy of not paying ransom to terrorists. Both the United States and the allies it had attempted to enlist in the embargo were embarrassed by this rogue operation. Embargoes can be successfully imposed in the modern world only where the originating government can control all sources of resupply.

Arms Race (65)

The competition between nations to maintain their real or perceived military superiority. Arms races have been part of the political landscape since steel weapons supplanted bronze in the ancient world. In the post–World War II era, the usual result of arms races—war—is no longer a viable alternative between the superpowers. This has not stopped them, however, from building their arsenals, including nuclear weapons, nor has it prevented other countries from increasing their military infrastructures far beyond any real need for self-defense. *See also* AEROSPACE AND DEFENSE INDUSTRY, 63; ARMS TRANSFER, 67; CUBAN MISSILE CRISIS, 71; MILITARY PARITY, 78; URANIUM, 84.

Significance   After 1945, the world arms race assumed new dimensions with the advent of nuclear weapons. Prior to this, serious arms races almost invariably resulted in war, with one side eventually prevailing. Following World War II, "the United States and the Soviet Union squared off in a kind of global chess match, the military power of each rapidly overshadowing that of every other country."[4] Both superpowers sought ultimate security by building large numbers of atomic devices, each seeking to bluff the other into not using their respective arsenals. Ironically, neither power seemed to realize that greater numbers of warheads do not a safer world make. The fact that war could no longer be conducted between nuclear states without the ultimate destruction of both parties was not publicly acknowledged by either government until the 1980s, when the "nuclear winter" scenario and the Chernobyl nuclear power plant disaster suddenly exposed the civil defense plans of both sides as self-delusional charades. By then, East and West possessed the means to destroy each other a hundred times over. Arms control discussions between the Soviets and Americans had begun as early as 1946, but in 1957, for example, President Dwight D. Eisenhower had suspended such talks because he was convinced that an agreement would give the Russians a "strategic advantage," even though "it was [later] discovered . . . the United States [had] always maintained a substantial lead over the Soviet Union."[5] The Cuban missile crisis of 1962 convinced Soviet planners that the United States enjoyed "an overwhelming lead in deliverable nuclear weapons,"[6] prompting a rapid buildup in Russian ICBMs. By 1967, despite large increases in their nuclear arsenal, "the Soviets may have concluded that in a wide open race . . . the United States might emerge distinctly better off militarily,"[7] due to its substantially larger economic infrastructure. Both sides appeared more willing to bargain for arms control during the administration of President Richard M. Nixon. With the 1979 Soviet invasion of Afghanistan and the election of President Ronald W. Reagan, the arms race resumed, as the Americans perceived themselves falling behind the Russians in both nuclear and conventional arms. This period ended with a series of Reagan-Mikhail Gorbachev summits, the first of which was held at Geneva in 1985. The 1987 Intermediate-Range Nuclear Forces Treaty eliminated an entire class of nuclear weapons for the first time, reducing the number of delivery vehicles in Europe, and offering the hope that mankind might finally see a day when arms are no longer a factor in relations between states.

Arms Sale (66)

The marketing of weapons and military technology, usually to overseas customers. Foreign arms sales bolster the defense industry by providing a profitable outlet for goods produced originally in response to Department of Defense contracts, and also aid the balance of trade figures of the United States. In addition, such sales may reduce the unit cost of certain weapons systems by increasing the number of items produced, may help maintain assembly lines that would otherwise remain idle, may help test untried weapons systems in combat situations, and may be used to bolster U.S. foreign policy aims. The major arms producers market their wares through trade fairs in Europe and elsewhere, and through presentations made directly to interested governments or parties. See also AEROSPACE AND DEFENSE INDUSTRY, 63; ARMS EMBARGO, 64; ARMS TRANSFER, 67; RESEARCH AND DEVELOPMENT (R&D), 83.

Significance The sale and marketing of arms to foreign states has been a part of the world since the late nineteenth century, when arms merchants helped create the conditions that led to World War I. While such sales provide positive benefits to the U.S. economy (and to the economies of France, Israel, Czechoslovakia, and South Africa, among others), the merchants of death have much to answer for. By selling (or allowing the sale of) weapons and support technology to Third World countries, the United States and the industrialized world have directly or indirectly supported wars, skirmishes, and internal uprisings that otherwise could not exist or sustain themselves; and have helped maintain in power ruthless dictatorial regimes which may ultimately not share U.S. foreign policy aims. The recent trend in providing "first-line" equipment (i.e., weapons currently being used by the U.S. military as their primary systems, or newly developed weapons and technology not sponsored by or for the Department of Defense, where "the American company . . . simply sells management and technical knowhow" to the foreign user[8]) has created a "brain drain" to profitable overseas markets.

Arms Transfer (67)

The donation or sale of weapons from existing inventory to a foreign military establishment. The paradigm for such a program is the Lend Lease Act of 1940, which transferred 40 "obsolete" U.S. destroyers to Great Britain to help bolster its war against German submarines. Such transfers are often made for "credits," which are either never repaid by the receiving country or for which goods may ultimately be traded. Arms transfers can be handled much more quickly than the purchase of new weapons from the defense industry, and are often intended to fill urgent, temporary needs. The host country's inventory is then replenished by ordering replacements. *See also* AEROSPACE AND DEFENSE INDUSTRY, 63; ARMS EMBARGO, 64; ARMS SALE, 66; RESEARCH AND DEVELOPMENT (R&D), 83.

Significance　　The arms transfer system is a peculiarity of modern defense strategy, used by both superpowers to strengthen their European pacts, to provide support for Third World allies, and often to generate short-term political gains. The transfer of first-line weapons systems to unstable states has, however, resulted in some unfortunate long-term aspects, including the loss of major military technology to the opposing superpower, or even the use of such weapons against allied states or the originating power itself. Such transfers, if used unwisely or precipitously, can also destabilize previously stable areas of the world, creating new sources of conflict between the superpowers. "A significant segment of the population" believes "that traffic in arms fosters conflict and is often a direct cause of the outbreak of violence."[9] Arms transfers are supported heavily by the defense industry lobby, which benefits directly when depleted stockpiles must be replenished.

Asymmetrical Weapons Systems (68)

Arms which supposedly give one state military superiority over another in specific areas of defense, a term commonly used in statistical warfare. Asymmetrical weapons systems are difficult to evaluate in terms of parity, effectiveness, and capability. *See also* MILITARY PARITY, 78.

Significance Asymmetrical weapons systems can mask the perceived parity of the superpowers, and the term itself is often used as a buzzword during arms-control negotiations. As Richard K. Betts indicates, the "significance of static indices is uncertain when force structures are asymmetrical"; thus, "net equivalence depends on which indices seem most salient."[10] The manipulation of such data is often used to demonstrate either military superiority or inferiority, depending on the political necessity of the moment. In reality, few weapons systems remain asymmetrical for long in the modern world, since any temporary advantages can usually be easily overcome by the opposing superpower.

Civilian Control of the Military (69)

The ability of a free nation to employ its military power in defense of freedom. The exercise of civilian control over the military is a basic democratic political concept, extending the checks and balances that maintain our system of government. *See also* DEPARTMENT OF DEFENSE (DOD), 72; NATIONAL SECURITY COUNCIL (NSC), 79.

Significance The relationship of the civilian sector of society to the military is as relevant today as it was 200 years ago. National decisions made exclusively by and for the benefit of the military lead to repression and the crushing of a free and open government. In a democracy, "the military are professionals in the employ of the state, [and] professional ethics as well as democratic parliamentary institutions guarantee civilian political supremacy."[11] Our nation was "founded by men who believed devoutly in civilian control of the military, . . . vigorous able people fleeing from the militaristic repressions of Europe."[12] Curiously, totalitarian states such as the Soviet Union appear to be as much concerned over civilian control as the Western democracies. The U.S.S.R. has long injected agents of the ruling Communist party at all levels of its military structure, specifically to ensure that the Bolshevik Revolution could not be overthrown by some ambitious officer or clique. In the Western democracies, civilian control of the military ensures that the will of the people, as represented through their elected officials, shall be carried out.

Commission on Strategic Forces (70)

A government body appointed by President Ronald W. Reagan to examine the defense condition of the United States in the 1980s. The Scowcroft Commission, as it was popularly known, made its initial report in 1983, with the approval of four former secretaries of defense and other high-ranking officials.[13] As adopted by the Reagan administration, it made three major recommendations: limiting deployment of the MX missile; development of a small, single-warhead ICBM (the Midgetman); and "an arms control structure which emphasizes the enhancement of strategic stability."[14] In its final report to the president in March of 1984, the commission stated that "it is important to focus, in this final report to you, on the arms control aspects of [the] earlier recommendations."[15] Retired Lt. Gen. Brent Scowcroft headed the blue-ribbon group. *See also* ARMS CONTROL AND DISARMAMENT, 238; ARMS RACE, 65; DEPARTMENT OF DEFENSE (DOD), 72; MILITARY PARITY, 78; STRATEGIC ARMS REDUCTION TALKS (START) AND INTERMEDIATE-RANGE NUCLEAR FORCES (INF) TALKS, 266.

Significance   The Reagan administration created the Commission on Strategic Forces to justify the president's intention to begin "the largest strategic arms buildup in the history of the United States."[16] But the commission concluded that the United States was not nearly as vulnerable as 1979 figures had first indicated; more importantly, it argued strongly in its final report that arms control negotiations constituted a vital and necessary adjunct to the research and development of new weaponry. Although SALT II was eventually abandoned by President Reagan, the SALT structure remained largely intact in the START talks, still influencing attitudes toward arms control even during the height of the renewed cold war of the early 1980s. As the commission observed, "We can not foresee an end to U.S.-Soviet competition. . . . What we can and must do, through a combination of arms control and weapons programs, is reduce the chances that such crises will result in nuclear war."[17]

Cuban Missile Crisis (1962) (71)

A military and political confrontation between the U.S. and U.S.S.R. that led both countries to the brink of nuclear war. In October 1962, President John F. Kennedy, responding to intelligence reports of a buildup of Soviet troops and short-range nuclear weapons in Communist Cuba, issued an ultimatum to Soviet Premier Nikita Khrushchev to withdraw the missiles from the Western hemisphere or face serious military consequences. After the United States had imposed a limited naval blockade on the island, and the Russians had responded by sending several of their ships to the area, the two sides finally reached a face-saving "compromise." The United States agreed never again to attack Cuba, in exchange for a Soviet pledge never to base its nuclear warheads there. Russia withdrew already existing missiles, the U.S. blockade was cancelled, and both sides claimed victory. *See also* ARMS CONTROL AND DISARMAMENT, 238; ARMS RACE, 65; HOT LINE AGREE- MENTS, 249; LIMITED TEST BAN TREATY (LTBT), 251; MILITARY PARITY, 78; NONPROLIFERATION, 225.

Significance   The Cuban missile crisis was the logical outcome of 15 years of cold war politics between the two superpowers, and it brought the world closer to nuclear holocaust than it has ever been, before or since. The Russians "blinked" first because of the over- whelming superiority of the United States in deliverable nuclear war- heads; this resulted in a renewed arms race, as the Soviets resolved never to be put in this situation again. The crisis also ultimately cost Premier Khrushchev his job. Both superpowers were so frightened by their postmortem analyses of the crisis that they began hurried con- sultations to improve communications links between their capitals, concluding the first of several Hot Line Agreements the following year. Arms control suddenly attained new respectability, as one method in which the conflicting powers could prevent such "brink- manship" in the future. Subsequent negotiations led in 1963 to the Limited Test Ban Treaty, the first successful arms pact concluded by the two superpowers in the post–World War II era.

Department of Defense (DOD)   (72)

That branch of the U.S. government responsible for managing the nation's military forces and materiel. The Department of Defense consists of a civilian administrative structure, headed by the secretary of defense (a Cabinet official), plus various undersecretaries and other staff, superimposed over the Joint Chiefs of Staff, the military heads of the four major services (the army, navy, air force, and marines). The secretary of defense and the chairman of the Joint Chiefs of Staff also serve as permanent members of the National Security Council, which advises the president on military policies and strategy.[18] The Joint Chiefs were restructured during the second term of President Ronald W. Reagan to give them more real authority over the services during combined military operations. *See also* AERO- SPACE AND DEFENSE INDUSTRY, 63; CIVILIAN CONTROL OF THE MILITARY, 69; JOINT CHIEFS OF STAFF, 197; NATIONAL SECURITY COUNCIL (NSC), 79.

Significance   Almost every aspect of governmental policy—military, diplomatic, budgetary—is touched upon in some way by the Department of Defense. Other than entitlement programs, defense spending accounts for the largest single portion of the federal budget. President Reagan inaugurated a new round in the arms race with his proposals for substantial increases in defense spending, much of it funded through deficit financing. The sudden availability of billions of dollars for new arms resulted in an emphasis on expensive, "high tech" weapons systems that often did not work as planned, could only be produced with massive cost overruns, and required a level of operator sophistication that could not be met with today's uneducated recruits. Administration critics have questioned whether the U.S. defense posture was actually improved by some of these weapons; one system, the Sergeant York gun, had to be scrapped completely after an investment exceeding $2 billion. A permanently established civilian "defense industry" actually conducts the production and research on new weapons, with the DOD awarding contracts on a competitive basis, and providing appropriate oversight;[19] the U.S. Congress also maintains an oversight function through House and Senate Defense Committees. The size, influence, and lobbying capabilities of both the DOD and the civilian defense industry give them enormous influence over arms control negotiations, the conduct of U.S. foreign policy, and U.S. politics, particularly in a negative sense, by slowing or vetoing certain kinds of actions. During President Reagan's second term, the Defense Department was rocked by a number of scandals involving bribes, influence peddling, and kickbacks.

Détente   (73)

The unspoken mutual recognition that neither the United States nor the Soviet Union intends to take hostile military action against the other. Although relations between the U.S. and U.S.S.R. have fluctuated since World War II, from the depths of the Cuban missile crisis to the heights of SALT I and the INF treaty, détente (or "peaceful coexistence," as it is called by the Russians) has made a virtue of necessity. The Cuban missile crisis caused both superpowers to reexamine their priorities, and slowly to come to the realization that the logical outcome of the cold war was a hot war in which both sides would be utterly destroyed by an exchange of nuclear weapons. Some form of détente was the only practical solution to this political and military dilemma. *See also* ARMS CONTROL AND DISARMAMENT, 238; ARMS RACE, 65; CUBAN MISSILE CRISIS, 71; GENEVA SUMMIT, 248; INTERMEDIATE-

RANGE NUCLEAR FORCES TREATY (INFT), 250; MILITARY PARITY, 78; STRATE-
GIC ARMS LIMITATION TALKS I (SALT I), 264.

Significance   Détente has always been an uncertain stepchild of the
cold war between the United States and the Soviet Union, but gradually flourished in the post–World War II era as the superpowers
became more civilized. The near disaster in Cuba in 1962 forced both
military leaders and politicians to face the realities of the nuclear age
for the first time. Ironically, it was the conservative President Richard
M. Nixon, together with adviser Henry A. Kissinger, who successfully
concluded substantial new negotiations with the Russians, including
the ABM treaty, the Interim Agreement, and other accords.[20] Kissinger, who won a Nobel prize for his efforts, was forced to defend the
administration against charges by Republican and Democratic hawks
that the Russians were using the talks to further their own military
posture. President Ronald W. Reagan renewed the arms race and
downplayed détente, but was ultimately forced to realize that we cannot have "détente in one part of the world and aggravation of conflicts
in another."[21] His 1985 Geneva Summit with Soviet General Secretary
Mikhail Gorbachev ultimately led to the 1987 INF treaty, which eliminated intermediate-range nuclear missiles in Europe, and which set
the stage for further negotiations on wholesale reductions of both
superpowers' nuclear arsenals.

Escalation   (74)

Raising the level of hostilities in a military or political conflict. "Escalation dominance . . . is the ability, actual or perceived, to take a conflict
to a higher level of violence in the expectation of enforcing an improved outcome."[22] Bernard Brodie says that it represents, "above all,
a nation's determination to show its enemies that it is not more unwilling than they to move towards 'higher levels.'" [23] An "escalation
ladder" is a "deterrent which is purely counterforce and not warwin-
ning; [it] is no sufficient deterrent against an enemy whose threats . . .
are not restricted to pure counterforce."[24] In other words, an enemy
who can inflict unacceptable losses, and who is willing to go to the
highest rung of the "ladder of escalation," cannot be deterred.
"Limited escalation . . . controls the process of escalation in order to
limit damage." As Arthur M. Schlesinger points out, "We need . . . a
series of measured responses to aggression which . . . have prospects
of terminating hostilities before general nuclear war breaks out."[25] He
warns, however, that to ensure restraint the United States would always
have to hold some of the enemy's most valued assests as "hostages."[26]

See also ARMS RACE, 65; ESCALATION OF WAR, 15; MILITARY PARITY, 78; WAR GAMES, 207.

Significance   Escalation theory is sometimes used in war games to predict the likely outcome of an armed conflict. Such "what if?" scenarios are based upon relative military strength, political climate, and, most importantly, the will of the opponents. Escalation dominance is not viable, however, unless backed with the means and the will to carry out the threat. Since the highest rung of the escalation ladder is obviously the use of nuclear weapons, the justification for proliferation of such weaponry is that it provides a "deterrent" to all-out nuclear war. However, as McGeorge Bundy states: "There is an enormous gulf between what political leaders really think about nuclear weapons and what is assumed in . . . simulated strategic warfare. In the real world . . . one hydrogen bomb on one city . . . would be . . . a catastrophic blunder; ten bombs on ten cities would be a disaster beyond history."[27] Thus, the use of escalation scenarios can, under perverted circumstances, dull the perception of the gamesplayers into believing the real world is itself a political or military game, thereby increasing the risk of an actual nuclear conflict.

Hawks vs. Doves   (75)

The continuing debate between those who support a large military establishment and its potential use to support the political aims of the United States, and those who favor a smaller military infrastructure with more limited foreign policy goals. While some U.S. politicians, such as the late Senator Henry M. Jackson (D-Wash.), have embraced the term "hawk," the public perception of hawkishness or dovishness depends largely on the prevailing political mood of the time, and on the willingness of certain politicos to tar others with labels they may or may not accept. Conservatives often call liberals with whom they disagree "doves," and liberals may label their opponents "hawks," but whether those so labelled will agree with such pejoratives is questionable. In fact, not one prominent U.S. politician will publicly support a "weak" U.S. defense posture; rather, the argument is over levels of degree and funding, or over specific programs; and the shouting on both sides may become so vehement as to overshadow the virtues or demerits of either position. The media play a large (and sometimes unwitting) role in applying such labels to public figures. *See also* ARMS CONTROL AND DISARMAMENT, 238; ARMS RACE, 65; MILITARY PARITY, 78.

Significance   The issue of hawks vs. doves crosses party lines, having more to do with such self-perceived labels as "liberal" and

Arms Control, Disarmament, and Military Security

conservative" than with political affiliation. Those at the extremes of
the U.S. political spectrum tend to voice such opinions most loudly.
Arthur Macy Cox, for example, states: "The main barrier to strategic
arms control has been the American hawks, who oppose the concept
of nuclear equality. The American hawks want to restore . . . superiority. . . . The sane approach would be to negotiate a treaty which
would reduce and control nuclear weapons systems"[28]; ironically, it is
the self-proclaimed "hawk," Ronald W. Reagan, who seems to have
embraced this position. On the other side, the Committee on the
Present Danger, a bipartisan group formed in 1976 to inform the
public "about the dangers of détente and the need to increase our
military power," states: "Unless decisive steps are taken to alert the
nation, and to change the course of its policy, our economic and
military capacity will become inadequate to assure peace with security.
. . . The principal threat to our nation, to world peace, and to the
cause of human freedom is the Soviet drive for dominance based
upon an unparalleled military buildup."[29] The hawks vs. doves debate
has the power to polarize both the U.S. public and the government.
Barry M. Blechman believes that "the U.S. public broadly supports
the maintenance of a 'strong' military posture; the precise definition
of 'strong' varying in response to events and the position adopted by
the President and other national leaders."[30] An obvious solution to
the debate is strong leadership at the presidential level to ensure the
nation's support for the administration's stated foreign policy goals.
Without such leadership and the reestablishment of a foreign policy
and defense consensus among the major U.S. parties, the U.S. body
politic runs a real risk of breaking into polarized factions, thus
"freezing" into place the governmental impasse between the executive
and legislative branches so characteristic of the administration of
President Ronald Reagan.

Korean Airlines Flight 007 Incident   (76)

The deliberate shooting down by Soviet military forces of a commercial jetliner which had strayed over Russian air space. On September
1, 1983, KAL flight 007 was downed by Soviet interceptors after it had
crossed into Siberia. Sixty-one Americans were aboard, including conservative U.S. Congressman Larry McDonald (D-Ga.). The plane appeared to lose its bearings not long after leaving Anchorage, Alaska,
wandering over the Kamchatka Peninsula for more than two hours
before finally being downed by a single air-to-air missile. Secretary of
State George Shultz called the act "barbaric," but the Russians responded by insisting "that the airliner had been on a spy mission for
American and Korean intelligence services, and that the destruction

of the plane, while regrettable, was completely justified."[31] On July 3, 1988, the U.S. cruiser *Vincennes* shot down an Iranian Airbus over the Persian Gulf, killing 290 civilians, and raising a storm of controversy. *See also* CIVILIAN CONTROL OF THE MILITARY, 69; GENEVA SUMMIT, 248; IRAN-IRAQ WAR, 126.

Significance   The KAL disaster was the nadir of the mini–cold war that started with the 1979 Soviet invasion of Afghanistan. Representing an almost complete breakdown of Russian air defenses in Siberia, it also proved a public relations disaster for the U.S.S.R. Several years earlier, another Korean airliner had been forced to land in Siberia on a frozen lake, after it too had violated Soviet airspace. The resulting shake-up of the Soviet military command had persuaded surviving officers never to let another craft penetrate Soviet defenses. Then, on a night when a U.S. intelligence plane was circling just outside Russia's Kamchatka bases, one of KAL 007's pilots apparently keyed the wrong data into his guidance computer. Through a combination of errors, including the inattention of the chief pilot and the failure of the Soviet command structure to verify which craft had penetrated their space, an innocent commercial airliner was destroyed. In the resulting brouhaha, a number of high-ranking Soviet military officers were transferred or retired, the U.S.S.R. lost considerable face around the world, and President Ronald W. Reagan's proposed Strategic Defense Initiative and military buildup received considerable support in the U.S. Congress. U.S.-Soviet relations were not restored to any semblance of normality until the 1985 Geneva summit. The 1988 U.S. downing of an Iranian airliner was compared by some observers around the world to the KAL 007 incident.

Long Term Defense Program (LTDP)   (77)

A proposal made at a 1978 NATO conference to strengthen allied conventional forces in Europe. In response to Soviet deployment of the intermediate-range SS-20 missile in 1976, a Long Term Defense Program was proposed in May of 1978, to increase monetary support for the NATO conventional forces, which are used to deter potential Soviet aggression.[32] The NATO defense ministers agreed to a 3 percent increase in defense outlays annually for each member, although in reality only the United States has actually contributed that much (and more). *See also* DEEP STRIKE, 189; INTERMEDIATE-RANGE NUCLEAR FORCES TREATY (INFT), 250.

Significance   The NATO Long Term Defense Program is often used as an example of Allied consensus on conventional deterrent strategy.[33] Conventional forces aid in preventing escalation to the

highest "rung" of the nuclear ladder. Given the overwhelming pre-
ponderance of Soviet conventional weapons in the European theater,
reliance on such forces alone cannot provide sufficient deterrence to
the possibility of nuclear or chemical warfare. Still, when used in
conjunction with nuclear retaliatory systems, the LTDP plan remains
a major and necessary part of overall NATO defense strategy. This
kind of program will assume even more importance when the provisions of the INF treaty have been completely carried out, as the
medium-range nuclear missiles upon which NATO so heavily relied
are removed and destroyed.

Military Parity (78)

A perceived balance in the weapons and defense capabilities of two or
more states. A realistic estimate of military parity can only be achieved
by actually comparing the relative strengths, weaknesses, effectiveness, and capabilities of the opposing forces. Since a great many vari-
ables are included in such equations, including the will of political
leaders to use their forces, such judgments can be notoriously faulty.
See also ARMS RACE, 65; ASYMMETRICAL WEAPONS SYSTEMS, 68; PROXY FORCES
WARFARE, 133.

Significance Real military parity in the prenuclear era was rare,
and judgments of such parity often proved wrong by subsequent
events. In both World War I and World War II, France's defensive
fortifications along its border with Germany were judged by most
strategists to have offset Germany's military superiority in other areas; German military leaders disagreed with these assessments, and
quickly demonstrated why. Nations are usually superior in one area
and deficient in another, making real comparisons between their
forces impossible. Further, the outcome of real military clashes is
often determined by superior strategic sense, by the willingness of
generals or politicians to commit their forces, by boldness, even by
luck. In the post–World War II era, military parity exists between the
superpowers due to a general realization that the nuclear arsenals of
both sides are capable of destroying the other completely and irrevo-
cably. As Raymond Garthoff states, "Strategic parity between the
United States and the Soviet Union has existed, and will continue to
exist, so long as each has the recognized capability to deal the other a
devastating retaliatory strike after receiving a first strike."[34] Because
of the prolonged stalemate in a relationship that normally would have
ended in war during previous eras, the United States and the Soviet
Union have been forced to wage mini-wars through client proxies,

generally unsuccessfully, and have gradually come to an accommodation that will allow them to continue their struggle with economic weapons in the future.

National Security Council (NSC) (79)

An advisory group to the president of the United States on national security matters. Proposed by President Harry S Truman, and enacted into law by the National Security Act of 1947, the National Security Council (NSC) includes as permanent members the president, vice-president, secretary of state, secretary of defense, chairman of the Joint Chiefs of Staff, and the director of the Central Intelligence Agency (who reports to the NSC), plus a White House-based staff that has grown larger with each succeeding administration. The group is chaired by the national security adviser, a presidential appointee responsible only to the chief executive. The relationship of the NSC to other governmental agencies has varied with the interest of each president in national security. *See also* COMMISSION ON STRATEGIC FORCES, 70; DEPARTMENT OF DEFENSE (DOD), 72; JOINT CHIEFS OF STAFF, 197.

Significance The National Security Council responds uniquely to the will and personality of the president, reflecting his foreign and security policy needs and perceptions. President Harry S Truman, for example, commissioned a 1949 landmark study (NSC–68) which concluded that the two superpowers (as a result of the U.S.S.R.'s acquisition of the atomic bomb) "might now deter each other . . . and devote a fair amount of attention to the counterforce possibility."[35] President Dwight D. Eisenhower placed a "premium . . . on [the NSC's] consensus prior to presidential decisions," which led to a proliferation of council committees and agencies. President John F. Kennedy "employed the National Security Council . . . as [his] personal staff rather than [as] an interagency decision-making board."[36] In 1962, he used the council to back his decision to sell wheat to the Soviets, thereby bypassing Congress, and setting a precedent that has continued to this day. The administration of President Ronald W. Reagan was notorious for its abuses of the NSC, particularly in the Iran-Contra affair, where the president circumvented the recommendations of both his secretary of state and secretary of defense to carry out ill-advised and poorly organized intelligence operations, actions which may well have violated both the law and the dicta of common sense. A reexamination of the NSC's role in U.S. government is long overdue.

Nicaraguan Civil War (1979–) (80)

The ongoing military and political conflict in Nicaragua between the ruling left-wing party, the Sandinistas, and the right-wing rebels, the Contras. After the deposition of President Anastasio Somoza in 1979, the leftist rebels, the Sandinistas, assumed power under the presidency of Daniel Ortega. The remnants of the old regime fled to the hills, forming a new resistance movement popularly called the Contras. The newly installed administration of President Ronald W. Reagan called for both military and humanitarian aid for the Contras, whom Reagan called the new "freedom-fighters in Nicaragua," denouncing the Sandinistas as Communists. The U.S. Congress has funded such aid haphazardly. Reagan's efforts to support the Contras led the National Security Council, through Colonel Oliver North, to mount an extralegal effort to sell arms to Iran and give the profits to the Contras (the Iran-Contra affair or "Irangate"). Following this scandal, Congress rejected President Reagan's request for military assistance in 1988. *See also* CUBAN MISSILE CRISIS, 71; HAWKS VS. DOVES, 75; NATIONAL SECURITY COUNCIL (NSC), 79.

Significance   The Nicaraguan conflict "constitutes a crisis in American foreign policy, not because it poses a threat to U.S. national security in any direct way, but because [Nicaragua] has the potential to become a Soviet client."[37] Conservatives fear another Cuba in the Western Hemisphere, and argue that only by keeping pressure on President Ortega's government can Nicaragua be prevented from falling into the Soviet camp. Liberals respond by saying that the Nicaraguans not only have the right to determine their own style of government, but more importantly, would be less likely to bolster ties with the Soviets if less pressure and more aid came from the United States. The Nicaragua-Contra conflict is symptomatic of deep-seated differences between hawks and doves in U.S. politics, and of the way in which the superpowers use such bush wars to further their own international agendas.

Nonaligned States (81)

Nations that choose not to be associated politically or militarily with either the West or the East. The first Conference of Nonaligned Countries (Belgrade, Yugoslavia, 1961) stated that they must: "1) pursue an independent policy based on peaceful coexistence; 2) not participate in any multilateral military alliance; 3) support liberation and independence movements; and 4) not participate in bilateral military alliances with the Great Powers."[38] Subsequent conferences have included: Cairo (1964), Lusaka (1970), Algiers (1973), Colombo (1976),

Havana (1979), New Delhi (1982), and Harare, Zimbabwe (1986). *See also* ARMS RACE, 65.

Significance The nonaligned movement began at the height of the cold war period. In 1955, 25 Third World leaders met in Indonesia to seek some method of establishing a bargaining position with the superpowers. By the 1980s, about 100 nations considered themselves nonaligned, including most, though not all, of the Third World nations. U.S. conservatives have accused the nonaligned movement of furthering the ends, directly or indirectly, of the Soviet Union; but the reality of Third World politics seems much more muddled and directionless. In fact, both superpowers routinely regard the Third World as impotent and ineffectual, and use Third World countries for their own economic, political, and military purposes, virtually at will. Conversely, both East and West reserve issues they consider vital—such as arms control negotiations—exclusively to themselves. Where nonaligned Third World countries have been involved in such discussions, the results have almost always been meaningless.

Nuclear Stockpiles (82)

Nuclear weapons or warheads stored in strategic locations for deployment in the event of war. Nuclear stockpiles are maintained in both East and West at processing facilities, and moved according to the needs of changing weapons systems and changing political winds. *See also* INTERMEDIATE-RANGE NUCLEAR FORCES TREATY (INFT), 250; NONPROLIFERATION, 225; URANIUM, 84.

Significance Nuclear stockpiles have grown steadily in both the U.S. and U.S.S.R. during the post–World War II era, now numbering about 30,000 warheads each, and seem destined to continue rising unless arms control negotiations significantly reduce nuclear arsenals. Even after the reductions suggested in 1983, NATO had "over 4,000 warheads . . . on the [European] continent, and a substantial stockpile . . . stored in the U.S. . . . for deployment in Europe in time of crisis. . . . Although nuclear weapons must be stockpiled in central locations in peacetime for security reasons, such stockpiling makes wartime deployment difficult and provides attractive targets."[39] The 1987 INF treaty eliminated intermediate-range nuclear missiles in Europe, but allowed both superpowers to keep the warheads and reuse them for other purposes, including long-range missile systems. Antinuclear activists in both Europe and the United States have protested the storage of nuclear warheads in close proximity to civilian populations.

Research and Development (R&D) (83)

The invention and construction of new weapons or weapons technology by the defense industry. Research and development into major weapons has become so expensive that it is now largely funded by governments, working (in the West) through competitive contracts awarded to independent contractors. Hundreds of millions of dollars annually are spent by the Department of Defense on weapons development; an equal sum is presumably spent by the Soviet Union, although it has publicly admitted that R&D figures are a secret part of its defense budget. Private companies do produce new weapons on their own initiative, but these tend to be targeted toward more individual use, for sale to small armies or groups in Third World countries and elsewhere. *See also* AEROSPACE AND DEFENSE INDUSTRY, 63; ARMS RACE, 65; ARMS SALE, 66; ARMS TRANSFER, 67; STRATEGIC DEFENSE INITIATIVE (SDI), 141.

Significance   Research and development into the Strategic Defense Initiative and other weapons systems now commands such a large monetary contribution from the U.S. government that it threatens to limit scientific investigation into other areas of research of potentially greater long-term interest to the human race. Engineers and scientists find themselves becoming involved in the arms race whether they wish to or not; federal funds for other kinds of serious investigation have gradually evaporated as billions of dollars are poured into SDI. A number of scientists have questioned: (1) whether programs such as SDI are technologically feasible; (2) whether it is wise for the government to put all of its scientific eggs into one basket; or (3) whether such wholesale diversion of the limited number of scientific and engineering minds of the United States into one program is really to the long-term benefit of this country, particularly vis-à-vis its future economic competition with Japan and the other technological giants of the Far East and Europe.

Uranium (84)

An element vital to the production of nuclear arms and the fueling of nuclear power plants. Access to a secure and reliable supply of uranium (and its derivative, plutonium) is crucial to the superpowers' overall defense strategy. Conversely, denying weapons-grade uranium or plutonium to those states that have not developed the atom bomb is a long-standing policy of both the superpowers and most of the industrialized world, as overseen by the International Atomic Energy Agency. *See also* INTERNATIONAL ATOMIC ENERGY AGENCY (IAEA), 219;

NONPROLIFERATION, 225; NUCLEAR POWER PLANTS, 230; NUCLEAR STOCK-
PILES, 82; THRESHOLD NUCLEAR POWERS, 236.

Significance   Only those nations that have adequate supplies of uranium and the technology to use it can build atomic weapons. Threshold nations, such as India and Israel, which have access to uranium supplies and have a developing nuclear power industry, can automatically use such bargaining chips with the superpowers to secure themselves a privileged relationship. The knowledge to construct nuclear weapons is generally available; but it "is not so much a question of having access to the necessary knowledge, but rather obtaining sufficient uranium or plutonium and working it into a functional weapon"[40] that is the problem. It is to the benefit of all mankind that such supplies be available only to nations already possessing nuclear weapons, and that they not be allowed to fall into the hands of terrorists or extremist political groups.

4. Collective Security

Arab League (85)

A pan-Arabian regional organization, created in 1945, to strengthen relations amongst the Arab states, coordinate political activities, protect national sovereignty and independence, and promote social, cultural, and economic cooperation. The Arab League—which was originally founded by Syria, Jordan, Iraq, Saudi Arabia, Lebanon, Egypt, and Yemen—now represents most independent Arab states. The Arab League Charter prohibits the use of force as a means of resolving interstate conflicts. If disputes arise (e.g., over independence, sovereignty, or territorial integrity), and the member-states enjoy recourse to the Council (of the Arab League), the decision of the council is binding. Supreme decision-making authority rests with the Majlis, or council, which convenes biannually and consists of a representative from each state. Binding decisions require unanimous agreement, while majority rulings are nonobligatory. The organization's secretariat, which is headed by a secretary-general, is based in Tunis. *See also* COLLECTIVE SECURITY, 88; INTERNATIONAL ORGANIZATION, 91; REGIONALISM, 96.

Significance The Arab League, like many regional alliances, has been plagued by internal conflict and division. Over the years, the Arab League has spearheaded Arab opposition to Israel. Indeed, in 1948, it declared war on Israel. However, the organization proved unable to coordinate the military actions of the various Arab parties. Disagreements over the conduct of the war and the Palestinian question exacerbated tensions and disunity amongst the member-states. Following the Arab defeat in the 1948–1949 war, the Arab League suffered a major loss of influence. Since then, it has supported Syrian opposition to the Hashemites of Jordan and Iraq in the early 1950s, strongly condemned Egyptian President Anwar el-Sadat's peace overture toward Israel in 1977, and bitterly denounced the peace treaty between Egypt and Israel in 1979. Incensed over the Camp David accords, the Arab League suspended Egypt's membership and transferred its headquarters from Cairo to Tunis. Despite its claim of representing the Arab world, it has failed to moderate differences between rival states, as illustrated by its failure to prevent Iraq from invading Iran in 1980. In recent years, however, the Arab League has demonstrated increased unity. In 1982, for example, it held a summit meeting in response to the expulsion of the Palestine Liberation Organization from Beirut by the Israelis. Although some observers were impressed by this apparent new show of Arab unity, "it remains to be seen," according to one expert, "whether this display of camaraderie was a true test of Arab intentions, or merely another temporary arrangement provoked by the war in Lebanon."[1] Still, the Arab League does boast several tangible accomplishments, among them: the establishment of an Arab Common Market, an Arab Development Bank, an Arab States Broadcasting Union, an Anti-Narcotics Bureau, and an Arab Press. In addition, it has functioned skillfully as a caucusing group at the United Nations, and has won recognition of Arabic as an official language of that international body.

Central Intelligence Agency (CIA) (86)

The primary federal agency charged with gathering and assessing information acquired by the national intelligence community that may contribute to effective foreign and defense policy. The Central Intelligence Agency, created by the National Security Act of 1947, is under the aegis of the National Security Council (NSC) and the president. Its duties include research, espionage, and a wide range of functions covering overt (open) and covert (secret) activities. The CIA is headed by a civilian director, appointed by the president with Senate approval, who frequently participates in NSC meetings at the behest of the president. At times, the CIA has exceeded its congressional mandate, engaging in a variety of clandestine activities (e.g., political assassinations, coups and revolutions, and extensive surveillance of U.S. citizens). Although the Congress has established a watchdog select committee to oversee CIA operations, it has achieved mixed results. For example, no one outside the CIA's most "classified" circles knows precisely the amount of its budget or how it is spent, how many agents it employs and in which areas, or the nature and extent of its activities in various countries. Indeed, outside the intelligence community, few know much about intelligence products or processes. This may explain, for example, why there are so few major pressure groups with either knowledge or sufficient power to influence the formulation of intelligence policy. Despite several well-known agency failures (e.g., the Bay of Pigs), the United States, like most major and minor powers, recognizes the importance of maintaining an effective intelligence-gathering network. *See also* COUNTER-INTELLIGENCE, 40; INTELLIGENCE COMMUNITY, 42; INTELLIGENCE CYCLE, 43; NATIONAL SECURITY COUNCIL (NSC), 79.

Significance   The Central Intelligence Agency remained, by and large, unchanged until the early and mid-1970s. Since then, the CIA has been the subject of increased public and private scrutiny, culminating in a series of shocking revelations of wrongdoing. As a result, the CIA came to be viewed as a service function, an unfortunate but necessary evil. This resulted in major cutbacks in manpower, resources, and support personnel. In addition, numerous legal restrictions were imposed on the agency, in the form of federal laws, presidential executive orders, and agency guidelines. These measures dramatically altered the nature of CIA activities, which were, for the most part, limited completely to official covert operations. A new emphasis was placed on relatively clean, risk-free data collection. One major CIA target, argues agency expert Roy Godson, was covert action. In a real sense, notes Godson, "covert action had all the hallmarks of a dying art form."[2] Today, in spite of CIA protestations, there is ample evidence to suggest that the CIA is involved in covert operations in Nicaragua, El Salvador, and the Middle East. Under President Ronald W. Reagan, the CIA experienced a new resurgence, enjoying its largest buildup, both budgetary and personnel-wise, since the 1950s. In 1987, the CIA was rocked by charges that the agency played a salient role in the Iran-Contra affair, in which weapons were sold to the Iranians in exchange for release of U.S. hostages, with the profits being diverted to the Nicaraguan Contras, in direct defiance of the law.

Central Treaty Organization (CENTO)   (87)
A regional alliance instigated by the United States in 1955 to safeguard the Middle East against Communist aggression and to foster social and economic cooperation among its members. The Central Treaty Organization, which succeeded the ill-fated Baghdad Pact, closely parallels the aims of the North Atlantic Treaty Organization (NATO). Specifically, CENTO sought to formalize an alliance between Turkey, Iran, Pakistan, and Great Britain. Although the United States was not a formal party to the pact, it served as an

unofficial partner. In essence, CENTO represented a pivotal link in the chain of alliances between NATO and the Southeast Treaty Organization (SEATO), providing the members with vital arms and protection. The United States functioned as an active member of the alliance, participating in myriad committees and subcommittees, most notably in the areas of military planning, bilateral agreements, and strategic decisions. CENTO is headed by a council, which serves as the Supreme Organ of the Organization, assisted by four main committees (military, economic, countersubversion, and liaison) and a secretariat (headed by a secretary-general), based in Ankara. *See also* COLLECTIVE SECURITY, 88; INTERNATIONAL ORGANIZATION, 91; REGIONALISM, 96; SOUTHEAST ASIA COLLECTIVE DEFENSE TREATY, 98; TREATY, 99.

Significance The Central Treaty Organization proved minimally effective. Although it endorsed the principle of containment, it failed to enforce the peace and to prevent regional conflicts. In large part, CENTO's demise was precipitated by U.S. indifference and intransigence. Indeed, the United States did little to assist those states who were not the direct victims of Soviet aggression. This, in turn, resulted in a loss of confidence in America's resolve. In addition, CENTO was plagued by deep internal divisions, an inability to recruit members among the Arab world, and the lack of overt Communist aggression, all of which served to undermine the vitality of the alliance. Furthermore, the 1979 Iranian revolution, followed by the subsequent seizure of U.S. hostages by that country, culminated in Iran's withdrawal from CENTO, which raised serious questions about CENTO's future. Finally, in spite of its stated objectives, CENTO failed to promote social and economic cooperation among its members, which blunted its appeal to the Third World, which faced myriad problems, including poverty, illiteracy, disease, and malnutrition. Ultimately, CENTO proved both ineffectual and irrelevant. For example, in the case of Pakistan, the United States waffled on its pledges, refusing to provide that nation with the arms it sought to counteract the growing power of India, its principal adversary in the region. In the end, CENTO's rhetoric far surpassed its performance, leaving many of its members both embittered and disillusioned.

Collective Security (88)

A system of states that join together, usually by treaty, to renounce the use of force and pledge to take common action against any state(s) that breaches the peace. Collective security is based on the principles of deterrence and joint action—that is, if deterrence fails, then the members will coalesce, employing military action, to defeat the aggressor. Collective security is only applicable to the system itself; its purpose is to protect its members from other insiders. In this sense, it does not apply to external aggression. To be effective, collective security obligates the members to support each other, thus ensuring predictability and simplicity. In this regard, collective security eliminates any doubts as to what will occur in the event of armed aggression; the attacker knows that it will be met by unified opposition. Likewise, collective security promotes the peaceful resolution of disputes, since the use of force is strictly prohibited. Scant attention is paid to the reasons for using force, the issues behind the conflict, or the consequences of defeat for one side or the other. *See also* ALLIANCE, 2; INTERNATIONAL ORGANIZATION, 91; NATIONAL SECURITY, 56; TREATY, 99; TRUMAN DOCTRINE, 100; UNITED NATIONS, 101.

Significance   Collective security was first articulated, at least on the international level, by President Woodrow Wilson following World War I, when he proposed a League of Nations. Indeed, the principle of collective security was embodied in Article 16 of the League's Covenant, which stated: "Should any Member of the League resort to war in disregard of its covenants . . . it shall, ipso facto, be deemed to have committed an act of war against the other Members of the League."[3] Unfortunately, the League proved ineffectual, owing, in part, to ideological divisions and structural weaknesses. Although the major powers endorsed the principle of collective security, their actions were motivated by a desire to preserve the balance of power against specific opponents. The small states were equally culpable, as they showed little direct interest in collective security. The failure of the League of Nations underscores the difficulties inherent in any system of collective security. In part, the problem stems from a lack of consensus over what constitutes "aggression." The classic definition—that is, the "violation of territorial integrity and political independence"—has proven inadequate.[4] In addition, institutions such as the League of Nations or, for that matter, the United Nations, have found it difficult, if not impossible, to compel unified action. Although common action is not essential, collective security cannot succeed unless the major powers cooperate in action against an aggressor. In the past, states have been reluctant to act against a powerful neighbor, a close ally or friend, or the perceived victim of a conflict. For example, Albania refused to oppose Italy, its powerful protector, in 1935, while the Soviet Union would not condemn North Korea, an ideological ally in 1950. Like the League of Nations, the United Nations has been plagued by similar problems. According to its charter, the Security Council—which is primarily charged with the maintenance of world peace—may ask all members to invoke sanctions against aggressor states under Chapter VII. When the council is deadlocked, the General Assembly is empowered to authorize such collective action. However, any of the five major powers (the United States, Soviet Union, Great Britain, the People's Republic of China, or France) may block collective action by exercising its veto.

Colonialism (89)

The process of establishing and governing territories and peoples held in a dependent and inferior relationship by an external power. The term *colonialism* is often used together with imperialism (a conscious or unplanned state policy, in which one nation attempts to dominate or control another). In reality, colonialism is a manifestation of imperialism. Throughout history, colonialism has been motivated by economic gain, national prestige, social responsibility, political adventure, power politics, religious ties, and sheer avarice. Colonialism waxed strong until the late 1700s, at which point many Western Hemisphere colonies rebelled, due to geographical distance, political dissatisfaction, economic exploitation, and national pride. However, in the late 1800s, colonialism experienced a new resurgence in Europe, when various European powers turned their attention to Asia and Africa. By World War I, colonialism had begun to wane, a trend which was exacerbated by World War II and the establishment of the United Nations. In the end, colonialism collapsed, argues political scientist Forest L. Grieves, as a result of war, world opinion, the transplant of Western intellectual precepts, the nature of the nation-state system, and a buoyed sense of identity and nationalism.[5] *See also* INTERNATIONAL ORGANIZATION, 91; UNITED NATIONS, 101; WAR, 33.

Significance Colonialism, like imperialism, has sparked a fierce intellectual debate, one that has been marked by polemics on both sides. In the main, colonialism bequeathed a legacy of economic and political exploitation. The colonial powers saw these territories as a prime opportunity to control investment and trade, regulate currency and production, and manipulate labor. In addition, colonialism satisfied their desire for power and national triumph, a vehicle to achieve hegemony and influence. Ultimately, colonialism collapsed, fueled, in part, by the cry of self-determination and the rise of myriad independence movements. These newly independent states were bolstered by the principles enunciated in the Declaration Regarding Non-Self-Governing Territories of the United Nations Charter, which heightened their quest for nationhood. Indeed, by 1960, the number of new nation-states had more than doubled the membership of the United Nations. Despite these developments, colonialism has reemerged, albeit in new forms. Although the former colonial powers no longer physically occupy or govern these developing states, they wield enormous influence in many Third World nations. This is made possible, contends Leon P. Baradat, a specialist in international relations, by the fact that the industrialized powers own large shares in the major industries of many Third World countries.[6] In addition, foreign aid, with its attendant political strings, has enticed them into economic relationships similar to colonialism. Finally, Third World independence has, in many cases, been undermined by the role of international corporations, which have injected themselves into the political affairs of the emerging states. These corporations frequently operate outside the legal system, unfettered by legal restraints, owing to their corporate structure and wealth. As Baradat notes, "The power relationship between the international corporations and the host countries is frequently so uneven that the developing nations find themselves needing the companies more than the companies need them. . . . Their [the corporations'] role in Third World countries has often led to improper involvement in the domestic and international political affairs of the host country, stimulating charges of oppression, exploitation, and neocolonialism."[7]

Domino Theory (90)
This theory postulates that if one state falls, then those states near and around it will also fall like a row of dominos. The domino theory was cited on sundry occasions to justify U.S. intervention in Vietnam. The phrase itself was coined by President Dwight D. Eisenhower, who, in 1954, explained the necessity of containment in Asia as follows: "You have a row of dominos set up, you knock over the first one, and what will happen to the last one is certainly that it will go over very quickly."[8] In a later speech, President Eisenhower elaborated on the domino theory, observing: "Strategically, South Vietnam's capture by the Communists would bring their power several hundred miles into a hitherto free region. The remaining countries in Southeast Asia would be menaced by a great flanking movement. The freedom of 12 million people would be lost immediately and that of 150 million others in adjacent lands would be seriously endangered. The loss of South Vietnam would have grave consequences for us and for freedom."[9] This view, which was reiterated by three U.S. presidents, held that the loss of South Vietnam would result in the collapse of such nations as Laos, Cambodia, and Thailand, which would undermine the security of the United States and the entire free world. Specifically, President Eisenhower feared that the fall of Vietnam, coupled with Laos to the west and Cambodia to the southwest, would

spell the surrender and enslavement of millions. Materially, warned Eisenhower, it would result in the loss of valuable deposits of tin and vast supplies of rubber and rice. Militarily, it would mean that Thailand, which enjoyed a buffer territory between itself and the People's Republic of China, would be exposed on its entire eastern border to infiltration or attack. Indeed, if Indochina fell, cautioned President Eisenhower, its collapse would threaten not only Thailand but Burma and Malaysia, with serious risks to East Pakistan, South Asia, and Indonesia. *See also* APPEASEMENT, 3; BALANCE OF POWER, 4; INTERVENTION, 19; NATIONAL SECURITY, 56; WAR, 33.

Significance   The domino theory, as applied to Asia, was of equal concern to the Soviet Union, for the Russians were deeply concerned about Chinese objectives in Asia. In the case of Vietnam, U.S. decision makers argued that South Vietnam was of dual importance to the United States—that is, not only was it strategically vital to U.S. policy, but the consequences of "losing Vietnam" could pose a serious threat domestically and internationally. As political scientists Richard H. Foster and Robert V. Edington note, "If the United States could prevent the fall of the South Vietnamese domino, it would show the world in general, and the communist world in particular, that it was willing to interject its power to prevent communist governments from coming into existence in that area of the world."[10] Thus, a victory by South Vietnam would actively discourage the Soviets from attempting to topple other Southeast Asian dominos, thereby reinforcing the U.S. goal of containment. Like most theories, the domino theory was not without its critics, who maintained that the Vietnamese conflict was, in fact, a civil war—not a battle between the forces of communism and democracy—and that circumstances in the neighboring states were sufficiently different, as to deny the validity of the theory. In the end, the verdict proved inconclusive. When the United States withdrew from Vietnam in 1973, Communist forces did seize control of Laos, Kampuchea (formerly Cambodia), and South Vietnam. However, for more than a decade following these events, no additional dominos have fallen under Communist control.

International Organization (91)
Institutional structure, established on a global basis, to organize and regulate international relations. International organization, in contrast to supranational organization (a system in which states are subordinate to the organization, which has the authority to dictate policy within specifically defined limits), seeks to develop and implement

policy among states, and does not exist independently from them. There are two main types of international organization: those structures composed of governments (e.g., North Atlantic Treaty Organization) and those composed of private individuals and groups (e.g., Rosicrucian Order). The number of both types has grown sharply since World War II. Approximately 90 percent of present international organizations (2,400) are nongovernmental, while the remaining 10 percent (300) are governmental and far more influential. International organizations were created to promote national security, economic development, and social intercourse. Today, they take myriad forms and serve sundry purposes. *See also* COLLECTIVE SECURITY, 88; REGIONALISM, 96; TREATY, 99; UNITED NATIONS, 101.

Significance International organizations, argue political scientists Walter S. Jones and Steven J. Rosen, can be divided into global and nonglobal organizations.[11] Global organizations may be multipurpose (e.g., United Nations) or single-purpose or -function, of which there are numerous types. These include: economic (e.g., Economic and Social Council); security (e.g., Security Council); anti-imperial (e.g., Trusteeship Council); nutrition (e.g., Food and Agricultural Organization); transportation—sea and air (e.g., International Maritime Organization and International Civil Aviation Organization); communications—mail and telegraph (e.g., Universal Postal Union and International Telecommunication Union); and judicial (e.g., International Court of Justice). Subglobal organizations may be classified into intrabloc, regional, and integrating organizations. These, too, fall into several categories. Intrabloc includes economic (e.g., International Monetary Fund) and security (e.g., North Atlantic Treaty Organization) organizations. Regional comprises economic (e.g., European Economic Community), security (e.g., Rio Treaty), and sociocultural and economic (e.g., Bogotá Pact) organizations. Integrating encompasses economic (e.g., European Coal and Steel Community) and judicial (e.g., European Court of Human Rights) organizations. Clearly, nation-states have influenced these international organizations to advance their own foreign policy interests and objectives. Given the present East-West conflict, most countries view these organizations as important institutional forums in which to pursue their goals and to resolve their differences. Moreover, these organizations are highly adaptive, quite capable of adjusting to meet changing political realities. Although one should not expect too much or, for that matter, too little, from these organizations, they wield considerable influence on the international stage. This is particularly true of organizations such as the United Nations, which is extremely prized by Third World countries. Although the United Nations lacks authority and autonomy, it has shaped the actions of many states.

Monroe Doctrine (92)

A principle of foreign policy, wherein the United States asserted its steadfast opposition to European intervention in the Western Hemisphere and its willingness to refrain from any involvement in European affairs. The Monroe Doctrine, which was a unilateral declaration, was enunciated by President James Monroe in an 1823 message to Congress, and was later abrogated by the events of World War I and World War II. This declaration, which represented the commitment of the United States to an isolationist foreign policy, reflected "a U.S. focus on domestic affairs, geographical isolationism from Europe of the United States, European preoccupation with political affairs within Europe, and the strength of British sea power, which imposed a *pax Britannica* on the oceans and indirectly served U.S. interests."[12] The Monroe Doctrine, which was enforced militarily by Great Britain, was initiated in direct response to the stated goals of the Holy Alliance of Prussia, Austria, France, and Russia to assist Spain to reclaim her Latin American colonies that had secured their independence following the Napoleonic wars. This led President Monroe to declare that the United States would "consider any attempt on their [any European powers] part to extend their system to any portion of this hemisphere as dangerous to our peace and safety."[13] *See also* DOMINO THEORY, 90; INTERVENTION, 19; NATIONAL SECURITY, 56; WAR, 33.

Significance   The Monroe Doctrine reflected the United States' growing nationalism and suspicions of Britain's hemispheric objectives. Subsequently, the Monroe Doctrine was expanded through the Polk Restatement and the Olney (Richard), Roosevelt (Theodore), and Lodge (Henry Cabot) Corollaries. The Polk Restatement (1845) asserted that "no future European colony or dominion shall with our consent be platted or established on any part of the North American continent."[14] The Olney Corollary (1895) proclaimed: "The United States is practically sovereign on this [South American] continent, and its fiat is law upon the subject to which it confines its interposition . . . because . . . its infinite resources combined with its isolated position render it master of the situation and practically invulnerable as against any or all other powers."[15] The Roosevelt Corollary (1904) affirmed: "Chronic wrongdoing, or an impotence which results in a general loosening of the ties of civilized society, may in America, as elsewhere, ultimately require intervention by some civilized nation."[16] The Lodge Corollary (1912) announced that "the United States would be willing to undertake action to prevent a non-hemispheric power from gaining acquisition of Latin American territory that could be used as a naval base or for other military purposes."[17] The Monroe Doctrine dominated U.S. foreign policy through World War II, after which the United States was forced to abandon its policy of isolationism. In recognition of its postwar position, the United States had no choice but to assume a new and expanded international role, one for which it was ill-suited at the time. Since then, U.S. military and defense power has continued to evolve, to the point where it has become a major superpower—the defender of the free world and the protector of the global balance of power.

North Atlantic Treaty Organization (NATO)   (93)

A regional military alliance created in 1949 for the collective defense of North America and Western Europe. The North Atlantic Treaty Organization, which was established at the conclusion of World War II, reflected Western determination to prevent Soviet aggression and to ensure the security of the region. NATO includes sixteen members: Belgium, Canada, Denmark, France, Federal Republic of Germany, Greece, Iceland, Italy, Luxembourg, Netherlands, Norway, Portugal, Spain, Turkey, United Kingdom, and the United States. Created under the authority of the North Atlantic Treaty, NATO functions as a cooperative framework in military, political, economic, and social matters. NATO maintains that an attack on any member will be considered to be an attack against all members. The alliance, which consists of a complex civil and military organizational structure, includes a Council and a Military Committee of three commands (Allied Command Europe, Allied Command Atlantic, and Allied Command Channel) and the Canada-U.S. Regional Planning Group. *See also* BIPOLARITY, 6; COLLECTIVE SECURITY, 88; REGIONALISM, 96; TREATY, 99.

Significance   The North Atlantic Treaty Organization reflects the world's bipolar distribution of power—that is, the division of states into two blocs, one led by the United States, the other by the Soviet Union. For most of its history, NATO unflinchingly supported U.S. policy, in spite of occasional ideological and strategic differences. In recent years, however, NATO has become increasingly independent, frequently challenging U.S. initiatives. At the time of NATO's creation, Europe was virtually powerless. As a result, it became dependent on the United States for its defense, relegating itself to a subordinate role. All major policy decisions were made by Washington, usually in terms of the West's vital interests. This produced both bitterness and, at times, acrimony. Today, the situation is considerably different. Europe has recovered its postwar economic health and developed renewed confidence. Modern Europe bears little resemblance to the defeated, divided, and demoralized Europe of 1945. As a result, Europe has demanded a greater voice in the determination of NATO policies and decisions. This move was led by France, which insisted upon a more equitable distribution of power. As political scientist John Spanier notes, Europe's desire for increased power is based both on equality and fear. According to Spanier: "As the United States became more vulnerable, they [Europeans] had to ask themselves whether they could continue to rely in the indefinite future upon American protection against the Soviet Union. Without sufficiently large and credible national nuclear forces of their own, they would continue to be dependent upon American power for their national security."[18] This led them to ask: What if the Soviets demanded concessions considered vital by the Europeans but not by the United States? Could the British or the French, with their relatively small strategic forces, successfully challenge Soviet superiority? In addition, the reconfiguration of NATO is partially due to the different geographic position of the members and the diverse historical experiences of the United States and Europe since World War II. Moreover, many European nations have expressed deep concern over the United States' recent emphasis on the Third World and what they perceive to be "a major diversion of American resources and attention away from Europe."[19] Finally, Europe has become deeply concerned about the issue of nuclear weapons—specifically, the unwillingness of the United States to surrender its primacy in this area. Conversely, the United States has become strongly critical of its European partners' unwillingness to support its foreign policy initiatives (e.g., the war in Nicaragua) and their seeming unwillingness to assume greater responsibility for their own defense.

Organization of African Unity (OAU) (94)

A regional organization formed in 1963 to promote African solidarity, economic development, and conflict resolution. The Organization of African Unity (OAU) consists of all 50 independent African states, except South Africa. The OAU Charter lists six main goals: (1) the sovereign equality of nations; (2) respect for the sovereignty and territorial integrity of states; (3) noninterference in the internal affairs of countries; (4) opposition to political assassination and subversion; (5) support of independence movements; and (6) nonalignment with major superpower blocs. An ardent advocate of national liberation, the OAU has assisted liberation movements in Angola, Mozambique, Zimbabwe, and Namibia. In addition, the OAU serves as a caucusing bloc in the United Nations, and has sponsored a campaign to expel South Africa from the United Nations. *See also* ALLIANCE, 2; COLLECTIVE SECURITY, 88; CONFLICT, 10; REGIONALISM, 96.

Significance   The Organization of African Unity enjoys widespread support within the region and is closely aligned with several prominent liberation movements, among them: (1) the African National Congress (South Africa); (2) the Pan African Congress (South Africa); (3) *Polisario* (Spanish Sahara); and (4) the South-West African Peoples Organization (Namibia). Although most OAU states share similar political values and a common purpose, it functions, more or less, as a loose association of separate states, whose Assembly of Heads of State meets annually, with a secretariat based at OAU headquarters in Addis Ababa. The OAU boasts a mixed record of accomplishment. It successfully excluded South Africa from the United Nations Economic Commission for Africa and UNESCO, spearheaded a drive for an arms embargo against that country, organized the first African Economic Summit, and circulated for ratification the African Charter on Human and People's Rights. On the other hand, it has failed to resolve the dispute between Somalia and Ethiopia, work out the conflict between Zaire and Angola, prevent an attack on Tanzania by Uganda, and end the civil war in Chad. Despite its efforts, the OAU has failed to prevent or control hostilities in the region. In part, the problem stems from organizational paralysis, internal dissension, and inadequate resources, as well as limited authority, ideological conflicts, and cultural cleavages. Presently, the future of the OAU remains uncertain. However, as political scientist David W. Ziegler notes, these and other problems only underscore the fact that "it is difficult to accept the claim that regional organization can succeed where global organizations have failed. . . . The problems of agreeing on what constitutes aggression, organizing a timely response, and getting states to participate in collective action when it is not clearly in their self-interest have been too serious for collective security to overcome."[20]

Organization of American States (OAS)   (95)

A regional organization composed of the United States and most Latin American nations, which determines major social, political, economic, and defense policies for the Inter-American system. The Organization of American States (OAS) was created by the Ninth

International Conference of American States at Bogotá in 1948, but was substantially changed by charter amendments defined in the 1967 Protocol of Buenos Aires. The OAS charter was initially ratified by 21 American republics, although the Castro government (but not Cuba, which still remains a member) was subsequently expelled from the organization in 1962. The OAS, which now comprises 32 members, including several newly independent countries, seeks to promote political unity, economic growth, and social understanding. The OAS is predicated on three main principles: national sovereignty, state equality, and political nonintervention. Charged with implementing the Inter-American Treaty of Reciprocal Assistance (Rio Pact), the OAS plays an important peacekeeping function in the region, both in terms of resolving disputes and preventing aggression. See also ALLIANCE, 2; INTERVENTION, 19; MONROE DOCTRINE, 92; REGIONALISM, 96.

Significance   The Organization of American States has, since its inception, been mired in controversy, owing, in part, to U.S. attempts to persuade the organization to actively oppose communism, both from within and outside the region. In this regard, the OAS has long been dominated by the United States, which is the major partner in the organization. Despite this fact, the OAS has occasionally exercised marked independence, as it did during the 1982 Falklands War, where the United States supported Great Britain, while many OAS states championed the Argentinian cause. In recent years, the OAS, like other international organizations, has experienced increasing division and discord, as the Falkland Islands War demonstrates. Far from acting with a united front, the OAS was bitterly split; some states expressed strong support for Argentina, while others refused to do so. For this reason, the OAS has steadfastly resisted U.S. demands to serve as a mediator in the present conflict between the United States and Nicaragua. Instead, the United States convinced the Contadora countries (Mexico, Venezuela, Colombia, and Panama) to use their influence to resolve the situation. Likewise, the United States induced the 11-member Cartegena group to address the Latin American debt crisis. Despite its close ties with the United States the OAS has, with increasing frequency, opposed several recent U.S. initiatives. For example, in 1983, it refused to support U.S. intervention in Grenada, which forced the United States to seek approval of a little-known Caribbean alliance called the Association of East Caribbean States. Moreover, in 1985, 24 Latin American countries opposed the U.S. embargo against Nicaragua, urged that it be lifted, and promised to assist that nation. Ultimately, however, the main challenge confronting the OAS today, argue political scientists Ernest E. Rossi and Jack C. Plano, involves "the problem of dealing with subversion and indirect aggression in the region without stifling the peaceful economic and social revolutions needed to produce progress."[21]

Regionalism (96)

The concept that states situated in geographical proximity or sharing common goals can mutually cooperate through a limited-membership organization to solve political, military, and practical problems. Regionalism constitutes a middle-range approach to problem solving, with unilateralism (where states act individually) on one side and universalism (where all states act in concert) on the other. There are several types of regional organizations, among them: (1) military-alliance systems (e.g., North Atlantic Treaty Organization, Southeast Asian Treaty Organization, Western European Union, Warsaw Pact Treaty Organization); (2) economic associations (e.g., European Community, European Free Trade Association, Benelux, Latin American Free Trade Association, Central American Common Market); and (3) political groupings (e.g., Organization of American States, Council of Europe, Commonwealth of Nations, Arab League, Organization of African Unity). Regional organizations seek to promote peace among their members by diffusing political rivalries, ideological conflicts, and economic competition. Regionalism is based on the premise that such organizations are more likely to achieve their objectives than collective security organizations, in that their members share a variety of common interests or similar problems. This enables them to better understand and mediate regional disputes. *See also* ALLIANCE, 2; COLLECTIVE SECURITY, 88; INTERNATIONAL ORGANIZATION, 91; TREATY, 99; UNITED NATIONS, 101.

Significance   Regionalism has, to some extent, reduced tensions in many parts of the world (e.g., the dispute between Iraq and Kuwait). In most cases, collective security organizations are incapable of resolving interstate conflicts. Likewise, individual nations often lack the ability to deal with deep-seated divisions. Thus, the regionalists argue that pragmatic solutions are most likely to be found at the regional level. This approach also minimizes the impact of superpower intervention, as regionalism provides a valid justification to exclude the major powers. Although no regional organizations are exclusively devoted to peacekeeping, many groups have taken concrete steps in the name of peace. For example, the Organization of African Unity, the Arab League, and the Organization of American States have all attempted to marshal their resources to solve regional problems. At its inception, the United States expressed strong support for regionalism. Indeed, President Richard M. Nixon, in his 1971 State of the

World Message, remarked: "It is no longer possible to . . . argue that security or development around the globe is primarily America's concern. The defense and progress of other countries must be first their responsibility and second a regional responsibility."[22] In recent years, however, regionalism has suffered a series of major setbacks. Key organizations, such as the Organization of African Unity, have failed to resolve many long-standing regional disputes (e.g., the conflicts between Somalia and Ethiopia, Angola and Zaire, Tanzania and Uganda, Libya and Chad) that have plagued the region. Moreover, many of these organizations have been wracked by numerous internal problems, which have prevented them from preventing or controlling conflict.

Rio Treaty (Inter-American Treaty (97) of Reciprocal Assistance)

A regional self-defense pact, signed in Rio de Janeiro in 1947, to protect the Western Hemisphere against armed aggression. The Rio Treaty, which includes 21 signatories (except for Cuba, under Fidel Castro, whose government was excluded from membership in 1962), views "an armed attack by any States against an American state" as justification for collective action. In addition, it provides that when two-thirds of the American republics agree to resist external aggression, all states must actively support that decision, either with troops or supplies. The Rio Treaty not only opposes direct or indirect military intervention, but condemns any other form of interference or threat against a member-state, be it political, economic, or cultural. In sum, the Rio Treaty seeks to safeguard the territorial sovereignty of signatories by resisting all forms of military occupation, temporary or permanent, on any grounds. At its establishment, the Rio Treaty sought to join the United States and all Latin American states in an alliance supporting the Monroe Doctrine. Prompted by the fear of Communist subversion, the Rio Treaty was reinforced by the 1948 Bogotá Charter of the Organization of American States (Resolution 32), which declared "international Communism . . . incompatible with the concept of American freedom," and implored the signatories to steadfastly oppose foreign-backed propaganda and threats.[23] This requirement effectively voided the United Nations Security Council's authorizing power (Article 53 of the Charter) in matters requiring regional collective action. *See also* COLLECTIVE SECURITY, 88; MONROE DOCTRINE, 92; ORGANIZATION OF AMERICAN STATES (OAS), 95; REGIONALISM, 96.

Significance The Rio Treaty culminated a half-century effort to develop a cooperative approach to problems of regional defense and to secure multilateral support for U.S. hemispheric objectives, as embodied in the Monroe Doctrine of 1823. The Rio Treaty was the first major security alliance entered into by the United States and served as a model for the establishment of the North Atlantic Treaty Organization and the Southeast Asia Treaty Organization treaties. At the time, the United States hoped that the Rio Treaty would deter Soviet aggression in the Western Hemisphere and prevent the spread of Communist ideology and expansion. In proposing the Rio Treaty, the United States acknowledged that henceforth the security of that nation would be entwined with that of Latin America and paved the way for sundry other regional alliances. Although the United States endorsed the principle of nonintervention, it has not always honored its commitment, as exemplified by U.S. intervention in Guatemala, Cuba, the Dominican Republic, El Salvador, Haiti, and Nicaragua. In this regard, Melvin Gurtov, an authority on international relations, observes: "Nonintervention has been acceptable to American administrations only so long as Latin 'instability'—the 'Communist threat'—has not jeopardized U.S. business and political interests. At that point, American officials have consistently put the need of 'collective' defense ahead of the nonintervention principle."[24] In such cases, the United States has emphasized collective self-defense over nonintervention, insisting on the "right" of both self-defense and the defense of an "attacked" state.

Southeast Asia Collective Defense Treaty (98)

A mutual-security pact promulgated in 1954 that binds the signatories to assist one another to resist military aggression or subversive activities in Southeast Asia and the South Pacific. The Southeast Asia Collective Defense Treaty, which is also known as the Manila Pact, originally included: Australia, Great Britain, France, New Zealand, Pakistan, the Philippines, Thailand, and the United States. To implement the treaty, the signatories created the Southeast Asia Treaty Organization (SEATO), which was headquartered in Bangkok and met regularly to discuss a wide range of mutual concerns. SEATO was precipitated by several major historical developments, among them: the triumph of Communist forces in China (1949), the invasion of South Korea by the North Koreans (1950–1953), and the defeat of the French in Indochina (1953). In response to these events, the United States intervened in Vietnam, requesting the assistance of SEATO to prevent the spread of communism. SEATO refused, insisting that South Vietnam was not a member of the alliance. Following U.S. withdrawal from Vietnam in 1973, SEATO collapsed, and, in 1977, the organization was dissolved. However, as a result of a special protocol to the treaty, the Southeast Asia Collective Defense Treaty was expanded to include Cambodia, Laos, and South Vietnam. The member-states refused, however, to admit Hong Kong, South Korea, and Taiwan, as they were unwilling to ensure their security. *See also* ALLIANCE, 2; COLLECTIVE SECURITY, 88; DOMINO THEORY, 90; TREATY, 99.

Significance   The Southeast Asia Collective Defense Treaty was, for all intents and purposes, a U.S.-sponsored mutual-security system. From its inception, SEATO was wracked with problems. Some nations, such as India, refused to join the alliance, arguing that communism posed no major threat to the region. Other countries, such as Pakistan, did sign the treaty, hoping to use the alliance to obtain arms, in the event of a war with India, which it viewed as far more serious than the threat posed by the Soviet Union. Unlike the North Atlantic Treaty Organization (NATO), SEATO proved to be a "paper tiger," one that was incapable of concerted action in defense of its own security. In this regard, SEATO failed to develop an effective command structure, an allied military strategy, or a major commitment of forces by member-states. SEATO disintegrated for sundry reasons, chief of which was its inability to enlist the support of most nations in the region (e.g., India, Burma, Ceylon, and Indonesia). Its failure to do so, contends political scientist John Spanier, resulted from the fact that "they had just emerged from Western colonialism and were unwilling to be tied again to the West through a military alliance. They preferred to remain neutral in the struggle between the Western powers and the Sino-Soviet bloc."[25] In reality, SEATO was a non-Asian alliance designed to protect Asia from internal and external aggression, which explains, in large part, why it was doomed to failure. Like SEATO, the Southeast Asia Collective Defense Treaty has been plagued by myriad problems, both institutional and ideological, requiring the United States to assume primary responsibility for maintaining the security of the region.

Treaty   **(99)**
A contractual agreement between two or more states that establishes, explains, or alters their mutual duties and obligations. Generally, treaties are of two types: bilateral (between two states) and multilateral (among three or more states). Most treaties are bilateral, creating what is called "particular" international law (which binds only the two signatories). Multilateral treaties, which are usually called "general" international law, can create rules that bind not only the specific parties but also the nonsignatories. In such cases, multilateral treaties may prescribe a commonly accepted norm. For example, Article 2 (6)

120

of the United Nations Charter states: "The Organization shall ensure that states which are not Members of the United Nations act in accordance with these Principles so far as may be necessary for the maintenance of international peace and security."[26] Typically, treaties involve such issues as peace, territorial cession, commerce, alliance, friendship, or other matters. In the United States, treaties enjoy the force of law, as defined by Article VI of the United States Constitution, under the "supreme law of the land" clause. Although a treaty can be negotiated by the president, it must undergo "advice and consent" of the Senate, in which consent requires a two-thirds vote of the members present. *See also* ALLIANCE, 2; COLLECTIVE SECURITY, 88; FORCE, 41; INTERNATIONAL LAW, 18.

Significance   Treaties promote the orderly conduct of interstate relations. International law delineates, in specific detail, how treaties are to be established and interpreted. The number and diversity of treaties have expanded greatly in recent years, as states have negotiated agreements on a wide variety of new problems. Although treaties are legally binding on the signatories, states enjoy the right to abrogate them where circumstances have changed markedly from when the treaties were concluded. In 1919, for example, Germany signed the Versailles treaty, under which it promised to disarm. At the time, the Germans were weak and divided, the victims of isolation and occupation. By 1934, the situation had changed, and the Germans began to rearm, citing the principle of *rebus sic stantibus*—namely, that states have the right to renounce a treaty when they determine that changing circumstances render the treaty void. Although this provision was uncommon in treaties negotiated in the late nineteenth and early twentieth centuries, most recent treaties include such a clause. For example, the Non-Proliferation Treaty of 1968 (Article X) states: "Each Party shall in exercising its national sovereignty have the right to withdraw from the Treaty if it decides that extraordinary events, related to the subject matter of this Treaty, have jeopardized the supreme interests of its country."[27] Despite this loophole, treaties foster predictability in interstate relations, freezing the status quo until it no longer obtains.

Truman Doctrine   (100)
A U.S. foreign policy statement, enunciated by President Harry S Truman, to assist states threatened by Soviet expansion or subversion. The Truman Doctrine was precipitated by Soviet military pressure on Iran and Turkey, which had been successfully resisted, and the fear that the Soviets were planning a major attack on Greece, which, in the

president's view, would seriously undermine the security of Western Europe. As a result, President Truman urged Congress to appropriate $400 million in economic assistance and military supplies for Greece and Turkey and to authorize the deployment of U.S. civilian and combat forces to provide both nations with essential financial and military support. In President Truman's words: "The United States must be willing to help free people to maintain their free institutions and their national integrity against aggressive movements that seek to impose upon them totalitarian regimes."[28] The Truman Doctrine not only provided support for nations threatened by foreign aggression but also offered assistance to free governments that were faced with internal subversion. *See also* BALANCE OF POWER, 4; BIPOLARITY, 6; MONROE DOCTRINE, 92; NATIONAL SECURITY, 56; NORTH ATLANTIC TREATY ORGANIZATION (NATO), 93.

Significance   The Truman Doctrine marked the beginning of a new era in U.S. foreign policy. The president viewed containment—that is, the prevention of Soviet expansion—as the best means of preserving the global balance of power. Additionally, in 1947, Congress passed the Marshall Plan, a comprehensive economic-aid program designed to assist the recovery of Western Europe and to strengthen its security against Soviet intervention. Shortly thereafter, the Congress approved the establishment of the North Atlantic Treaty Organization, a military alliance between the United States and Western Europe, which committed the United States to the defense of its allies against Soviet aggression. The Truman Doctrine maintained that the world was divided into two opposing systems: one predicated on freedom, the other on totalitarianism. President Truman believed that world peace and international order were indivisible. "If aggression were allowed to proceed," insisted the president, "then the fabric of global security would unravel, and American security would inevitably be jeopardized."[29] The Truman Doctrine was not without its critics. Indeed, Professor Hans J. Morganthau, who headed the "realist" school, accused it of "sentimentalism" and "moralism."[30] Journalist Walter Lippmann, another realist, termed the Truman Doctrine "a strategic monstrosity," one that was incapable of altering the political situation in Eastern Europe.[31] On the other hand, John Foster Dulles, President Dwight D. Eisenhower's secretary of state, opposed the Truman Doctrine for different reasons, arguing that it constituted a "passive policy," one that allowed the Soviets to dictate the place and terms of conflict.[32] Secretary of Agriculture Henry A. Wallace, the leader of the "dove" school, asserted that "a great part of our conflict with Russia is the normal conflict between two strong and sovereign nations that can be solved in normal ways."[33] Instead, Wallace advocated a policy of international cooperation, as exemplified by the United Nations, rather than a worldwide anticommunist crusade. Interestingly, Senator Robert A. Taft (R-Ohio), the leading conservative of the time, also objected to the Truman Doctrine, characterizing the North Atlantic Alliance as "a treaty by which one nation undertakes to arm half the world against the other half," and predicting that "this treaty . . . means inevitably an arms race."[34] President Truman dismissed these criticisms, insisting that the Truman Doctrine did not presage the beginning of an international ideological crusade—that there were indeed limits to U.S. interventionism. Still, the United States must, wherever possible, argued Truman, use its economic and political influence to prevent the expansion of world communism. In President Truman's view, this was best accomplished through massive economic assistance. After all, he maintained, "the seeds of totalitarian regimes are nurtured by misery and want. They spread and grow in the soil of poverty and strife."[35] In the end, he argued, global freedom ultimately depends on a comprehensive attack on the economic conditions that give rise to totalitarian governments.

United Nations (101)

An international organization, established in 1945, to foster world peace and global understanding. The United Nations' modern roots date back to the Conferences at Münster and Osnabrück that produced the Peace of Westphalia (1648) and inaugurated the nation-state system; the Congress of Vienna (1815), which convened to explore the problems of post-Napoleonic Europe; and the Concert of Europe (1815–1914), at which the great powers of Europe assembled—over a hundred-year period—to resolve their differences "in concert." The United Nations, which succeeded the League of Nations, was spearheaded by the governments of the United States, Great Britain, the Soviet Union, and China. Born out of the ashes of World War II, the United Nations' Preamble expresses the determination of "the peoples of the United Nations . . . to save succeeding generations from the scourge of war, which twice in our lifetime has brought untold sorrow to mankind."[36] Specifically, the United Nations seeks to promote "tolerance in human relations, the maintenance of international peace and security, and the economic and social advancement of all peoples."[37] The United Nations, which now comprises 159 member countries, spanning six official working languages (Chinese, English, French, Russian, Spanish, and Arabic), is permanently headquartered in New York. It is headed by a secretary-general, who oversees a staff of more than 6,000 specialists (recruited worldwide). Structurally, it retains many features of the League of

Nations, and includes the General Assembly (a forum for the discussion of world peace and security), the Security Council (the principal instrument for the establishment and maintenance of international peace), and the Economic and Social Council (a central clearinghouse and administrative body that coordinates such policy areas as health, education, and human rights). *See also* COLLECTIVE SECURITY, 88; UNITED NATIONS: GENERAL ASSEMBLY, 103; UNITED NATIONS: SECURITY COUNCIL, 105; WORLD GOVERNMENT, 108.

Significance   The United Nations, unlike the League of Nations, is better suited to the maintenance of collective security, in that it possesses more elaborate and ambitious provisions for sanctions and confers upon the Security Council the authority "to identify the aggressor, to order members to engage in nonmilitary coercion, and itself to put into action the military forces presumably to be placed at its permanent disposal by members of the organization."[38] Still, as political scientist James L. Ray points out, its effectiveness remains largely untested. Despite these provisions, the United Nations has failed to marshal the military forces necessary to the achievement of peace. Moreover, since every permanent member of the Security Council (the United States, the Soviet Union, Great Britain, France, and the People's Republic of China) enjoys the right to veto actions of the council, it is virtually impossible to impose sanctions against one of the major powers. Although the United Nations boasts a proud record of accomplishment (e.g., in agricultural development, international finance, world health, and educational, scientific, and cultural organization), it has been beset by myriad problems and difficulties, which are, by and large, the product of the nature of the organization and international political realities. These include, among others: (1) the myth of sovereign equality and membership problems; (2) parliamentary diplomacy, bloc voting, and the veto; (3) administrative isolation, internationality, and the political role of the secretary-general; (4) inadequate finances, spiraling budgets, disputes over assessments, and inflationary woes; (5) program coordination, overlapping jurisdictions, bureaucratic empire-building, and political wrangling; and (6) collective security, peacekeeping, international compliance, and ideological divisions. In the end, the United Nations can only act, maintains Forest L. Grieves, a prominent political scientist, "where the Big Powers have important and immediate foreign-policy interests. . . . Further, it can act in other areas only so long as it has at least tacit Big Power support."[39] Despite its failings, the United Nations continues to enjoy widespread international support, providing a much-needed forum for debate, discussion, interaction, and, at times, action.

United Nations: Dispute Settlement Procedures (102)
Tools and methods employed by organs of the United Nations to resolve international crises and settle interstate conflicts. Dispute settlement procedures are governed by the United Nations Charter, which states: "All Members shall settle their international disputes by peaceful means in such a manner that international peace and security, and justice, are not endangered" (Article 2). According to the Charter, if a dispute arises, the parties shall "first of all, seek a solution by negotiation, enquiry, mediation, conciliation, arbitration, judicial settlement, resort to regional agencies or arrangements, or other peaceful means of their own choice" (Article 33). The Charter empowers the Security Council, at its discretion, to request the parties to solve their differences by the aforementioned means. Further, the Charter (Article 34) allows the Security Council to investigate the claims of the parties, in order to determine whether the dispute is likely to jeopardize the maintenance of peace and security. If the parties are unable to resolve the matter, they may bring the dispute before the Security Council or the General Assembly (Article 35). Where the dispute involves a question of international law, the disputants are encouraged to present their case before the International Court of Justice (Article 36). After reviewing the dispute, the Security Council is authorized to determine whether the situation poses a threat to world peace and order (Article 37). If so, the Security Council may decide whether to take any action (under Article 36) or to recommend those terms of settlement that it deems advisable. In addition, the Charter provides that the secretary-general may bring any dispute before the Security Council (Article 99). See also CONFLICT, 10; UNITED NATIONS: GENERAL ASSEMBLY, 103; UNITED NATIONS: INTERNATIONAL COURT OF JUSTICE (ICJ), 104; UNITED NATIONS: SECURITY COUNCIL, 105; UNITED NATIONS: UNITED NATIONS EMERGENCY FORCE (UNEF), 106.

Significance   Despite these dispute settlement procedures, the Security Council is not always able to resolve a conflict. In such cases, the United Nations may approve a commission of inquiry and mediation or a U.N. representative or mediator to visit the scene of the dispute to ascertain the facts and to seek an on-the-spot settlement. If the dispute intensifies, portending major power participation, the United Nations may employ "preventive diplomacy" in the form of a U.N. "presence" or police force. Despite these actions, the disputants do not always honor the decisions of the United Nations. Indeed, in his 1982 status report on the actions of the United Nations, Secretary-General Javier Pérez de Cuéllar concluded that the Security Council's decisions "are increasingly defied or ignored by those that feel themselves strong enough to do so."[40] For example, Israel and South

Africa have frequently disregarded Security Council resolutions in favor of what they perceive to be their national interests. However, they are not alone. Argentina, for example, ignored a 1982 Security Council demand for a cease-fire in the Falkland Islands, while Iraq and Iran have consistently dismissed Security Council demands to conclude their long-standing conflict. Still, these and other nations recognize the costs inherent in defying the recommendations of the Security Council. Obviously, defiance brings with it both institutional condemnation and the loss of international prestige. On the other hand, all nations are motivated by their own national interests. As a result, it is unrealistic to expect that nations will sacrifice their short- and long-term interests, even in favor of international law and world peace. Compliance is far more likely where consensus is high and the issue is only marginally important.

United Nations: General Assembly (103)

The primary forum within the United Nations for the discussion of international problems. The General Assembly consists of 159 nations, including the original 51 countries. For voting purposes, each member has one vote. On "important" questions, including those involving world peace and security, a two-thirds majority of those present and voting is required. On lesser matters, decisions are made by a simple majority. The General Assembly is a recommendatory body; it possesses no power to enforce its decisions. The Assembly's agenda is defined by the United Nations Charter. It can make recommendations to member-nations, the Security Council, or both. In addition to its initiatives in the area of peace and security, it sponsors a broad range of international programs (e.g., economic, social, cultural, educational, health, and human rights). Among its myriad responsibilities, the General Assembly is actively involved in the trusteeship system, and determines and approves the United Nations budget. *See also* CONFLICT, 10; UNITED NATIONS, 101; UNITED NATIONS: SECURITY COUNCIL, 105; WORLD GOVERNMENT, 108.

Significance The General Assembly, unlike the Security Council, is based on the principles of egalitarianism, parliamentarianism, and majoritarianism. Indeed, it is the only major U.N. organ in which all members are equally represented. This equality pervades the entire General Assembly, including its seven major special committees. Often called a "Global Parliament," or "Town Meeting of the World," its operations are conducted according to parliamentary rule, which, at times, impedes the decision-making process. Although it lacks law-making authority, the General Assembly is ideally suited to the twin functions of debate and discussion. The General Assembly operates on the basis of consensus, which, in turn, necessitates compromise. On most important matters, consensus depends upon coalition-building. The General Assembly, given its lack of formal power, attempts to wield influence through the passage of resolutions (often called "manifestos"), declarations, and conventions. Although it plays a secondary role to the Security Council in the area of international peace and security, the General Assembly enjoys a dispute settlement function, which is particularly important when the Security Council is mired in deadlock or a crowded agenda. The General Assembly exercises this function through discussion, recommendation, tendering good offices, mediation, conciliation, commissions of inquiry, and appointment of individual mediators. Like the Security Council, the General Assembly's effectiveness has been undermined by several structural weaknesses. Although numerous proposals have been advanced to expedite the deliberative process, few have met with approval. Robert E. Riggs and Jack C. Plano, two experts on the United Nations, have proposed the following recommendations to streamline General Assembly procedures: (1) reduce the time wasted during each session; (2) expedite the "general debate" with which each Assembly opens; (3) speed up committee work, and organize it better; and (4) accelerate the debate and voting process in the Assembly and its main committees.[41] In recent years, the General Assembly has become increasingly influential, as a result of veto deadlocks in the Security Council, the influx of new members, broad interpretation of its Charter powers, its budgetary authority, its supervisory control over other bodies, and the fact that it is the only principal U.N. organ in which all members are represented.

United Nations: (104)
International Court of Justice (ICJ)

The principal judicial organ of the United Nations. The International Court of Justice succeeded the Permanent Court of International Justice (PCIJ), which existed from 1922 to 1946. All members of the United Nations are automatically parties to the Statute of the Court, as are three nonmembers—Liechtenstein, San Marino, and Switzerland. The court decides cases submitted by U.N. members, as well as matters contained in the charter or treaties. Although it renders judgments and issues advisory opinions, the court's decisions are binding only between the parties concerned and in respect to a particular dispute. If one party fails to heed the court's judgment, the other party may seek recourse to the Security Council. All questions are decided by majority vote and cannot be appealed. The 15 judges are elected for nine-year terms by the General Assembly and Security Council, with five judges elected every three years. Retiring judges are eligible for reelection. In rendering its decisions, the court applies treaties, international customs, general principles of law, judicial decisions, and, where the parties concur, the teachings of highly qualified international jurists. In addition, the court may, with the consent of the parties, order a decision *ex aequo et bono* (based on justice and fairness). The court remains permanently in session, except during vacations, and is headquartered in The Hague, Netherlands. *See also* CONFLICT, 10; INTERNATIONAL LAW, 18; TREATY, 99; UNITED NATIONS, 101; WORLD GOVERNMENT, 108.

Significance The International Court of Justice plays a dual role in the international system—that is, it is both the "constitutional court" of the United Nations and the court of law among nations. Despite its successes over the years, the court faces several problems, chief of which are limited compulsory jurisdiction and compliance. The Committee of Jurists, of the Permanent Court of International Justice, recognized these difficulties, albeit begrudgingly, when it drafted the Statute in 1921. Indeed, the committee understood the political improbability of compulsory jurisdiction, realizing that such a requirement would severely limit its membership. Thus, it approved an interim agreement, by which nations could freely accept limited compulsory jurisdiction in regard to specific matters, with or without reservation, and predicated on reciprocity. These conditions, which are known as the Optional Clause, have, for the most part, failed to produce widespread support for compulsory jurisdiction. As for compliance, most members honor the decisions of the court, owing to its ability to issue either declaratory judgments (which resolve points of law, interpret rights, or clarify existing law) or executory judgments (which find for one party rather than another and require one side to make remedial or compensatory action). Since compliance is voluntary, the court often renders decisions based on various political considerations, knowing that its judgments may have important political consequences. Thus, the court may, on occasion, fail to act, or modify its action, if it concludes that a decision is likely to provoke organizational or internecine strife. This is especially true in cases involving ideological disputes, where there is little, if any, likelihood that a particular ruling will achieve the desired result.

United Nations: Security Council (105)

The principal peacekeeping organ of the United Nations. The Security Council consists of 15 members, five of whom are permanent (the

United States, Soviet Union, Great Britain, France, and the People's Republic of China). The ten temporary members are elected by the General Assembly for two-year terms, representing five different regions in the world. On procedural matters, a nine-vote majority is required to carry. However, on substantive issues, the vote of all five permanent members is necessary. Countries not represented on the Security Council may, where they are parties to a dispute, be invited to participate in the deliberations. If a Security Council member is party to a dispute under consideration, that member must abstain from voting on questions directly related to the outcome of the proceedings. According to Chapter VII of the United Nations Charter, the Security Council is empowered "to determine the existence of any threat to the peace, breach of peace, or act of aggression and shall make recommendations, or decide what measures shall be taken in accordance with Articles 41 and 42, to maintain or restore international peace and security." The Security Council, which operates on a permanent basis, is headed by a president, who rotates monthly among the members. *See also* PEACE, 24; UNITED NATIONS, 101; UNITED NATIONS: DISPUTE SETTLEMENT PROCEDURES, 102; UNITED NATIONS: GENERAL ASSEMBLY, 103; WAR, 33.

Significance   The Security Council was conceived as the primary peacekeeping vehicle. However, that organ has failed to realize the high expectations of its framers, who hoped that it would unite the great powers and smaller nations in the common pursuit of peace. Forty years later, that goal has yet to be achieved. The problem stems, in part, from the nature of the cold war, ideological divisions, territorial ambitions, accumulated suspicions, national duplicity, saber rattling, blatant threats, and armed conflict. In addition, its failure is partly explained by the cumbersome procedures and apparatus of the Security Council itself, which has thwarted effective collective action. Structurally, the Security Council is hampered by several vagaries in the charter. For example, the charter does not define what constitutes a "procedural" or "nonprocedural" question. As a result, a permanent member can force a matter to be declared "nonprocedural" by opposing the preliminary motion to declare it "procedural," and then exercise its veto to kill the measure once it is ruled "nonprocedural." Functionally, the Security Council has usually favored a nonconfrontational approach to conflict resolution, one that involves deliberation, investigation, recommendation, conciliation, interposition, appeal, and enforcement. On most occasions, note political scientists Robert E. Riggs and Jack C. Plano, "the Council has handled situations under Chapter VI of the Charter as simple disputes rather than considering collective action under Chapter VII, even where both sides to the dispute have been engaged in extensive military actions."[42] As to the future, the actions of the Security Council will, in all likelihood, be influenced by practical politics, the cold war, budget limitations, the expanding role of the General Assembly, shifting alliances, and the imperatives of a war-torn world.

United Nations: (106)
United Nations Emergency Force (UNEF)

A nonfighting, military peacekeeping force created by the General Assembly during the 1956 Suez War, to temporarily supervise the Suez Canal area and the withdrawal of Anglo-French and Israeli forces from Egyptian territory. The United Nations Emergency Force, at its peak, comprised nearly 6,000 officers and troops, representing ten countries. Since then, the term "UNEF" has been used to refer to any U.N.-sponsored nonfighting "presence," which may vary markedly in form and purpose. The UNEF embodies five main principles: (1) that it consist of contingents from "neutral" nations; (2) that its function be defined by the United Nations; (3) that the host country approve its presence; (4) that the force serve an exclusively nonfighting, conventional role; and (5) that the financial costs be borne by a special levy on all U.N. members. The UNEF operated continuously from 1956 to 1967, at which point Egypt requested the withdrawal of the contingent in response to escalating tensions in the area. The UNEF was reconstituted as UNEF II in the wake of the 1973 Arab-Israeli War, and functioned until 1979, when its mandate expired. *See also* NEUTRALITY, 22; PEACE, 24; POWER, 27; UNITED NATIONS, 101.

Significance   The United Nations Emergency Force, which was conceived by General-Secretary Dag Hammarskjöld, was established "to prevent local disputes or power vacuums from becoming extensions of inviting escalations of the Cold War."[43] This concept later became known as "preventive diplomacy" (an effort to prevent major party involvement in conflicts or potential conflicts by diffusing tensions, thereby preventing possible strife or combat). The UNEF operated effectively for over a decade. Some experts, such as James L. Ray, contend that the withdrawal of UNEF troops in 1967 set the stage for the outbreak of the 1967 Middle East war. Clearly, UNEF efforts contributed to improved relations between Israel and Egpyt, which culminated in the 1978 Camp David accords and the March 1979 peace treaty. This resulted in the first peace settlement between Israel and any Arab nation, and included provisions for an Israeli withdrawal from the Sinai by April 1982. Although Israel and Egypt requested that UNEF II be reconstituted to assist in the implementation of the peace treaty, their efforts were thwarted by Soviet and Arab opposition, which prevented subsequent U.N. involvement. In addition to the Middle East, the United Nations has sent peacekeeping forces to the Congo (1960), Yemen (1963), Cyprus (1964), and the Middle East (1973 and 1978). All told, prior to 1973, the United Nations was involved in 12 peacekeeping operations. Since 1970, the UNEF II participated in the Sinai, the UNDOF (United Nations Disengagement Observer Force) in the Golan Heights, and the UNIFIL (United Nations Interim Force in Lebanon) in Lebanon. Although this approach to peacekeeping, argues Ray, is "a rather mundane, tentative and piecemeal approach compared with the grander sweep of collective security,"[44] the UNEF and other U.N. peacekeeping forces have played a salient role in preventing the outbreak of hostilities or limiting their expansion.

Warsaw Pact (107)

A regional military alliance established by the Soviet Union and its Eastern bloc allies in 1955 to provide a united military command. The Warsaw Pact, which was prompted by the rearmament and entrance of West Germany as a full member of the North Atlantic Treaty Organization (NATO), is dominated by the Soviet Union, which provides over half the forces committed to the Warsaw Pact. The treaty originally comprised eight nations: Albania, Bulgaria, Czechoslovakia, the German Democratic Republic, Hungary, Poland, Romania, and the Soviet Union. Created to promote "friendship, cooperation, and mutual assistance," the Warsaw Pact stipulates that if one member is attacked, the others will take whatever steps are required, including military force. Headquartered in Moscow, the treaty reflects the bipolarization of the international community. It has emerged as the most important Soviet alliance in the post-Stalin (Joseph V.) years. In recent decades, the Warsaw Pact nations have become increasingly assertive, particularly on economic matters. *See also* ALLIANCE, 2; BIPOLARITY, 6; COLLECTIVE SECURITY, 88; NORTH ATLANTIC TREATY ORGANIZATION (NATO), 93.

Significance The Warsaw Pact has served to solidify Soviet control over Eastern Europe and has enabled the Soviet Union to position over 500,000 troops in the region. In the process, the Soviets have standardized military hardware and incorporated its allied forces under a unified, Soviet-headed command. The Warsaw Pact, which closely mirrors the text of NATO, requires the members to safeguard the advances of socialism. Although the treaty grants decision-making authority to the signatories, through the Joint Secretariat, all major policy decisions are made by the Joint Armed Forces Command, which reports to the Soviet General Staff and is led by a Soviet marshal. In reality, the Warsaw Pact serves as an instrument of Soviet expansion—that is, it is designed to expand Soviet influence and to safeguard its political and military interests. In recent years, the members have, on several occasions, voiced criticism, albeit quietly, of Soviet primacy in the alliance. Overall, the Warsaw Pact has helped to equalize the East-West balance, in the wake of German rearmament, and provided the Soviets with an international forum from which to "legitimize" its policy actions. Still, the Warsaw Pact has fallen short of Soviet expectations. Jack C. Plano, an authority on international relations, points out that "growing polycentrism in East Europe during the 1970s and 1980s has weakened it [the Warsaw Pact] by preventing development of its full structure and anticipated role as a unified military group."[45] For example, Albania ended its participation in 1962 and withdrew from the alliance in 1968, and the People's Republic of China, which once served as a "permanent observer," has also severed its association. As Plano notes, "Dissatisfaction of other members with Soviet domination of the alliance has sapped its unity, and the decreasing fear of war along with growing trade relations between East and West Europe have weakened its role."[46] Like other regional alliances, the Warsaw Pact has evolved in response to the evolving nature of the East-West conflict and has become little more than a symbol of U.S.-Soviet military rivalry.

World Government (108)

A single supreme global political authority to promote peace and reduce conflict. Although world government is a theoretical construct—that is, there are few, if any, historical examples, it remains a popular, yet controversial idea. In reality, its closest approximation was the ancient Roman Empire, with its *pax Romana*. Despite the paucity of historical examples, theorists have, since the creation of the modern state system, advocated various forms of world government. For example, Dante, in his epic poem *The Divine Comedy*, and also in his *De Monarchia*, proposed the idea of a universal kingdom. Although many writers associate world peace with world government, the two are not indivisible—that is, it is quite conceivable that a world government would not be able to prevent war (e.g., civil war). Most proposals for a world government include several common features, among them: a world legislature, a global police force, elimination of existing armies, disarmament, peaceful settlement of conflicts, and rule of law. Although numerous proposals have been advanced, most modern advocates of world government favor the creation of a federation in which the central authority would be vested with specifically designated powers while other government powers would remain with the various constituent units. Internationally, the United World Federalists are the major proponent of world government. *See also* CONFLICT, 10; FORCE, 41; PEACE, 24; UNITED NATIONS, 101.

Significance   World government boasts myriad defenders and detractors. Although its supporters sometimes engage in hyperbole, world government may represent a positive alternative to the present international system. For example, even if world government does not eliminate war, there is ample reason to believe that it might reduce its likelihood. In this regard, world government is far more likely to promote global peace and order than the present system. Moreover, it is clear that a central authority, vested with sufficient power, could markedly reduce international violence. In addition, world government could greatly contribute to increased unity, by curtailing abuses inherent in the current nation-state system. Finally, world government would, in all likelihood, promote a heightened moral consciousness, given its opposition to war and violence. On the other hand, world government raises a host of questions, and this explains, in part, the resistance to it. Political scientist David W. Ziegler, a specialist on international relations, posits four main criticisms of world government: (1) people are attached to their culture, language, and traditions; (2) people fear disruption of their economic system; (3) people believe that a large political unit will be less responsive to their wishes; and (4) people who benefit from existing arrangements, such as those with jobs in government, fear they will lose income or power.[47] For these and other reasons, opposition to world government appears to be deeply ingrained. In the end, advocates of world government are left with one fundamental question—namely, how to secure the support of over 160 diverse states in favor of a "higher authority" that would abolish their national sovereignty. Needless to say, the answer to this question will ultimately determine the future of world government.

5. Conventional Wars and Weapons

Afghan War (1979–)   **(109)**

The Soviet invasion and occupation of Afghanistan. The Afghan War was instigated by the Soviet Union on December 27, 1979, when 50,000 Russian troops landed at the capital city of Kabul, ostensibly to assist in "maintaining order," but actually to overthrow Marxist Prime Minister Hafizullah Amin, who was showing signs of independence from Moscow. The Communists had taken power in Afghanistan on April 27, 1978, installing Nur Muhammad Taraki as prime minister; he was replaced by Amin, Minister of Foreign Affairs and leader of a rival faction, on September 16, 1979. According to Anthony Arnold, "Amin's most grievous sin in Soviet eyes may have been a refusal to accede to demands that he issue a formal invitation for the full-fledged invasion that followed."[1] Amin was replaced as Soviet puppet leader by Babrak Karmal, and in 1986 by Najibullah. Soviet occupation forces quickly increased to over 100,000 men, but despite their overwhelming superiority in training, materiel, support forces, and intelligence, the Russian army was soon stalemated in a guerrilla war strikingly reminiscent of the Vietnam War. *See also* FIGHTER AIRCRAFT WARFARE, 123; HELICOPTER WARFARE, 125; VIETNAM WAR, 143.

Significance   The Afghan War was a major political and tactical blunder by the aging Soviet leadership under President Leonid Brezhnev. International reaction was swift and condemnatory, damaging or destroying decades of carefully cultivated Soviet relations with the West and Third World countries. The 1980

135

Moscow Olympics, which were to have been a major propaganda coup, instead became a major embarrassment, as most of the Western states withdrew. Arnold has speculated that "Soviet military officers could have wanted to expose their units to combat conditions as a means of giving them real-life experience";[2] however, much like the Americans before them in Vietnam, they soon found themselves unable to control either the population, which remained universally hostile, or the countryside, where the mountainous terrain provided ample opportunity for the Mujahedeen ("holy warriors") to attack Soviet emplacements or convoys in small, sharp engagements, and then to withdraw before the better-equipped but cumbersome Russian forces could retaliate. As the war progressed, reports reached the West of massive disillusionment among Soviet enlisted men in Afghanistan. The United States has been the largest supplier of small arms to the Afghan rebels; most observers believe that the decision of the U.S. government to supply the Mujahedeen with hand-held Stinger ground-to-air missiles was a turning point in the war, since it enabled relatively unsophisticated soldiers to down Soviet gunship helicopters, jet bombers, and supply aircraft easily, thereby severely hampering the Russian ability to provide air cover for their operations. This, combined with the accession of Soviet General Secretary Mikhail Gorbachev in 1985, led the Soviet government to announce in March 1988 that it would withdraw its forces within the next year, leaving the puppet government to stand or fall on its own merits. U.S. President Ronald W. Reagan linked this withdrawal to the negotiation of further arms control agreements with the Soviets. The last Russian troops returned to their native soil on February 14, 1989.

Aircraft Carrier Warfare (110)

The use of huge "flat-top" ships as mobile launching and landing bases for bombers, jet fighters, helicopters, and strike forces. Aircraft carrier groups are central to U.S. naval strategy; such groups typically consist of one or more nuclear-powered carriers (CVNs), surrounded by layers of support ships which provide antisubmarine, anti-aircraft, and antimissile defense. A typical CVN carries an air group consisting of approximately 100 attack and reconnaissance planes and helicopters, and is capable of achieving a speed in excess of 30 knots.[3] "An Alfa Strike is . . . the carrier's knockout punch . . . [in which] every available aircraft in the wing takes part."[4] The United States has led the world in the development, deployment, and construction of aircraft carriers in the post–World War II period. *See also* FALKLAND

ISLANDS WAR, 122; GRENADA INVASION, 124; IRAN-IRAQ WAR, 126; LIBYAN
AIR RAID, 127; VIETNAM WAR, 143.

Significance   Aircraft carrier strategy has been the subject of much
debate in recent decades. In the late 1970s supporters of the carrier
group concept proposed, "in a study known as 'Sea Plan 2000,' a
somewhat . . . ambitious objective of 631 ships. . . . At the heart of this
force were to be 15 aircraft carriers, their escorts, and replenishment
ships, for a total of 222 ships."[5] Critics, however, including ex-
Secretary of Defense Frank Carlucci, have argued that adding more
carrier battle groups to the fleet is counterproductive, since they
would be "sitting ducks" in any nuclear conflict, and since the United
States currently has sufficient groups to cover its conventional needs.
Harlan K. Ullman and R. James Woolsey state that "decisions will
have to be made before the end of the 1980s about what, if anything,
should replace the large deck aircraft carriers. If the United States
plans to maintain 15 carrier battle groups into the future, replacement ships will have to be on the building ways in the 1990s."[6] The
Russians constructed their first aircraft carriers in 1967, and have
since added two helicopter ships, four conventional carriers, and, in
1983, their first nuclear-powered carrier.[7] Soviet General Secretary
Mikhail Gorbachev scrapped an additional CVN on which construction had started early in 1988. Great Britain was on the verge of
selling or scrapping its remaining two carriers in 1982 when the Falkland Islands War broke out, forcing the British government to recon-
sider its decision after their usefulness was demonstrated there.

Antisatellite Systems (ASAT)   (111)
Space-, sea-, or ground-launched interceptor rockets that have the
capability of locating and destroying an opponent's surveillance satellites. Beginning in the 1970s, both the Soviet Union and the United
States began developing and deploying ASAT systems. "Two current
programs for space intercept are the Army-sponsored program 505
and the Air Force-sponsored program 922. The 505 is based on Kwa-
jelein Island in the Pacific, is built around the surplus Nike-Zeus
missiles, and appears to be dormant. The 922 program is based on
Johnston Island and combines the Thor missile with an upper stage
which expands the normally window-limited ascent capabilities of earlier satellite interceptors."[8] Several different methods of satellite destruction have been proposed. The use of X-ray energy appears to
offer the largest potential kill radius. An alternative proposal employs
clusters of energetic particles directed at a target in a shotgun blast

pattern to cause the satellite's destruction. A third possibility is the use of small nuclear or conventional bombs. A fourth alternative is the crashing of rocket- or jet-fighter-launched pellets, or a small unarmed rocket, into a satellite at high speeds. *See also* DIRECTED ENERGY WEAPONS WARFARE, 121; SPACE WARFARE, 136; SPY SATELLITE WARFARE, 138.

Significance   In 1983, the Soviets proposed extending their own self-imposed moratorium on ASAT testing to both superpowers. The administration of U.S. President Ronald W. Reagan, bolstered by public opinion polls, and wary of verification problems associated with a proposed treaty, demurred, and in 1984 announced it was resuming ASAT tests. In July of that year the Soviet Union again urged the United States to negotiate a ban on ASAT weapons. The Soviet offer was quickly accepted by the White House, but was linked by Reagan to discussions on reducing strategic and intermediate-range nuclear forces. "In retrospect, the Soviet offer . . . appears to have been part of a well-orchestrated peace campaign and not meant to elicit a positive response from Washington. . . . Mikhail Gorbachev played on this theme heavily [however, and] . . . was clearly willing to work on a new agenda for negotiations on offensive as well as space weapons."[9] Most experts agree that it is far easier to develop systems to destroy spy or "Star Wars" satellites than it is to maintain them.

Antisubmarine Warfare (ASW)   (112)

The detection and/or destruction of hostile submarines. Antisubmarine warfare "involves at least four activities that proceed in logical sequence: intelligence, detection, location, and destruction. Ocean surveillance is the strategic problem of detecting, locating, and identifying missile ships or submarines, while tactical ASW is the problem of destroying the hostile vessels."[10] *See also* FALKLAND ISLANDS WAR, 122; SUBMARINE WARFARE, 142.

Significance   Unlike their predecessors of World War I and World War II, nuclear submarines are fast, silent, and capable of staying submerged for long periods of time at great depths. Their role in the modern age has been expanded even further, with the addition of nuclear missiles, to that of "submarine versus city";[11] such vessels are capable of launching their deadly cargoes from great distances. Traditional ASW tactics employed aerial surveillance combined with destroyer forces and carrier groups, the latter "actively seeking out submarines [with the] particular . . . task of destroying missile [carrying] submarines."[12] These have been expanded in recent decades to include more passive defenses, including spy satellites (now capable of using infrared and other sensors to detect submarine wakes in mid-ocean), and permanent underwater sensors and monitors stationed on the continental shelves of both Russia and the United States. Such sensing devices make close approaches by missile-carrying submarines to either land mass difficult, an important factor in increasing the margin of time available to either side in making decisions during a nuclear crisis.

Antitank Guided Missiles (ATGMs) (113)

Precision-guided, rocket-powered munitions designed to disable or destroy mobile armored vehicles. ATGMs are relatively new systems, having first seen widespread use in the Yom Kippur War (1973) between Israel and its Arab neighbors, particularly in the massive tank battles that occurred on its western front with Egypt. The tank has traditionally, since its first use in World War I, been "in both its strategic and tactical applications . . . a terror weapon . . . , because it combines within itself the tactical elements of protection, mobility, and firepower to a higher degree than any other weapons system."[13] The new antitank weapons combine wire- or laser-tracking devices with highly concentrated, armor-penetrating explosives to produce an extremely accurate and effective defensive system which can be deployed by both infantry and in other armored vehicles. Tank designers have responded to these new weapons by drastically increasing armored plating, both in thickness and in strength, and by redesigning vulnerable areas of the vehicle to resist or deflect incoming missiles. *See also* AFGHAN WAR, 109; ARAB-ISRAELI WARS, 114; ARMORED VEHICLE WARFARE, 115; IRAN-IRAQ WAR, 126.

Significance The history of antitank weapons reflects the history of conventional warfare: it is always cheaper and easier to develop countermeasures to expensive new weapons systems than it is to develop the weapon itself. "The real revolution in antiarmor weapons came not with the initial deployment of ATGMs in the 1970s but with their proliferation in the 1980s. . . . Given the widespread proliferation of ATGMs in the U.S. Army (and in the rest of NATO), even if we assume much lower hit probabilities than those achieved in test conditions, the greatly increased number of ATGMs will result in the destruction of large numbers of Soviet tanks."[14] What is true for the Soviet Union is also true for the United States, however, particularly since Warsaw Pact tanks outnumber those of NATO by a margin of three or four to one, and since the Soviets are generally conceded by most experts to have a much superior armor-plating system. Under such circumstances, one is forced to wonder how much deterrence will be provided by conventional NATO armored vehicles when the

INF treaty is implemented, removing much of the short-range umbrella that U.S. strategists had counted upon to provide retaliation at some level short of total nuclear war.

Arab-Israeli Wars (1948–) (114)

A series of political and military conflicts between Israel and its Arab neighbors. The proclamation of Israel's independence in 1948 resulted in immediate conflict between the Jewish settlers and the indigenous Arab population, supported by the armed forces of Egypt, Jordan, and Syria; and set the pattern for future confrontations when the hastily assembled Israeli Army soundly beat its poorly trained and equipped Arab counterparts. This was followed in 1956 by Egypt's occupation of the Suez Canal, which prompted an Israeli attack on Egyptian forces in the Sinai desert; after a brief occupation, Israeli tanks were withdrawn under intense international political pressure from the United States and the Soviet Union. The 1967 Six-Day War, in which Israel launched a preemptive air and ground attack when it became obvious that Egypt was about to do the same, resulted in Israeli occupation of the Sinai, Gaza Strip, Golan Heights, the West Bank of the Jordan River, and the east bank of the Suez Canal. In 1973, Egypt and Syria attacked Israel during the Yom Kippur holy days; after initial successes, the Arab armies were beaten back. Israel later agreed to return the Sinai to Egypt as part of a peace treaty negotiated by U.S. President Jimmy Carter (1978). Terrorist activities by the Palestine Liberation Organization (PLO) continued to plague Jewish security forces, however, eventually resulting in Israel's disastrous 1982 invasion and occupation of southern Lebanon; after three years of harassment and resistence by Palestinian guerrillas, the Jewish forces were forced to withdraw in 1985. By 1988, riots, civil disturbances, and political unrest in the occupied West Bank and Gaza Strip had grown to the point where Israel was forced to deploy much of its army permanently in these areas just to maintain order. *See also* ANTITANK GUIDED MISSILES (ATGM), 113; ARMORED VEHICLE WARFARE, 115; CONVENTIONAL WEAPONS, 120; FIGHTER AIRCRAFT WARFARE, 123; REMOTELY PILOTED VEHICLE WARFARE, 135.

Significance A permanent solution to the Arab-Israeli conflicts seems as far removed in the 1980s as it did in the 1940s. Centuries of ethnic and religious hostility between the two groups, combined with the displacement of indigenous Arab populations in Palestine by Jewish settlers, have made both sides increasingly intractable, as the suffering and deaths have mounted ever higher. The major world powers have also contributed their full measure to the conflict: "The last gasp of British and French intrigue [in the region] was the ill-advised Suez War of 1956, which saw the United States and the Soviet Union emerge as the major forces operating regionally. . . . The Soviets' clumsy efforts leading to the 1967 war, a classic example of misperception and disinformation creating conditions that soon careened wildly out of control, could have excited a superpower confrontation had it not been for the unexpected swiftness and decisiveness of the Israeli victory."[15] The Israeli dominance of the region is due, according to Michael I. Handel, to "the superior quality of the Israeli Army,"[16] including both training and equipment; but this military superiority has been accompanied, in the 1980s, by a harsh and growing repression of the Arabs still living within Israel's boundaries. In recent decades, both major superpowers have used their clients (the Soviets supporting the Arabs, the Americans the Israelis) to test conventional weapons systems and strategies; thus, the Yom Kippur War served as a kind of proving ground for new Soviet and U.S. antitank weapons. During the same time period the Israelis developed a large domestic small arms industry, exporting a large number of such weapons to the world market. The Israeli attempt to develop a modern jet fighter, the Lavi, was finally scrapped in the mid-1980s after an investment of hundreds of millions of dollars.

Armored Vehicle Warfare (115)

The use of tanks and other armor-plated troop transports or weapons-carrying vehicles in modern military strategy. Armored vehicles "strengthen defense with their antiarmor firepower and their ability to conduct counterattacks before the enemy has had an opportunity to consolidate any gains."[17] They are also an essential part of offensive military planning, being used to break through fortified enemy positions, to protect and lead infantry forces into battle, and to destroy opposing armored vehicles and emplacements. *See also* AF-GHAN WAR, 109; ANTITANK GUIDED MISSILES (ATGM), 113; ARAB-ISRAELI WARS, 114; IRAN-IRAQ WAR, 126; VIETNAM WAR, 143.

Significance   Armored vehicles have proven most useful in traditional, large-scale battles involving large numbers of troops, artillery, armored vehicles, and/or static fortifications. Although tanks were first used by the British in World War I, it was the German High Command which, in 1940, developed the blitzkrieg ("lightning war") strategy, which used waves of bombers and fighter aircraft combined with quick, concentrated thrusts of fast, heavily armed tanks to overwhelm enemy lines at carefully calculated points, penetrate them, and "pinch" (surround) entire segments of opposing armies. In more recent military history, huge tank battles took place between Arab and Israeli forces in 1956, 1967, and 1973; in the 1973 Yom Kippur War, the Israelis, because of "impulsive and uncoordinated tank charges,"[18] initially suffered devastating tank losses, when the Egyptians used their recently acquired antitank missiles. "Later the Israelis returned to the combined arms formations which had been so successful in 1967, and deployed infantry and artillery to nullify the advantage of the Egyptian missileers."[19] In the Iran-Iraq War, the Iraqis have employed their superiority in armored vehicles to prevent the Iranians from overwhelming their outmanned defensive lines. In Vietnam and Afghanistan, however, both the Americans and Soviets discovered the limitations of armored vehicle warfare. In both cases the inhospitable terrain severely limited the mobility of tanks and other armored transport; the absence of concentrated enemy forces, and the use by the enemy of the standard guerrilla techniques of harassment, the mining of roads and trails, and small, quick attacks rather than full-scale battles, made response by armored vehicles problematical at best.[20] With the signing of the INF treaty (1987), and the elimination of medium-range nuclear missiles in Europe, armored vehicles will inevitably assume more importance in Europe to the long-term strategic postures of both East and West. J. A. English states that the Soviets, to prevent NATO from organizing a coherent defense in depth, have developed "the concept of the Operational Maneuver Group (OMG). Historically rooted in the Mobile group concept of the 1941–1945 war on the Eastern Front, the OMG is a tank-heavy formation of division size designed to carry the battle deep into the NATO rear on the first or second day of an offensive. The subsequent disruption and devastating psychological shock of a number of OMGs erupting throughout the operational depth of the defense will, the Soviets hope, sap the NATO soldier's will to fight and hasten the political collapse of the Alliance before nuclear weapons are likely to be used."[21] Since Soviet tanks outnumber those of NATO forces by a factor of three or four to one, according to most experts, conservatives in the United States have attempted to link proposed arms control agreements on nuclear missiles to reductions by the Soviets of their conventional Warsaw Pact units, including infantry and armored vehicle deployments; Soviet General Secretary Mikhail Gorbachev has responded favorably to such ideas.

Battleship Warfare (116)

The military use of large, heavily armored and weaponed warships in the modern period. Following World War II, most of the battleships then in service were either scrapped by the world's navies, or mothballed (i.e., decommissioned, preserved against rust and other deterioration, and stored indefinitely at ports designed for that purpose). Three U.S. *Iowa*-class vessels were recommissioned at the onset of the Korean War in 1950, joining the *Missouri*, which had remained in active service after 1945. All saw extensive duty throughout that conflict, but were decommissioned again in 1957. The *New Jersey* was recommissioned in 1968 and saw brief duty during the Vietnam War before again being retired. The administration of President Ronald W. Reagan proposed reactivating the *New Jersey, Iowa, Missouri,* and *Wisconsin,* the first three of which had been recommissioned by the end of his term, with major upgradings of their offensive and defensive weapons systems.[22] *See also* ARAB-ISRAELI WARS, 114; VIETNAM WAR, 143.

Significance　　The Reagan proposal to recommission the United States' four remaining battleships created a storm of controversy that has raised serious questions concerning the role of such vessels in modern naval strategy. Proponents have pointed to the immense firepower of the ships, whose batteries of 16-inch guns, combined with their mobility, make them a potent threat in support of onshore operations. The *New Jersey* was used in this fashion to shell positions miles inland during the U.S. Marine incursion into Lebanon in 1983–1984. Unfortunately, although the huge guns proved as deadly as advertised, "the old silk bags of powder charges threw off the aim,"[23] rendering the operation largely ineffectual. Supporters have also noted that the thick steel plating covering these ships renders them virtually invulnerable to antiship missiles and most conventional weapons. Critics of the reactivation have pointed to the cost of modernization, which, with the addition of ship-to-ship missile batteries and antiship missile defense systems, now totals more than $300 million apiece; to the vessels' vulnerability to nuclear torpedoes or bombs; to their relative slowness compared to other capital ships, due to their heavy armor plating; and to the limited role these ships can play in a navy where most strategic planning has revolved around aircraft carrier groups. Proponents have countered with the Surface Action Group (SAG) plan, which "would operate either in loose coordination with a carrier battle group or to escort an amphibious force or an underway replenishment group. . . . With a battleship as the centerpiece, the SAG would operate with destroyers and frigates for antisubmarine and limited antiair protection."[24] However, since battleships cannot keep up either with nuclear-powered carriers or their escorts, their presence would likely make such a task force a sitting duck to the enemy. Consequently, many experts believe that the decision to reactivate the mothballed battleships has been an expensive—if nostalgic—excursion into a military never-never land.

Biological (Bacteriological) Warfare (117)

The use of naturally occurring or specially engineered bacteria, viruses, or other organisms to kill or incapacitate a target population. Among "the lethal biological agents that might be considered for military use are the viruses of Eastern equine encephalitis, yellow and Rocky Mountain spotted fever, and the bacteria causing anthrax, plague, cholera. . . . Incapacitating biological agents that might be considered . . . are the viruses of chikungunya fever, dengue fever, and Venezuelan equine encephalitis. The latter causes severe headache, nausea, and prostration, but has a [low] case fatality rate."[25] *See also* BIOLOGICAL WEAPONS CONVENTION (BWC), 240; CHEMICAL WARFARE, 119; GENEVA PROTOCOL, 247.

Significance   The potential use of biological agents in modern warfare has received nearly universal condemnation from religious leaders, politicians, and concerned citizens alike, yet production of such weapons by the superpowers has continued unabated. Critics have pointed out that such research involves the deadliest toxins known to man, being produced by laboratories located primarily in urban areas, with questionable control mechanisms; and that a leak or containment rupture could have deadly effect on surrounding civilian populations. In addition, the use of gene-splicing techniques to create new or variant organisms without natural, or even synthetic control agents or antidotes, raises profound moral questions, since even the most unlikely of accidents could release upon the Earth a modern plague of unimaginable ferocity. James N. Constant tells us that "lethal biological weapons have the potential of killing human populations over large areas even on a par with nuclear weapons. The threat is more formidable since the technology for such weapons is considerably less complex than the comparable technology for producing nuclear weapons. The substitution of lethal biological weapons for nuclear warheads is a distinct possibility."[26] Reports of inadequate security and containment procedures had proven sufficiently alarming by 1988 that the U.S. Congress began a series of hearings into the matter, seeking to force the Department of Defense to disclose (and tighten) its oversight provisions. The outlawing of such weapons has long been advocated, most notably in the Biological Weapons Convention (1972), but the major producers of bioweapons, the two superpowers, have long refused to sign such a treaty, since enforcement is virtually impossible without massive and reciprocal on-site inspections. Many experts believe that the real threat with such weapons lies in their very existence, and their possible theft and use by terrorists for political blackmail or murder.

Bomber Warfare (118)

The use of aircraft to drop explosive devices over enemy territory. The first use of aircraft for bombing purposes occurred during World War I, when propeller-driven fighters and transports were converted into bombers by adding racks under their wings, or by using flight personnel to roll or drop bombs over the side. By the advent of World War II, an extraordinary array of bombing aircraft and techniques had been developed, and were used to great effect as part of the Germans' blitzkrieg strategy. It was the United States, however, which produced the finest series of bomber aircraft in the war, culminating in the B-29 Superfortress, a four-engine heavy plane with a top speed of 357 miles per hour, equipped with the superior Norden bombsight for accuracy. "Postwar jet-powered bombers, designed for high-altitude, long-range strategic bombing, include the B-36 (1946), the largest and heaviest warplane ever built, and the B-52 Stratofortress (designed by Boeing). In Vietnam, the B-52 was the backbone of the Strategic Air Command, and was used extensively for high-altitude, radar-directed night bombing missions."[27] One hundred U.S. B-1 bombers, designed to replace the aging fleet of B-52s, began entering service in the late 1980s, but generated much controversy, both over their high per-plane cost, and a myriad of technical problems. Both series of planes have been retrofitted to carry cruise missiles. In 1988 the U.S. Air Force rolled out for public viewing a prototype of its B-2 Stealth bomber, a flying wing design, which will become operational in the 1990s. The Soviet equivalent of the B-1 is the Blackjack bomber. *See also* ARAB-ISRAELI WARS, 114; FALKLAND ISLANDS WAR, 122; IRAN-IRAQ WAR, 126; STEALTH AIRCRAFT, 139; VIETNAM WAR, 143.

Significance   The role of the aircraft bomber in modern warfare is currently a subject of much debate. U.S. President Jimmy Carter scrapped production of the B-1 bomber, but President Ronald W. Reagan promptly reinstated it after assuming office in 1981. The B-1 can carry, in "three weapons bays, varying combinations of nuclear air-to-ground missiles, conventional or nuclear free-fall bombs, and auxiliary fuel," using "electronic jamming equipment, infrared countermeasures, radar location and warning systems, advanced avionics and low observable technology to defeat hostile defensive systems."[28] However, critics have questioned the aircraft's performance, citing an almost continuous "after-the-fact" parade of upgrades and retrofits, due to crashes, leaky fuel tanks, inadequate radar and electronic equipment, and a consistent failure to meet the aircraft's touted performance standards. All of these contributed to huge cost overruns for the program. A U.S. Defense Department report released in 1988 indicated that the B-1 has yet to meet half of its proposed mission goals, and will require a huge continued investment in the future. Supporters have responded by pointing to the obsolescence of the B-52, and by noting that, unlike nuclear missiles, aircraft can be both dispatched *and* recalled during an international crisis. Concerning the B-2 flying wing, currently under development, Brian Beckett tells us that "Stealth bombers are likely to cost several times B-1's price (around $200 million per plane), and there is no guarantee that Soviet progress in radar and defensive technology will not make the whole project obsolete by the time it is perfected. Considerations such as these make the future of the manned bomber . . . [un]certain. . . . All Reagan has succeeded in doing is to postpone the final commitment until Stealth's viability is known, and to give the Air Force a partially modernized fleet in the meantime."[29]

Chemical Warfare (119)

The use of lethal or incapacitating gases, sprays, or toxins to kill or paralyze enemy forces. Toxins, poisonous substances created by living organisms, do not reproduce, and are therefore classed by some experts as "chemical" rather than "biological" weapons. Chemical weapons were first used by the Germans during World War I, with limited effectiveness. Their use prompted such horror among the combatants, however, that in 1925 the major powers signed the Geneva Protocol, banning the use of chemical weapons on the battlefield, but not their development or stockpiling. Lethal chemical weapons include the "nerve" gases, developed by Germany during World War II, which cause a breakdown of respiration and other functions: death results from asphyxiation. VX and GB (Sarin) are other nerve agents stockpiled by the United States. Sarin is a spray which "evaporates to create a respiratory hazard for unprotected personnel. . . . even a small droplet of VX can be fatal." Incapacitating agents include the U.S. agent BZ, "a psychochemical solid that can be dispersed as an aerosol to be inhaled by enemy personnel. It affects both physical and mental processes, causing blurred vision, disorientation, and confusion." The "principal short-term incapacitant now in military use is CS . . . first synthesized in the U.S. in the 1920s . . . exposure . . . causes intense pain in the eyes and upper respiratory tract, progressing to the deep recesses of the lungs and giving rise to feelings of suffocation and acute anxiety. . . . In humid weather, moderately heavy skin exposure can cause severe blistering."[30] Defoliants, such as Agent Orange, were first developed during World War II and subsequently used extensively by the United States in Vietnam. *See also* BIOLOGICAL (BACTERIOLOGICAL) WARFARE, 117; GENEVA PROTOCOL, 247; IRAN-IRAQ WAR, 126.

Significance   Nerve gases and other chemicals have generally been regarded as among the most abhorrent weapons of war, although such opinions have not stopped the two superpowers and many other states from maintaining large research and development programs and stockpiles of these devices, none of them prohibited by the Geneva Protocol. Many experts believe that the threat from chemical and biological weapons is greater than from nuclear weapons, since mustard and other nerve gases are relatively cheap and easy to produce, requiring no great expertise or technological infrastructure. It is not surprising, therefore, to find chemical weapons being employed for the first time in 70 years by both Iraq and Iran in their stalemated war, despite the fact that both parties are signatories to the protocol. Supporters of the chemical weapons program of the United States have pointed to huge Soviet stockpiles of such weapons, and to the fact that Russian soldiers in Europe have been elaborately trained and equipped to deal with chemical attack and defense. As Owen Carrow states, "Why should it be thought demeaning to be made to vomit but heroic to be disembowelled by a flying shard of steel?"[31] Opponents point to U.S. and Soviet production accidents of the 1950s and 1960s which claimed the lives of livestock and possibly of innocent civilians, to reports of lax supervision and oversight of such facilities, and to a questionable military need (any conventional conflict in Europe, they say, would quickly escalate to the use of nuclear weapons). Questions have also been raised about the United States using Agent Orange and other defoliants in the Vietnam War, which may have had serious, long-term adverse health effects, both on the indigenous civilian populations and on U.S. soldiers.

Conventional Weapons   (120)

Personnel, equipment, or armaments used in defensive or offensive warfare, which do not directly require the use of nuclear weapons. Conventional weapons may include ships, aircraft, armored vehicles, guns, nonnuclear missiles, nonnuclear warheads, and armies, navies, marines, and other personnel, and the strategies for deploying them, including communication, command, and control bases and networks.

See also AFGHAN WAR, 109; ARAB-ISRAELI WARS, 114; COMMAND, CONTROL, AND COMMUNICATION (C3), 185; FALKLAND ISLANDS WAR, 122; IRAN-IRAQ WAR, 126; VIETNAM WAR, 143.

Significance   In a world where the use of nuclear weapons has become unthinkable and improbable, conventional weapons have continued to play the major role in all the wars and military confrontations that have taken place since World War II. Conversely, few such conflicts in the modern period have seen clear and decisive results, due primarily to self-perceived and imposed limitations placed by the superpowers on all conventional wars of the last 45 years, even those in which they have not been directly involved. As conventional weaponry has become more sophisticated, destructive, and expensive, it has also increasingly failed to provide the security that each nation seems to require. Even those conflicts that have seemingly resulted in clear-cut victories (e.g., the Six-Day War of 1967 between Israel and its Arab neighbors), have produced long-term stalemates, continued political tension, and, inevitably, further military clashes. The two superpowers have not been immune from this military impotence, having both been involved in the last two decades in costly, frustrating, demoralizing guerrilla wars which they could not win, and from which they ultimately had to withdraw, leaving the real combatants still on the fields. As John I. Alger has pointed out, ours "is a nuclear age and a nuclear peace, but it is also an age of many small wars. The term *small war*, like 'limited war,' is relative; it refers to wars in which the major powers do not directly confront each other on the battlefield. Like any war, however, small wars are as deadly serious as any human activity can be."[32] As long as such conflicts exist, the demand for conventional weapons will continue unabated.

Directed Energy Weapons Warfare   (121)

The use of high-energy lasers or particle beams as agents of destruction. Among other requirements directed energy weapons need secure space, air, or ground bases, plus detection, tracking, and damage-assessing capabilities. In their present state they remain highly susceptible to destruction or disruption through electronic jamming, decoy devices, missiles, ramming agents, and other lasers. Such weapons form the heart of former U.S. President Ronald W. Reagan's Strategic Defense Initiative ("Star Wars"). *See also* ANTISATELLITE SYSTEMS (ASAT), 111; SPACE WARFARE, 136; SPY SATELLITE WARFARE, 138; STRATEGIC DEFENSE INITIATIVE (SDI), 141.

Significance   Directed energy weapons have become theoretically possible only within the last decade, but serious questions remain about their potential use and development. Kosta Tsipis states: "Practical space-based directed energy weapon systems are not within the visible technological horizon. Even if eventually they could be developed, the cost of emplacing, supplying, and maintaining them would be prohibitive, they would be fatally vulnerable during their embryonic stage, and even if emplaced and made operational, most probably they could be defeated by active and passive countermeasures and countertactics of a determined opponent." He concludes that airborne laser antisatellite systems appear feasible within the near future, and anti-aircraft laser and particle beam systems also may be possible, but that both suffer from excessive sensitivity to countermeasures, and are not cost-effective when compared to more conventional defenses.[33] Brian Beckett adds that "doubts on . . . the military feasibility of beam devices have far from disappeared; they have simply lessened in the face of increasing evidence of their ultimate plausibility."[34] Proponents have responded by pointing to an ongoing Soviet development program for such weapons, and by saying that all new weapons systems have been opposed at their outset. They have further stated that if such weapons *can* be developed, the first nation to do so will immediately gain an advantage over the rest. The United States, they say, cannot afford to finish second in such a race.

Falkland Islands War (1982)   (122)

A conflict between Great Britain and Argentina to determine the sovereignty of the Falklands (or Malvinas), a small group of islands in the South Atlantic. Argentina has claimed the islands since the British occupied them in the 1830s. By the end of the nineteenth century, several thousand English sheep farmers had settled the two main islands. After World War II, successive British governments sought a compromise with Argentina, but the latter insisted upon full sovereignty. With increasing domestic pressure on the military dictatorship, Argentine President Leopoldo Galtieri rashly invaded the islands on April 2, 1982, easily displacing the small British force. British Prime Minister Margaret Thatcher immediately ordered a military response, and within a month a hastily organized fleet had set sail. After clashes which resulted in the loss of several ships on both sides, and the decimation of Argentina's air forces, British marines quickly landed and occupied the main island in a lightning series of quick marches and precision attacks. The Argentine garrison surrendered on June 14, 1982. *See also* AIRCRAFT CARRIER WARFARE, 110;

BOMBER WARFARE, 118; FIGHTER AIRCRAFT WARFARE, 123; MINE WARFARE, 129; SUBMARINE WARFARE, 142.

Significance   The Falklands Islands War provided some interesting military lessons for the modern world. Britain appeared at the outset to be at a disadvantage, due to the distances involved, the absence of a landing strip in the Falklands which could accept large aircraft, and the lack of support ships. The U.K.'s two surviving aircraft carriers, one already sold to Australia, the other slated to be scrapped, were hastily refurbished, as were several merchant vessels. Britain's air support, consisting mainly of slow, seemingly outdated Harrier jets, were given no chance against the Argentine F-4s and Mirage fighters. But the Argentine Air Force was also stretched to the limit, its fighters operating at extreme range, with only ten minutes' flying time over the Falklands; thus, despite several initial successes, the Argentines soon found themselves outclassed by the Harriers, more than one-third of their planes eventually being destroyed. The Harriers, with their ability to take off vertically, hover, and land on the smallest strip of flat land, were ideal for this type of conflict. The Argentine Navy suffered several serious losses, the most damaging being the torpedoing of the cruiser *Belgrano,* with the loss of hundreds of lives; the British fleet lost several frigates and destroyers to bombs and Exocet missiles. Argentina's ground forces were also outclassed, being poorly trained, equipped, and led. The British forces were allowed to land virtually unopposed, and soon had overrun a key Argentine outpost, in the only seriously contested land battle of the war. Thereafter they moved inland in a quick series of forced marches; the Argentine troops at Stanley (the capital) were surrounded within days. A key element in the successful British operation was their almost total control of the Western media, which they skillfully manipulated to Argentina's disadvantage. The Argentines left behind thousands of almost undetectable plastic antipersonnel mines, strewn randomly over the beaches and hillsides, thus rendering entire sections of the islands uninhabitable for decades. The Argentine defeat resulted directly in the displacement of the military regime there; the succeeding civilian government has maintained its claim over the islands, but has stated it will not use force to reclaim them. The British have thus been left with the prospect of spending hundreds of millions of pounds annually to maintain a defense force on and around the Falklands, with no solution in sight. Although claiming neutrality, the United States provided Britain with satellite intelligence data, and allowed British jets to refuel at U.S. island bases.[35]

Fighter Aircraft Warfare (123)
The use of fast, light jet planes for close-in ground support and air-to-air combat. Fighter aircraft were first developed during World War I from slow, propeller-driven biplanes. By World War II a wide variety of aircraft had been designed to serve specific purposes. Those "with a high rate of climb, good maneuverability, and short range, [developed] to stop longer-range enemy bombers, were called interceptors. Those [with] sufficient range to accompany bombers, and sufficient maneuverability to be competitive with interceptors, were called escort fighters. Pursuit planes were small fighters having a high speed and a limited radius of action. Short-range fighters designed for high speed interception of enemy aircraft in good visibility daylight were called day fighters."[36] Jet-propelled fighter craft were first developed by the Germans at the end of World War II, but saw only limited action until the Korean War. The first supersonic jet, the F-100 Super Sabre, was tested in 1953. The F-105 Thunderjet was used extensively during the Vietnam War, as was the F-4 Phantom jet. The United States presently employs F-15, F-16, and A-10 fighters in the air force, and A-6, A-7, F-4, and F-14 fighters in the navy. The Soviets rely on the MiG-25, reputedly one of the fastest aircraft in the world.[37] Under development by U.S. designers for production in the 1990s is the F-117 Stealth fighter, its design characteristics a closely guarded secret. See also AFGHAN WAR, 109; ARAB-ISRAELI WARS, 114; BOMBER WARFARE, 118; FALKLAND ISLANDS WAR, 122; GRENADA INVASION, 124; LIBYAN AIR RAID, 127; STEALTH AIRCRAFT, 139; STRATEGIC AIR COMMAND (SAC), 140; VIETNAM WAR, 143.

Significance   Fighter aircraft are an integral part of conventional air defense strategy. The jet fighter "represents a highly unwelcome and persistent threat. . . . Engagement by enemy fighters is most unsettling to attack crews—particularly the less well-trained and disciplined crews—and hence the presence of a fighter threat can frequently produce results quite disproportionate to the actual threat imposed." Analysis of the Vietnam War, the Middle East wars, and other post–World War II engagements "all suggest that the attack mission is greatly enhanced when supported by escort fighters. It is therefore surprising that in most of today's modern air forces the tactics of fighter escort are seldom practiced; there is evidence to suggest that the Soviet Air Force may be an exception."[38] The most recently developed superpower fighters, including the U.S.'s new Stealth aircraft, the F-117, have proven increasingly costly to build and maintain, with highly sophisticated, computer-operated systems that require large support infrastructures and years of pilot training to operate well. Due to high development costs, there has been a tendency in recent decades to combine several different functions into one aircraft type, producing compromises in design that have satisfied none of the services that use the planes, and which have raised serious questions about their actual utility in any large-scale conflict.

Grenada Invasion (1983) (124)
An attack by U.S. military forces on a tiny island state in the Caribbean. The Grenada invasion was presaged by installation of a Marxist government in 1979, under the leadership of Prime Minister Maurice Bishop, who promptly sought Cuban assistance to develop the island's economy, to build an airstrip capable of handling large military planes (and tourist jets), and to provide arms and training for his growing military/police forces. Bishop was overthrown by radical elements of his own party on October 14, 1983, and murdered on October 19. The assassination prompted U.S. President Ronald W. Reagan, citing a request for assistance from the Organization of Eastern Caribbean States, and from Grenadan Governor General Sir Paul Scoon, to order an invasion of Grenada on October 23, ostensibly to rescue U.S. medical students and restore democratic rule. "Grenadan casualties were estimated as 45 killed, 337 wounded, and 68 captured unwounded. The Cubans lost an estimated 25 dead, 57 wounded, and 634 captured. U.S. losses amounted to 26 killed (five from noncombat causes) and 122 wounded (14 due to friendly fire)." U.S. naval forces included: one aircraft carrier with embarked air wing, one missile cruiser, one missile destroyer, two destroyers, two missile frigates, six amphibious ships, and three auxiliaries. The U.S. Air Force's Military Airlift Command flew 750 missions, carrying 18,000 passengers and 8,800 tons of cargo.[39] *See also* AIRCRAFT CARRIER WARFARE, 110; FIGHTER AIRCRAFT WARFARE, 123; HELICOPTER WARFARE, 125; SPECIAL FORCES WARFARE, 137.

Significance From a military perspective, the Grenada invasion was little more than a short, three-day exercise by U.S. forces, remarkably similar to the joint-forces wargames conducted by the U.S. military on a regular basis. The Reagan administration heavily restricted media access to the island while the invasion was in progress, claiming military security needs, but also thereby thwarting any stories that might have countered U.S. government claims of heavy Cuban troop build-ups on Grenada. In fact, however, later independent analyses of the operation confirmed that few of the 700 Cubans on Grenada were military personnel, most being construction workers working on the new airstrip. Public reaction to the invasion was predictable. Many U.S. liberals and overseas allies were horrified at President Reagan's blatant violation of international law; others, such as columnist Carl Rowan, supported the intervention, saying, "I think a lot of liberals and blacks put ourselves in the place of these Caribbean leaders."[40] Senator Gary Hart (D-Colo.) "vowed to oppose any further extension of U.S. military involvement in this small island country."[41] Other lawmakers supported the operation when "faced with massive public support of the action, the apparent evidence of danger in Grenada provided by the returning students, the discovery of Cuban and Soviet weapons, and the popularity of Reagan's . . . speech."[42] The *New York Times*, on the other hand, observed that "when all is done, pacifying Grenada will prove only the obvious about American power. The enduring test for Americans is not whether we have the will to use that power but the skill to avoid having to. A President who felt he had no other choice . . . should not be celebrating a victory. He should be repairing the prior political failures and forestalling the bitter harvest to come."[43] According to Richard A. Melanson, the Grenada incursion demonstrates that "U.S. military power could be employed prudently as long as the objectives were limited and could be achieved swiftly, decisively, and at a reasonably low cost; it was clearly closer to containment than to world order politics." But, he adds, it did not help Reagan rally public or congressional support for his more controversial Central American policies.[44] Significantly, U.S. promises to provide extensive economic development aid to the new, more moderate Grenadan government which emerged after the invasion were never fulfilled; unemployment there remains staggeringly high, affecting more than 30 percent of adult males.

Helicopter Warfare (125)

The military use of specially modified autogiro aircraft supported by rotating airfoils rather than fixed wings. Modern helicopters can be employed as fast, highly mobile troop transports, dropping soldiers ahead of battle lines and then retrieving them; or as heavily armed and armored attack gunships bristling with heavy machine guns and air-to-ground missiles. The first widely used troop-carrying helicopter was the twin-rotor CH-21 [cargo helicopter] *Shawnee*. The UH-1 [utility helicopter] *Iroquois* was utilized extensively during the Vietnam War, as was the turbojet-powered CH-47 *Chinook*, a medium transport aircraft with twin rotors. The AH-1 [attack helicopter] *Cobra*, developed during the 1960s, was capable of speeds up to 220 miles per hour.The UH-60A Sikorsky *Black Hawk,* widely used by the U.S. Army, can carry 11 combat-equipped troops, plus a crew of three. Also used by U.S. military forces are the HH-60A *Night Hawk,* to perform unescorted day/night missions, and the AH-64 *Apache,* an advanced attack copter capable of flying in adverse weather conditions.[45] The Soviet Union uses similarly designed and styled helicopters, part of a series originally conceived by the late Mikhail Mil (1930–1970), culminating in the most recent model, the Mi-28 *Havoc,* expected to be operational in the late 1980s.[46] *See also* AFGHAN WAR, 109; FALKLAND ISLANDS WAR, 122; FIGHTER AIRCRAFT WARFARE, 123; GRENADA INVASION, 124; IRAN-IRAQ WAR, 126; MINE WARFARE, 129; VIETNAM WAR, 143.

Significance   Helicopter warfare has greatly changed the face of battle in the last two decades. Originally, helicopters were used only for troop transport or medical rescue missions, being slow and somewhat vulnerable to ground fire. By the early 1960s, however, new technological developments had provided these planes with greatly enhanced mobility and offensive and defensive power. When equipped "with antiarmor missiles, [helicopters] have most of the advantages of ground-mounted ATGMs without many of the vulnerabilities. They have achieved impressive kill ratios in situations where they have been tested against attacking tank formations. . . . The mobility and firepower of the attack helicopter greatly reduce the ability of the attacker to penetrate the defense or exploit a breakthrough."[47] Thus, it is not surprising that "in many ways the helicopter was the ideal vehicle for the guerrilla war in South Vietnam. . . . As the U.S. involvement . . . grew . . . so the helicopter came to play an increasingly important role in the Army counterinsurgency operations . . . reconnaissance . . . logistic support . . . casualty evacuation and the recovery of damaged vehicles and aircraft. . . . Finally the gunship helicopter was evolved to meet the Army's need for fire support during close-range jungle firefights and to escort vulnerable troop carrying assault helicopters. Vietnam became the helicopter's war, and many thousands of these machines were deployed. . . . Losses were on a similarly massive scale, with over 16,000 helicopters brought down by enemy fire or by accidents."[48] Similarly, helicopters proved invaluable to the Soviet war effort in Afghanistan, where the rugged terrain and lack of good roads made their mobile firepower utterly necessary in both offensive and defense situations. The introduction of U.S.-supplied, hand-held Stinger ground-to-air missiles to the guerrillas was a turning point in that conflict, with both copters and jet aircraft proving extremely vulnerable to their heat-seeking sensors. Without adequate air cover, the Soviets soon found themselves in a war they could not win.

Iran-Iraq War (1980–1988) (126)

A military conflict between the fundamentalist Islamic regime of Iran and the Arab-supported state of Iraq. Following the Iranian ouster of Shah Mohammad Reza Pahlavi in January 1979, and the assumption of power by the Ayatollah Khomeini, Iraqi President Saddam Hussein ordered his troops to invade Iran on September 22, 1980, ostensibly to recover land long-claimed by Iraq, but occupied for decades by the Shah. Hussein clearly expected an easy victory, due both to the Iraqi army's superiority in equipment and training, and to the chaotic political situation in Iran, which had seen its entire top echelon of military officers executed or replaced. Iraqi forces soon had occupied a major Iranian city and hundreds of square miles of Iranian territory. By 1982, however, Iranian troops had recaptured Khorramshahr, and driven the Iraqi forces back across its border. Thus began a series of punches and counterpunches that continued for years, with neither side able to gain a decisive advantage over the other. The attacks have spread to neutral shipping in the Persian Gulf, with both states trying to sink or disable tankers that are carrying revenue-generating petroleum from the other's oil wells. Both countries have also used long-range land-to-land missiles to terrorize each other's capitals in attacks reminiscent of the World War II V-2 bombings of London. Observers have also been struck by the similarities between this war and the trench warfare of World War I, with huge casualties generated by the Iranian human wave attacks, with the use of mustard gas by both sides, and with the elaborate system of defensive structures built by the Iraqis along the Shatt-al-Arab waterway. By the late 1980s, the advantage appeared to tilt to Iran, when it broke through Iraq's series of moats and trenches, drove within ten miles of Basrah, Iraq's second largest city, and occupied the Fao Peninsula, thus providing Iran with a launching point for Exocet antiship missiles aimed at ships in the harbor of Kuwait, Iraq's ally in the war. In early 1988, however, Iraq retook all the Iraqi lands occupied by Iran, drove the Iranian forces back across the international borderline, and launched a series of attacks against Iranian cities and forces designed to force Iran to the bargaining table. A cease-fire agreement was finally reached on August 20, 1988. *See also* AFGHAN WAR, 109; BOMBER WARFARE, 118; CHEMICAL WARFARE, 119; MINE WARFARE, 129.

Significance The Iran-Iraq War originated in long-standing border disputes between two fundamentally opposed regimes and cultures, and continued for eight years because the Ayatollah Khomeini, Iran's fanatical leader, refused to sign a truce with Saddam Hussein, despite entreaties from other Moslem leaders. Iran managed through its posturings to isolate itself diplomatically: "The Soviet Union, France, the

United States, Egypt, and the Arab traditional alliance were all determined that Iraq not be defeated militarily by Iran. . . . Given the dimensions of the support Iraq was receiving and given Iran's denial of essential military equipment, Iran's ability not only to stand firm but also to pose a serious threat to Iraq was impressive. . . . As a consequence, . . . the Reagan administration, preoccupied as it is with containing a perceived Soviet threat in the area, became the de facto ally of the Soviet Union in opposing the Iranian pressure against Iraq. . . . With regard to Afghanistan, however, the American government is supporting rebel groups that look to the Iranian government as a model."[49] Muriel Atkin insists that "from Moscow's perspective, the Iran-Iraq War could well leave the Soviet Union a loser regardless of which side wins. . . . [Moscow has] repeatedly urged the combatants to cease fighting and resolve their differences . . . and at the same time favored whichever combatant was on the defensive."[50]

Iran has always been able to use its oil revenues, however, to buy arms from the People's Republic of China and other sources. A major concern to both superpowers and their allies is continued "reliable Western access to Persian Gulf oil reserves. The physical vulnerability of the international oil-delivery installations and oil-transport systems to damage from acts of sabotage or war is manifest. These physical threats are secondary, however, to those that would be posed by Soviet political control over the West's oil supply."[51] To secure the flow of oil to the West, the administration of U.S. President Ronald W. Reagan agreed to allow several Kuwaiti tankers to fly the U.S. flag, and to provide military escorts to these and other U.S. ships. Several other countries, including France, Britain, and the Soviet Union, have also provided military escorts for their own vessels. The U.S. decision proved controversial after the accidental bombing of the USS *Stark,* which was hit by an Exocet missile from an Iraqi plane on May 17, 1987. Another controversy broke out when members of President Reagan's inner circle were accused of secretly selling arms to Iran in exchange for U.S. hostages, the so-called Iran-Contra affair. From a military point of view, the war has been noteworthy only for the millions of military and civilian casualties it has inflicted on both sides, with over a million deaths, making it the bloodiest conflict waged by any state since World War II. It has also consumed an estimated $200 billion in resources, mostly in petroleum revenues, money which could have been used to develop these desperately poor Third World states.

Libyan Air Raid (1986) **(127)**
A U.S. bombing attack on Libya on April 14, 1986. The Libyan Air Raid was prompted by the administration of President Ronald Rea-

gan, in retaliation for repeated terrorist attacks on and threats against U.S. citizens and establishments throughout the world. U.S. F-111F jets were launched from their bases in Britain, and refueled in flight; several U.S. carriers with their support ships and aircraft were also involved. Utilizing special laser-guided "smart bombs," the planes attacked air fields and barracks where the supposed terrorists were lodged, radar and missile emplacements on the Libyan coast, and several targets in the major cities of Tripoli and Benghazi. Libyan leader Muammar Qaddafi's own quarters were bombed, apparently in an overt attempt to kill him, leaving him wounded and his 18-month-old child dead. *See also* BOMBER WARFARE, 118; FIGHTER AIRCRAFT WARFARE, 123; PRECISION-GUIDED MUNITIONS (PGM), 132.

Significance   The Libyan Air Raid appeared, on the surface, to be an immediate reaction by U.S. forces to various terrorist incidents of the previous two years, which had culminated in a Libyan-organized bombing attack on a German nightclub frequented by U.S. soldiers; and to U.S.-Libyan naval clashes of the preceding months. On closer examination, however, the Reagan administration's decision appears part of a deliberate policy of using "U.S. military forces in limited, episodic fashion to suppress civil disorders, to rescue American civilians from overseas conflict zones, to intimidate hostile governments, or to otherwise 'project power' in the pursuit of U.S. foreign policy. Such activities which are generally confined to Third World areas are termed 'peacetime contingency operations'—'peacetime' in the sense that they fall short of an all-out global conflagration on the scale of World Wars I and II."[52] U.S. allies were noteworthy by their absence, only Britain providing full moral and material support; U.S. planes were forced to bypass the airspace of both France and Spain. Malcolm Spaven believes there were several other reasons for the American attack: "First . . . is inter-service rivalry. . . . A Pentagon official said that 'the Libyan attack provided a good proving ground for the F-111Fs to be flown in the Mediterranean . . . understandably, after the all-Navy action in Libya last month, the Air Force wanted a piece of the action.' . . . The fact that Libya has large numbers of Soviet-built weapons . . . would give U.S. forces experience in employing electronic countermeasures and untested new weapons, and assessing the performance of Soviet weaponry." Also, "the inevitable British support for the actions could be used as a stick with which to beat America's less staunch European allies and remind them who is really in charge. . . . The inevitable reaction of European governments has been to strengthen their resolve to do something against Qaddafi in order to try to dissuade Reagan from further military strikes."[53] And, in fact, Libyan terrorist activities around the world showed a noticeable decline in the year following the raid; whether such approaches will have any long-term effect is problematical. "The challenge for Washington might truly be seen not only as one of understanding the length and breadth of low-intensity conflict phenomena but also of understanding how the full policy repertoire might best be integrated and applied to meet the threat."[54]

Marine Air-Ground Task Forces (MAGTF)   **(128)**
Specially trained amphibious assault groups organized, trained, and supervised by the U.S. Marine Corps. The MAGTF "combine flexibility and mobility, and are specifically organized for each task. The three basic elements . . . are the Marine Amphibious Unit (MAU), the Marine Amphibious Brigade (MAB), and the Marine Amphibious Force (MAF)." The MAU, which is comprised of 2,500 men who can be transported aboard three to five ships, carries two to three weeks of supplies, utilizes a battalion landing team, and includes a support air squadron of about eight *Cobra* attack helicopters or six *Harrier* fighter-attack aircraft and twenty medium- and heavy-lift helicopters. The MAB is a regimental landing team consisting of approximately 18,000 men and one Marine Aircraft Group (MAG). Air support includes 90 fixed-wing aircraft and 100 helicopters. It requires 20 ships for deployment and carries a month's supplies. The MAF consists of a marine division and a marine airwing (50,000–58,000 personnel total), and utilizes some 250 fixed-wing tactical aircraft and 300 helicopters. It requires 30 to 40 ships for deployment and carries about two months' supplies. There are three MAFs: one on the west coast (for Southwest Asia deployment), a second on the east coast (covering the Caribbean, Mediterranean, and Atlantic), and a third in Japan.[55] *See also* HELICOPTER WARFARE, 125; SPECIAL FORCES WARFARE, 137.

Significance   The "expansion and modernization" of U.S. amphibious assault forces was a major defense goal of the administration of President Ronald W. Reagan. Former Secretary of Defense Caspar Weinberger, in his annual report to Congress in 1985, said: "We have developed a comprehensive, long-term plan . . . [which] calls for a major increase in amphibious lift capability, with a goal of achieving the lift to support the assault echelons of a Marine Amphibious Force (MAF) and a Marine Amphibious Brigade (MAB) by 1994—an increase of roughly one-third over today's capability. The plan integrates . . . with the scheduled introduction of new Marine Corps equipment—CH-53E helicopters, JVX advanced vertical-lift aircraft, heavier artillery pieces, and improved ground vehicles. . . . The plan also develops a new concept of operations calling for launching amphibious assaults from points over the horizon, where assault ships would be less vulnerable to enemy counterattacks. . . . In wartime, amphibious forces provide a global capability for forcibly establishing lodgments ashore."[56] The concept remains untested in battle.

Mine Warfare (129)

The use of land- or sea-based explosive devices that detonate when disturbed. Mines were defined during World War I as "explosives placed under or projectiles fired from under the surface of the ground." Booby traps are designed to explode when what appears to be a harmless object is moved or stepped upon, while claymores, which may be detonated either by electronic commands or triggered by trip wires, explode in a fan-shaped pattern. The command-detonated mine was first used by World War II guerrilla forces who converted unexploded bombs. Antipersonnel mines and booby traps were commonly used by the Viet Cong against U.S. forces in that war. Sea-based mines may either be tethered in place, held by an anchor or cable, or free-floating, and may detonate on contact or be exploded by the magnetic field of a ship passing nearby. For this reason, most minesweepers have hulls made entirely of wood, fiberglass, and/or plastic. Mines may also be cleared by specially equipped helicopters dragging sleds that detonate the mines. Minelayers will seed their fields in geometric patterns to prevent the exit or entry of foreign vessels, particularly enemy submarines, into certain protected waters; friendly vessels may be given charts showing "clear" passages through which they may safely transit waterways or enter ports;[57] mines may be lain by ships constructed for that purpose, by submarines, and by specially converted aircraft. *See also* FALKLAND ISLANDS WAR, 122; HELICOPTER WARFARE, 125; IRAN-IRAQ WAR, 126; SUBMARINE WARFARE, 142.

Significance Mine warfare has received short shrift in modern military strategy, except in the Soviet Union and Great Britain, both of which have maintained an active minesweeping fleet. The massive buildup of the U.S. fleet during the administration of President Ronald W. Reagan ignored the development of minor vessels in favor of reactivating battleships and constructing capital ships. Consequently, most U.S. minesweepers still in service date from World War II, although several new vessels are scheduled to enter the fleet in the 1990s. Thus, the use of sea-based mines by Iran against Persian Gulf shipping in the mid-1980s caught U.S. strategists by surprise, and forced them to scramble for solutions to this cheap but very effective form of naval warfare. U.S. mine war strategy is based on a variety of countermeasures, including minehunter ships, helicopters with drag sleds, and the Honeywell mine neutralization system (MNS).[58] The small, plastic antipersonnel mines strewn randomly over the beaches and hills of the Falkland Islands by the Argentine forces during their war with the British cannot be detected except by direct contact (when they explode), or through visual sighting. Since the Argentines failed to map their minefields, vast stretches of the islands will thus remain uninhabitable by anyone for generations.

Missile Cruiser Warfare (130)

The use of capital vessels armed with missiles and missile defense systems in modern naval warfare. Except for aircraft carriers and a handful of reactivated American battleships, cruisers are the largest warships currently being used by the world's navies. Until World War II, naval firepower was measured by the size and number of guns carried by a particular vessel; hence the trend toward larger and larger battleships, ships which could carry massive 16-inch guns with an effective range of 20 or more miles. Following that conflict, the development of ship-to-ship and ship-to-air missiles made such huge guns obsolete, simultaneously obviating the necessity for a larger ship structure to support them. Today, virtually all cruisers from the major powers carry missiles of all kinds, and defensive systems against both air- and sea-launched antiship missiles. U.S. vessels are "armed with *Standard* surface-to-air and *Harpoon* surface-to-surface missiles, and with antisubmarine rockets (ASROC) for use against submarines."[59] The *Harpoon* is the principal antiship weapon of the United States. The *Aegis* surface-to-air weapon system "is the U.S. Navy's primary defensive missile system for the late-1980s and beyond. . . . Designed primarily to defend against anti-ship cruise missiles and missile launcher platforms, it will be installed aboard a new class of guided missile cruisers and destroyers. . . . *Aegis* will be capable of defending a task force which includes a carrier and several other types of ships."[60] The *Tomahawk* cruise missile is designed to be launched from submarines as well as cruisers and destroyers. The USN's vertical launch system (VLS), which provides improved missile launching capability, is "based on a modular design, the basic unit being a launcher module containing eight missile cells."[61] The Soviets use similar shipborne missile systems of the SA-N class (#1–9), with the SA-N-9 now in use aboard the *Frunze* battlecruiser class.[62] *See also* AIRCRAFT CARRIER WARFARE, 110; BATTLESHIP WARFARE, 116; GRENADA INVASION, 124; IRAN-IRAQ WAR, 126.

Significance   Missile cruisers are the heart of the United States naval defense program. Former Secretary of Defense Caspar Weinberger has stated that "guided missile cruisers will be the centerpiece of our future area defense capability. The *Aegis* system . . . incorporates the most advanced technologies available for detecting and intercepting high-speed cruise missiles at sea. . . . These capabilities will substantially increase the air defense firepower of our battle groups against coordinated antiship cruise missile saturation attacks."[63] The first ship with these capabilities was the *Ticonderoga*, which was commissioned in 1984; an additional 26 ships will join the U.S. fleet by the early 1990s. In its first known combat use, the *Aegis* system shot down an Iranian passenger plane over the Persian Gulf on July 3, 1988, killing all 290 persons aboard; the Pentagon blamed crew error arising from psychological stress.

North American Air Defense Command (NORAD)   (131)

A joint U.S.-Canadian early-warning radar and detection system to provide notice against a surprise Russian attack. NORAD is "based at Colorado Springs on the edge of the Rocky Mountains and has a massive battle headquarters blasted out of the solid granite of Cheyenne Mountain. . . . A third of a mile into the mountain are fifteen steel structures shock-mounted on springs, in which the staff of NORAD can operate 'buttoned-up' for up to one month with autonomous life-support systems."[64] NORAD utilizes satellite systems in orbit over the Soviet Union and elsewhere to spot ICBMs within 90 seconds of launching, and ground-based radar systems from Alaska to Florida to monitor other activities in every part of the world. NORAD does not itself control any of the retaliatory forces of the United States, but passes its information on to the relevant civilian authorities. *See also* ANTISATELLITE SYSTEMS (ASAT), 111; SPY SATELLITE WARFARE, 138.

Significance   The North American Air Defense Command performs a necessary role in providing early detection of potential sneak attacks or first strikes. In the last 20 years, however, NORAD has become heavily dependent on computers and programming which are now technologically obsolete, and which badly need replacing and updating. As a result, breakdowns and false signals are not uncommon, and have raised concern among outside observers who fear the possibility of an "accidental" nuclear war arising from computer malfunction or from the potential misreading of falsely reported computer data. "In November 1979 a computer at NORAD . . . was loaded with simulated data indicating that a nuclear attack on the U.S. was in progress and NORAD briefly took it for real. . . . In June 1980 a faulty microchip repeated the alarm and three days later there was a deliberate false alarm to locate the faulty microprocessor. In each case the alert lasted less than two minutes. NORAD's Commanding General, James V. Hartinger, said . . . 'We can contact every one of our sensors in less than sixty seconds. . . . No, no, no. There is no way a flock of geese could start a nuclear war.'"[65] In response, Senator Gary Hart (D-Colo.) has stated: "In 1980 Sen. Barry Goldwater and I led a Senate Armed Services Committee investigation into the continuing serious problems with the computers of NORAD . . . during one eighteen-month period, NORAD experienced 151 false alarms—one of which lasted a full six minutes, or one-fifth the time it would take an ICBM-launched warhead to reach its target. . . . Further, no one . . . knows how reliable Soviet personnel and computers are. This ignorance only underscores the importance of taking joint and immediate steps to reduce the likelihood of starting a nuclear war by mistake."[66]

Precision-Guided Munitions (PGMs) (132)

Bombs and other munitions which can be guided very precisely to their targets with computer-assisted technology. PGMs have "dramatically increased single shot kill probabilities. With accuracies expressed in terms of circular error probable (CEP) as low as 10 feet, these systems vary widely in role and sophistication. . . . Wire-guided anti-tank missiles, like the American TOW [are an example]. . . . PGM now being deployed on strike aircraft have still more sophisticated guidance systems and can deliver larger charges. . . . Other PGM under development in the US include laser-guided artillery projectiles and multiple independently maneuvering sub-munitions (MIMS) which would use a terminal guidance system to attack individual targets. American and, reportedly, Soviet research efforts are also concentrating on the development of high-powered lasers as destructive weapons."[67] Precision-guided munitions were used by U.S. aircraft in the 1986 Libyan Air Raid, in an attempt simultaneously to kill or injure Libyan President Muammar Qaddafi, and to destroy Libyan radar emplacements and missiles. *See also* ANTITANK GUIDED MISSILES (ATGM), 113; ARAB-ISRAELI WARS, 114; ARMORED VEHICLE WARFARE, 115; CIRCULAR ERROR PROBABLE (CEP), 182; LIBYAN AIR RAID, 127.

Significance Precision-guided weapons have forced military strategists to change their concepts of conventional war. The "concentration of forces on the battlefield is less desirable, and . . . larger and expensive systems—such as battle tanks and aircraft—have become increasingly vulnerable to far less expensive weapons carried by small units. . . . The introduction of large numbers of PGM . . . is thought especially relevant to Central Europe, where the primary military problem has long been seen as that of defense against a concerted attack by Warsaw Pact armored forces."[68] Such weapons do have potential technical and tactical limitations, including maintenance problems, operation of relatively sophisticated equipment by unsophisticated or poorly trained soldiers, and performance in urban areas; in the Libyan raid, for example, the attack on Qaddafi's compound was less successful than those on coastal radar and missile sites. The relationship between such weapons and their nuclear counterparts is also somewhat uncertain. "It could become difficult to differentiate levels of conflict escalation or to structure arms control agreements in terms of the nature of weapons employed."[69] In fact, many experts believe that any effort by the superpowers to control or monitor such weapons would quickly bog down in technicalities. Michael Moodie, in a discussion of arms transfers, believes that "the weapons most frequently debated as to their impact on stability are precision guided munitions. On one hand . . . because of the so-called defensive qualities of PGMs, they will be a stabilizing factor. . . . On the other, . . . the acquisition of those systems will not proceed in a balanced manner, thus giving some states at least a temporary great increase in firepower that could upset existing military balances."[70]

Proxy Forces Warfare (133)
The use of the military forces of a client state to substitute for one's own forces in combat, either by collusion, or by deliberate intent. Proxy warfare, which "began to flourish in the post–World War II international environment . . . has three characteristics. . . . First, the system is essentially bipolar (limited to the two superpowers serving as patrons); second, the onset of nuclear weapons makes direct superpower confrontation extremely unattractive; and third, the world today consists almost exclusively of nominally independent nation-states, which . . . guard their sovereignty closely."[71] The Russians, most notably in Angola, have used Cuban and East German proxy troops and "advisers" to support takeovers and coups in states which they consider advantageous to the Soviet cause. The United States has used proxy warfare much more sparingly in the post–World War II period, most notably with the Contras in Nicaragua; other commentators regard both the Mujahedeen guerrillas in Afghanistan and the UNITA forces of Jonas Savimbi in Angola as examples of other U.S.

proxies. *See also* AFGHAN WAR, 109; ARAB-ISRAELI WARS, 114; VIETNAM WAR, 143.

Significance   The use of third-party troops as proxies in bush wars limits the possibility of such conflicts escalating into a major confrontation between the superpowers. Christopher Lamb tells us, however, that a "shift in the geopolitical balance of power from a clear U.S. superiority to a questionable equilibrium has directly influenced the use of proxies by encouraging the Soviet Union to intervene with them in an increasingly unrestrained fashion." He concludes that "the United States will have to either meet the challenge or drastically devalue the nature and scope of its security interests. [Other options to consider are:] to build up U.S. limited-war capability, especially the logistical support necessary for moving large numbers of troops and large amounts of equipment quickly and far. . . . Multilateralize Western response to Soviet interventions. . . . Build on British, French, and local military facilities in the area, and cultivate and bolster the most reliable friends in the area. . . . The choice is to enlist proxies and allies or acquiesce to Soviet proxy interventions, which certainly will continue."[72] Meanwhile, the client states involved in proxy conflicts almost inevitably lose, no matter what the formal outcomes of the wars, with their economies, populations, and ecologies destroyed or severely damaged by the conflict itself. Vietnam, for example, although it won the war against the U.S.-supported proxy forces of South Vietnam, was left in a serious economic depression from which it has yet to emerge; several generations of almost constant fighting have condemned Vietnam to virtual economic servitude, a perpetual basket case of the Third World.

Rapid Deployment Forces (RDF) Command   (134)
A U.S. strike command designed to move large numbers of U.S. troops quickly and efficiently to parts of the world where regularly established support bases are unavailable. The RDF concept was developed in 1977 under the administration of President Jimmy Carter, and was expanded by the administration of President Ronald W. Reagan, with all RDF efforts placed under one command. "Subsequently designated the Rapid Deployment Joint Task Force (RDJTF), the command was formally established in December 1979. . . . After extensive consideration and debate, the RDJTF was elevated to the level of unified command on 1 January 1983 and renamed the U.S. Central Command."[73] Of particular concern to U.S. strategists is the Persian Gulf area, with its mix of volatile Middle Eastern politics and easily interdictable oil supply lines; consequently, RDF forces have been

permanently stationed in the Indian Ocean, where they can easily reach any part of the Middle East. *See also* AIRCRAFT CARRIER WARFARE, 110; HELICOPTER WARFARE, 125; IRAN-IRAQ WAR, 126; MARINE AIR-GROUND TASK FORCES (MAGTF), 128.

Significance   The development of the Rapid Deployment Forces network is an essential part of current U.S. defense strategy. As former Secretary of Defense Caspar Weinberger has noted, it makes both political and military sense "to be prepared to launch counter-offensives in other regions [of the world,] and try to exploit the aggressor's weaknesses wherever they exist."[74] William W. Kaufmann adds: "Unlike the infrastructure for Europe, the one leading into the Persian Gulf area is distant and cannot be considered reliable. Indeed, just when the United States might want to use bases in Africa and the Middle East, some of the host countries could conceivably deny access to them. In the circumstances, as long as the Persian Gulf remains a key contingency for force planning purposes, it makes sense to have a way of establishing a lodgment in the area that will permit the subsequent buildup of land-based forces arriving by air and sea. Carrier battle groups and Marine amphibious units provide just such an alternative to the current base structure."[75]

Remotely Piloted Vehicle (RPV) Warfare   (135)

The use of remote-controlled, pilotless aircraft for wartime surveillance, decoying, and bombing, and for peacetime testing of other weapons systems. "A drone is a similar type of vehicle, but is pre-programmed to fly a certain course at a certain height, or to fly a pattern of courses and heights. It is not fully remote controlled, but it might be possible to alter its flight pattern by remote control."[76] RPVs were used extensively during the Vietnam War; Israel has also utilized drones against their Arab neighbors, both as decoys and for surveillance. *See also* ARAB-ISRAELI WARS, 114; VIETNAM WAR, 143.

Significance   Remotely piloted vehicles have become a necessary part of modern warfare. To be effective, they require: "First, all the technical sensors of the manned aircraft as well as sensors to replace human vision . . . ; second, reliable communication links that will transmit all those stimuli back to a distant operator; third, an operator who is capable of reacting as skillfully as aircrew would do; and fourth, complex links back to the RPV that will faithfully transmit each of those reactions and activate the controls and equipment of the vehicle."[77] It has been suggested that RPVs "will probably have the greatest impact in strike and electronic warfare roles. Recoverable RPV can be used as support jammers and chaff dispensers to degrade an adversary's surface radar network, while strike RPV armed with PGM could be used against a variety of fixed targets, such as defense sites, command centers and air fields, and—further into the future— against mobile targets."[78] RPVs have also assumed a major role in the testing of new anti-aircraft missile systems, since these expendable flying machines can be made to assume the characteristics of far more expensive aircraft at a much lower unit price.

Space Warfare (136)

The use of military satellites, antisatellite weapons, and ballistic missile defense systems to control regions of outer space, and to defend against space- or Earth-launched weapons. Space has long been used for military purposes by both superpowers, primarily for surveillance, but also to provide early warning of missile launches, weather data, scientific research, navigation, and communications. An antisatellite weapons program was initiated by the United States as early as 1960, with a proposal to put a satellite interceptor program (SAINT) into orbit on an Agena/Atlas-Centaur booster combination. The program was later abandoned, and replaced by a Nike-Zeus missile armed with a nuclear warhead guided by ground-based radar. The Nike-Zeus system, however, had a "ceiling of only about 350 miles, and was superseded by . . . Program 437, which used the Thor intermediate-range ballistic missile to launch a nuclear warhead up to . . . 800 miles. . . . Two missiles were maintained at Johnston Island . . . [and the program] remained operational until 1975."[79] Both the Soviet Union and the United States have developed more sophisticated anti-satellite systems in the 1980s, based upon two concepts: the destruction or blinding of satellites by lasers or particle beams, and the destruction of satellites by collision with pellets or small missiles launched from high-altitude jet planes. *See also* ANTISATELLITE SYSTEMS (ASAT), 111; SPY SATELLITE WARFARE, 138; STRATEGIC DEFENSE INITIATIVE (SDI), 141.

Significance   The military use of space has been a fact of life since the beginning of the space age in 1957. Both superpowers have maintained extensive, ongoing research programs into space weapons and counterweapons, while steadfastly proclaiming their firm intentions of never using them. One-third to one-half of the experiments conducted on manned space flights since 1961 have been devoted to military purposes; it is no accident that a large majority of early astronauts were drawn directly from the military services of both superpowers (this has diminished somewhat in the space shuttle era). Concerning the development of antisatellite weapons, Rep. George E.

Brown, Jr. (D-Calif.) has stated: "Shortly after the Reagan Administration entered office, it announced a plan to deploy a large force of ASAT weapons. The device was an 18-foot missile that would be launched from high-flying (F-15) jets. . . . Initial plans called for 112 of these 'satellite killers,' enough to destroy all Soviet satellites in near-Earth orbit. The system would be fully operational by 1987. . . . The U.S. is enormously dependent on military satellites for arms control verification, communications, early warning and intelligence gathering. As a nation we are more dependent on satellites than is the Soviet Union. It would be extremely dangerous for the U.S. to encourage a competition with the Soviets in weapons designed to destroy satellites. . . . In 1985, Congress passed into law the Brown-Coughlin amendment establishing a U.S.-Soviet moratorium on ASAT testing . . . thus blocking the development and . . . deployment of the weapon. Frustrated . . . and recognizing that Congress' position was now firmly established, the Air Force decided [in its budget proposal for 1989] to abandon the fight. President Reagan's Strategic Defense Initiative (SDI) program still threatens to provoke a spiraling arms race in space. . . . But that program has a long, difficult road ahead of it."[80] Christopher Bertram notes, however, that "even in peacetime, the use of space for reconnaissance, communications, electronic intelligence, ocean surveillance and navigation has burgeoned,"[81] and will continue to do so at an even greater rate in the future. The development of Soviet and U.S. space stations in the 1990s will provide permanent platforms for manned habitation in space, and will undoubtedly increase man's direct military participation there, particularly with surveillance programs, direct antisatellite intervention from space, and, potentially, the stationing of nuclear bombs, enormously powerful lasers, and other destructive weapons in perpetual orbit.

Special Forces Warfare (137)

The use of specially trained Army Ranger Battalions and Navy SEAL (Sea-Air-Land) teams to provide cross-service coordination and security assistance during military crisis situations. Special Forces work "with foreign armed forces to augment their defense capabilities," provide a "flexible, tailored alternative where the use of conventional forces might not be appropriate or feasible," and are used during "major conflicts as an adjunct to conventional forces, utilizing special skills in unconventional warfare, psychological operations, intelligence, and surgical, direct action operations."[82] *See also* FALKLAND ISLANDS WAR, 122; GRENADA INVASION, 124; HELICOPTER WARFARE, 125; VIETNAM WAR, 143.

Significance   Special Forces played an important role in President Ronald W. Reagan's expansion of U.S. military forces. The use of terrorism by overseas political groups, the radicalization of the Middle East, the prevalence of bush-war operations throughout the Third World, have made the availability of such groups a desirable strategic option. Thus, it is not surprising that SEAL teams were used during the 1983 U.S. invasion of Grenada to secure landing beachheads. Former Secretary of Defense Caspar Weinberger has said: "Revitalizing our Special Operations Forces (SOF) remains one of this Administration's highest priorities, [reflecting] our recognition that low-level conflict—for which SOF are uniquely suited—will pose the threat we are most likely to encounter throughout the end of this century. . . . We have sought to build a force capable of meeting its global responsibilities by forming a new Special Forces Group, new SEAL Teams, and a Special Operations Aviation Task Force. Our program also includes procuring additional MC-130 Combat Talon aircraft and HH-60D helicopters, and a new naval special warfare craft. We have also begun research and development of follow-on naval and air systems, . . . and are improving SOF training, particularly in critical skills such as language and area orientation on which the success of special operations often depends."[83] Most other developed countries also maintain some equivalent of special forces, the British having long been recognized as being paramount in the training of elite commandos. The South Koreans developed a special 15,000-man antiterrorist brigade to counter North Korean threats to the celebration of the September 1988 Summer Olympic games at Seoul. The ill-fated attempt by the Carter administration to use special forces to rescue U.S. hostages in Iran (April 24, 1980), failed when several aircraft crashed into each other on the Iranian desert, resulting in eight Americans dead, and the loss of both helicopters and other transport craft.

Spy Satellite Warfare   (138)

The use of reconnaissance and surveillance satellites for a variety of military purposes. Spy satellites have routinely conducted sweeps of important military and civilian targets since the beginning of the space age. These can be divided into surveillance, "a regular monitoring activity," and reconnaissance, "a search for specific intelligence, possibly of a more urgent nature. Although the tasks are different, they are increasingly combined on a single satellite platform equipped with several sensors."[84] The United States relies heavily on the KH-11 (Key Hole) series reconnaissance satellite, which uses a "digital imaging device"—the KH-12 is reportedly under development. The Soviets use photo-reconnaissance satellites in their multipurpose Cosmos series. In addition, both superpowers utilize Elint (electronic intelligence) satellites (commonly known as "ferrets"), which can locate radio transmitters, eavesdrop, and monitor missile test sites. Satellites fitted with Elint communications equipment are also used for ocean surveillance by both nations.[85] *See also* ANTISATELLITE SYSTEMS (ASAT), 111; SPACE WARFARE, 136; STRATEGIC DEFENSE INITIATIVE (SDI), 141.

Significance　　Spy satellites provide a necessary safeguard in the nuclear age against sneak attack or other military surprises. This being the case, it is clear that "if either the United States or the Soviet Union were to be deprived of the use of military satellites in a time of crisis she would find herself at a marked disadvantage. Both have come to rely on the capabilities of satellite systems to provide the instantaneous warning and information needed in a contemporary war."[86] The very act of destroying or disabling a spy satellite network might, therefore, in itself provoke a nuclear war. Satellite surveillance also provides part of the means for verifying adherence to arms control treaties between the superpowers.

Stealth Aircraft　　　　　　　　　　　　　　　　(139)

Military airplanes which have been specially modified to reduce the radar echoes they create to near zero, thereby increasing the chances that they may successfully penetrate enemy airspace without detection. Stealth technology is a stepchild of the military buildup initiated by President Ronald W. Reagan, and of the computer age, utilizing components and systems that did not exist even ten years ago. Several different aircraft are reportedly under development: the advanced technology B-2 bomber (ATB), scheduled for deployment in the 1990s; the F-117 jet fighter; and a high-altitude spy plane. Stealth aircraft rely "on deception rather than speed to outwit their opponents and are designed to present the lowest possible optical, radar and infrared 'signatures' to enemy sensors. A product of Northrop, the prototype B-2 bomber has a carefully-shaped airframe incorporating much non-metallic composite material, and eliminates as many echo-producing corners as possible."[87] A prototype F-117 fighter crashed in the Nevada desert in 1987, but the crash site was quickly cordoned off by military security. The Reagan administration publicly displayed the first prototype of the B-2 bomber in 1988, revealing a flying wing aircraft reminiscent of an experimental craft tested by the U.S. Air

Force in the late 1940s. *See also* BOMBER WARFARE, 118; FIGHTER AIRCRAFT WARFARE, 123.

Significance   Details surrounding the Stealth program have been closely guarded by the U.S. military establishment, to prevent Soviet development of similarly designed aircraft. Reportedly, prototypes have been test-flown only at night, when spy satellites cannot see them, and kept shrouded in hangars during the day.

> The Stealth program remains shrouded in secrecy further obscured by controversy about the relationship between the prospects for the ATB . . . and the continued requirement for [the] B-1 [bomber]. . . . Although the exact shape of the future bomber program seems likely to continue to be a matter of controversy, if only because of the large costs of manned aircraft, the place of manned bombers in the strategic program seems secure for the indefinite future. . . . The central question is whether the B-1B will be followed as planned by a single-minded focus on the Stealth bomber, or [whether] additional B-1 bombers will be built beyond the 100 now projected.[88]

Critics have raised questions concerning the high unit cost of the planes, the sophisticated technology needed to fly the aircraft (the B-2 is inherently unstable, and can only be flown with advanced computers), and the long-term viability of the cloaking measures the craft employs. Supporters have pointed to the need for an effective nuclear deterrent that can be recalled before it reaches its target, something missiles are unable to do.

Strategic Air Command (SAC)   (140)

A special U.S. Air Force unit designed to guarantee nuclear retaliation against the Soviets in case of a surprise attack. Following World War II, as a part of the massive reorganization of the U.S. armed forces, which took place in 1946–1947, leading to the separation of the air force as an independent service, the Strategic Air Command was formed to "carry out the all-important nuclear delivery mission, and the Tactical Air Command, or TAC, assumed the ground support mission."[89] "Almost from its establishment in March, 1946, the Strategic Air Command was given priority over the Air Defense Command and the Tactical Air Command."[90] By the last two years of his second term, however, U.S. President Dwight D. Eisenhower had concluded "that American reliance on the survivability of the SAC bomber force was becoming increasingly tenuous. . . . The president stepped up efforts to make American nuclear forces less vulnerable to a devastating first strike . . . [which included such measures] as the continuous deployment of a portion of the SAC bomber force in the air."[91] The SAC fleet now consists of several hundred aging B-52 bombers, 100 B-1 bombers (some of them not yet fully operational, due to continuing technical problems with these planes), and an unknown number of B-2 Stealth bombers, a few of which may already be operational. *See also* BOMBER WARFARE, 118; FIGHTER AIRCRAFT WARFARE, 123; STEALTH AIRCRAFT, 139.

Significance   The United States has long relied on a vision of a Strategic Air Command which is ever-vigilant against the threat of an all-out Soviet first strike. Former Secretary of State Henry A. Kissinger offered these thoughts, however, pertaining to the competition between the Strategic Air Command and its intraservice rivals: "It is only natural for the best crews, the best equipment, and the choicest bases to be assigned to our retaliatory force. The penalty for our preoccupation with the strategic striking force is that it turns the mode of operation which is necessary for all-out war into the pattern for the conduct of limited war as well." The problem, as Kissinger sees it, is one of choice. By giving priority for weapons, transportation, and other necessities to SAC, we have, in effect, committed ourselves to its vision of war at the expense of all other alternatives, including limited war. He concludes, however, that "it is not that the belief in the importance of strategic striking forces is wrong; indeed, the Strategic Air Command must continue to have the first claim on our defense budget. It is only that the overemphasis on total solutions reinforces the already powerful tendency against supplementing our retaliatory forces with subtler military capabilities which address themselves to the likelier dangers and involve a less destructive strategy."[92]

Strategic Defense Initiative (SDI)   (141)

The 1983 "Star Wars" proposal of U.S. President Ronald W. Reagan to develop a space-based defensive umbrella against incoming ballistic nuclear missiles. The Strategic Defense Initiative proposes to stop Soviet missiles through a combination of early satellite detection, focused laser and/or particle beams, small interceptor missiles, and other means. An antiballistic missile (ABM) defense system, also called the Ballistic Missile Defense (BMD), is not a new idea, having been hotly debated in the 1960s, and again in 1972, with the signing and ratification of the ABM treaty emerging from SALT I. "In principle, a ballistic missile could be countered during any of the four phases of its flight trajectory: the boost, postboost, midcourse, and terminal phases. . . . In any phase of flight, a defensive system must perform the following functions: surveillance and acquisition, discrimination, pointing and tracking, interception and destruction, damage assessment, and battle management. . . . SDI envisions a layered defense that would attempt to counter ballistic missiles in all four phases of flight. Each layer would serve as a backup to deal with the missiles . . . that leak through the defensive layers directed at earlier phases of flight."[93] Although both the United States and the Soviet Union have long had the capability of stopping missiles in the midcourse and terminal phases, it remains to be seen whether an effective boost-phase or postboost-phase intercept is possible. *See also* ANTISATELLITE SYSTEMS (ASAT), 111; SPACE WARFARE, 136; SPY SATELLITE WARFARE, 138.

Significance   The Strategic Defense Initiative was President Ronald W. Reagan's major defense proposal in his eight years in office, and it immediately proved divisive, with most conservatives supporting SDI and most liberals opposing it. In his speech, Reagan declared: "What if free people could live secure in the knowledge that their security did not rest upon the threat of instant U.S. retaliation to deter a Soviet attack, that we could intercept and destroy strategic ballistic missiles before they reached our own soil or that of our allies?"[94] McGeorge Bundy replied: "The friends of arms control will do well to focus intense and continuing effort on the prevention of any premature weaponization of space. Unless and until the tests of survivability, cost-effectiveness, and contribution to stability can be persuasively met, the case for going slowly in space is overwhelming."[95] In a more vehement response, Senator Edward M. Kennedy (D-Mass.) stated: "The key to containing offensive strategic developments lies not in defensive technology, but in the successful negotiation of reductions in nuclear weapons. President Reagan has attempted to sell the Strategic Defense Initiative with the argument that it will eliminate the need for offensive nuclear weapons. Given that a leakproof defense is technologically impossible, nothing could be further from the truth. An arms race in defensive technology can *only* succeed in stimulating the offensive arms race as each side seeks to deploy countermeasures and greater numbers of offensive weapons to overwhelm any defense. The best way to reduce the threat posed by offensive weapons is to have an immediate, mutual, and verifiable nuclear freeze followed by major weapons reductions."[96] The scientific and technical communities have also split into several camps, some fervently supporting Reagan's initiative, but a majority stating either that the technology proposed by Reagan is unfeasible, or wondering whether it is worth spending billions of dollars to find out, particularly when the system could be so easily and cheaply countered by the Soviets. Accurate satellite surveillance and the satellite tracking of ballistic missiles are crucial to SDI, but satellites are easily blinded or destroyed by lasers and small missiles, and cannot be readily defended. Destruction of even a handful of these all-seeing spies would quickly render the system ineffectual, and the failure to stop even 100 Soviet warheads (out of 25,000-plus available) would probably result in an end of the United States as we know it, if not human civilization itself. The Soviet Union has consistently and sometimes stridently denounced SDI as a violation of the ABM treaty.

Submarine Warfare (142)

The use during combat of vessels specially designed to operate for long periods underwater. The first operational submarines were built during the U.S. Civil War, but modern submarine warfare first surfaced during World War I, with the Germans initially scoring notable successes against the allies. By World War II, "the aggressive vessels of the war were the submarines, or U-boats. . . . Designed for operations under the water, these warships' primary mission was to locate and destroy ships of all kinds, including other submarines. . . . Since World War II, the Navy has been transformed by technological developments. . . . The nuclear warhead capable of being launched from under the sea has made the ballistic missile submarine (SSBN) a candidate for the next dominant warship."[97] "The U.S. Navy operates just over 90 nuclear-propelled attack submarines (SSNs) and 4 diesel-electric attack submarines. . . . The current goal is 100 SSNs. Some Navy authorities have estimated that requirements in the 1990s and beyond could be as high as 140 submarines."[98] "The submarine leg of the U.S. strategic offensive forces—often referred to as the triad—consists of 31 older strategic missile submarines (SSBN) armed with the Poseidon C-3 or Trident C-4 missile, and a small number of new, very large submarines carrying [a complement of 24] Trident C-4 missiles. The new submarines are being built at the rate of about one per year."[99] *See also* ANTISUBMARINE WARFARE (ASW), 112; FALKLAND ISLANDS WAR, 122; SPY SATELLITE WARFARE, 138.

Significance Missile-carrying submarines are now considered by many observers to be the strongest leg of the nuclear triad.

> Land-based silos are vulnerable to attacks from new, highly accurate missiles tipped with huge warheads. Modern anti-aircraft missile systems make bomber strikes an iffy proposition. But the submarine, moving silently through millions of square miles of dark ocean, is relatively invulnerable to attack. . . . Once an American submarine disappears beneath the waves, it is virtually impossible to track. Both superpowers are working furiously on methods to reliably detect submerged submarines, but the oceans are likely to remain opaque for a long while, and to nuclear warfare theorists, this is a good

thing. American antisubmarine warfare is far from perfect, but it is so much better than Russian means of detection as to approach destabilization of the balance of power. . . . Both sides are looking to outer space for more accurate and secure methods of strategic submarine detection.[100]

In the last decade, infrared satellite sensors capable of detecting submarine wakes have been developed by both superpowers, but their true efficiency is a closely guarded military secret.

Vietnam War (1945–1975)   143

A civil war in which North and South Vietnam, client states, respectively, for the Soviet Union /Red China and the United States/France/ Great Britain, fought for political control of Southeast Asia (Vietnam, Laos, and Cambodia), with North Vietnam finally establishing hegemony in 1975. The Vietnam War had its origins in French Indochina, which the Japanese occupied during World War II. With the fall of Japan, a radical group under the leadership of Ho Chi Minh proclaimed Vietnam's independence in 1945. The French returned within months, initiating a war that lasted until the French defeat in 1954. The French withdrawal resulted in the division of Vietnam into two states, a Communist regime centered at Hanoi, controlling the northern half of the country, and a southern regime at Saigon, ostensibly a democracy, but in reality a presidential dictatorship. Ho Chi Minh continued to press for Vietnam's reunification, and, following the assassination of South Vietnam President Ngo Dinh Diem in late 1963, ordered his troops to begin infiltrating in large numbers down the Ho Chi Minh Trail. The United States, which had long supported South Vietnam with weapons and training, began air strikes against North Vietnam in 1964, and inserted U.S. combat troops into the struggle a year later. By 1969, U.S. forces in Vietnam totalled over a half million men. In 1973, U.S. President Richard M. Nixon ordered the withdrawal of U.S. troops, but promised continued aid to the South Vietnam regime. Early in 1975, however, the Communists began offensives in both Cambodia and South Vietnam that led to the collapse of both regimes in April, and the official reunification of Vietnam in 1976. After clashes with the new Cambodian government, Vietnam invaded that country in 1978, installing a puppet government there in early 1979; they began withdrawing their troops in 1988. Vietnam also maintains a troop contingent permanently stationed in eastern Laos. See also AFGHAN WAR, 109; PROXY FORCES WARFARE, 133.

Significance   The Vietnam War was the United States' longest war, lasting from 1965 to 1973 (the actual time U.S. troops were involved).

It was also the first war the United States ever lost, despite the fact that it won most of the battles fought by its troops. In addition, Vietnam was "the first war brought into the family living room by television. . . . It was a war maddeningly without front lines, [fought] against an enemy who often wore civilian clothes, and had no clear objective other than the 'body count.' . . . It cost the lives of 57,939 Americans, $150 billion in U.S. military spending, and produced four million killed or wounded Vietnamese on both sides. . . . It was also the most divisive conflict for Americans since the [U.S.] Civil War, and perhaps the most misunderstood war in American history."[101] In his analysis of the war, John I. Alger tells us that "in the early 1960s, brinkmanship gave way to the principle of flexible response, a policy that consisted of a variety of reactions to Communist-inspired activities that threatened the free world. Economic aid to victims, boycott, show of force, military assistance programs, commitment of unconventional forces, and—ultimately—massive nuclear strikes were all components of the policy of flexible response. The problems of flexible response became apparent in Vietnam, where the policy led to escalation, the commitment of an increasing number and variety of forces and weapons in an effort to contain successfully an enemy who was willing himself to increase his commitment."[102] The result of the war was a generation of emotionally scarred veterans and their families, and a serious loss of faith in the U.S. political system. U.S. President Lyndon B. Johnson was virtually driven from office in 1969; Richard M. Nixon, his successor, became the first U.S. executive to resign his post in 1974, in the midst of the Watergate scandal. The U.S. political apparatus has remained polarized and largely ineffectual ever since. In Vietnam, there was no lack of victims. In the aftermath of the war, Hanoi found itself involved in wars with the People's Republic of China and the new Communist government of Cambodia, which it ousted in 1979. Having established itself as the new master of Indochina, however, Vietnam soon discovered the price of success, as it headed into a deep economic decline from which it has yet to arise, and became bogged down in an interminable, expensive, and probably unwinnable guerrilla struggle with rebel forces in Cambodia. The final victims of the war were the people of Vietnam, who suffered millions of casualties, including deaths, injuries, psychological traumas, and poisoning by biological agents. Tens of thousands have tried to escape from Vietnam since 1975, many of them dying in the attempt. The most pitiable of these human remnants are the tens of thousands of half-American Vietnamese, fathered and abandoned by U.S. soldiers, now outcast by their own people from a society that believes in racial purity, unwanted by either of the cultures that begat them.

175

6. Nuclear Weapons

Atomic Bomb (144)

A bomb whose energy derives from the fission of plutonium or uranium. The atomic bomb, as originally conceived, was a fission device—that is, a bomb in which the explosion occurs as a result of the breaking apart (or fission) of atoms of various elements (in this case, unstable uranium isotopes). When fission occurs, energy is produced, which in turn causes a chain reaction, the result of which is an atomic explosion. This type of explosion produces four deadly effects: first, intense heat, which results from the release of energy from the split atoms, igniting fires in the blast area, creating a fire storm; second, blast overpressure, and precipitates an enormous change in atmospheric pressure, and induces massive winds emanating from the blast area that wreak tremendous physical damage; third, prompt radiation, which releases subatomic particles (mainly neutrons and gamma rays) from the breakup of the uranium atoms, producing incapacitation or death; and fourth, residual radiation (often called "fallout"), which consists of the larger particles that are generated by the fission. This fallout, which includes such isotopes as strontium 90, is highly radioactive and poses a serious health hazard for an indefinite period. *See also* HIROSHIMA BOMBARDMENT, 147; MANHATTAN PROJECT, 149; NUCLEAR FISSION, 155; NUCLEAR WARHEAD, 166; URANIUM, 84.

Significance The atomic bomb represented the first step in the nuclear revolution. Although primitive, when measured by present standards, the "simple" fission explosion is the "dirtiest" type, in that it produces an immense amount of residual radiation. In addition, it is extremely inefficient, requiring an inordinate amount of fuel to produce the desired damage than do more recent nuclear devices. At the time, the atomic bomb constituted an unparalleled advance in modern weaponry, one that gave rise to an entirely new lexicon. In its day, argues defense strategist Donald M. Snow, "the atomic bomb seemed admirably suited to the task of destroying cities (and hence industry)."[1] Although some experts viewed it as simply a more efficient means for instituting an aerial bombardment, cooler heads prevailed. Most understood, however, that the fission bomb was not just another bomb; rather, it was a weapon of unprecedented destructive power—one that could not only decimate entire population centers but also inflict frightening damage—both short- and long-term—on the ecosystem. The atomic bomb has altered the nature of modern warfare, rendering conventional warfare obsolete and arming its possessors with the tools necessary to plunge modern civilization back into prehistoric times. Given the political and military advantages that such weapons hold, the atomic bomb established the basis for a massive arms race that shows few signs of abating. Despite mankind's present knowledge of nuclear weapons, and their attendant dangers, little progress has been made in halting their spread; if anything, the specter of an enlarged nuclear weapons family grows more frightening daily.

Cruise Missile (145)

A guided missile that employs aerodynamic lift to sustain powered flight through the atmosphere to its target. The cruise missile is an unmanned, dispensable vehicle programmed to transport explosives over a nonballistic trajectory to its mark. Like the propulsion system of a jet airplane, a cruise missile uses air as an oxidizer. Thus, the missile's engine propels the vehicle in a similar way to aircraft, avoiding ballistic paths. Unlike ballistic missiles, which fly considerably faster, the cruise missile is able to utilize a sophisticated guidance system, which ensures far greater accuracy. The cruise missile originated with World War II, but soon fell into disfavor. In the 1950s, the United States deployed the first nuclear armed cruise missiles. They were subsequently abandoned, however, owing to their large size and lack of reliability and accuracy. Instead, most experts advocated the development of ballistic missiles, which possessed numerous advantages over the cruise missile. As a result of technological advances in the 1960s and 1970s—in engine, guidance, and warhead miniaturization—weapons designers concluded that they could develop smaller cruise missiles, with increased range and accuracy. The cruise missile program was accelerated in 1967, when a Soviet SS-N-2 STYX cruise missile succeeded in sinking the Israeli destroyer *Elath*. The

first present-generation nuclear armed cruise missile—the TOMA-
HAWK Sea-Launched Cruise Missile (SLCM)—was inaugurated by
the navy in 1972. The air force followed in 1973 with the Air-
Launched Cruise Missile (ALCM). *See also* INTERCONTINENTAL BALLISTIC
MISSILE (ICBM), 148; MISSILE CRUISER WARFARE, 180; MISSILE SILOS, 199;
SUBMARINE-LAUNCHED BALLISTIC MISSLE (SLBM), 174.

Significance   The cruise missile, of which there are myriad types,
became increasingly popular in the late 1970s. Today, the United
States stands ready to deploy nearly 9,000 cruise missiles: 4,348
ALCMs (including Advanced Cruise Missile replacements); 4,068
SLCMs; and 565 Ground-Launched Cruise Missiles (GLCMs). Of
these, nearly 5,000 will be armed with nuclear warheads; only the
SLCM will be dual capable. The total cost of the present cruise missile
system is projected to be $25 billion, with each missile ranging from
$2 million to $6 million. In recent years, cruise missile technology has
progressed at a rapid rate, owing, in part, to Soviet advances against
low-flying objects. This led to a 1982 Defense Department decision to
terminate the ALCM (AGM-86B) procurement of 1,449 missiles after
1983 rather than the 4,348 that were planned, and to pursue instead
an Advanced Cruise Missile to fill the remaining orders, the cost of
which will probably not exceed the ALCM program. The actual number of ALCMs (both current design and advanced) to be procured will
be roughly equal.

Fallout   (146)

The descent to earth of radioactive particulate matter from a nuclear
cloud. Fallout occurs in two stages: early and late. Immediately after
an attack, in which weapons are detonated at ground level, millions
of tons of earth are contaminated by radioactive gases. These dust
particles remain in the lower atmosphere and are dispersed by the
winds to cause local early fallout. Late fallout is produced by the
explosion of nuclear devices at altitudes of 1,000 meters or greater.
The radioactivity that is generated mixes with upper atmospheric
levels, decays in intensity during its transit through the stratosphere
and troposphere, and ultimately is deposited, owing to wind and
weather conditions, throughout the world's soil and water systems.
Radionuclides, which are produced during this phase, eventually
become part of the human food chain. Early and late fallout pose
severe—and often, lethal—health risks to the population, both in the
short- and long-term. *See also* ATOMIC BOMB, 144; CIVIL DEFENSE, 183;
HIROSHIMA BOMBARDMENT, 147; NUCLEAR WAR, 23; NUCLEAR WINTER, 167;
SURVIVABILITY, 205.

Significance   Fallout, maintains Jennifer Learning, an authority on the radiation consequences of nuclear war, has three major effects.[2] Structurally, the energy caused by radiation destroys or damages the DNA in cell chromosomes. Morphologically, radiation injury to cells appears to resemble toxic injury from lack of oxygen or exposure to excessive temperatures. Functionally, radiation injury results in the death of the particular cell, destruction of its capacity to reproduce, or damage to subcellular structures. This may cause a lessening in function or a change in genetic material. Unfortunately, statistics fail to capture the severity of fallout on a society following a nuclear attack. The impact cannot be understood merely by focusing on estimates of fatalities and injuries, which fail to reveal the myriad other problems that are certain to develop. For example, fallout will also cause millions of genetic abnormalities and other harmful health effects, including thyroid nodules and thyroid cancer, which will appear in later decades. In addition to the medical problems caused by fallout, it will inevitably have a demoralizing psychological impact, which will take the form of fear, helplessness, and vulnerability. From an economic point of view, fallout will severely erode the industrial capabilities of the contaminated areas, as well as threaten the full utilization of uncontaminated areas. Clearly, fallout poses an ominous threat to the social fabric of the nation. For instance, it will clearly overload the demand for human services (e.g., hospitals, home care, and family assistance), as well as cripple the nation's ability to provide essential goods and services. Moreover, it will destroy societal morale, threaten public order, and produce widespread panic. For these reasons, scientists and weapons experts launched a serious effort to build a "clean" nuclear bomb.

Hiroshima Bombardment (147)

The decision by U.S. President Harry S Truman to drop the first nuclear bomb on Hiroshima, Japan, to bring World War II to a rapid conclusion. The Hiroshima bombardment, which marked the beginning of the atomic age, demonstrated the massive destruction that even a single bomb could wreak. The decision to drop the 14-kiloton (equivalent to 14,000 tons of TNT) on Hiroshima on August 6, 1945, resulted in over 135,000 casualties. Three days later, a second bomb— 20 kilotons—was dropped on Nagasaki, causing 64,000 deaths. According to official statements, President Truman ordered the bombings to end the war in the shortest possible time and avoid the enormous losses of human life that a protracted conflict would inflict. Despite subsequent criticism, the president defended his decision, arguing that the bombardment served to end the war, stop the fire raids, halt the blockade, and prevent the clash of great land armies. Truman maintained that, given his position and his constitutional responsibilities, he had no choice but to order the bombings of Hiroshima and Nagasaki, however tragic the consequences. *See also* ATOMIC BOMB, 144; NUCLEAR WAR, 23; SURVIVABILITY, 205.

Significance   The Hiroshima bombardment sparked a fierce public debate. Despite President Truman's contentions, many experts continue to question the wisdom of his actions. For example, Hanson W. Baldwin, a military affairs analyst, disputes the argument that "the atomic bomb achieved or hastened victory, and, more important, that it helped to consolidate the peace or to further the political aims for which the war was fought."[3] Historian Gar Alperovitz maintains that President Truman's decision was prompted by the administration's hope that "the display would move the Soviets to change their course of action in Central and Eastern Europe."[4] Journalist Fred J. Cook argues that "the dropping of the bombs meant the enthronement of naked force and reflected the growth of the military to a new degree."[5] Carroll Quigley, an academic, contends that "the use of the bomb by the United States precipitated an international arms race that subsequently . . . led to such pervasive and grave consequences as the growth of a specialized war machine dangerous to political democracy, the development of increasingly planned national economic systems vastly limiting individual freedom, and the destruction of traditional concepts of international law and the old relationships of the community of nations."[6] On the other hand, then Secretary of War Henry L. Stimson insists that "in the light of the alternatives which, on a fair estimate, were open to us, I believe that no man, in our position and subject to our responsibilities, holding in his hands a weapon of such possibilities for accomplishing this purpose [ending the war] and saving those lives, could have failed to use it and afterwards looked his countrymen in the face."[7] Historian Richard H. Rovere believes that "the dropping of the bombs has served as the principal preventative of a third major world holocaust . . . and that the new atomic powers of the postwar world have been so fully aware of the terrible dangers of nuclear weapons that they have time and time again turned away from the use of force, despite repeated provocations. Hiroshima and Nagasaki have thus become sacrifices to the maintenance of world peace."[8] Despite the above objections, most experts believe that, rightly or wrongly, Truman's decision was based on a desire to bring a prompt end to a frightful war and, secondarily, to achieve the benefits of a rapid victory.

Intercontinental Ballistic Missile (ICBM)   (148)

A land-based fixed or mobile rocket-propelled vehicle capable of delivering one or several warheads over intercontinental distances defined in SALT I and SALT II as in excess of 5,500 kilometers. The intercontinental ballistic missile has played a salient role in U.S. strategic forces since the late 1950s, and it constitutes an even more integral component of the Soviet Union's military arsenal. Less than 40 percent of U.S. megatonnage is carried by ICBMs, while over three-fourths of Soviet megatonnage is similarly carried. U.S. ICBMs are based both in the West (e.g., California) and in the Northern plains (e.g., North Dakota), far removed from densely populated centers, so as to lessen the number of civilian casualties in the event of an attack. According to strategic forces experts, the ICBM boasts four main advantages: (1) its extreme accuracy; (2) a large percentage of missiles prepared for immediate launch; (3) a high probability of missile survival under nuclear attack; and (4) a more secure communications link with command authorities.[9] Presently, the United States maintains 1,000-plus intercontinental ballistic missiles, which carry a total of 2,100 nuclear warheads; the Soviet Union possesses 1,398 ICBMs, which are capable of carrying 6,000 warheads. *See also* NUCLEAR WAR, 23; NUCLEAR WARHEAD, 166.

Significance   The intercontinental ballistic missile has been the subject of ongoing debate. The fixed-site ICBMs, for example, are theoretically vulnerable to attack, although no concrete tests have ever been conducted. On the other hand, the mobile ICBMs' great advantage is the inability of the enemy to target the missiles, thereby reducing the possibility of a preemptive attack. In this regard, President Ronald W. Reagan has endorsed the deployment of the MX (Peacekeeper) missile, a program proposed during the Carter administration. Critics of the MX led President Reagan to add a small mobile ICBM (SICBM, or Midgetman) to his request. Critics have attacked the MX on two points: First, that it is unnecessary and would serve as a destabilizing force, and second, that it cannot be based so as to be secure against enemy attack. Donald M. Snow, an authority on U.S. defense policy, contends that "the basing problem has been the most serious challenge to the MX program and has occasionally produced proposals of nearly comic dimensions."[10] The main problem, argues Snow, is that "the MX is a very large rocket, weighing 192,000 pounds, and this size and weight restricts where and how it can be deployed on land."[11] These concerns have generated a fierce debate in Congress, resulting in its refusal to appropriate funds for MX construction until a viable basing mode can be developed. Many critics doubt that such a mode can be devised and would prefer to discontinue the entire program. The Reagan administration was equally committed to the continuation of the MX, maintaining that it will ensure a much-needed strategic capability.

Manhattan Project (149)

A U.S. government-backed project, established in 1942 under the War Department, to develop an atomic bomb. The Manhattan Project was created in response to repeated warnings from scores of "refugee scientists" who claimed that Germany was in the process of developing an atomic bomb. Although their suspicions proved unfounded, their concerns were well justified, given the assumption that mid-twentieth-century scientific and technological advancements had paved the way for the development of atomic weapons. This view was echoed by atomic physicist J. Robert Oppenheimer, of the Manhattan Project, who stated: "We always assumed if they [atomic bombs] were needed they would be used."[12] The work of Oppenheimer and his colleagues created a new era in human history, one which saw the testing of the first atomic device at Alamogordo, New Mexico, in July 1945 and the destruction of Hiroshima and Nagasaki, Japan, a month later. Actually, the initial stimulus behind the Manhattan Project was born in 1939, when two Hungarian scientists, Leo Szilard and Eugene Wigner, prevailed upon Albert Einstein to sign a letter to President Franklin D. Roosevelt, urging the United States to accelerate its research activity in this area. Despite Einstein's prodding, little effort was made in this area until August 1942, when the Manhattan Project was launched. Directed by Brigadier General Leslie R. Groves, the Manhattan Project assumed vast proportions, spending over $2 billion and employing more than 150,000 persons. Huge facilities were erected at Oak Ridge, Tennessee and Hanford, Washington, while scientific research was conducted primarily at the University of Chicago and at Los Alamos, New Mexico. *See also* ATOMIC BOMB, 144; HIROSHIMA BOMBARDMENT, 147; NUCLEAR WAR, 23.

Significance The Manhattan Project provoked a storm of controversy in the scientific community. Szilard rallied scientific opposition to the use of the atomic bomb, arguing that the detonation of the yet untested weapon would seriously weaken U.S.-Soviet relations and precipitate an unprecedented arms race. Szilard endeavored to arrange an urgent meeting with President Harry S Truman, but failed. Instead, he was referred to James F. Byrnes, who was later to become secretary of state. Byrnes took sharp issue with Szilard, insisting that the United States had no choice but to test and, if necessary, use the atomic bomb to demonstrate U.S. determination in this vital area. In response to the pleas of Secretary of War Henry L. Stimson, President Truman established a special civilian advisory group (known as the Interim Committee), headed by Stimson, to advise him on the political, military, and scientific applications of atomic energy. This committee urged the president "to use the bomb against Japan as quickly as possible and without prior warning."[13] Scientific opposition continued to mount, culminating in the so-called Franck Report, which concluded that "the development of the new weapon could not long be kept secret and that its unexpected use would intensify the already present mistrust of the United States by the Soviet Union and surely lead to an arms race."[14] Meanwhile, Szilard persisted in his efforts to stop or delay the bomb, collecting signatures among scientists in Chicago and circulating numerous petitions. As a result of the controversy, General Groves initiated a poll of 150 atomic scientists in Chicago, 46 percent of whom supported "a military demonstration in Japan to be followed by a renewed opportunity for surrender before full use of the weapon is employed."[15] The results reinforced the recommendations of the Interim Committee, which in turn supported President Truman's decision to drop the bomb on Hiroshima and Nagasaki.

Multiple Independently Targetable Reentry   (150) Vehicle (MIRV)

The reentry vehicle of a ballistic missile which is armed with multiple warheads capable of striking three or more separate targets. The multiple independently targetable reentry vehicle evolved from the simple multiple reentry vehicle (MRV), which lacked the capability of independently directing the reentry vehicles to separate targets. Devised by the Soviet Union, MRV was a primitive system in which the bombs fell back to earth in a static, preestablished manner, similar to that of a cluster bomb. The MIRV represented a major refinement in multiple-warhead technology. Its unique feature is called the MIRV "bus"—a cylindrical device in the reentry vehicle that arranges the warheads around its outer wall in much the same way that bullets are secured in the chamber of a revolver. The bombs can be deployed individually over an extended period to different targets within a defined range known as the MIRV "footprint" (the largest area in which any MIRV rocket can release its payload). Thus, multiple targets can be attacked by a single rocket—not just one target, as is the case with single-warhead missiles. See also NUCLEAR WAR, 23; NUCLEAR WARHEAD, 166; REENTRY VEHICLE (RV), 169; STRATEGIC ARMS LIMITATION TALKS I (SALT I), 264.

Significance   The creation of the multiple independently targetable reentry vehicle profoundly influenced the nuclear revolution. According to Donald M. Snow, a defense systems expert, MIRV served: (1) to increase the number of nuclear bombs in the operational arsenals of the United States and the Soviet Union; (2) to accelerate changes in the weapons balance between the superpowers; and (3) to allow the reemergence of thought about counterforce targeting and the possible survivability of a nuclear war.[16] In many ways, argues Snow, MIRV represents the most destabilizing influence in the nuclear era—that is, "the ability to calculate offensive damage limitation [as a result of MIRV's capability] . . . allegedly erodes the basis of deterrence."[17] In other words, when both nations possess MIRV capability, as is presently the case, a hostile nation may decide that it is wiser to launch a first strike than to launch a counterattack which, in the end, increases the likelihood of war rather than prevents it. The United States tested the first MIRV in 1968 just prior to the opening of the first Strategic Arms Limitation Talks (SALT). Two years later, MIRV warheads were added to the U.S. military arsenal. In 1975, the Soviet Union deployed its own MIRVs. Although the MIRV was intended to stabilize mutual deterrence, it created an opposite effect, making it possible for one of the superpowers to launch a surprise attack on the other, thereby escalating the dangers of the arms race.

Mutual Assured Destruction (MAD)   (151)

A theory of strategic deterrence, often referred to as "mutual suicide," whereby one nation seeks to deter a nuclear attack by possessing the capacity to retaliate in kind to an adversary's first strike. The concept of "mutual assured destruction," as conceived by former Secretary of Defense Robert S. McNamara in the mid-1960s, was predicated on the ability of the United States to inflict "unacceptable damage" on the Soviet Union to prevent it from initiating a nuclear war. According to two of Secretary McNamara's top lieutenants, Alain Enthoven and K. Wayne Smith: "Once we are sure that, in retaliation, we can destroy the Soviet Union and other potential attackers as modern societies, we cannot increase our security or power against them by threatening to destroy more."[18] McNamara estimated the desired theoretical level of damage at from 20 to 25 percent of the population and 50 percent of industrial capacity. Thus, any Soviet leader who was sufficiently "mad" to risk 25 percent of the Soviet population would, in all likelihood, not be deterred by any further amount of damage that could be caused by a first strike. According to Secretary McNamara's calculations at the time, the United States required only 400 warheads to destroy 30 percent of the Soviet population and 76 percent of its industrial capacity. Since the United States possessed over 10,000 warheads, no additional warheads were necessary. McNamara did recognize that more than 400 would actually be needed, to compensate for failures in launching, weapons that missed their targets, and various Soviet countermeasures. *See also* FIRST STRIKE, 194; NUCLEAR WAR, 23; NUCLEAR WINTER, 167.

Significance   Mutual assured destruction is based on the assumption that once a specified level of deterrence is achieved, no further weapons are required. Theorists disagree, however, as to the actual level. For example, Secretary McNamara fixed it at from 20 to 30 percent of the population and 50 percent of industry, while former National Security Adviser McGeorge Bundy suggested a much lower figure, opining: "One bomb on a city would be a catastrophe without precedent."[19] In proposing this theory, McNamara sought to persuade government decision makers that the United States "should forget about winning a thermonuclear war, or even limiting damage to this country if deterrence failed, for there could be no winners and the horrors of survival in the aftermath of nuclear holocaust would be worse than death."[20] As envisaged by Secretary McNamara, mutual assured destruction was simply a device for determining the appropriate level of U.S. strategic forces. In this regard, the theory was consistent with the government's policy of targeting major industrial and military centers. McNamara invoked this theory as a means of rejecting requests for increases in strategic forces. It was not used, however, to restrict the development of strategic forces capable of attacking Soviet military targets. Clearly, the Kennedy administration possessed this capability and fully intended to develop and expand it in the future. In addition, the theory was never invoked in calculating war plans; the United States insisted on maintaining the option of attacking and destroying Soviet strategic forces before they were employed.

Nuclear Artillery (152)

A high-powered gun with a nuclear shell or warhead capable of wreaking enormous damage at short, medium, and long range. Nuclear artillery constitutes an important part of the U.S. weapons arsenal. These weapons originated with the creation of the colossal 280mm cannon, which was first dispatched to West Germany in 1953. Today, the United States boasts six different types of nuclear artillery warheads. Moreover, virtually every large artillery gun is capable of firing nuclear rounds. Presently, the United States has embarked on a massive modernization effort, with the goal of upgrading and replacing most early or outmoded artillery weapons. The utility of these weapons has been recognized by the U.S. Army, which possesses over 3,500 nuclear capable artillery guns. These include: 748 M114 155mm guns, 2,200 M109 155mm guns, and 1,046 M110 eight-inch (203mm) guns. Seven of the United States' NATO allies (Belgium, Greece, Italy, Netherlands, Turkey, United Kingdom, and West Germany) that possess nuclear artillery also employ U.S.-designed artillery, although many of their guns are obsolete. The most popular weapons include the standard M109 and M110 guns. Nearly 5,000 nuclear artillery shells are currently deployed, most of which are in Europe. *See also* NUCLEAR TECHNOLOGY, 163; NUCLEAR WARHEAD, 166.

Significance   Nuclear artillery is low yield; explosive capabilities range from about 0.1 kiloton (e.g., the W48) to about 12 kilotons (e.g., W33). Three warhead types are presently deployed: the 1–12 kiloton W33 eight-inch fission warhead, the 0.1 kiloton W48 155mm fission warhead, and the 1–2 kiloton W79 eight-inch enhanced radiation warhead. All three projectiles are fired as air bursts, with accuracies (for the W48 and W33) of 40, 100, and 172 meters CEP at short, medium, and long range. Nuclear artillery is fast approaching its practical limits in terms of accuracy, reliability, target acquisition, and noise. Today's guns possess greater range and muzzle velocity, while nuclear artillery projectiles now boast such features as timing and memory assemblies, fuse subcomponents, power supplies, electronic programmers, target sensors, and rocket motors in the shell. "Future artillery guns," contend nuclear weapons experts Thomas B. Cochran, William M. Arkin, and Milton M. Hoenig, "are being examined to provide important capabilities for responding rapidly and accurately to fire missions and reduced emplacement times."[21] Tomorrow's weapon, they argue, will feature short recoil cycle time, burst rate-of-fire, automatic ammunition handling, loading and resupply, and automated position location and weapons alignment.[22]

Nuclear Decision Making   (153)

The people, processes, and institutions that possess the authority to decide issues involving nuclear weapons. Nuclear decision making is lodged in those political leaders who are legally empowered to authorize their use. In the United States, this authority lies with the National Command Authority (NCA), a civilian body composed of the president and the secretary of defense, "or their duly deputized alternates and successors."[23] Ultimately, the president is empowered to make decisions concerning the use of military force. Final and total authority to make nuclear decisions in the Soviet Union rests with the Politburo; in Britain, the prime minister; in France, the president; and in the People's Republic of China, the Communist Party Central Committee. This control is safeguarded by various devices that prevent the unauthorized or accidental use of nuclear weapons and by rules that govern their security. In each nation, designated command operations and communications networks connect authorized personnel to the nuclear forces. In the United States—and probably in other countries—the deployment of nuclear weapons requires both voice and written commands (over Teletype) that are validated by codes and "authenticators." *See also* COMMANDER IN CHIEF, 39; NATIONAL SECURITY COUNCIL (NSC), 79; STRATEGIC AIR COMMAND (SAC), 140.

Significance Nuclear decision making in the United States is reinforced by five major command centers which are responsible for nuclear operations. These facilities collect and process information on planning, forces, intelligence, and early warning to ensure "informed" decisions involving the use of nuclear weapons. In the event that the NCA and its civilian successors were destroyed, the chain of command would continue to function, as the United States maintains a sophisticated network of airborne and other fallback command centers. In this regard, at least one airborne command center is always in the air, a policy that originated in 1962. Secret plans detail procedures for granting NCA authority to the succeeding military officers when civilian communication proves impossible. The Strategic Air Command (SAC) operates the largest fleet of airborne command centers, which are always manned by general officers prepared to assume the reins of the nuclear forces. The head of each nuclear-armed command (Atlantic, Pacific, Europe, Central [Middle East], and North American Aerospace Defense [NORAD]) possesses primary and alternate command posts ready to lead the armed forces. Three of the nuclear commands fly their own airborne command planes: *Scope Light,* based in Virginia, for the Atlantic; *Blue Eagle,* based in Hawaii, for the Pacific; and *Silk Purse,* based in Britain, for Europe.

Nuclear Equivalence (154)

A condition that exists when neither party possesses the nuclear capacity to inflict more damage than the other (sometimes referred to as parity). The concept of nuclear equivalence has become increasingly popular with the major nuclear powers, owing to its political acceptability. Although nuclear superiority may be more ideally desirable, neither the United States nor the Soviet Union possesses the political resolve or economic resources required to pursue this approach. Despite the popularity of nuclear equivalence, there is no consensus on the criteria for equivalence, either within the United States or between the United States and the Soviet Union. The Strategic Arms Reduction Talks (START), for example, centered around inputs— that is, achieving agreement over trade-offs in asymmetrical force structures. The two sides carefully skirted negotiating outputs involving operational capabilities. As political scientist Richard K. Betts notes, "Equality was manifestly defined in terms of numbers of launchers, but only implicitly, at best, in terms of stability, hard-target kill capabilities, assured destruction, or other measures of what the asymmetrical weapon inventories could actually do to the opponent in a war."[24] This was not an accident; it is far easier to measure technical inputs than hypothetical outputs. Moreover, a case could be made that each party's definition of its own interests may make it impossible to reach consensus on any clear definition of nuclear equivalence. In the United States, disagreement within the defense establishment may also preclude such a consensus. *See also* BALANCE OF POWER, 4; MUTUAL ASSURED DESTRUCTION (MAD), 151; NUCLEAR DECISION MAKING, 153; STRATEGIC ARMS LIMITATION TALKS I (SALT I), 264.

Significance   Nuclear equivalence is a difficult concept to define. Indeed, there are several major definitions of nuclear equivalence. For example, the minimalist definition, proposed by Soviet Premier Nikita Khrushchev in the late 1950s, and endorsed by some Western analysts, associates it with mutual second-strike capabilities (regardless of disparities in relative levels of destructive might). Thus, mutual assured destruction, even at unequal levels, constitutes equivalence. The Madison Avenue definition, although more complex, is predicated on exchange calculations—that is, it bases advantage on the simple perceptions of untrained elites. The definition is tied to several gross indices of striking power that are readily observable (e.g., size, numbers, and modernity of delivery vehicles). The best definition, contend many experts, is one that considers a distribution of forces that implies no net advantage in either counterforce or postattack capabilities or postexchange countervalue reserves. Clearly, it will be difficult, if not impossible, to achieve agreement on nuclear equivalence, due to the inability of the United States and the Soviet Union to approve an acceptable formula. Until this is achieved, there is scant likelihood that nuclear equivalence will be little more than a desirable goal, lacking in operational value.

Nuclear Fission (155)

The process by which the nucleus of an atom is split into two or more parts. Nuclear fission provides the explosive power (along with nuclear fusion) that fires a nuclear weapon. In a fission device, it is essential to create a chain reaction, whereby neutrons are emitted at high speed, and heat and radiation are released. To realize maximum efficiency in a nuclear explosion, it is necessary to produce a rapid increase in the number of fissions sought—that is, a rapidly multiplying chain reaction. To do so, it is critical to control leakage of neutrons out of the fissile material to prevent neutron-absorbing impurities in the fissionable material. Numerous heavy atomic nuclei are capable of being fissioned. However, only a small fraction of these are fissile (meaning fissionable by slow [or zero energy] neutrons, as well as fast [highly energetic] neutrons). Fission weapons must be produced with fissile materials—primarily U-235, Pu-239, U-233, or a combination of the three. Fission weapons are made with grades of enriched uranium (from an enrichment plant) or plutonium (produced in a reactor) which possess the fissile isotopes U-235 and Pu-239 at levels which cause efficient reactions and use a minimum of materials. These weapons do not require uranium or plutonium pure in the isotopes U-235 and Pu-239 to create an explosion, nor do they require uranium or plutonium in the form of a metal. *See also* ATOMIC BOMB, 144; HIROSHIMA BOMBARDMENT, 147; NUCLEAR WARHEAD, 166; URANIUM, 84.

Significance With the discovery of nuclear fission, scientists unearthed a potent force—one that threatens to destroy humankind if it is not harnessed intelligently. Two main design approaches are commonly used to produce a fissile explosion: the implosion technique and the gun assembly technique. In the implosion technique, a peripheral charge of chemical high explosives (HE) is uniformly detonated so as to compress (implode) a subcritical mass into a supercritical configuration. This technique is widely used in nuclear weapons involving the fissionable material Pu-239, U-235, or a combination of the two. It was employed in the first U.S. nuclear test (Trinity, July 16, 1945), as well as in "Fat Man," the second nuclear bomb, dropped on Nagasaki, Japan. The gun device involves two or more masses of fissionable material, each of which is less than the critical mass. A conventional explosive is used to propel the subcritical pieces of fissionable materials together, thereby assembling a supercritical mass. This method was employed in "Little Boy," the U-235 weapon that was dropped on Hiroshima, Japan. Today the W33 artillery-fired atomic projectile in the U.S. weapons arsenal uses this technique. Gun devices are theoretically simple to create and are highly reliable.

Nuclear Force Models   **(156)**
Alternative ways of viewing nuclear weapons and defense policy. Nuclear force models have long been the subject of fierce debate, reflecting conflicting assumptions, assessments, and goals. According to national security expert Morton H. Halperin, there are three distinct models: (1) Treating nuclear weapons as "regular weapons." This approach, which seeks to integrate nuclear weapons into all military planning, predominated during the Eisenhower administration. (2) Treating nuclear weapons as "special weapons." This view, which is predicated on the belief that first use should be carefully weighed, has characterized U.S. nuclear policy since the Kennedy administration. (3) Treating nuclear weapons as "explosive devices." This approach maintains that nuclear weapons may, in extreme circumstances, be used to demonstrate national resolve, but not to wage wars.[25] *See also* CONVENTIONAL WEAPONS, 120; NUCLEAR DECISION MAKING, 153; NUCLEAR WAR, 23.

Significance   Nuclear force models have played a salient role in the development of U.S. nuclear policy. The regular weapons model, as articulated in NSC 162/1 and endorsed by President Dwight D. Eisenhower in 1953, asserts that nuclear devices are superior weapons that may be used as "a matter of course" in any armed conflict. It rejects the view that because nuclear weapons are far more destructive, they are qualitatively different from other weapons. Advocates of this view contend that nuclear devices can and should be used just like other weapons—that "if employed on the battlefield, they can be used to defeat an enemy force."[26] Moreover, they claim that even if both sides employ nuclear devices, their use can be limited to the battlefield. In short, they argue that a two-sided nuclear confrontation could be "winnable," without creating large-scale devastation. The special weapons model maintains that nuclear devices are not just another weapon—that they are "special" weapons whose first use must be carefully considered. Adherents contend that a limited nuclear war would easily escalate into a general war, which could result in the destruction of the United States. As a result, these weapons should only be used as a last resort to prevent a battlefield defeat. Thus, the United States should strengthen its conventional forces, eschew unnecessary nuclear risks, and respond forcefully to low-level threats. This model shares several of the assumptions of the first model. It maintains that nuclear weapons can be used to avoid defeat in a conventional war by preventing the massing of troops. It also assumes that "on some occasions the United States can emerge as the clear victor from a nuclear battlefield that does not destroy the society being defended."[27] The nuclear explosive devices model asserts that nuclear devices will inevitably increase the risk of uncontrollable escalation, which could lead to the total destruction of the nation in which the war is waged. Although this model asserts that nuclear weapons are essential to U.S. security, they should not be regarded as weapons and should not be turned over to the military. If an enemy were to employ nuclear weapons on the battlefield, the United States should use, or threaten to use, nuclear devices against targets of strategic value to that side. Because the use of a single nuclear device would trigger massive escalation, many proponents of this model argue that "the United States should base its military plans, training programs, defense budgets, weapons deployments, and arms negotiations on the assumption that it will not initiate the use of nuclear weapons."[28] This model does not preclude the use of nuclear weapons, but does maintain that if such weapons are employed, they should be used as tools for ending a war, not as weapons to win a battle.

Nuclear Fusion (157)

A reaction in which nuclei combine to create heavier nuclei with the attendant release of energy. Nuclear fusion is one of two major processes (along with nuclear fission) that propel atomic weapons. Although many thermonuclear reactions exist, the primary one associated with nuclear reactions is that between deuterium (H-2 or D) and tritium (H-3 or T), two hydrogen isotopes, because the deuterium-tritium (D-T) reaction occurs more rapidly at achievable temperatures than other fusion reactions. Thermonuclear weapons—which are often referred to as "fusion" or "hydrogen" weapons—require that at least a portion of the release of energy derives from nuclear fusion. Fusion reaction rates are especially sensitive to temperature and are extremely small at average temperatures. Indeed, fusion weapons (or reactors) can only function at 10 to 100 million degrees Kelvin (the sun's interior temperature is 14 million degrees Kelvin). This accounts for the term "thermonuclear." In thermonuclear weapons, the necessary temperatures and density of fusion materials are created by a fission explosion. *See also* NUCLEAR WAR, 23; YIELD, 179.

Significance Nuclear fusion is a primary source of energy in thermonuclear weapons. Although the D-T reaction is critical, it is not necessary to use elemental deuterium and tritium (which are gases at ordinary temperatures) directly in an atomic weapon. The main thermonuclear material is usually lithium-6 deuteride, a solid chemical compound at average temperatures. In this instance, the tritium is manufactured in the weapon itself by neutron bombardment of the lithium-6 isotope during the fusion reaction. Tritium deteriorates radioactively (5.5 percent each year), giving lithium-6 deuteride the added plus of a longer storage life compared to tritium. In thermonuclear weapons, the fusion material can be incorporated directly into the fissile core, or external to the fissile core, or both. Generally, the energy released in the explosion of a large thermonuclear weapon derives from three sources: a fission chain reaction (the first stage); "burning" of thermonuclear fuel (the second stage); and the fission of the U-238 blanket, assuming one exists (the third stage), with approximately half the total energy produced by fission and the other half by fusion. In order to achieve tailored weapons effects or to realize specific space or weight limitations, different ratios of fission-yield-to-fusion-yield may be used. These range from nearly pure fission yield weapons to those where an extremely high proportion of the yield comes from fusion.

Nuclear Geography (158)

The study of the earth and its features as potential nuclear battlefields. Nuclear geography is of salient military importance. Military studies typically focus on political divisions, topographic considerations, natural resources, climatic forces, and economic determinants as measures of power and as indicators for strategy. Traditional military thinking holds that "geographic considerations, in their broadest sense, are the cause of most wars."[29] Thus, the military stands ready to wage all forms of war in all areas of the world, based on its scientific analysis of geographic factors. Yet, given the potent striking power of nuclear weapons, the existence of more or less permanent military alliances, and the unwinnable nature of nuclear war, this analysis may be somewhat anachronistic. Nuclear geography, argue nuclear weapons experts William M. Arkin and Richard W. Fieldhouse, is characterized by three main features: (1) the heightened awareness by the military of needing to know the exact position, area, and physical characteristics of land and water areas, and the air and space above them; (2) the global nature of the arms race has meant that conflict could break out anywhere, leading experts to define the most prominent as well as the most obscure sites around the world as having "vital" strategic importance; and (3) the new demands of the infrastructure require that all resources of a society be available to support war plans, thereby blurring the distinction between what is civilian and what is military.[30] *See also* NUCLEAR DECISION MAKING, 153; NUCLEAR WAR, 23.

Significance   Nuclear geography, as it relates to today's global realities, is primarily concerned with the day-to-day problems of access and position—that is, the two major nuclear powers, the United States and the Soviet Union, maintain the right of access to any area of the world in which their interests are threatened. Generally, superpower disputes do not occur over national boundaries and international space, but from access to these areas. Even so, traditional geographic concerns, such as "the importance of being an island nation, of lacking natural borders, or of having depth in resources for a prolonged mobilization" are still relevant in certain nonnuclear wars.[31] Military analysts are particularly interested in the relationship between traditional geography and current wartime planning, which explains, to a large extent, the "obsession" with nuclear targeting. Yet, geography does not necessarily correspond to the dictates of nuclear weapons. For this reason, it makes little sense to arbitrarily define weapons by ranges and then design war plans for them. For example, war scenarios for Europe often fail to account for the thousands of added warheads on submarines and in U.S. strategic forces that could attack any site that weapons in Europe could attack. Moreover, traditional geography is of limited value in a nuclear world, in that it often overstates the importance of a nation's size, as well as the ability of the United States and the Soviet Union to protect their allies and interests.

Nuclear Infrastructure (159)

A vast complex comprised of myriad command, electronic, testing, and research facilities. The nuclear infrastructure plays a salient role in preparations for nuclear war. Its operations—which are extremely diverse—are designed to promote preparedness. Major tasks include scientific research, information collection, and early-warning surveillance. For this reason, laboratories, test ranges, military bases, and communications transmitters are crucial components of the nuclear infrastructure. In this regard, nuclear weapons researchers William M. Arkin and Richard W. Fieldhouse argue that "the superior ability to detect and target the enemy's forces, to hide and communicate with one's own, and to control military operations has become more important than the weapons themselves."[32] Clearly, it is essential for a nuclear power, such as the United States, to be able to chart vital military operations, which is made possible by the existence of observatories, satellites, oceanographic laboratories, and electronic and technical facilities. *See also* CIVIL DEFENSE, 183; NUCLEAR LINKS, 160; NUCLEAR PRODUCTION COMPLEX, 161; RESEARCH AND DEVELOPMENT (R&D), 83.

Significance　　The nuclear infrastructure, note Arkin and Fieldhouse, consists of eight main categories of activities.[33] These include:

1. The arsenals (e.g., warheads, guns, aircraft, ships, and missiles) and the bases responsible for training, maintenance, storage, and supply of nuclear forces

2. The production complex that designs and manufactures nuclear warheads and radioactive materials

3. The research, development, and testing complex consisting of sundry laboratories and test facilities

4. The surveillance system whose facilities gather data related to nuclear weapons, primarily as part of ocean surveillance and monitoring foreign nuclear tests (a burgeoning complex of satellite tracking and control stations also buoys the nuclear arsenals)

5. The early-warning and "attack-assessment" complex of radars and processing stations that monitor and report attacks

6. The communications system that links all of the above

7. The planning and command structure that controls the nuclear battlefields

8. Civil defense

These activities—which are, at times, relatively obscure—require very close scrutiny. Since the nuclear infrastructure plays a pivotal role in the military complex, it is essential to question whether such systems merely assist key decision makers and weapons or control them. The nuclear infrastructure generates reams of technical information but provides few answers. It is up to the decision makers to act or not act on the data they are given. The countless analysts, planners, and technicians lack the mandate to lead. Rather, it is their responsibility to provide the nation's leaders with current and reliable information—information that could well spell victory or defeat.

Nuclear Links (160)

The units that connect the various components of the nuclear infrastructure. Nuclear links are essential to the success of any nuclear strategy. There are two main types of nuclear links: First, the relatively known and discernible set of base agreements, joint exercises and planning, military alliances, and programs of nuclear cooperation; and second, the more indirect, elusive, and understated, including the marshaling of science and technology, as well as the application of civilian resources for military purposes in the area of nuclear weapons. In this regard, civilian resources play an indispensable role in the nuclear infrastructure, particularly when a nation becomes embroiled in a protracted war. The nuclear infrastructure is all-encompassing, made possible by the myriad links that provide the necessary organization and support. *See also* NUCLEAR INFRASTRUCTURE, 159; NUCLEAR WAR, 23.

Significance   The nuclear links take many forms. There are those, for example, that involve the deployment of nuclear weapons. Although most remain secret, the United States presently has nuclear weapons in eight nations, despite the fact that no formal agreements exist between the nuclear powers and their foreign allies delineating specific port calls of nuclear-armed ships and submarines or the overflight of "neutral" nations with nuclear cargo. In the main, U.S. links with Britain and France directly involve nuclear weapons. In the case of other countries, these links appear to be nonnuclear. For example, several nonnuclear countries, such as Japan, the Scandinavian nations, and the countries in Latin America do not possess nuclear weapons, but provide technical facilities that play a salient role in the nuclear infrastructure. Interestingly, even adversaries are linked and assist each to improve the accuracy of their missiles. In addition to military support, civilian resources play a prominent role in the nuclear infrastructure. For example, nearly 95 percent of the communications that support U.S. nuclear weapons release orders are provided by U.S. commercial carriers. According to *Business Week*, for instance, "The Pentagon is 'hardening' all 21 major switching stations through which its messages are now carried by American Telephone & Telegraph Company and is installing electromagnetic pulse surge 'arrestors' at these stations."[34] In a real sense, the immense size and complexity of the nuclear infrastructure constitute its greatest limitation. Despite its sundry links, the system does not permit the collection or monitoring of all useful information. To counter this problem, both the military and civilian sectors continue to explore new technologies that will ensure improved communications and greater readiness.

Nuclear Production Complex (161)

Those government agencies, institutions, facilities, and individuals who design, manufacture, and test nuclear weapons. The production process varies from nation to nation, depending on its size, level, capacity, and commitment to nuclear proficiency. In the United States, the production process is directed by the Department of Energy (DOE), which comprises approximately 45,000 people, located in 36 laboratories and production centers, in 13 states. By contrast, the Soviet complex, about which relatively little is known, is operated by the Medium Machine Building Ministry, and is thought to closely rival the United States' production complex in size and level of technology. The British nuclear complex is administered by the Controller Research and Development Establishments, Research and Nuclear Programmes (CERN) in the Ministry of Defence, which consists of three major facilities and employs approximately 8,000 people. The French complex is supervised by the Commissariat à l'Énergie Atomique (CEA), encompassing ten nuclear weapons sites. As for the Chinese, little is known about which ministry controls the production process, although some 40 facilities have been identified. *See also* NUCLEAR LINKS, 160; NUCLEAR TECHNOLOGY, 163; RESEARCH AND DEVELOPMENT (R&D), 83.

Significance The nuclear production process has become a multibillion-dollar world enterprise. Worldwide, nuclear weapons research is limited to ten main laboratories. In the United States, all nuclear research, design, and testing is conducted at the Lawrence Livermore National Laboratory, in California; the Los Alamos National Laboratory, in New Mexico; and the Sandia National Laboratory, in Albuquerque, New Mexico. The Soviet research complex is based at the Arzamas Laboratory, south of Gorky, with additional facilities at Kyshtym, Moscow, Leningrad, and Semipalatinsk. In Great Britain, one laboratory, the Atomic Weapons Research Establishment at Aldermaston, specializes in the design of nuclear warheads. The major French laboratories include the Saclay and Grenoble Centers for Nuclear Studies, as well as those under CEA's military applications branch. As for production, uranium, plutonium, and tritium (for warheads) are produced at seven United States facilities. Soviet uranium and plutonium are manufactured at over ten main facilities, both civilian and military. British nuclear materials are produced primarily at Calder Hall, Chapelcross, and Windscale. The French manufacture materials at Marcoule, Miramas, and Pierrelatte. Chinese nuclear materials are produced at Lanzhou, Yumen, Baotou, Hong Yuan, Jiuquan, and Urumqui. As for testing, nuclear warheads are presently tested at five sites worldwide. All United States and British warheads are detonated at the Nevada Test Site; the United States also maintains a "readiness to test" facility at Johnston Island, near Hawaii. The Soviets have tested nuclear warheads at over 20 sites, among them East and West Kazakh, five sites in Siberia, Semipalatinsk, and two at Novaya and Zemlya (the Novaya Zemlya and Semipalatinsk sites are still active). The French detonate nuclear weapons at Mururoa Atoll in French Polynesia, while Chinese tests are conducted at Lop Nor.

Nuclear Superiority (162)

The capacity, as defined by a nation's leaders, to inflict greater nuclear damage, against an adversary, than one's opponent can inflict. Nuclear superiority challenges the desirability of nuclear equivalence (parity), in which neither side enjoys an advantage. Both the United States and the Soviet Union recognize the dangers implicit in allowing the other side to achieve nuclear superiority. Although the evidence remains unclear—and the statistics inconclusive—there is little doubt that both nations understand the coercive potential of nuclear superiority. Despite this fact, the United States and the Soviet Union continue to profess their commitment to nuclear equivalence, owing to various internal and external political considerations. Fearing that a massive arms buildup might lead to a dangerous escalation of the arms race, both nations have pursued policies calculated to enhance their positions, both offensively and defensively. At the same time, the United States and the Soviet Union have eschewed the stated goal of nuclear superiority. *See also* BALANCE OF POWER, 4; MUTUAL ASSURED DESTRUCTION (MAD), 151; NUCLEAR EQUIVALENCE, 154; NUCLEAR THREAT MYTH, 165; WINDOW OF OPPORTUNITY, 178.

Significance Nuclear superiority, however desirable, has given way—at least, publicly, to the goal of nuclear equivalance. For doves, this policy is wasteful but acceptable; for hawks, it is foolish but preferable to inferiority. Despite the desirability of nuclear superiority, both the United States and the Soviet Union recognize that such a policy precludes the possibility for negotiating a mutually acceptable arms reduction. Moreover, both sides recognize the dangers inherent in pursuing a policy of nuclear superiority, which would necessitate an unprecedented commitment of tax dollars. Clearly, such a commitment could wreak massive havoc in both countries and generate enormous political opposition. For these reasons, many U.S. decision makers have endorsed the goal of fortifying the conventional balance, which they perceive to be a better investment. The Soviets' strategic buildup is predicated on the belief that it is far easier to match U.S. increases with incremental commitments than to further cripple their already depressed economy by pursuing the goal of nuclear superiority. Moreover, both sides have become increasingly sensitive to the military dangers implicit in a runaway arms race. Interestingly, Richard K. Betts, a senior fellow at the Brookings Institution and an expert on defense issues, maintains that "one could argue that because a nuclear buildup would be cheaper than expansion of conventional forces, it is preferable. But the scale of effort . . . needed to establish an advantage large enough to give confidence in deliberate first use is tremendous, while the amount of conventional improvement to keep the Soviet conventional edge manageable is less than most assume."[35] Since true parity does not presently exist—that is, both the United States and the Soviet Union enjoy decided advantages in specific areas—future debate is likely to center around issues of technical advantage rather than nuclear superiority.

Nuclear Technology (163)

The development and application of scientific knowledge to the creation of increasingly sophisticated nuclear devices. Nuclear technology has, in recent years, seriously undermined efforts to halt the proliferation of such weapons, owing, in large part, to the potential commercial use of plutonium in the nuclear fuel cycle. In this regard, the major superpowers (i.e., the United States and the Soviet Union) have aggressively pursued the goal of technological superiority. To achieve this goal, they have expended billions of dollars in the search for ever more deadly weapon systems. Rapid improvements in technology, contends Arthur M. Katz, an expert in nuclear technology, is best reflected in the proliferation of nuclear warheads (i.e., multiple independent reentry vehicles, or MIRVs).[36] Clearly, this has resulted in increased accuracy and targeting flexibility. These developments, notes Katz, made possible a change from "a 'blunderbus' urban retaliation to a capability to destroy selectively critical military as well as civilian targets."[37] Nuclear technology has profoundly affected the current debate about nuclear policy in the United States and the Soviet Union, and is likely to intensify as this new technology provides a Pandora's box of unforeseen possibilities. Interestingly, this technology has also led to increased discussions of the possibility of a "controlled" nuclear war, which some see as an extension of conventional war. *See also* ATOMIC BOMB, 144; FIRST STRIKE, 194; NUCLEAR WAR, 23; RESEARCH AND DEVELOPMENT (R&D), 83.

Significance   Nuclear technology has dramatically transformed the nature of modern warfare. Prior to the invention of the atomic bomb, the nuclear alternative did not exist. Thus, military strategists were forced to rely on weapons delivered by medium and heavy bombers. That all changed with the discovery of nuclear weapons.

These weapons not only altered the nature of warfare, but profoundly affected domestic priorities in the nuclear nations, which reduced the percentage (but not in absolute terms) of government spending on social needs in favor of increased research and development in the military area. Today, most nuclear nations understand that the deployment of such devices would inevitably result in massive and indiscriminate damage not only to their enemies, but to the entire global community. Nuclear weapons pose myriad dangers to world peace and stability. The real danger, simply put, is that a nation will feel vulnerable to a first strike, and that in a crisis, both sides will conclude that they have little choice but to launch a preemptive strike. Obviously, neither side can wait to see whether the other will strike first. Fearing a first strike, each side will feel compelled to protect its retaliatory forces, and each will feel obliged to strike first. Despite these recent developments in nuclear technology, there exists the possibility that this knowledge could also serve to restabilize mutual deterrence (e.g., through the Midgetman ICBM). Since multiple warheads are chiefly responsible for undermining the stability of the strategic balance, many believe that it is still possible—with the requisite leadership and will—to return to earlier times when missiles were armed with a single warhead. The verdict is still out, but hope remains that both the United States and the Soviet Union will recognize the wisdom of such an approach.

Nuclear Terrorism (164)

The theft from, sabotage of, or attack on nuclear facilities by political dissidents or disgruntled individuals. Nuclear terrorism has, in recent years, received widespread attention, owing, in large measure, to the proliferation of nuclear weapons and its attendant dangers. According to a major international study, the likelihood of nuclear terrorism, however slight, is steadily increasing as a result of several factors, including "the growing incidence, sophistication, and lethality of conventional terrorism, the apparent evidence of state support, even sponsorship, of terrorist groups, and growing world-wide stocks of nuclear-weapons material."[38] Many experts are concerned that nuclear weapons may accidentally or deliberately fall into the hands of radicals or antigovernment forces as the result of war, revolution, or coup d'état. In fact, nuclear terrorism posed just such a threat to France and the People's Republic of China, two acknowledged nuclear powers, during the formative stages of their nuclear-weapons programs. Some authorities fear that political instability may provoke similar incidents in such crisis-ridden nations as South Africa and Pakistan. *See also* COUP D'ÉTAT, 11; NUCLEAR PROLIFERATION, 231; REVOLUTION, 29; TERRORISM, 31.

Significance   Nuclear terrorism poses a serious, but untested threat to world peace and security. Despite the paucity of celebrated incidents, several governments, including Israel, Iraq, and Iran, have conducted raids against foreign nuclear installations, while other countries, such as Libya and India, have reportedly contemplated similar actions. Obviously, the specter of nuclear terrorism has encouraged the international community to intensify its efforts to prevent the spread of nuclear weapons. In the United States alone, during the past decade, there have been more than 50 threats—many so serious that the Department of Energy was forced to establish a SWAT-like unit, the Nuclear Emergency Search Team (NEST), to cope with the problem. This unit, which is composed of research scientists and technicians, operates undercover, so as not to create unnecessary panic. Armed with radiation detectors concealed in briefcases and purses, the team scours a city in search of nuclear materials and devices. In 1975, for example, the team was dispatched to Los Angeles in search of a 20-kiloton atom bomb that an extortionist was alleged to have planted on Union Oil Company property. Although threats are easy to make, most experts contend that, though it is difficult, nuclear terrorists could steal the requisite nuclear material, then design and build a weapon. After all, nuclear reactors are not impenetrable. In addition, there are documented cases of nuclear shipments that have been either lost or misrouted. In 1970, for example, city officials in Orlando, Florida, received a ransom note with a design for a nuclear bomb that air force armament officers declared workable. The culprit was revealed to be a fourteen-year-old boy. Rep. Edward J. Markey (D.-Mass.), an expert on the politics of nuclear proliferation, maintains that "a crude, homemade bomb made from reactor-grade plutonium might only cause an explosion equal to several hundred tons of TNT, but such a blast would still be ten times more powerful than the largest conventional bomb dropped during World War II."[39]

Nuclear Threat Myth (165)

Those fictions or half-truths that give expression to popularly held beliefs about nuclear weapons and threats of nuclear war. The nuclear threat myth abounds, owing to a lack of public knowledge, as well as the deliberate efforts of individuals and groups who wish to exploit the situation to achieve their policy goals. For example, many Americans—knowledgeable observers included—believe that the United States has not seriously contemplated the first use of nuclear weapons in several decades and that it would only do so in the event of a major Soviet assault against Europe. This view, argues Morton H.

Halperin, a national security expert, is contradicted by the facts. According to Halperin, "the nuclear threat has been issued on nearly twenty occasions since the end of World War II . . . but it has been a secret one, hidden from review or assessment by the American public."[40] These include: Iran (1946), Berlin (1948), Korea (1953), Suez (1956), Lebanon (1958), *Pueblo* seizure (1968), Vietnam (1969), Arab-Israeli War (1973), Korea (1975), and the Persian Gulf (1981), among others. Admittedly, the purpose of such threats was not to achieve military victory, but to pressure the political leadership of the enemy. *See also* AEROSPACE AND DEFENSE INDUSTRY, 63; MILITARY-INDUSTRIAL COMPLEX (MIC), 48; NUCLEAR WAR, 23.

Significance   The nuclear threat myth is pervasive and widespread. Many experts believe that such threats serve a vital purpose and have played a salient role in resolving crises and preventing war. Moreover, they contend that the United States must continue to issue such threats if it hopes to protect its interests in key areas of the world. Although this view is not shared by all members of the national security bureaucracy, it is widely believed that world peace depends upon the willingness of the United States to take whatever steps are necessary to safeguard its interests. It is important to note, however, that while the Joint Chiefs of Staff and some well-respected citizens have advocated the tactical use of nuclear weapons (to avoid military defeat), no U.S. president has approved such use. Those presidents who did contemplate the use of nuclear weapons, did so for the same reason as did President Harry S Truman in 1945—namely to save lives and shorten the war. Thus, it is those in the national security bureaucracy, and not U.S. presidents, who believe most strongly in the usefulness of such threats. In Halperin's view, this position—which he describes as "unwarranted faith"—is "the greatest single obstacle to the adoption of a new American nuclear policy that would substantially reduce the possibility of nuclear war."[41] Moreover, the evidence strongly suggests that the resolution of these 20 crises was not the result of nuclear threats, but skillful diplomacy, a willingness to compromise, a realistic assessment of vital security interests, and the balance of conventional military weapons.

Nuclear Warhead (166)

The part of a missile, rocket, torpedo, projectile, or other weapon containing the nuclear or thermonuclear system. Nuclear-warhead technology proceeded apace following World War II, with a large turnover of increasingly complex weapons systems. Major advances in nuclear-warhead design (e.g., electronics miniaturization) occasioned more efficient applications of fissile materials and the development of small nuclear warheads. The fabrication of small warheads, coupled with major advances in warhead delivery systems, paved the way for the widespread acceptance of nuclear weapons within the U.S. armed forces. New warhead designs were marked by increased control, efficiency, and safety, resulting in improved mobility, greater accuracy, better range, and additional lethality. *See also* NUCLEAR TECHNOLOGY, 163; RESEARCH AND DEVELOPMENT (R&D), 83; URANIUM, 84.

Significance   Nuclear-warhead technology has become increasingly sophisticated and competitive. The typical life of a warhead, argues weapons expert Thomas B. Cochran, spans some 30 years, encompassing seven distinct phases: (1) weapons conception; (2) program study or feasibility study; (3) development engineering or full-scale development; (4) production engineering; (5) first production; (6) quantity production and stockpile; and (7) retirement.[42] Approximately 10 to 20 percent of a weapon system's cost is the warhead, although this figure may vary markedly. By the mid-1990s, total U.S. warhead production will exceed 28,000. Despite the steady escalation in the quantity and quality of nuclear warheads, recent evidence reveals several major problems, both in research and production. These include difficulties associated with need, scheduling, cost, and effectiveness. In many cases, the news media have paid scant attention to these concerns, although some have been identified in various congressional reports. For example, in 1983, both the House and Senate appropriations committees found that "some build levels appear excessive in relation to military capabilities and requirements, as well as realistic assessments of deployment requirements in the current world political climate."[43] In addition, the committees questioned the rate of the retirement program "particularly for those systems that would alleviate materials production requirements and those systems that are considered to be near or at a state of obsolescence."[44] In response to these and other questions, the Congress has, on various occasions, held up funding for individual warheads (e.g., SENTRY antiballistic missile warhead). Additional funding has been reduced for some warheads (e.g., W87 MX warhead), for test status and production reasons. In other cases, Congress has deleted funds for certain warheads (e.g., W81 STANDARD-2 missile warhead), pending the resolution of sundry design defects.

Nuclear Winter (167)

Describes the ecological disaster that could occur as a result of a nuclear war. The nuclear winter thesis was first articulated by astronomer Carl Sagan and other scientists in the early 1980s in the hopes of forging a broad public consensus on the impermissibility of nuclear war. According to Sagan, "There is a real danger of the extinction of humanity. A threshold exists at which the climatic catastrophe could be triggered. . . . A major first strike may be an act of national suicide, even if no retaliation occurs."[45] Simply put, Sagan and his cohorts contend that severe nuclear explosions, involving less than half the warheads currently stockpiled by the United States and the Soviet Union, would trigger massive fires, both in forests and particularly in cities. These fires would produce smoke and soot, which the intense heat would propel into the stratosphere. At that point, natural forces, such as rain, would prove incapable of driving it down. As a result, the soot would, in all likelihood, drift around the Earth for a year or more, blotting out the sun. This would create a sudden and profound cooling, with summer temperatures plummeting to an average of 25°C (which is equivalent to a drop from 75°F to 32°F), the average difference between winter and summer). Thus, every summer would be like winter—a "nuclear winter." Crops would perish, animals would die, and lakes and rivers would freeze. In the end, the northern hemisphere or, for that matter, the entire planet, would revert to prehistoric times. This would expose most, if not all, of the unfortunate survivors outside the target areas to lethal doses of radioactivity, pyrotoxins, and cancer-producing ultraviolet light, creating a freezing black winter lasting at least a year. *See also* FALLOUT, 146; FIRST STRIKE, 194; NUCLEAR WAR, 23; SURVIVABILITY, 205.

Significance   The nuclear winter argument has provoked widespread controversy in the scientific community. Indeed, numerous physicists, meteorologists, astronomers, chemists, and biologists have attempted to prove whether or not a nuclear winter could lead to the destruction of the human species. Their efforts have failed to produce a consensus, as the projected consequences can only be artificially simulated with highly complex models that are at best only partially understood. For example, research scientists at the National Center for Atmospheric Research (NCAR) in Boulder, Colorado, take strong exception to the nuclear winter scenario. These studies, which the NCAR insists are based on more geographically realistic models than those of Sagan and his supporters, contend that "despite the continued potential for serious nuclear winter effects, there does not seem to be a real potential for human extinction. . . . The idea of automatic suicide is now unsupportable given that a scenario of weeks of continuous subfreezing temperatures on a continental scale is no longer plausible."[46] As a result of these and other studies, the debate over possible biospheric disruption from nuclear war continues unabated. The Sagan thesis rests on many imponderables: the quantity of burnable fuel in cities, the amount of soot it would generate, the heights to which the soot would travel, and the period of time it would remain. Clearly, different assumptions will produce vastly different conclusions. Still, most scientists agree that a nuclear war will, at some level, produce a biospheric catastrophe.

Nukespeak **(168)**

A popular term coined to emphasize the importance and desirability of nuclear weapons. Nukespeak, argues linguistic scholar Paul Chilton, seeks to promote the goals and objectives of those who support the development and deployment of nuclear arms. According to Chilton, nukespeak serves to define the parameters of the nuclear debate, in that "the bounds for possible thought about the nuclear issue are influenced in a more positive way—in the sense that both official and popular utterances about nuclear weapons and war are familiarized and made acceptable."[47] Nukespeak, notes Chilton, reflects three main claims: (1) There exists a specialized lexicon for discussing nuclear arms and war, replete with acceptable metaphors and grammatical rules. (2) The vocabulary is neither neutral nor descriptive, but is ideologically biased in favor of the nuclear option. (3) This language matters, in that it shapes how people view the subject and the arguments they advance.[48] *See also* AEROSPACE AND DEFENSE INDUSTRY, 63; MILITARY-INDUSTRIAL COMPLEX (MIC), 48; NUCLEAR WAR, 23.

Significance Nukespeak, insist its critics, is "a controlled response directed by the state in conjunction with other interested parties . . . who see it as a means of constraining possible thought on the nuclear phenomenon."[49] Moreover, they suggest that "in spite of the technical theorizing, most talk about nuclear weapons reflects irrational, not to say, superstitious, processes of thought. Myths, metaphors, paradoxes, and contradictions exist."[50] On the other hand, nukespeak advocates take strong exception, asserting that whether one likes it or not, the nuclear age is a modern-day reality; to dismiss it or to pretend otherwise is to court destruction. Instead, they opine, it is critical to understand the ways in which these weapons have altered conventional warfare and to use this new technology in a wise and prudent manner. Further, they argue that nuclear weapons—in and of themselves—do not pose a threat to international peace and order. Indeed, they can serve to promote stability and freedom and prevent the possibility of World War III. That is, the destructive power of these weapons is so enormous that they may, in fact, serve as a deterrent to war. Opponents of this view label these arguments as propaganda, pointing out that "the association of 'Life' with weapons of death and destruction is bizarre . . . rather it is the typical stuff of which western propaganda is made."[51] For example, the very naming of weapons systems underscores this fact. The LGM-30F/G is also called the "Minuteman," a term that refers to the brave militiamen of the American Revolutionary War. The uranium bomb dropped on Hiroshima, Japan was called "Little Boy," and was later "promoted" to "Corporal," and still later to "Sergeant" (both were tactical, short-range missiles). The plutonium bomb dropped on Nagasaki, Japan, was dubbed "Fat Man." Nukespeak has attempted to "humanize" nuclear weapons in other ways. For example, Chilton observes that "they have fathers (Edward Teller, 'father of the H-bomb'); they grow from infants ('baby nukes') to old age (NATO's allegedly 'aging' forces) in a family ('the ICBM family'); they retire ('retiring Polaris force') and make way for the young ('new generation MX ICBMs')."[52]

Reentry Vehicle (RV)   (169)
A nuclear warhead that is fashioned to reenter the Earth's atmosphere from space. The reentry vehicle seeks to reduce the impact of environmental factors, such as atmospheric density and wind, which may affect the missile's trajectory. Although RVs may minimally affect missile speed and accuracy, research findings reveal theoretical accuracies of over 250 feet CEP (circular error probable). A ballistic missile system may carry one or more reentry vehicles, which may be independently targeted. Where a missile system carries several RVs that are not independently targetable, the system is called a multiple reentry vehicle (MRV) system. In a multiple independently targetable reentry vehicle system (MIRV system), the various reentry vehicles are carried on a "bus," which releases the RVs separately following predetermined changes in orientation and speed, propelling each RV to an independent target. See also MULTIPLE INDEPENDENTLY TARGETABLE REENTRY VEHICLE (MIRV), 150; NUCLEAR WARHEAD, 166; RESEARCH AND DEVELOPMENT (R&D), 83; SUBMARINE-LAUNCHED BALLISTIC MISSILE (SLBM), 174.

Significance   Reentry vehicles are currently deployed on the Poseidon, Trident, Titan, and Minuteman missile systems. Presently, all deployed missile RVs are ballistic, although future RVs (e.g., Peacekeeper/MX) may be nonballistic or Maneuvering Reentry Vehicles (MaRVs). The MaRV boasts several distinct advantages, including the ability to correct its flight path after reentry as well as the ability to attack mobile targets (e.g., ships and mobile missiles). Additionally, a MaRV-fitted missile coupled with an autonomous sensor could reach the prospective target and maneuver in order to attack a nonfixed target. Since 1982, Congress has appropriated approximately $100 million per year for maneuvering RVs. In this regard, the Department of Defense has launched a major research effort, focusing on such areas as nosetip ablation/erosion studies, materials development, maneuvering subsystems, decoys, and other penetration aids. The newest RV, the Mk-12A, has been retrofitted on over 300 Minuteman missiles, replacing the MK-12, which was developed in the mid-1960s. The Mk-12A, which possesses a larger yield warhead, increased accuracy, and an improved arming and fusing system, reflected the air force's belief that it was vital to offset continual Soviet hardening of its strategic targets.

Stockpile Reliability (170)
The dependability of weapons and other military hardware in a nation's arsenal. Stockpile reliability has become an increasing concern in recent years, owing to persistent reports of various design defects. Indeed, such flaws have been discovered in several types of tactical and strategic warheads, as a result of added inspection, testing, and accidents. Common problems include: the corrosion of fissile material, ineffective mechanical arming systems, and the sensitivity or deterioration of chemical explosives. According to one study, "these design failures have rendered numbers of stockpiled warheads inoperable and have increased the workload of the production complex in order to rework or replace the defective warheads or components."[53] Test explosions have served to correct many of these problems, although some still remain. *See also* NUCLEAR PRODUCTION COMPLEX, 161; NUCLEAR STOCKPILES, 82; NUCLEAR TECHNOLOGY, 163; RESEARCH AND DEVELOPMENT (R&D), 83.

Significance   Stockpile reliability is key to a nation's military strength. Thus, reports of design defects have caused considerable alarm within the U.S. defense establishment. In 1983, for example, a study sponsored by the Office of International Security reported several such problems. According to the study, weapons engineers discovered that the W47/Polaris SLBM contained noticeable corrosion in the fissile material of the warhead, leading them to conclude that "the corrosion would have resulted in either a dud or a much reduced yield."[54] Their conclusion was confirmed through observations of other warheads. In the case of the W56/Minuteman ICBM, flaws were unearthed in the mechanical arming system, which failed to fully complete its operation, resulting in a possible dud. The W45/Terrier (MADM or Little John), according to the study, was plagued by problems resulting from corrosion of its fissile material and with its chemical high explosive. This corrosion served to alter the geometry of the warhead. In the case of the W52/Sergeant, scientists revealed potential hazards of the unpredictable high explosive. In all cases, these design problems were corrected and the problems remedied. Still, there is a widespread belief that numerous other systems are plagued by equally serious flaws. For this reason, weapons analysts continue to remain concerned about stockpile reliability. To combat the problem, they have called for increased testing, which has yielded a wealth of useful data. The results of these tests have forced design modifications, which are calculated to produce greater stockpile reliability.

Strategic Bomber (171)

A manned offensive weapon designed for nuclear attack against key targets. The strategic bomber, one of the legs of the United States' triad system, was inaugurated in 1945, when President Harry S Truman ordered a nuclear bombardment against the Japanese cities of Hiroshima and Nagasaki, to hasten the end of World War II and reduce casualties. The strategic bomber constituted the sole U.S. nuclear delivery system until the late 1950s and the advent of the modern missile age. Today, manned bombers are but one component of the U.S. strategic bomber force, which now includes the air-launched cruise missile. The strategic bomber, contends defense expert Donald M. Snow, possesses five main advantages.[55] First, controllability. The manned bomber is the only vehicle that can be retrieved after it is launched—that is, it can be recalled to base, thereby reducing the likelihood of accidental war. Second, payload size. A bomber can carry a far heavier payload than can a rocket. Third, accuracy. A manned bomber can, in most cases, penetrate close to its target, achieving remarkable accuracy. Fourth, flexibility. A bomber would take hours to reach its target(s) in the Soviet Union. Thus aerial reconnaissance of sites attacked by missiles would occur before the bombers approached them. That reconnaissance would be used to redirect the bombers if they were dispatched to targets already hit. Fifth, competitive slowness. A manned bomber represents the most effective second-strike weapon in the United States' triad force and, as such, poses no direct threat to Soviet missile silos or other launch vehicles. It simply takes too long for such a vehicle to approach the target to constitute a threat. After penetrating Soviet airspace, the bomber would have ample opportunity to release its missiles or become airborne. *See also* ATOMIC BOMB, 144; CONVENTIONAL WEAPONS, 120; HIROSHIMA BOMBARDMENT, 147; TRIAD, 176.

Significance   The strategic bomber, in spite of myriad advantages, boasts one major shortcoming—namely, its inability to penetrate Soviet airspace. To counteract this weapon, the Soviets have devised the most intricate air defense system ever invented. As a result, many defense specialists have questioned the practicality of the strategic bomber. This concern, combined with the advanced age of present aircraft, has fueled the controversy and resulted in demands for increased modernization of the bomber force. A prime example is the B-52 bomber (the centerpin of the Strategic Air Command), whose airframe is decaying, thereby raising questions as to its ability to penetrate Soviet air defenses. Indeed, the "newest" models were produced in 1962, albeit with upgraded equipment. Many defense critics contend that the United States should reduce its reliance on the B-52, purchasing instead the B-1 bomber or the more expensive modified version, the B-1B bomber. As is true of most new weapons systems, the B-1 has sparked heated debate. Opponents maintain that it will only be able to penetrate Soviet airspace until the early 1990s, at which point it will be little more than an extremely costly cruise missile carrier. Other experts advocate the adoption of the advanced technology bomber (ATB), also called the B-2 Stealth bomber, which was unveiled by the U.S. Air Force in 1988 in a public ceremony in California, and revealed to have an unusual flying wing design. Still other critics favor the air-launched cruise missile (ALCM), a pilotless airplane under development in the United States, which has been faulted for its lack of reliability and the problems it may pose for arms control agreements. The administration of President Ronald W. Reagan urged Congress to build all three systems.

Strategic Nuclear War Plans   **(172)**
Options and strategies—based on projected enemy strength—for possible use in the event of a nuclear attack. The strategic nuclear war plan of the United States, called the Single Integrated Operational Plan (presently SIOP-6), was instituted on October 1, 1983. Developed by the Joint Strategic Target Planning Staff (JSTPS) at Offutt Air Force Base in Omaha, Nebraska, the plan includes detailed instructions ranging "from a show of force to a trans/post SIOP environment."[56] The JSTPS coordinates U.S. nuclear forces to attack strike targets identified as preplanned "options" under the aegis of the National Command Authority (NCA). Nuclear contingency plans have changed dramatically since the immediate period following

World War II, when bombers were targeted to strike at industrial centers, transportation links, and other bombers. Beginning in the 1960s, options for "limited" nuclear war were drafted, drawing distinctions between attacks on military (counterforce targets) from those on cities (countervalue targets). According to one report, "damage-limiting counterforce strikes would presumably destroy the enemy's nuclear forces with the countervalue attack retained for revenge."[57] By 1974, "more selective options, relatively small scale, were added to the existing large-scale operations."[58] Upon becoming president, Jimmy Carter initiated a review of the nuclear targeting policy (PD-18) that resulted in the countervailing doctrine, a strategy that emphasized "that no plausible outcome [of a Soviet nuclear attack] would represent a success—or any rational definition of success."[59] During the past eight years, the Reagan administration has stressed "making improvements in the command and control system to bolster post-attack control over nuclear forces as the first priority and called for greater coordination of theater and strategic plans."[60]
See also CIVILIAN (COUNTERVALUE) TARGETING, 184; COUNTERFORCE TARGETING, 187; NUCLEAR FORCE MODELS, 156; NUCLEAR THREAT MYTH, 165; NUCLEAR WAR, 23.

Significance   Strategic Nuclear War Plans underwent considerable change with the adoption of the strategy of limited war as the basis of U.S.-Soviet nuclear strategy. Current policy resulted from an exhaustive intelligence examination which concluded that Soviet planners believed that a protracted nuclear war was possible. In this regard, U.S. options for exact targeting or escalation control is predicated on the Soviet Union pursuing a strategy other than the massive show of nuclear force. According to the 1984 edition of *Soviet Military Power*, "Priority targets of all Soviet forces would be the enemy's nuclear delivery systems and weapons, nuclear C3, air defenses and politico-administrative centers."[61] In reality, little is known about the Soviet Union's actual nuclear-war plans. For this reason, U.S. planners have concluded that selective targeting makes necessary U.S. weapons and nuclear plans. Drawing on Soviet military writings, U.S. planners have identified the following ten basic rules that may reflect Soviet thinking on the subject[62]:

1. Preemption consistently has been the preferred Soviet strategic option

2. Second strike has been the residual option if the Soviets do not succeed in preempting

3. Launch on warning was adopted as the second option (after preempting) in 1966–1967

4. Nuclear forces are the first targets in a nuclear exchange to be destroyed in their entirety

5. Neutralization of nonnuclear military forces is a secondary objective to be carried out by whatever means possible

6. Destruction of the enemy political control system and the preservation of Soviet state power and control are high priorities

7. Industrial and other economic targets important for sustaining warfare would be a high priority in a world war

8. Defense of the Soviet homeland is the overall objective of any military operation

9. A prolonged nuclear war is possible

10. Victory is a theoretical possibility, although it is rarely defined in the context of nuclear war

Strategic Nuclear Weapons (173)

Long-range weapons intended for nuclear attack against strategic sites or for active defense against such an attack. Strategic nuclear weapons vary markedly from theater nuclear weapons (TNWs), which include those weapons aimed at a specific geographic area with the goal of destroying key bases and support facilities. There are numerous types of strategic weapons: intercontinental missiles (both land- and sea-based); long-range heavy bombers and their carried weapons (bombs and air-launched missiles); long-range cruise missiles not carried on bombers; and homeland defense missiles (both ground- and air-launched). In U.S. defense parlance, these weapons are targeted on the Soviet Union to prevent an attack or respond if one occurs. Currently, there are 2,149 warheads on more than 1,000 land-based strategic missiles, an additional 4,960 on submarine-launched missiles, and over 2,580 to be carried on strategic bombers. These weapons are often called "force loadings." Unlike TNWs, which are "dual capable"—that is, they can be armed with conventional or nuclear warheads—nearly all strategic systems are armed only with nuclear warheads. The strategic bomber force includes the FB-111 and B-52; interceptors, the F-4, F-15, and F-106; land-based missiles, the Titan II, Minuteman II, and Minuteman III; and submarine-based missiles, the Poseidon and Trident I. *See also* CRUISE MISSILE, 145; INTERCONTINENTAL BALLISTIC MISSILE (ICBM), 148; NUCLEAR WARHEAD, 166; STRATEGIC DEFENSE INITIATIVE (SDI), 141; THEATER NUCLEAR WEAPONS (TNW), 175.

Significance In theory, strategic nuclear weapons are designed to provide a nation with the means to repel a nuclear attack. In reality, however, such a defense is highly questionable given the existence of ballistic missiles, against which there are no sure means of defense. Still, experts have continued to debate the efficacy of strategic nuclear weapons, most vocally during the antiballistic missile (ABM) controversy in the late 1960s, and in the more recent debate surrounding President Ronald W. Reagan's Stategic Defense Initiative (SDI). Most strategic nuclear weapons are of intercontinental range, deliverable by land-and sea-based missiles and bombers. These three types of weapons form the basis of the United States' triad system, each of which varies in range, yield, accuracy, reliability, and survivability. Of these weapons, virtually all U.S. land-based missiles (95 percent), one-third of the bombers, and one-half of the submarines are permanently ready for war. In the case of the Soviets, their readiness level is considerably less—no bombers remain on alert, while only 15 percent of the submarine force is located outside home waters on a regular basis. On the other hand, nearly 5,000 Soviet warheads could be launched at a given moment.

Submarine-Launched Ballistic Missile (SLBM)   (174)
A ballistic missile carried in and capable of being launched by a submarine, which provides mobility and covering for a missile force. The submarine-launched ballistic missile, one of the legs of the United States' triad system, is regarded as the nation's primary strategic deterrent. A potent retaliatory system, the SLBM is believed to be invulnerable to preemptive attack. For this reason, the SLBM nullifies the "use them or lose them" strategy, thus reducing the possibility that an adversary will initiate a nuclear war. Nearly one-half of the missile-carrying submarines of the United States are located in areas that would allow them to launch an attack against the Soviet Union. The Soviets are virtually powerless to destroy these vessels, which are protected by millions of square miles of ocean. In this realm, the United States boasts clear advantages over the Soviet Union, which explains why it continues to invest a large percentage of its resources in the nation's SLBM force. U.S. preeminence is buttressed by two main factors. First, the coastlines of the United States possess sundry natural ports that are accessible throughout the year. The Soviets, on the other hand, have far fewer ports, most of which are ice-logged for prolonged periods. Second, most U.S. ports open directly into either the Pacific or Atlantic oceans, enabling U.S. submarines to find protection in the open ocean. By contrast, Soviet submarines are forced to navigate through narrow bodies of water (e.g., Baltic Sea, Barents

Sea, Kuril Islands), which permits the United States to monitor Soviet fleet movements. *See also* ANTISUBMARINE WARFARE (ASW), 112; SUBMARINE WARFARE, 142; TRIAD, 176.

Significance   The submarine-launched ballistic missile is not without its disadvantages, two of which are most pronounced. First, historically, the SLBM is far less accurate than the intercontinental ballistic missile. In this regard, it is considerably more difficult to program the SLBM's guidance system, since the ocean is not nearly as stable a launching pad as dry land. As a result, U.S. defense planners view the SLBM as more effective for attacking soft countervalue targets, such as cities, where extreme accuracy is less important. To meet this problem, the U.S. recently inaugurated the Trident submarine, the largest submarine ever built by the United States, which approaches the accuracy of land-based missiles. Second, the SLBM has been faulted for its precarious communications system. It is extremely difficult to converse effectively with a submerged submarine. This problem, which exists even in peacetime, could become particularly acute in a wartime situation, where it could prevent the issuing or canceling of launch orders. Although the problem is solvable, through the use of an "extremely low frequency" (ELF) communications system, this option has failed to garner political support. The Reagan administration endeavored to modernize the SLBM force, arguing that the Poseidon submarine, the backbone of the U.S. submarine force, requires additional upgrading. Despite these criticisms, the SLBM will, in all likelihood, remain the centerpin of the United States' strategic deterrent, owing to its imperviousness to preemptive attack.

Theater Nuclear Weapons (TNWs)   (175)

Nuclear weapons designed to destroy military bases and support facilities. Theater nuclear weapons include: cruise missiles, atomic demolition munitions (nuclear land mines), bombs and depth charges on nonstrategic aircraft, and short-range ballistic missiles used in surface-to-surface and surface-to-air missions. TNWs differ sharply from strategic nuclear weapons, which are used to attack an enemy or to defend a nation's homeland. TNWs are not merely used for tactical surprise or advantage, but the elimination of major targets. These weapons have experienced a variety of name changes. The Reagan administration, for example, referred to TNWs as "intermediate-range" and "nonstrategic" nuclear forces, owing to the negative connotation of the term "theater," particularly in Europe (where it is used as "theater of war"). Many Europeans fear that U.S. policy seeks to limit the use of such weapons to Europe, exempting U.S. territory in a nuclear conflict initiated in Europe. The term "theater" is frequently used synonymously with "tactical," which connotes short-range weapons. *See also* CONVENTIONAL WEAPONS, 120; CRUISE MISSILE, 145; NORTH ATLANTIC TREATY ORGANIZATION (NATO), 93; STRATEGIC NUCLEAR WEAPONS, 173.

Significance Theater nuclear weapons were added to the North Atlantic Treaty Organization (NATO) defense plan in Western Europe in the mid-1950s, to bolster inadequate NATO manpower levels. Simultaneously, the Eisenhower administration proposed several multilateral (e.g., Southeast Asia Treaty Organization or SEATO) and bilateral (e.g., with Nationalist China) defense pacts to dissuade hostile states from challenging U.S. military power. Many observers perceive TNWs as weapons that could be restricted to a single theater or geographical area. Unlike the United States, the Soviet Union does not draw a distinction between TNWs and strategic nuclear weapons. In recent years, budgetary cutbacks in the defense arsenal of the United States have severely affected that nation's theater forces, resulting in major slowdowns, reductions, and abandonment of some theater weapons. Most political leaders and defense analysts, however, recognize the importance of TNWs, whose main purpose is to influence the nature of a tactical maneuver or battle. Presently, tactical nuclear warheads are deployed on sundry missile and rocket systems, artillery, aircraft, and land mines, which possess explosive yields varying from .01 kiloton to over one megaton. Most TNWs are dual capable—that is, they can be armed with nuclear or conventional warheads. Only two systems are solely nuclear capable: the Navy SUBROC (W55) antisubmarine rocket and the Army Pershing 1a (W50) missile.

Triad (176)

The three components of the strategic nuclear forces of the United States. The triad consists of land-based intercontinental ballistic missiles (ICBMs), submarine-launched ballistic missiles (SLBMs), and manned bombers, which have recently been supplemented by air-launched cruise missiles (ALCMs). Each leg of the system, both in terms of capabilities and characteristics, complements the others. The triad developed more or less by accident, reflecting the activities of the three services during the 1950s. At the time, the air force possessed manned bombers and was conducting research that would result in the ICBMs, while the navy was exploring the idea of launching rockets from submarines. Their efforts culminated at about the same time, resulting in a U.S. offensive force composed of three distinct components, which came to be known as the triad. Each leg of the system boasts both offensive and defensive advantages.[63] The ICBMs provide: (1) full target coverage; (2) high degree of accuracy (depending on model); (3) assured ballistic penetration; (4) rapid targeting capability; (5) constant survivable command and control; (6) highest degree of reliability (98 percent); (7) highest degree of alert (90 percent-plus); (8) hardened silos; (9) postattack survivability; (10) quickest reaction time; and (11) low operating cost. The SLBMs offer: (1) highest degree of survivability (60 percent of forces at sea); (2) assured ballistic penetration; (3) tenuous communications link; (4) high degree of reliability; (5) ability to withhold from initial attack; and (6) invulnerable to detection or attack. The manned bombers ensure: (1) survivability of forces on alert (30 percent); (2) recallable after take-off; (3) flexible targeting to include mobile targets, targets of opportunity, and multiple targets separated by long distances; (4) highest degree of accuracy; (5) vulnerable to air defenses; and (6) ability to withhold from initial attack. U.S. defense planners have assiduously avoided disproportionate reliance on any one component, so as to promote stability and deterrence, as well as to reduce the risks of technological surprise. *See also* CRUISE MISSILE, 145; INTERCONTINENTAL BALLISTIC MISSILE (ICBM), 148; STRATEGIC NUCLEAR WEAPONS, 173; SUBMARINE-LAUNCHED BALLISTIC MISSILES (SLBM), 174.

Significance   The triad concept forms the basis of the strategic nuclear force of the United States. Offensively, each leg can be deployed against the Soviets' targets independently, using a different method of approach. This makes it far more difficult to defend against those forces, than were the United States to rely on a single component. Defensively, each system is launched from a different medium, making it extremely difficult to attack or destroy all three simultaneously. This "planned redundancy" has, in the process, promoted increased stability. Each leg boasts the ability to deal a crushing retaliatory blow against the Soviet Union in the event of attack, whether or not the other legs function. This redundancy is said to exist because if all three components succeed, they could duplicate each other's efforts. However, this redundancy is viewed as a hedge against any one or possibly two of the components becoming vulnerable to a preemptive attack. Some military experts, such as Admiral Gene LaRocque, USN, retired, question the mythos that has developed around the triad: "The Triad of the bombers, the missiles, and the missiles in the submarines has grown to such proportions that it has become the Holy Trinity. It's ridiculous, because it's just something that grew like Topsy. The navy was going ahead with its submarines, the air force was going ahead with its bombers and its land-missiles, and they got the happy idea, well there are three of us, so we'll call it a Triad. . . ."[64] LaRocque concludes that "anyone who suggests cutting one out is [attacked as though] he's going to take one of the legs out of a stool. They resort to all sorts of paradigms to suggest that you can't touch any of the weapons systems."[65] Most experts contend that the triad possesses sundry advantages and disadvantages in terms of reliability, accuracy, safety, and responsiveness. For this reason, the United States has, in recent years, attempted to modernize each component of the triad, recognizing that recent developments in military technology demand new and ever more sophisticated systems.

Weapon Effects Simulation (177)
The act or process of imitating the behavior and consequences of nuclear weapons. Weapon effects simulation was inaugurated following the passage of the Limited Test Ban Treaty of 1963, which permitted only underground testing of nuclear weapons. As a result, the effects of these weapons can only be simulated. This has led the Department of Defense (DOD) and the Department of Energy (DOE) to establish facilities in which weapon effects research can be conducted. Some simulations involve underground nuclear tests (effects tests) carried out by DOD; others employ radiation simulators (for X-rays and gamma rays), high explosives, shock tubes, and natural disturbances; still others use high-powered computers. The Defense Nuclear Agency (DNA) is the principal agency involved in weapon effects simulation, managing the entire DOD Nuclear Weapon Effects program. The goal of the program is "to assess the ability of aircraft, missiles, and electronics to withstand nuclear explosion effects."[66] It also studies the ways in which military personnel and equipment react and could be protected against the effects of nuclear explosions (e.g., neutron flux, blast, thermal shockwaves). In addition, the program analyzes the indirect environmental consequences of nuclear detonations (e.g., the formation of ice clouds, fallout, and rain-out). *See also* FALLOUT, 146; LIMITED TEST BAN TREATY (LTBT), 251; SURVIVABILITY, 205.

Significance Weapon effects simulation has generated myriad scientific investigations. For example, the DNA is actively engaged in studying the effects of nuclear weapons on people. This research, which is conducted at the Armed Forces Radiobiology Institute at Bethesda, Maryland, conducts animal experimentation to analyze the response of cells, tissues, and blood systems, and nervous systems to dangerous levels of ionizing radiation. The Air Force Weapons Laboratory (AFWL), at Kirkland Air Force Base, New Mexico, is the primary laboratory for nuclear weapon effects simulation. It carries out all DNA-sponsored air force research on the impact of nuclear weapons, and supervises the world's most extensive glue-laminated wood structure, called "Trestle EMP," to protect airborne electronics against electromagnetic pulse (EMP). In addition to EMP, many other nuclear effects are also studied. For example, the AFWL simulates radiation, blast, and shock effects of nuclear explosions. To research X-ray effects, simulation investigations are conducted by the Naval Surface Weapons Center at White Oak, Maryland, while the Army Pulse Radiation Facility at the Ballistic Research Laboratory, Aberdeen Proving Ground, Maryland, "provides a radiative environment simulating a portion of the nuclear weapons ground environment to determine the nuclear vulnerability of army equipment and systems."[67] In addition to using man-made simulators, natural disturbances can also simulate various nuclear effects. For example, the Air Force Geophysics Laboratory, at Hanscom Air Force Base, Massachusetts, has initiated a program that employs "natural and artificial phenomena such as aurora and metal releases in the atmosphere . . . to simulate important aspects of atmospheric conditions following nuclear detonations."[68]

Window of Opportunity (178)

A theory that postulates that the Soviet Union will exploit the present alleged nuclear imbalance to extract military and political concessions from the United States. The window of opportunity is predicated on the assumption that the United States, owing to a purported lack of nuclear parity, is at the mercy of the Soviet Union, which recognizes that it only has a short period of time to exploit its advantage. This theory was particularly popular during the late 1970s, when writers and politicians alike charged that the United States had allowed its nuclear forces to deteriorate to a dangerously low level. To close the window, experts advocated the development of the MX missile system. In their view, this system would prove accurate enough to counteract Soviet land-based missiles and match in kind the Soviet Union's threat to American missile power. According to this theory, the MX would seriously erode Soviet power, as 80 percent of their nuclear weaponry is ground-based (in fixed silos), as compared to 25 percent of the U.S. force. In addition, the MX would counteract the vulnerability of the United States' Minuteman missiles, by rendering them mobile and shifting them from one protective shelter to another, thus concealing their location from the Soviets. *See also*

BALANCE OF POWER, 4; BALANCE OF TERROR, 5; MILITARY-INDUSTRIAL COMPLEX (MIC), 48; NUCLEAR SUPERIORITY, 162; NUCLEAR THREAT MYTH, 165; PREVENTIVE WAR, 28.

Significance   The window of opportunity theory presumes the risk of a Soviet first strike and the vulnerability of the Minuteman, neither of which are proven assumptions. Moreover, it is based on the dependability of the U.S. MX missile system. However, as James Fallows, an authority on national defense, notes: "Each new MX plan has been presented with solemn assurances that the imperfections in each previous scheme have all been worked out. Because of the constant reworking of these schemes, not to mention the inherent Rube Goldberg nature of the mobile basing system, many groups are not quite sure."[69] Indeed, since the late 1970s, the United States Air Force has proposed at least six schemes for basing the MX, at costs ranging from $30 to $80 billion, the actual amount of which is unknown. In reality, both sides' calculations of nuclear vulnerability are based on extrapolations from extremely limited test results, as opposed to actual experience or exhaustive testing. Thus, the nuclear capabilities of both superpowers remain uncertain, leading some experts to question the charge of vulnerability. Still, most defense strategists contend that the United States must proceed on the basis of theoretical vulnerability. In this regard, they believe that in order to counter the problem, the United States must reassess its present intercontinental ballistic missile system (ICBM), which they contend is critical if the United States is to close the window. Major recommendations include: (1) dismantle the ICBM force; (2) do nothing about the force; (3) protect the force more effectively; (4) develop a corollary capability to offset the Soviets' capacity to destroy U.S. ICBMs; or (5) free ICBMs from their fixed sites and make them mobile.[70] Still, many policy experts, such as Rep. Ronald V. Dellums (D-Calif.), dismiss the window argument, insisting: "The claim that our strategic forces have a 'window of opportunity' in the 1980s is without foundation. The only element of our strategic deterrent triad that is even theoretically becoming vulnerable is the land-based ICBMs . . . and I stress theoretical. . . . The overall strategic deterrent of the United States is not vulnerable."[71]

Yield   (179)

The energy released in a nuclear blast, generally measured in terms of kilotons or megatons (a megaton equals a thousand kilotons). The yield of most early nuclear weapons ranged from 10 to 20 Kt. Today, a megaton warhead is simply an ordinary-sized weapon in the nuclear arsenals of the United States and the Soviet Union and, to a lesser extent, in the nuclear armories of France, the People's Republic of China, and the United Kingdom. The designs of these early weapons were relatively conservative, producing an adequate amount of nuclear or fissile material to guarantee a sufficient yield without imposing excessive demands on the implosion or gun used. For example, the "Gadget," which was tested at Alamogordo, New Mexico, in 1945, had a yield of 22 ± 2 Kt. With a plutonium core weighing approximately 13.5 pounds (6.1 kg), it was imploded by 5,000 pounds of high explosive. The nuclear weapon, "Fat Man," which was dropped on Nagasaki, Japan, on August 9, 1945—and was similar in design to the "Gadget"—weighed 10,800 pounds with fins and had a yield of 22 ± 2 Kt. The yield of "Little Boy," the nuclear weapon which destroyed Hiroshima, Japan, on August 6, 1945, is less known, with estimates ranging from 12 to 15 Kt, and weighing 8,900 pounds. Today, a single warhead—weighing less than one-fifth of either of the bombs used against Nagasaki or Hiroshima—possesses anywhere from 10 to 100 times the amount of explosive power used to destroy these two cities. *See also* ATOMIC BOMB, 144; HIROSHIMA BOMBARDMENT, 147; NUCLEAR STOCKPILES, 82; NUCLEAR WARHEAD, 166.

Significance   Yield-wise, the smallest nuclear device in the U.S. stockpile is the W54, which is a fission implosion weapon. It is presently deployed as a warhead in the Special Atomic Demolition Munition (SADM), and is currently employed as the warhead for the FALCON missile (retired in 1972) and the Davy Crockett rocket (retired 1971). By contrast, the Super Oralloy bomb, the largest fission device ever detonated, boasted a yield of 500 Kt. This is larger than most thermonuclear weapons which are presently part of the U.S. stockpile. The most potent warhead ever tested had a yield of approximately 58 megatons, and was detonated in the final series of atmospheric tests conducted by the Soviet Union in 1962. Blast represents about 50 percent of the energy that a nuclear explosion produces. For example, a single one-megaton bomb would destroy all houses up to two miles from the point of burst. The fires that would ensue would most likely ravage an area far larger than the actual damage caused by the blast. The remainder of the energy of the bomb occurs in the form of nuclear radiation.

7. Nuclear Strategy

AirLand Battle (ALB) (180)

A U.S. Army strategy for NATO defense, one of the so-called deep strike initiatives. AirLand Battle (and its futuristic successor, Air Land Battle 2000) "involves conducting simultaneous deep attacks into the depth of oncoming Warsaw Pact formations at strategically vulnerable points while fighting an overall defensive battle across the entire front."[1] The strategy is outlined in *U.S. Army Manual* FM 100-5 as revised in 1982. See also DEEP STRIKE, 189; WAR OF ATTRITION, 208.

Significance The AirLand Battle plan stresses an aggressively offensive defense for Europe, one which if implemented would require substantive changes in the existing deployment and organization of NATO forces. Critics (including members of the U.S. armed forces) have suggested that the emphasis on offensive incursions into Warsaw Pact territory is not only diametrically opposed to traditional allied defense strategies, but would actually leave Western frontal positions vulnerable in the event of a Soviet attack, either with conventional and/or nuclear forces. As James A. Blackwell, Jr., points out, while "Air-Land Battle operations [are] theoretically possible . . . insufficient logistics capabilities are on hand in Europe to support wideranging and continuous manuever."[2] ALB remains unproven as a defense strategy, and also delineates the many differences between the NATO alliance states in agreeing to some long-term, coherent, viable military strategy acceptable to all of the allied services.

Center for Defense Information (CDI) (181)

A private, bipartisan organization that monitors governmental arms control and spending policies. The Center for Defense Information "opposed the Reagan defense spending increases and called for more intensive congressional oversight and improved Department of Defense planning."[3] *See also* INTERNATIONAL INSTITUTE FOR STRATEGIC STUDIES (IISS), 196.

Significance Private organizations such as the Center for Defense Information are representative of a growing concern at the grassroots level with arms control and disarmament. Operating as a coalition with such congressional groups as the Military Reform Caucus, founded in 1981 by Senator Gary Hart (D-Colo.) and Congressman G. William Whitehurst (R-Va.), the CDI has served as a fiscal and political watchdog representing a segment of U.S. society that believes in a more responsive and responsible defense establishment. Conservative critics have dismissed it as a tool of the so-called liberal bloc, but the CDI itself disavows any particular political affiliation.

Circular Error Probable (CEP) (182)

A measure of warhead accuracy used in statistical warfare and with strategic weapons design and production. Circular error probable is "the radius of a circle centered at the expected impact point such that, on the average, 50 percent of the missiles of a specified class may be expected to hit within this circle."[4] The lower the figure, the more accurate the system. The CEP formula is employed during the design, fabrication, and testing of missiles, with the aim of identifying (and eliminating) error potential, and producing an effective and accurate weapons system.[5] *See also* DAMAGE ASSESSMENT, 188; PROBABILITY OF KILL (PK), 203; SURVIVABILITY, 205.

Significance Warhead accuracy, as measured by circular error probable and other mathematical functions, is of great concern to military and political leaders alike. The ability to hit a target accurately enough to destroy it, particularly if that target consists of other missile or communications systems, is central to the West's long-term defense strategy of mutually assured destruction. Also, while kill probability (PK) may be increased with higher individual yield or with larger numbers of warheads aimed at a particular target, warhead accuracy remains one of the most critical and valuable measurements of overall weapons systems effectiveness, and is one area where U.S. technical proficiency has clearly outshone the Soviet military machine.[6]

Civil Defense (183)

The protection, dispersement, and sustenance of civilian populations during times of attack. Civil defense is a concept as old as war itself, since there is no point to conflict unless some remnant of one's own society can survive to rebuild. The protection of women, children, the elderly, and the sick and wounded from bombardment and direct attack has often been considered a point of honor, a mark of civilization between warring nations. As late as 1939, U.S. President Franklin D. Roosevelt believed that "armed forces [should] in no event and under no circumstances undertake bombardment from the air of civilian populations or unfortified cities."[7] The subsequent destruction of London, Dresden, Hiroshima, and Nagasaki made a mockery of such sentiments. The administration of President Dwight D. Eisenhower began a nationwide effort to construct fallout shelters in cities and to encourage individuals to build shelters in their homes, but during the 1970s most such projects were abandoned. The administration of President Ronald W. Reagan proposed massive evacuations of civilian populations in the event of nuclear attack, a plan that was called unworkable by its critics. Both the Soviet Union and the People's Republic of China maintain widespread civil defense facilities. *See also* CIVILIAN (COUNTERVALUE) TARGETING, 184; COUNTERFORCE TARGETING, 187; SURVIVABILITY, 205; SURVIVALIST MOVEMENT, 206.

Significance   The nuclear winter scenario has left most experts with a dim view of civil defense plans. Desmond Ball's response is typical: "Is it really possible to conduct a strategic nuclear exchange . . . without significant civilian casualties, . . . casualties [that would] range from 2 to 20 million?"[8] Modern nuclear strategy includes both "counterforce" targeting (military sites) and "countervalue" targeting (cities and industrial plants). The "essence of countervalue in deterrence lies in being able to inflict 'unacceptable damage' on the enemy—a level of damage to his own country which no rational leader would run the risk of incurring."[9] Reginald Bretnor points out that the decentralization of urban centers is a necessary prerequisite to any realistic civilian survival in the nuclear age, but that "most nations have done precisely the reverse. No real effort has been made to decentralize great cities and the supply, water and power networks on which they depend. . . . We should not need to be reminded that it is far, far harder to cut off the food supplies of a million families working wheat fields or rice paddies than to shut off the supply lines to a great city."[10] Further, as George H. Quester states, "We know for certain that humanity can survive repeated rounds of conventional war. We have no real way of knowing whether or not humanity can meaningfully survive a war once it becomes nuclear. . . . If . . . warheads are . . . detonated in the second, third, sixth, and tenth weeks of a war. . . it is not so clear how anyone will be able . . . to begin providing for the necessities of life."[11] Finally, in response to proposals for increasing civil defense efforts, Dr. Howard Hiatt, of the Harvard School of Public Health, declares, "I would spend all [the money allocated] on morphine. Civil defense money is worse than wasted now. It misleads. It [lets] people believe they can escape in a nuclear war. They can't."[12]

Civilian (Countervalue) Targeting (184)

In nuclear strategy, the bombing of urban and/or industrial complexes, as opposed to strictly military objectives. Civilian, or countervalue, targeting does not require the same kind of pinpoint accuracy as counterforce (i.e., military) targeting, since it is designed primarily to destroy a country's economic and social infrastructure. Large urban areas are readily destroyed, first by blast damage, and secondarily with fire storms and radiation poisoning. Thus, a "hit" anywhere near a large city will probably result in long-term disruption of communications and commerce, and widespread decimation of the population. *See also* CIRCULAR ERROR PROBABLE (CEP), 182; COUNTERFORCE TARGETING, 187; MUTUAL ASSURED DESTRUCTION (MAD), 151; WAR OF ATTRITION, 208.

Significance   The threat of civilian targeting is the ultimate deterrent to nuclear war. In most conventional wars, bombs can be most effectively used on purely military objectives, including weapons emplacements, troops, and bases, and on some secondary targets, particularly arms factories and transportation facilities, such as harbors or rail yards. Centers of population without such structures have traditionally been immune from attack. In the nuclear era, the concept of "neutral" civilian areas has become irrelevant; although warheads can be specifically targeted to strictly military objectives, the aim of nuclear war is the total destruction of one's enemy, including his economic and social centers. The Rand Bomb Damage Computer Model "predicts . . . fatalities only and leaves out those due to thermal and radioactive effects. . . . It also gives no idea of levels of casualties, social disintegration and general misery that would follow even the use of a Hiroshima-sized weapon upon any population";[13] and yet the picture it produces is one of utter devastation. It is the "not knowing" that makes deterrence possible and the dangers of actual nuclear conflict so chilling. The possibility with the nuclear winter scenario that most higher forms of life could be decimated or even exterminated in an atomic war, and that the remnants of humankind would be reduced at best to a sustenance level, has convinced many political and military leaders in both East and West that some agreement must be reached by the Soviet Union and the United States to prevent the possibility of a nuclear holocaust. As George H. Quester says, "The United States [and, by implication, the Soviet Union] preserves peace, in the nuclear age, by threatening millions of innocent people, on the expectation (not so badly founded, so far as anyone can tell) that doing so will deter the potentially guilty from initiating wars and aggressions."[14] While this strategy has worked for more than 40 years, it remains a very dangerous philosophy, one which does not really take into account accidents, malfunctions, madmen, terrorists, or conflicts in or with other states.

Command, Control, and Communication (C3)　　　　(185)

Three elements in a network to provide coordinated military management in both peace and war. Command, Control, and Communication (C3), also called Command, Control, Communication, and Intelligence (C3I) and Command-and-Control (C&C), uses "the World-Wide Military Command and Control System (WWMCCS), inaugurated in 1962, and consisting now of 35 mainframe computer systems at more than 25 command posts located around the world."[15] Tied into this system are all current U.S. military command structures, plus the Strategic Air Command (SAC) always-airborne command post, "Looking Glass," and NEACP ("Kneecap"), the National Emergency Airborne Command Post, by which the president would be evacuated in time of crisis, and from which he would issue commands to the National Command System to unify the nation's defense effort. *See also* EMERGENCY ACTION MESSAGES (EAM), 191; FAIL-SAFE MECHANISMS, 193; JOINT CHIEFS OF STAFF, 197; LAUNCH-ON-WARNING (LOW), 198; NATIONAL EMERGENCY AIRBORNE COMMAND POST (NEACP), 201; WHITE HOUSE SITUATION ROOM, 209.

Significance　　　The command and control network, which "interlinks the land-based, sea-based, and bomber strategic forces to the proper command authority, and consists of cable connections, ground, airborne, and satellite radio connections,"[16] is only as valuable as its ability to withstand nuclear attack and conduct an adequate response. One of the major problems with C3 is that the time frame for answering a supposed or actual threat has shrunk in recent decades to ten minutes or less (the time it would take submarine-based missiles to impact major command and communications targets). This has led both East and West to develop a launch-on-warning strategy that severely limits the options of both sides. The perceived instantaneous ability to knock out central command posts, either through direct hits or via an electromagnetic nuclear pulse, has theoretically made the logic of a first strike overwhelming, if one presumes that nuclear war is itself a logical outgrowth of disputes between nations. Proponents of C3 upgrading, however, favor being "in a position to negotiate with the other side to end an unplanned, unwanted, and potentially suicidal superpower military confrontation before it spins out of control."[17]

Counterdeterrent Strategy (186)

A plan to deter nuclear war by convincing potential opponents that an attack by them on one's own atomic arsenal would be too costly or too risky. The counterdeterrent ability of the United States "depends upon the relative vulnerability of [the superpowers'] military forces, leadership, economy, and population to various types and levels of nuclear attack."[18] *See also* FIRST STRIKE, 194; LAUNCH-ON-WARNING (LOW), 198; RETALIATORY STRIKE, 204; SURVIVABILITY, 205.

Significance According to the Office of Technical Assessment, the objective of U.S. counterdeterrent strategy is "to avoid nuclear attack on this nation while preserving other national interests. To accomplish this, our strategy has attempted to achieve three major goals: (1) deter the Soviets from nuclear attack on the United States by convincing them that the outcome would be unacceptable to them; (2) convince the Soviets that we will attempt to preserve our national interests by means short of nuclear war, but that attacks on those interests might well lead to nuclear war; and (3) terminate nuclear war, if it cannot be avoided, at the lowest possible level of violence and on terms most favorable to us."[19] As Samuel P. Huntington says, such "military forces can contribute to deterrence in three ways. First they . . . deter simply by being in place; second, [they] deter by raising the possibility of a successful defense; [and] third . . . they deter by threatening retaliation."[20]

Counterforce Targeting (187)

In nuclear strategy, the bombing of strictly military objectives, as opposed to civilian (countervalue) targeting. In counterforce targeting, "(1) only the forces which would be used in a potential enemy's unjust aggression would be threatened; and (2) other deaths expected to result from carrying out the threat would be accepted only as side-effects."[21] Typical targets of counterforce strategy would be "bombers and their bases, ballistic-missile submarines and their shore facilities, ICBM silos, ABM and air defence installations, command and control centers, and nuclear stockpiles."[22] *See also* CIRCULAR ERROR PROBABLE (CEP), 182; CIVILIAN (COUNTERVALUE) TARGETING, 184; MUTUAL ASSURED DESTRUCTION (MAD), 151; WAR OF ATTRITION, 208.

Significance   The United States has long advocated counterforce strategy as a means of controlling nuclear war. Such reasoning assumes that "other (i.e., civilian) deaths" would be incidental to the bombing of purely military targets. However, the reality of nuclear conflict is such that few observers accept the premise that destruction could be limited so easily, or that either superpower would readily restrict their atomic forces to just military targets when so many warheads are available to both sides. MAD (mutual assured destruction) proponents hold that only by maintaining the threat of all-out nuclear war at the highest level can the Soviets be deterred from risking an attack. Counterforce strategists maintain that the threat to military targets is a sufficient deterrent in itself, and that such targeting keeps escalation possibilities to a minimum. Such theorists hope that a nuclear war could be "limited" while other solutions are being sought. The correctness of either strategy is probably unknowable without the hard data generated by an actual field test.

Damage Assessment   (188)

In nuclear strategy, the determination of the actual effectiveness of a missile strike. Damage is assessed through information "derived from the missile itself (through radio links which transmit data in 'real time') or from satellites." Information that is relayed in "non-real-time" (or after launch) "has [a] disadvantage [in] that the entire . . . force may have been . . . focused on targets which may have already been destroyed."[23] *See also* CIRCULAR ERROR PROBABLE (CEP), 182; CIVILIAN (COUNTERVALUE) TARGETING, 184; COUNTERFORCE TARGETING, 187; PROBABILITY OF KILL (PK), 203; SURVIVABILITY, 205.

Significance   Proper damage assessment allows military planners to distribute more effectively strategic missile forces; and the measuring of such effectiveness with missile tests allows strategists to check targeting specifications, maximum yields for particular warhead configurations, and the results of war game scenarios. In addition, the defensive systems making such assessments perform a wide variety of other functions, including surveillance, tracking, interception, destruction, and evaluation (assessment) of ballistic missile strikes,[24] a key element of President Ronald W. Reagan's Strategic Defense Initiative.

Deep Strike (189)

A series of conventional defense initiatives proposed for NATO forces. Deep strike "has come to describe different methods that NATO could employ to attack and thus destroy, disrupt, and delay the Soviet-Warsaw Pact, second-echelon forces moving toward the line of battle"[25] by, in essence, counterattacking selective targets deep behind Soviet lines. Deep-strike strategies include: AirLand Battle (ALB) (and the futuristic AirLand Battle 2000); the Emerging Technologies Initiative (ETI); Follow-on-Forces Attack (FOFA); and perhaps Counter-Air 90. *See also* AIRLAND BATTLE (ALB), 180; EMERGING TECHNOLOGIES INITIATIVE (ETI), 192; FOLLOW-ON-FORCES ATTACK (FOFA), 195.

Significance Deep-strike strategies assume that existing NATO forces are insufficient to stem a massive Soviet conventional attack, and that Russian penetration of Western Europe can only be halted by counterattacks on Warsaw Pact support forces, behind enemy lines. Some of the European allies of the United States are not enthusiastic over this philosophy, since it interferes with their own image of NATO as a purely defensive organization. Other critics have pointed out what they perceive to be serious flaws in the proposed plans, including problems with logistics, command and control capabilities, resupply, and the expense of upgrading existing defensive modes with new weapons and technology.

Dense Pack (190)

A silo-basing scheme that would supposedly preserve some MX missiles from Soviet attack. The administration of President Jimmy Carter had predicted a five-year "window of vulnerability" during the mid-1980s, at which time the United States would be least able to defend itself against a first strike by Soviet missile forces. To counteract this, the Carter administration proposed basing the new MX missile in multiple protective shelters (MPS), with some 200 missiles (each carrying multiple warheads) shuttled daily among 4,000 hardened silos spread over a large expanse of desert. In 1982, the Townes Commission rejected this strategy, and proposed the dense-pack system, by which 100 MX missiles would be placed in super-hardened silos, so closely situated to one another that an attack on one would interfere (through shock waves and the electromagnetic pulse phenomenon) with other missiles aimed at proximate targets. Thus, some of the missiles would survive to launch a counter-strike. The scheme was rejected by Congress later the same year, and the 1983 Scowcroft Commission report discounted the entire "window of vulnerability" scenario. *See also* COUNTERFORCE TARGETING, 187; FIRST STRIKE, 194; MISSILE SILOS, 199; PROBABILITY OF KILL (PK), 203; SURVIVABILITY, 205.

Significance   The dense-pack deployment plan was scotched both for reasons of cost and questions of feasibility. The proposal also clearly violated the SALT agreement, but was justified by President Ronald W. Reagan on the grounds that excavations for the new missiles would not really be silos, but "hardened capsules," and would, in any event, not be completed until after the expiration of SALT II.[26] The question of land-based silo vulnerability has not been resolved. Increased missile accuracy, plus the development of MIRV technology (allowing the targeting of multiple warheads against each site), suggest that land-based missiles are not likely to survive an all-out first strike by either side.[27] Christopher Bertram points out that the "simplest and most obvious solution to the problem [of protection] would be to phase ICBM out of the strategic arsenal. However, for reasons of cost, secure command and control, accuracy of delivery, flexibility and political balance, fixed-site land-based missiles will probably continue to form a major part of the strategic forces of both superpowers."[28]

Emergency Action Messages (EAMs)   (191)
Commands to initiate a nuclear strike, relayed from C3 (Command and Control) posts to field forces in times of attack. More than "forty different communications systems are assigned to the World Wide Military Command and Control System (WWMCCS)" for relaying these messages,[29] which may be sent to submarine, bomber, and missile forces. Once launched, bomber forces are maintained by "positive launch control" in airborne holding positions until properly coded EAMs are received. Permissive Action Links (PAL) are coding devices whose "unlocking allows unit commanders to use the proper numerical firing code."[30] *See also* COMMAND, CONTROL, AND COMMUNICATION (C3), 185; FAIL-SAFE MECHANISMS, 193; NATIONAL EMERGENCY AIRBORNE COMMAND POST (NEACP), 201; WHITE HOUSE SITUATION ROOM, 209.

Significance   Emergency action messages are part of the extraordinarily complex fail-safe mechanisms employed by command and control (C3) units. As Arthur Macy Cox points out: "One of the greatest risks we face is accidental launch of nuclear weapons resulting from breakdowns in the communications systems and insufficient time for reliable human decision making."[31] Such accidents could be caused by computer glitches in the early-warning radar systems employed by both superpowers; erroneous reports in these computers are common enough to have caused several alerts in the last decade, including three during one eight-month period in 1980. Concern has also been raised by tests that have shown that at least one-third of the military operators of missile silos may ignore launch signals due to moral qualms, and by speculation that a madman could use a missile submarine or bomber for blackmail or to start World War III. Although the EAM system represents an honest effort to limit the use of nuclear weapons to responsible political leaders, no system is perfect, and while the possibility of accidents exists, however slim, the world continues to live on the edge of nuclear *Götterdämmerung*.

Emerging Technologies Initiative (ETI) (192)

One of several strategies using the deep-strike philosophy that have been proposed by NATO for the defense of Europe. ETI was first suggested at a NATO summit meeting in May 1982. The broadest of the deep-strike initiatives, it exploits the West's technological superiority to offset the Warsaw Pact's edge in conventional arms, focusing particularly on areas of "target acquisition, situation assessment, precision guidance, and munition lethality."[32] By employing such technology, the West could supposedly hold off Soviet forces until reinforcements were sent from the United States. *See also* AIRLAND BATTLE (ALB), 180; DEEP STRIKE, 189; FOLLOW-ON-FORCES ATTACK (FOFA), 195; WAR OF ATTRITION, 208.

Significance The Emerging Technologies Initiative, as with all of the deep-strike schemes, has been under fire at one time or another as supporting an offensive rather than the more traditional defensive stance which the NATO allies have found most comfortable. Other critics have pointed out that ETI would require putting the bulk of new development funds into untried technologies rather than toward the modernization of existing conventional forces. The question of who would develop these weapons or technologies is also important, since many Europeans feel themselves falling further and further behind both the Americans and the Japanese in computer-oriented systems, and regard the ETI scheme as one more proprietary U.S. weapons system that they would be forced to buy. The controversy generated by the deep-strike proposals has thus far prevented them from being adopted as official NATO policy.

Fail-safe Mechanisms (193)

Those devices, maneuvers, and tactics that are employed by command and control to prevent nuclear accidents and unprovoked launchings. Fail-safe devices may include the Hot Line Agreements, Emergency Action Messages (EAMs), Permissive Action Links (PAL), and other communicative processes. *See also* COMMAND, CONTROL, AND COMMUNICA-

TION (C3), 185; EMERGENCY ACTION MESSAGES (EAM), 191; HOT LINE AGREE-
MENTS, 249.

Significance   Fail-safe mechanisms are essential in preventing an
accidental nuclear war. Former Senator Gary Hart (D-Colo.) sees the
prevention of "the possibility of a nuclear exchange through accident
or miscalculation" as one of the prime imperatives for future arms
control talks. To this end, he recommends that "talks on prevention
should seek to: (1) update the 1963 'Hot Line Agreement' to ensure
instant, continuous, and secure communications between the two
heads of government during a crisis [in fact, the Hot Line Agreements were updated and modernized in 1988]; (2) update and extend
the 1971 U.S.-Soviet agreement on accidental nuclear war to provide
accurate and reliable notification of any accidental launch; and (3)
establish a jointly staffed crisis control facility in which personnel
from the United States and the Soviet Union would monitor all nuclear weapons-related activities, including missile tests launches."[33]
According to George H. Quester, "good" military hardware includes
"permissive action links (PAL) that make it impossible to fire nuclear
weapons without the approval of higher command authority, or the
enhanced command and control links that also ensure that the president and high-ranking officers can communicate with each other
during a crisis."[34] He sees one of the "major problems with deterrence
[as] the fear of an irresponsible launching of a nuclear attack."[35]
Fail-safe mechanisms help ensure against both the irrational acts of
madmen and the irreversible accidents of nature.

First Strike   (194)

The launching of an all-out nuclear attack without warning, ostensibly to destroy the enemy's ability to retaliate. A first (or preemptive)
strike capability depends upon the vulnerability of an enemy's command and control network, weapons systems (including ICBM sites),
intelligence, communication, and delivery systems (including submarines and bombers), as well as the attacking force's willingness to risk
a retaliation that may involve its own annihilation. *See also* COMMAND,
CONTROL, AND COMMUNICATION (C3), 185; COUNTERDETERRENT STRATEGY,
186; LAUNCH-ON-WARNING (LOW), 198; PROBABILITY OF KILL (PK), 203; RE-
TALIATORY STRIKE, 204.

Significance   A first-strike scenario may become tempting if one
superpower believes the other is vulnerable in any of the above areas.
Conversely, preemptive strikes may become compelling if a greatly
superior defense system, one that will upset the balance of power, is
implemented by an opponent, or if one state begins developing a

major offensive system not possessed by another. An example of such an imbalance used to the advantage of one superpower is the Cuban missile crisis of 1962, where the United States was able to force the Soviet Union to remove its missiles from Cuba through the threat of nuclear war, an event which many experts believe almost happened. Senator Albert Gore (D-Tenn.) believes that "SALT II resolved the first-strike problem in principle by means of a numerical equilibrium between MX missiles in protective shelters and the number of permitted Soviet warheads. But the treaty's failure and the subsequent crisis over MX . . . ruled out a return to that particular solution."[36] George H. Quester adds that our "first worry, as always, must be an actual Soviet capacity for a splendid first strike. If the accuracies of Soviet multiple-warhead missiles allow for a very good kill-ratio against the U.S. land-based missile silos, they could then be combined with new breakthroughs in Soviet antisubmarine warfare (ASW) capability to leave all of the U.S. strategic force too vulnerable."[37] Other defense experts discount such a possibility, however, by pointing out that the number of warheads and delivery systems available to both sides is too great to risk the possibility of self-annihilation; and that, in any event, even a "successful" attack by one side would probably result in massive radiation poisoning and a severe nuclear winter effect covering the entire Northern hemisphere, causing almost as much damage on the attacking nation as the recipient.

Follow-on-Forces Attack (FOFA) (195)

A deep-strike initiative for European defense that employs conventional bombing strikes far behind enemy lines in response to a Warsaw Pact attack. FOFA is a "concept developed at Supreme Headquarters, Allied Power Europe (SHAPE) in the early 1980s under the direction of General Bernard Rogers," and subsequently approved by NATO's Defense Planning Council in November 1984, "to target Warsaw Pact follow-on forces throughout the depth of pact territory with highly accurate conventional weapons."[38] *See also* AIR-LAND BATTLE (ALB), 180; DEEP STRIKE, 189; EMERGING TECHNOLOGIES INITIATIVE (ETI), 192; WAR OF ATTRITION, 208.

Significance   The follow-on-forces attack scheme relies heavily, as with all the deep-strike strategies, on the successful implementation of technologies that currently either do not exist or that are untried on the battlefield. "If such technology continues to show promise, then predeployed forces can and will have greater utility in deterring and defeating Soviet attack."[38] Deep-strike initiatives continue to be controversial, however, involving a philosophy of defense that strikes many of the U.S.'s European allies as having a blatantly offensive nature. Such new technologies are also extraordinarily expensive to develop, require skills that many U.S. soldiers seem incapable of learning, are subject to frequent breakdown, cost more than conventional weapons to maintain, and often do not work as planned.

International Institute for Strategic Studies (IISS)   (196)

A center formed to study the growing complexity of security in the nuclear age. IISS was "originally founded in 1958 by a group of British analysts, academics, politicians, journalists, and men of the Church. Since 1964, the Institute has become fully international. Its membership [1986] extends to more than seventy countries. . . . Its researchers come from a variety of different countries, and its . . . support from a number of countries in America, Europe and Asia." IISS publishes *Strategic Survey*, an overview of the year; *Survival*, the Institute's journal, "containing original articles, documentation and book reviews"; *The Military Balance*, a "quantitative assessment of the military strength and defense spending of every country with armed forces"; and the *Adelphi Papers*, a "series of monographs analyzing current and future problems of international security concern, written by experts from many nations."[39] *See also* CENTER FOR DEFENSE INFORMATION (CDI), 181; NUCLEAR PLANNING GROUP (NPG), 202.

Significance   The International Institute for Strategic Studies sees its purpose as performing research, propagating information, and, through its annual conference, seminars and lectures, providing a "forum for discussion and debate on international security problems"; and "its prime responsibilities [as] the analysis of the complexities of international security and conflict and the injection of new thinking into the debate. . . . The Institute has become, over the years, a forum of discussion for the international constituency concerned with security, military and political conflict and arms control. Among its members . . . are a growing number from third-world countries."[40] Such international organizations serve as nonpartisan sounding boards for the ideas, concerns, and desires of individuals from many different countries, all concerned with disarmament, arms control, and the problems of survival in the nuclear age.

Joint Chiefs of Staff   (197)

The heads of the four branches of the U.S. military—the army, the navy, the air force, and the marine corps—together with the chief of staff to the secretary of defense. The Joint Chiefs of Staff were created by the National Security Acts of 1947 and 1949. They are subordinate to the secretary of defense, and work closely with the Department of Defense; they also have seats on the National Security Council. The Joint Chiefs coordinate (with the secretary) the nation's defense spending, planning, strategy, joint operations of the services, and deployment of U.S. armed forces in the case of attack. *See also* COM- MAND, CONTROL, AND COMMUNICATION (C3), 185; NATIONAL SECURITY COUN- CIL (NSC), 79; NUCLEAR PLANNING GROUP (NPG), 202.

Significance   The Joint Chiefs of Staff were established to provide coordinated, high-level military advice to the president, and to carry out the orders of the civilian leaders of the government. Thus, they serve not only as heads of their respective military branches but also as political creatures, appointed by the president, and essentially serv- ing at his pleasure. Traditionally, the Joint Chiefs have had relatively little effect as a military group, each service resisting efforts to coor- dinate its actions with the others; rather, they have been used by many presidents as sometime effective lobbyists before congressional com- mittees for increases in military expenditures. The administration of President Ronald W. Reagan made a strong effort to reorganize the Joint Chiefs, giving them an increased support staff and more power to effect joint military operations, even over the objections of com- manding officers in the individual services; the lasting results of this shake-up have yet to be seen. Critics have lambasted the Joint Chiefs for their long-standing inability to manage internecine rivalries which have, on occasion, caused embarrassment, fatal accidents, or even outright military defeats, and which certainly have worked against the integration of the armed forces "envisioned by the National Security Acts."[41]

Launch-on-Warning (LOW)   (198)

The launching of strategic offensive nuclear missiles immediately upon receiving notice that the enemy has launched an attack. Launch- on-Warning (LOW) is one of several strategies developed to counter a preemptive first strike. Others include: hardening ICBM missile silos (thus reducing their vulnerability to first strikes), spreading one's launching platforms over a wide enough area that some are certain to escape attack, making one's delivery vehicles mobile, and the launch- through-attack (LTA) strategy, whereby "missiles would be launched when the full scope of the attack became clear."[42] *See also* CIVILIAN (COUNTERVALUE) TARGETING, 184; COUNTERDETERRENT STRATEGY, 186; COUNTERFORCE TARGETING, 187; FAIL-SAFE MECHANISMS, 193; FIRST STRIKE, 194; MISSILE SILOS, 199; RETALIATORY STRIKE, 204.

Significance   The launch-on-warning strategy increases the risks of nuclear war. As Fred Iklé states, "The more we rely on launch-on-warning (or, for that matter, the more the Soviets do), the greater the risk of accidental nuclear war. . . . No one can understand in sufficient detail all the possible malfunctions, unanticipated events and human errors that might interact . . . to confound the redundant warning systems or to bypass the safeguards against an unintended release of the command to launch a missile salvo."[43] And, in fact, errors have been frequently observed in the radar warning computers of the United States, causing numerous alerts and other glitches. The launch-on-warning philosophy reduces the president's decision-making window to ten minutes or less.

Missile Silos (199)

Structures housing land-based intercontinental ballistic missiles (ICBMs). Missiles are deployed in "underground concrete- and steel-reinforced silos. By 1967, the United States had . . . 1054 ICBMs [but] since 1982 the number has actually decreased slightly, as the U.S. has begun to dismantle the oldest and least reliable of these systems (the Titan II)."[44] *See also* COUNTERFORCE TARGETING, 187; DAMAGE ASSESSMENT, 188; DENSE PACK, 190; FIRST STRIKE, 194; RETALIATORY STRIKE, 204; SURVIVABILITY, 205.

Significance   The ongoing controversy over the effectiveness of silo-based launching systems concerns their potential survivability in a nuclear war. Robert Travis Scott cites strength of the silo as one of the "four major factors [determining] the probability that an ICBM silo can survive."[45] Since their inception, missile silos have been hardened to withstand approximately 2,000 pounds per square inch. Increasing silo hardness further would involve enlarging them at considerable extra cost (in violation of the SALT agreements); at the same time, Soviet warhead accuracy (and MIRV technology) has improved and "more than [made] up for silo hardening."[46] Strengthening silos has only led to an escalation of efforts to make them more vulnerable. Christy Campbell points out that "it is possible, given the CEP, the overpressure yield at impact, the reliability factor, and the estimated 'hardness of the target,' swiftly to calculate the amount of force necessary to smash the enemy's fixed-site weapons (their positions known and precision mapped by satellite)."[47] Thus, many observers now believe that both superpowers would be better off limiting their land-based missiles, and concentrating on other missile delivery systems that are inherently less vulnerable.

Monitoring Devices (200)

The equipment or means by which states can determine the violation of agreements, the disposition of enemy forces, the development of new weapons systems, the long- or short-term intentions of the enemy, and any other appropriate needs. Monitoring is dependent on ready access to data that can give accurate readings, and may include: spy satellites, on-site verification, electronic eavesdropping, seismometers, radar, surveillance aircraft, espionage, the perusing of published documents, and other measures or devices. *See also* ANTISATELLITE SYSTEMS (ASAT), 111; ARMS CONTROL AND DISARMAMENT, 238; NATIONAL TECHNICAL MEANS (NTM), 253; SPY SATELLITE WARFARE, 138.

Significance An essential part of nuclear strategy is the ability of one side to determine what its opponents are doing, a fact that has made monitoring devices necessary to modern states. Further, as Jack C. Plano and Roy Olton point out, "Inspection is a key ingredient of any disarmament agreement because the security of each participant depends on the compliance of all to the terms of the accord."[48] Beginning with the Limited Test Ban Treaty (1963), most such documents have required verification by "national technical means" (i.e., external verification). The INF treaty of 1987 departs from this pattern to allow on-site verification by both sides. Both the Soviets and the Americans conduct widespread surveillance activities on each other and on both sides' client states; the Soviets are believed to have upgraded their armed forces over the past two decades by (in part) stealing or buying Western military advances and secrets. "Monitoring military budgets to verify arms-control agreements has been suggested since the Hague Peace Conference of 1899. The Soviet Union advanced more than 20 such proposals between 1948 and 1977, but in all instances means of verification were either unspecified or were so vague as to be unacceptable to the West."[49] This was reiterated by President Ronald W. Reagan in his 1987 summit with General Secretary Mikhail Gorbachev, where he continually reiterated, "Trust—but verify!" In a world where trust is a commodity in short supply, monitoring will continue, with or without disarmament agreements, for the indefinite future.

National Emergency Airborne Command Post (201)
(NEACP)

The always-airborne Boeing 747 jet operated by SAC (Strategic Air Command) together with "Looking Glass" to provide command, control, and communication (C3) functions in times of national crisis. NEACP provides the National Command Authorities and the commander in chief of the Strategic Air Command with a "survivable airborne command-and-control system that will operate during the pre-, trans- and post-attack phases of a nuclear war. As a survivable emergency extension of . . . ground control centers, the E-4B Airborne Command Post provides high confidence in U.S. ability to execute and control [enemy] forces in a nuclear environment."[50] *See also* COMMAND, CONTROL, AND COMMUNICATION (C3), 185; EMERGENCY ACTION MESSAGES (EAM), 191; JOINT CHIEFS OF STAFF, 197; WHITE HOUSE SITUATION ROOM, 209.

Significance Survivable command posts such as NEACP and "Looking Glass" are central to the C3 strategic system, and must be capable of "withstand[ing] attack and continu[ing] to support decision making and control of our strategic forces." Former Secretary of Defense Caspar Weinberger, in his annual report to the Congress (1985), stated that although "fixed command centers are our most capable command and control assets in peacetime, during crises, and in the early stages of a nuclear attack . . . our airborne command centers . . . are more likely to survive a nuclear attack."[51] Critics have questioned, however, whether any airborne system can survive the electromagnetic nuclear pulse that the Soviets would undoubtedly deliberately attempt to generate at the beginning of a first-strike attack. It is entirely possible that NEACP and other similar measures are no more than an exercise in ultimate futility.

Nuclear Planning Group (NPG) (202)

A council under the direction of the North Atlantic Treaty Organization that concerns itself with questions pertaining to nuclear defense. The NPG was organized "in 1963 as NATO's nuclear elite, and includes all member nations of NATO in its councils."[52] The Nuclear Planning Group is primarily concerned with NATO's nuclear defense strategy, and the stockpiling of U.S. nuclear weapons in Europe. In October 1977, the NPG "set up a working . . . High Level Group (HLG) to study the problem of Theatre Nuclear Force (TNF) modernization."[53] *See also* DEEP STRIKE, 189; JOINT CHIEFS OF STAFF, 197.

Significance The United States has used the Nuclear Planning Group to create its own agenda for the nuclear defense of Western Europe. By February 1978, the HLG arm of the NPG was focusing primarily on long-range TNF "rather than the whole spectrum of theater nuclear weapons. . . . They were not . . . seen in a war-fighting context but rather as being essential for linkage to the U.S. strategic deterrent."[54] Christy Campbell adds, "In contrast to the U.S., few Europeans have actually been involved in [defense policymaking]. . . .

Faced with a nuclear inventory fast approaching obsolescence and the build-up of Soviet power, this small circle of planners urged their political clients to embrace the latest products of American technology."[55] The proprietary nature of such decisions, with European states being forced to buy expensive, complicated, and sometimes unworkable military equipment manufactured only by U.S. vendors, has caused a great deal of resentment among the NATO allies, who look upon their role as primarily defensive, and who dislike being pushed toward blatantly offensive roles.

Probability of Kill (PK)   (203)

The likelihood that any particular warhead will destroy its target, as determined by a series of complicated mathematical formulae. PK "is the single-shot kill probability or the chance that a single warhead will destroy the target . . . and can be calculated from the target's lethal radius (LR), the warhead's accuracy in circular error probable (CEP) and the attacking missile's reliability (R)."[56] The chance of a target surviving an attack by one warhead (Ps) equals the kill probability subtracted from 1; the number of warheads attacking one target is the many-shot or n-shot kill probability (Pkn). James N. Constant lists the elements of single-shot kill probability as follows: Pl (launch); Pg (guidance); Pf (fuse action); Pw (detonation); Pd (damage). Probability may be increased by raising the accuracy of guidance, by increasing the lethal radius, or by increasing the number of warheads, or all three.[57] *See also* CIRCULAR ERROR PROBABLE (CEP), 182; DAMAGE ASSESSMENT, 188; FIRST STRIKE, 194; MISSILE SILOS, 199; RETALIATORY STRIKE, 204; SURVIVABILITY, 205.

Significance   Increasing kill probability is something both superpowers have striven for, particularly in recent decades; the extent to which one is able to increase such probability also increases the likelihood of attempting a knockout first strike. One reason that no such strike has been tried by either superpower is the problem of fratricide, or the accidental detonation or disruption of one warhead by another. Christy Campbell states that "in theory, a one-warhead–one-target relationship would be the counterforce 'ideal' as there would be no need to increase kill probability by sending more than one warhead to any target. . . . This overlooks the reliability problem, however, since nothing would be accomplished if the warhead failed to arrive or to detonate."[58] Complicating the reliability problem is the potential impact of the electromagnetic pulse generated by the explosion of other warheads nearby. Such uncertainties have made any realistic determination of kill probability very difficult. Without a reliable gauge of PK, the chances of a precipitous nuclear strike remain remote.

Retaliatory Strike (204)

A nuclear attack made in retaliation to a first or preemptive strike. Counterforce or retaliatory capability is measured by one's command, control, and communication protection, the vulnerability of one's military forces, and the will of one's government and people to seek a meaningless revenge. *See also* COMMAND, CONTROL, AND COMMUNICATION (C3), 185; FIRST STRIKE, 194; MISSILE SILOS, 199; SURVIVABILITY, 205.

Significance The entire superpower balance of power is based on the theory that either side could survive a knockout first strike with sufficient resources remaining to launch a retaliatory strike that would destroy the aggressor. George H. Quester states, for example, that deterrence "would cease to exist, if either side could use its military forces so effectively as to preclude second-strike retaliation by the enemy's nuclear forces."[59] The United States possesses a triad of forces that are "designed to maintain a major retaliatory capability [with] a high degree of confidence that the assured destruction mission could be carried out."[60] These forces are protected through a variety of means, including hardened silos, wide-ranging nuclear missile submarines, low-flying cruise missiles, electronic camouflaging techniques, antiballistic missiles, and other technologies. The nuclear winter scenario has increased the likelihood that even a first strike would create serious problems for an aggressor state, with a retaliatory strike merely adding to widespread ecological damage in the Northern hemisphere; scientists have speculated that the detonation of only a hundred warheads could initiate a nuclear winter sequence, perhaps causing the extinction of all higher forms of life if both superpowers used their entire arsenals.

Survivability (205)

The ability of a nation's defense systems to withstand an attack. Survivability is one of the key elements of counterdeterrent strategy. Samuel P. Huntington tells us that "the ability of a country to use its nuclear forces for extended deterrence purposes depends upon its own vulnerability to a nuclear response"[61]—in other words, how well it can absorb the damage from a knockout first strike, maintaining its capability to respond with a retaliatory strike of its own. *See also* DAMAGE ASSESSMENT, 188; DENSE PACK, 190; FIRST STRIKE, 194; PROBABILITY OF KILL (PK), 203; RETALIATORY STRIKE, 204.

Arms Control, Disarmament, and Military Security

Significance   The survivability of U.S. nuclear forces, particularly its land-based ICBMs, has been debated vociferously over the last two decades. Scientists such as Carl Sagan have termed the entire debate meaningless, contending that even a minimal nuclear exchange or first strike would cause irreparable damage to the entire world ecosphere, particularly in the Northern hemisphere. Congress and the president, on the other hand, have taken the view that the U.S. nuclear arsenal has prevented a World War III, and that, pending a verifiable arms control agreement, the United States must do everything in its power to protect the missiles it already has. The issue of survivability came to a head with the debate over the MX missile. By 1983, the Scowcroft Commission had determined that the "window of vulnerability" affected primarily the land-based missile system, and recommended "long-term emphasis on more survivable and more stable strategic forces, featuring the development of a new, much smaller single-warhead ICBM [the Minuteman]."[62] The debate is likely to continue until (or unless) land-based ICBMs are phased out.

Survivalist Movement   **(206)**
A confluence of U.S. grass-roots organizations and individuals who believe a Soviet nuclear attack on the United States is both inevitable and survivable, and that one must make preparations for that day. The survivalist movement arose spontaneously in the 1970s as an outgrowth of the disillusionment many Americans felt over the Vietnam War, the Watergate scandal, and the increase in the nuclear arsenals of both superpowers. Well-meaning individuals in the United States moved to remote areas of the country, often in the Pacific Northwest, and began accumulating food, water, firearms, and medicines. Others joined extreme right-wing political or religious organizations such as the Posse Comitatus and The Order, which believe in a neo-Nazi philosophy of survival of the fittest, and extermination of liberals, Jews, Blacks, Roman Catholics, and other minorities. *See also* CIVIL DEFENSE, 183; SURVIVABILITY, 205.

Significance   The survivalist movement has romanticized the idea of nuclear conflict and its aftermath, and ignored scientific evidence that nuclear winter would either make survival impossible, or reduce life to such marginal levels that no one would want to live in such a world. The survivalists tie into such basic U.S. myths as the struggle for the Western frontier, the defense of oneself and one's family against savages and the elements, and the stopping of the Communist menace. To these the neo-Nazis would add a fourth, the

240

purity of the white race. Such themes can be seen in the several dozen survivalist novels published in the 1980s (exemplified by Jerry Ahern's 15-volume *The Survivalist* series), in films such as *Red Dawn*, and in *The Turner Diaries*, the propagandistic bible of the extremist groups. Legitimate organizations such as the Mormon church have long promoted the storage of food, water, and other supplies in case of local or national emergencies. These reasonable and praiseworthy activities have been twisted by some into a philosophy of hate and paranoia, and the actions of such militaristic groups have caused grave concern to law-enforcement officials and civil libertarians alike.

War Games (207)

Scenarios devised by military strategists to predict the outcome of armed conflict, including nuclear war. War games are a logical outgrowth of game theory, which places each participant or player in situations of conflict and competition where they must use decision strategies to maximize gains and minimize losses. Through the use of such activities, one can practice basic elements of strategy, troop deployment, and military conflict, and test an opponent's will, ability, and forces, in a series of fictitious engagements that can explore alternatives to each created scenario. The popularity of such devices can be seen in the board games which companies such as Avalon Hill began producing in the late 1950s, each of which simulated a real-life battle (for example, the 1944 Allied invasion of Europe) for thousands of avid fans; by the 1980s, these scenarios had been developed into computer games. Similarly, military strategists have used both mathematical equations (e.g., circular error probable and probability of kill) and simulated battlefield scenarios to test theories, new ideas, and possible responses and outcomes in both board and computer simulations. *See also* AIRLAND BATTLE (ALB), 180; CIRCULAR ERROR PROBABLE (CEP), 182; DEEP STRIKE, 189; EMERGING TECHNOLOGIES INITIATIVE (ETI), 192; FOLLOW-ON-FORCES ATTACK (FOFA), 195; PROBABILITY OF KILL (PK), 203.

Significance   War games allow military planners to test scenarios that cannot actually be played out in real life without causing a nuclear holocaust. As James N. Constant states, "The task of game theory is to (1) discover the rules of the game, and (2) apply these rules to the prediction of the game outcome.... [A] cardinal objective ... is to destroy [the] opponent while . . . minimizing side effects and retaliation possibilities.... [Two key factors are the adversary's] ability and motivation to play the game. . . . The game ends when one or both adversaries accept the futility of any further play."[63] A 1985 conference at the Naval War College in Rhode Island, to discuss "the role of conflict termination as it applies to U.S. military strategy formulation," concluded that "nothing is certain in war, and particularly nothing is certain when operational plans are constructed for the full range of possible alternative conflict scenarios which, hopefully, will never occur. As a result, assumptions are a necessary evil for developing plans and alternative strategies. The point is that viable military plans and strategies must be built on realistic assumptions."[64] Other observers, however, believe that the military establishment has based major strategic decisions on war-game scenarios without regard to, or knowledge of, the real-life political needs of either the United States or the world as a whole. Other critics have pointed out the desensitizing nature of such games and the fantasies they create, and the possibility that some of those who play them will come to look at real-life developments as just another series of scenarios. To disregard, for example, the nuclear winter possibility, while simultaneously developing stratagems for winning an atomic war, strikes many observers as the height of irrationality, a disregard of basic scientific facts.

War of Attrition (208)

A conflict in which both sides overrate their own capabilities, and seek to wear down each other by causing as much damage as possible to the opponent's military capabilities. The war of attrition, or "tug-of-war" as it is known in strategical parlance, "most closely resembles a game of 'chicken,' wherein young men drive automobiles directly at each other to see who will be the first to veer off the collision course. The major difference . . . is that the material costs of the 'war' are not borne minute by minute, but are to be found in the continually increasing risk of disaster."[65] Edward N. Luttwak describes pure attrition as "only techniques and tactics, and there is no action at all at the operational level. All that remains are routinized techniques . . . to bring firepower-producing forces within range of the most conveniently targetable aggregations of enemy forces."[66] *See also* AIRLAND BATTLE (ALB), 180; DEEP STRIKE, 189; EMERGING TECHNOLOGIES INITIATIVE (ETI), 192; FOLLOW-ON-FORCES ATTACK (FOFA), 195.

Significance   The NATO strategy of forward defense is "designed to engage the attacking Warsaw Pact forces in large-scale battles of attrition along the inter-German border."[67] Critics have pointed out that adopting such tactics is foolhardy in light of the enemy's suspected superiority in firepower, and "virtually guarantees defeat."[68] The U.S. advocacy of a deep-strike strategy, the implementation of operational (as opposed to attritional) maneuvers keyed to the enemy's perceived weaknesses, was prompted by perceived weaknesses in NATO's purely defensive stance, and has caused much controversy and debate among the United States' European allies.

White House Situation Room (209)

The basement headquarters in the White House where the president conducts command-and-control operations. The Situation Room "since President Kennedy's time . . . has been equipped to receive all important traffic and can communicate directly to virtually all points,"[69] including U.S. strategic nuclear forces and the Soviet Union, through several "hot lines." *See also* COMMAND, CONTROL, AND COMMUNICATION (C3), 185; EMERGENCY ACTION MESSAGES (EAM), 191; JOINT CHIEFS OF STAFF, 197; NATIONAL EMERGENCY AIRBORNE COMMAND POST (NEACP), 201.

Significance   The White House Situation Room is a vital link in the command-and-control network. At all times the president has access to the latest data from the various warning systems, and may, in turn, send his own orders and requests directly to such command centers as the National Military Command Center (NMCC) (located in the Pentagon), and to the Strategic Air Command, which controls the always-airborne command posts, NEACP and "Looking Glass." In an emergency situation, the president would retreat first to the Situation Room, and secondly via helicopter to Camp David or one of the air command planes. Should he fail to escape the Situation Room (an increasingly likely possibility with short-range, submarine-launched missiles), command would fall to his constitutional successors (in order, the vice-president, speaker of the House of Representatives, president pro tempore of the Senate, and the cabinet officers, in descending order by seniority of creation of the department).

8. Nuclear Proliferation

Atomic Energy Act of 1946 (210)

An act of the U.S. Congress that established the Atomic Energy Commission and banned the dissemination of information on nuclear weapons and technology. In a reaction to the development and use of nuclear weapons by the Manhattan Project during World War II, Congress attempted to regularize the conduct of nuclear experimentation and weapons production with the Atomic Energy Act of 1946. The law established the Atomic Energy Commission (AEC) as a semi-independent body under the aegis of five civilian commissioners; the AEC was given control of atomic bomb development and production, and was empowered to conduct or monitor research on the peaceful uses of nuclear energy. The act also restricted dissemination of information on atomic technology, banning both its export to other countries and its use for peaceful purposes by commercial enterprises.[1] *See also* ATOMIC ENERGY COMMISSION (AEC), 211; ATOMS FOR PEACE PROPOSAL, 212; BARUCH PLAN, 213; EUROPEAN ATOMIC ENERGY COMMUNITY (EURATOM), 216; INTERNATIONAL ATOMIC ENERGY AGENCY (IAEA), 219; NONPROLIFERATION, 225; NUCLEAR POWER PLANTS, 230; NUCLEAR PROLIFERATION, 231.

Significance The Atomic Energy Act of 1946 represented the first attempt to restrict the spread of atomic weapons, by the only government that then had them. By 1953, both the Soviet Union and Britain had exploded their first bombs, and it became obvious to the new U.S. government of President Dwight D. Eisenhower that the act had failed. This prompted the Atoms for Peace initiative in December of that year, by which the United States proposed to share its technology with other countries for peaceful purposes only; and the Atomic

Energy Act of 1954, which revised the AEC's charge to allow the development of commercial nuclear power plants.

Atomic Energy Commission (AEC) (211)

An agency of the U.S. government that regulated the development of nuclear energy between 1946 and 1975. The Atomic Energy Commission was established by the Atomic Energy Act of 1946, in an attempt by Congress to impose civilian control over the Manhattan Project, the secret wartime effort of the United States to build a nuclear bomb. The act created a semi-independent agency governed by five civilian commissioners appointed by the president, with congressional oversight by the Joint Committee on Atomic Energy. The commission would manage the development and production of nuclear weapons, and maintain the government monopoly on atomic facilities, fissionable materials, and nuclear research. The act also banned the dissemination of information on nuclear power technology (amended by the McMahon Act in 1954 to further the Atoms for Peace plan), and charged the agency to develop proposals on the free exchange of scientific information and the control of nuclear technology for peaceful purposes only, on the elimination of nuclear weapons, and on the creation of effective international inspection procedures to ensure compliance by other nations. The Atomic Energy Act of 1954 amended the original legislation to permit the building of privately controlled nuclear power plants for peaceful uses, under license from the AEC. The government could now sell fissionable material to private licensees.[2] The Price-Anderson Act of 1957 removed an obstacle to the operation of such facilities by limiting the insurance liability of the industry in the event of an accident, with the U.S. government underwriting the difference. The AEC was split in 1975 into two new agencies that reflected its developmental and regulatory roles: the Energy Research and Development Administration (ERDA, later to become the Department of Energy), and the Nuclear Regulatory Commission (NRC). *See also* ATOMIC ENERGY ACT OF 1946, 210; ATOMS FOR PEACE PROPOSAL, 212; BARUCH PLAN, 213; NONPROLIFERATION, 225; NUCLEAR POWER PLANTS, 230; NUCLEAR PROLIFERATION, 231; NUCLEAR REGULATORY COMMISSION (NRC), 232.

Significance   The Atomic Energy Commission was conceived as one means of transferring control over the development of nuclear energy in the United States from the military, which had secretly constructed the nation's first atomic weapons, to a presumably more benign civilian body; it also was charged with maintaining U.S. monopoly over nuclear energy and weapons technology, and with preventing other nations from building atomic bombs. In fact, the agency was never able to reconcile its seemingly contradictory aims of building atomic weapons while simultaneously trying to restrict their spread, and later of promoting atomic power while regulating the nascent nuclear power industry. The 1954 act admitted the failure of the containment policy of the United States, and changed the agency's focus to more domestic concerns. Curiously, the act contains 31 references to the "health and safety of the public," but not one statement in either the law or the discussions surrounding it as to what those safety measures should be. "Nobody really ever thought that safety was a problem. They assumed that if you just wrote the requirement into the Act that it be done properly, [then] it would be done properly."[3] That the agency had allowed gross safety violations in the construction of some plants became evident with a series of accidents during the 1970s and 1980s, particularly at Browns Ferry (1975) and Three Mile Island (1979). These mishaps, combined with the Soviet Chernobyl disaster (1986) and continuing cost overruns, forced the nuclear power plant industry to cancel most new construction projects, and put pressure on the NRC, the AEC's regulatory successor, to "get tough" on safety violations.

Atoms for Peace Proposal (1953)   (212)
A program to share U.S. nuclear power plant technology with other nations of the world. The Atoms for Peace plan was proposed by U.S. President Dwight D. Eisenhower in December 1953, to the United Nations General Assembly, when it became obvious that the provisions of the Atomic Energy Act of 1946 had failed to stop other nations from developing nuclear weapons. The plan lifted "the U.S. moratorium on atomic cooperation with other states. In return for sharing U.S. know-how, the beneficiary states would have to undertake not to divert any assistance received towards military ends. This obligation was to be made verifiable by a system of safeguards, including on-site inspection by international officials."[4] President Eisenhower's proposal led in 1956 to the establishment of the United Nations International Atomic Energy Agency (IAEA), to monitor the use of fissile materials for peaceful purposes; similarly, the United States, following passage of the McMahon Act in 1954, began concluding agreements with other states that allowed the United States to inspect civilian nuclear power sites in those countries. See also ATOMIC ENERGY ACT OF 1946, 210; BARUCH PLAN, 213; EUROPEAN ATOMIC ENERGY COMMUNITY (EURATOM), 216; INTERNATIONAL ATOMIC ENERGY AGENCY (IAEA), 219; NUCLEAR SUPPLIERS GROUP (NSG), 233; THRESHOLD NUCLEAR POWERS, 236.

Significance   Atoms for Peace represented the United States' realization that the atomic genie had escaped its bottle, and could never again be replaced. The Atomic Energy Act of 1946 had banned the dissemination of information on nuclear technology. Now, the AEC and the Eisenhower administration would assist nations in constructing nuclear power plants, provided they in turn would agree to on-site inspections to ensure that the materials were not being used for military purposes. This "represented the first successful major effort to subject undertakings among nations to verification by outside authorities in place of the historic reliance on the good faith of each nation."[5] Nothing in the program prevented beneficiary states from building a nuclear weapons program on their own, so long as "it was carried out in installations and with materials wholly distinct from those provided by the U.S.,"[6] although few countries have taken advantage of this loophole. The IAEA, established by the United Nations in 1956 to monitor the use and transportation of fissionable materials, has proved an effective watchdog agency in Europe and elsewhere.

Baruch Plan (1946) (213)

A proposal by U.S. statesman Bernard Baruch to achieve international nuclear disarmament. One of the initial charges made by the Atomic Energy Act of 1946 to the newly formed Atomic Energy Commission was the drawing up of a plan for the elimination of nuclear weapons in the world. Subsequently, Bernard Baruch proposed to the AEC in June of 1946 that an international atomic energy agency be created, with the authority to monitor all forms of nuclear technology development; upon erection of the agency, the United States would destroy its atomic bombs, the only such stock then extant. The Soviet Union, which had already begun work on a bomb of its own, responded with proposals demanding the destruction of all existing nuclear weapons before negotiations commenced, with self-regulation by the individual states. Negotiations broke off in 1948. *See also* ATOMIC ENERGY ACT OF 1946, 210; ATOMIC ENERGY COMMISSION (AEC), 211; INTERNATIONAL ATOMIC ENERGY AGENCY (IAEA), 219; NONPROLIFERATION, 225; NUCLEAR PROLIFERATION, 231.

Significance   According to Joseph Kruzel, "the real problem with the Baruch Plan was not the mechanism of control or the mode of inspection, but the fact that it proposed much more than arms limitation. [It] was a scheme for limited world government."[7] It also provided for on-site inspection by an international agency presumably influenced by the United States, something the Soviets had never allowed historically, and would not allow until the 1987 Intermediate-Range Nuclear Forces (INF) Treaty. Consequently, despite its good intentions, the plan never had any real chance for success.

Breeder Reactors (214)

Reactors that produce more nuclear fuel than they consume. The Fermi breeder reactor, proposed to the AEC in 1955 as a solution to the United States' projected uranium shortage, was to be fueled with uranium and plutonium, arranged in such a way that an excess of neutrons produced by fission would enrich the uranium surrounding the core, thereby converting some of this fuel to plutonium. The net result would be a sort of nuclear perpetual motion machine, in which the spent uranium fuel would generate extra plutonium that could be recycled into nuclear bombs and other power plants, *ad infinitum*. *See also* INTERNATIONAL NUCLEAR FUEL CYCLE EVALUATION (INFCE), 220; NUCLEAR POWER PLANTS, 230.

Significance   Given the finite amount of uranium ore available to the United States and other world powers, breeder reactors are considered essential to the production of nuclear warheads, as well as the long-term continuance of the nuclear power industry. They also pose significantly higher operational risks, including the possibility of sodium explosions in reactor cores during certain kinds of accidents (the 1986 nonnuclear steam explosion at the Soviet Chernobyl facility breached the plant's containment walls, scattering radioactive material as far as Western Europe). A potentially greater hazard is the availability of plutonium and enriched uranium to those who might be able to use them to construct makeshift atomic bombs. Most "burner" reactors use a particular kind of uranium, and produce an isotope of plutonium, which cannot easily be converted to weapons use without highly sophisticated enrichment facilities, now limited to the major nuclear powers; should these facilities become commonplace, particularly in unstable parts of the world, the threat of nuclear terrorism could very well become a terrifying reality.

British Labour Party Manifestos (215)
on Nuclear Weapons

A series of official policy statements from one of Britain's major political parties advocating unilateral nuclear disarmament. Following the Labour Party's disastrous electoral defeat in 1979, the party leadership was left in chaos, prompting an attempt by Labour's left wing to assume control. Although ultraleftist Tony Benn was defeated by Michael Foot for the party leadership, the leftists managed to force a series of manifestos through the party conferences of 1980–1982. These included planks that, if actually put into effect, would ban cruise missiles in Britain, scrap Britain's small Polaris submarine force, eliminate all U.S. military bases in Britain, and keep U.S. ships with nuclear weapons from docking at British ports. Labour's leaders toned down these policies during the 1983 election, but were accused by Prime Minister Margaret Thatcher of potentially leaving Britain defenseless. The ensuing Labour defeat was the worst electoral showing of any British party in 30 years. Neil Kinnock, who succeeded Foot in 1983, also ran on a nonnuclear plank in the 1987 elections, with modifications that would allow continued British membership in NATO, and the retention of nonnuclear U.S. bases on British soil. Labour again lost. *See also* GREEN PARTY MOVEMENT, 217; NEW ZEALAND'S ANZUS WITHDRAWAL, 224; NUCLEAR FREEZE MOVEMENT, 227; NUCLEAR-FREE ZONES (NFZ), 228.

Significance   The British Labour Party manifestos on nuclear weapons represent the first time a major political party from the nuclear powers has proposed the unilateral nuclear disarmament of its own atomic forces, and the banning of U.S. or NATO nuclear weapons from its soil. Labour's 1983 election platform stated: "This means the rejection of any fresh nuclear bases or weapons on British soil or in British waters, and the removal of all existing nuclear bases and weapons, thus enabling us to make a direct contribution to an eventually much wider nuclear-free zone in Europe. We will propose that Britain's Polaris force be included in the nuclear disarmament negotiations in which Britain must take part. We will, after consultation, carry through in the lifetime of the next parliament our nonnuclear defence policy."[8] The loss of British bases would be a severe blow to the United States' (and NATO's) European defense strategy; thus, despite Labour's lack of success in three recent elections, the possibility of a future Labour victory must be viewed seriously by Western military planners as a potential disaster in long-term U.S.-British relations, and as symptomatic of a general trend among socialist-oriented parties in the West toward promoting a nuclear-free Europe.

European Atomic Energy Community (Euratom)   (216)

An association of European states to monitor and manage the development of nuclear power in the European Economic Community. Euratom was created in tandem with the EEC in 1955 as a European counterpart to the U.S. Atomic Energy Commission. At the time of its founding, the Americans were pushing the Atoms for Peace program as a way of sharing its nuclear technology with the rest of the world, and Euratom was organized partially to develop nuclear power plants for an energy-poor Europe. As Louis Armand, its first president, stated: "The U.S. does not immediately need atomic energy, since it has abundant and cheap conventional energy. . . . In this case, why not set up in Europe a large complex of industrial nuclear power stations, making use of the experience already acquired in the U.S.?"[9] Ironically, Euratom built only three power stations, "but it did stimulate the European dialogue about nuclear power."[10] Later, under the Non-Proliferation Treaty (1968), Euratom was given the task of monitoring radioactive materials used by the EEC states, a function handled elsewhere by the International Atomic Energy Agency. *See also* ATOMIC ENERGY COMMISSION (AEC), 211; ATOMS FOR PEACE PROPOSAL, 212; INTERNATIONAL ATOMIC ENERGY AGENCY (IAEA), 219; NON-PROLIFERATION TREATY (NPT), 226.

Significance   Euratom began life as a promoter and developer of atomic energy, but its role changed markedly with the Non-Proliferation Treaty. Under this agreement, the "problem of controlling the use of radioactive materials was assumed by the International Atomic Energy Agency in Vienna, and by Euratom for the European Community. This, of course, involves on-site inspection."[11] Prior to this time, Euratom had, like its U.S. counterpart, the Atomic Energy Commission, regulated the nuclear power industry in Europe, but now its role was expanded to provide safeguards and accountings of all nuclear materials used throughout the EEC. This role was expanded under the Nuclear Materials Convention (1981).

Green Party Movement (217)

A loose group of political parties in Western Europe that share a pro-environment and antinuclear philosophy. The Greens (*Die Grünen*) arose from a confluence of environmental movements in West Germany. Herbert Gruhl, a member of the German parliament for the Christian Democrats, resigned his seat in 1978, and formed the Green Action Future, proclaiming "We are neither the left nor right; we are in front."[12] The Greens' initial effort to win seats in the German state legislatures failed, but in March of 1979, the party held a founding convention in Frankfurt, approving a platform with two major planks: a nuclear-free Europe (including the elimination of atomic power plants), and a decentralization of European governments into regional groups.[13] In 1979, they elected representatives to the European Parliament, and by 1983 had secured representation in the German parliament. Since then Green parties have sprung up in Belgium, the Netherlands, and most other European countries, and in British Columbia, Australia, and Japan. *See also* BRITISH LABOUR PARTY MANIFESTOS ON NUCLEAR WEAPONS, 215; LATIN AMERICAN NUCLEAR-FREE ZONE TREATY, 223; NUCLEAR FREEZE MOVEMENT, 227; NUCLEAR-FREE ZONES (NFZ), 228; SOUTH PACIFIC NUCLEAR-FREE ZONE TREATY, 235.

Significance   The Greens were initially discounted by many observers as a political force, but soon proved that their pro-environment and antinuclear stances had touched deep reservoirs of feeling in the German people. Their presence in the German parliament gave them a very vocal platform for their antinuclear views, ideas that became increasingly popular in Europe in the 1980s, particularly when Soviet General Secretary Mikhail Gorbachev began moving the Russian state away from nuclear confrontation in 1985. The Greens support unilateral nuclear disarmament, a European nuclear-free zone, and the banning of atomic power plants on the continent. Unfortunately, the party itself consists of so many different factions and subdivisions that it has consistently failed to agree on any long-term political strategies or clearly defined goals, other than nuclear disarmament and protection of the environment. It thus seems doomed by its own factiousness to forever remain a minority force in German politics.

Indian Nuclear Test (1974) (218)

An underground atomic explosion conducted by India, ostensibly for "peaceful purposes." In December of 1971, Pakistan attacked India in the latest of a long series of conflicts that had begun in 1947. India quickly established its superiority by conquering East Pakistan, which declared its independence as Bangladesh. The United States sent a naval task force under the USS *Enterprise* into the Bay of Bengal to demonstrate its support for Pakistan. As Eliot A. Cohen states, "One cannot overemphasize the intensity of the bitter Indian reaction to the *Enterprise* affair. . . . It had a major impact on military thinking . . . and is remembered as a humiliating experience, all the more so because it occurred at just the moment of India's greatest military-political triumph."[14] Subsequently, India decided to expand its military and naval forces, and conducted its first (and only) underground nuclear explosion in May of 1974. It has consistently declined to sign the Non-Proliferation Treaty. *See also* NONPROLIFERATION, 225; NONPROLIFERATION TREATY (NPT), 226; NUCLEAR PROLIFERATION, 231; NUCLEAR SUPPLIERS GROUP (NSG), 233.

Significance   The explosion of India's first atomic bomb, in 1974, shocked the world, especially since the late Prime Minister Jawaharlal Nehru had been among the first of world leaders to call (two decades earlier) for the abolition of nuclear weapons. India's intransigence in refusing to sign the Non-Proliferation Treaty (NPT) is due both to its long-running conflicts with the people's Republic of China and Pakistan (the People's Republic of China has the bomb, while Pakistan is considered a threshold nation), and to its own posturing as the pre-eminent military power in the Indian Ocean. India continues to insist that its nuclear research is for peaceful purposes only, while protesting that the NPT legitimizes "nuclear weapons and their monopoly by those nations that [have] already developed them."[15] However, "Pakistan's unwillingness to join the NPT has less to do with threats to its national security from an existing nuclear weapon power than with fears of the nuclear weapon potential of India—its principal adversary," despite its "sympathetic attitude in the late 1960s towards international efforts to check the proliferation of nuclear weapons."[16] The Indian test prompted formation of the Nuclear Suppliers Group.

International Atomic Energy Agency (IAEA)   (219)

An independent agency of the United Nations that monitors both the development of nuclear energy for peaceful purposes and compliance with the Non-Proliferation Treaty (NPT). The International Atomic Energy Agency grew from U.S. President Dwight D. Eisenhower's 1953 proposal to the U.N. General Assembly for an "Atoms for Peace" plan, by which the United States would share its nuclear technology with other countries. The Statute of the International Atomic Energy Agency, signed on October 26, 1956, stated that the agency "is authorized to establish and administer safeguards designed to ensure that special fissionable and other materials, services, equipment, facilities, and information made available by the Agency . . . are not used in such a way as to further any military purpose" (Article III).[17] It was also charged with assisting the research and development of atomic energy for peaceful purposes, with helping underdeveloped parts of the world to obtain nuclear power plants, with encouraging scientific exchanges, and with establishing safety standards. Under the Non-Proliferation Treaty of 1968, IAEA became the primary agency monitoring (and assisting with) compliance. *See also* ATOMIC ENERGY ACT OF 1946, 210; ATOMIC ENERGY COMMISSION (AEC), 211; ATOMS FOR PEACE PROPOSAL, 212; EUROPEAN ATOMIC ENERGY COMMUNITY (EURATOM), 216; NON-PROLIFERATION TREATY (NPT), 226; NUCLEAR POWER PLANTS, 230; NUCLEAR SUPPLIERS GROUP (NSG), 233.

Significance   The International Atomic Energy Agency has assumed an increasingly large role in the safeguarding of nuclear materials worldwide, particularly after 1963, when the Soviet Union dropped its opposition to the idea. "Thereafter, the safeguards responsibilities of the supplier states under existing bilateral agreements were tranferred to the IAEA . . . by means of 'safeguards transfer agreements.' Any bilateral agreement concluded since 1963 has invariably incorporated a standard provision according the IAEA responsibility for establishing and administering safeguards under the agreement."[18] The Non-Proliferation Treaty established IAEA as the primary agency to establish safeguards procedures with signatory states. "Non-nuclear weapon states [NNWS] undertook to conclude safeguards agreements with IAEA with a view to preventing the diversion of nuclear materials from peaceful uses to nuclear weapons or other nuclear explosive devices."[19] In this, according to Benjamin N. Schiff, "IAEA has succeeded. . . . The evidence shows that no state has diverted materials from a peaceful nuclear program under Agency safeguards into a military [one]."[20]

International Nuclear Fuel Cycle Evaluation (220) (INFCE) (1978–1980)

A study of nuclear power generation that sought to find ways to limit the possibility that commercial atomic fuel could be converted into nuclear weapons. The concern felt in international circles by the mid-1970s over the proliferation of enriched uranium and plutonium, both capable of being used to build atomic bombs, prompted the United States to pass the Nuclear Non-Proliferation Act of 1978, which limited exports of these materials. Simultaneously, U.S. President Jimmy Carter proposed the International Nuclear Fuel Cycle Evaluation (INFCE), "to devise means to minimize the proliferation of nuclear weapons without jeopardizing energy supplies or the development of atomic energy for peaceful purposes."[21] Forty countries participated in the two-year study, which completed its work in February of 1980. *See also* BREEDER REACTORS, 214; INTERNATIONAL ATOMIC ENERGY AGENCY (IAEA), 219; NONPROLIFERATION, 225; NON-PROLIFERATION TREATY (NPT), 226; NUCLEAR NON-PROLIFERATION ACT OF 1978 (NNPA), 229; NUCLEAR POWER PLANTS, 230; NUCLEAR PROLIFERATION, 231.

Significance   INFCE was designed "to buy time for Carter's diplomatic maneuvers . . . [and] would also focus the world's attention on the gravity of the proliferation problem and perhaps develop 'proliferation-resistant' fuel cycle technologies."[22] Its final report concluded that, "although certain measures could make misuse of the nuclear fuel cycle more difficult, there is no technical way to produce nuclear energy without at the same time producing fissile material usable for weapons."[23] In other words, while the reactor-grade plutonium derived from the spent fuel of reactor cores contains a mix of plutonium isotopes generally undesirable for the production of military weapons, it nonetheless can be converted to such uses with some difficulty, provided one has the technical facilities to do so. Limiting such technology, and the distribution of enriched uranium and plutonium, lies at the heart of any nonproliferation strategy.

Iraqi Nuclear Power Plant Raid (1981) (221)

The destruction of a commercial atomic energy plant in Iraq by Israeli jets, ostensibly to prevent Iraq from developing a nuclear weapons capability. Israeli warplanes struck the Osirak reactor near Baghdad on June 7, 1981, utterly destroying the main building. The power plant, being built with French technicians, was nearing completion, but had not yet been fueled with enriched uranium. One foreign worker was killed. The Iraqi reactor, Israel claimed, "was intended to produce atomic bombs for possible use against Israel."[24] Israeli Prime Minister Menachem Begin indicated that the raid had also destroyed a secret, underground nuclear weapons facility designed to shield the Iraqis from inspection by the International Atomic Energy Agency. The raid was condemned by most other nations, including the United States and the Soviet Union. *See also* INTERNATIONAL ATOMIC ENERGY AGENCY (IAEA), 219; ISRAELI NUCLEAR BOMB EXPOSÉ, 222; NONPROLIFERATION, 225; NON-PROLIFERATION TREATY (NPT), 226; NUCLEAR PROLIFERATION, 231.

Significance   The Iraqi nuclear plant raid "powerfully illustrated something American strategists had known for over three decades: that the worldwide proliferation of nuclear technology gravely endangered global peace and stability in general, and U.S. strategic interests in particular."[25] In the eyes of many experts, the possibility of a terrorist state or unstable ideological government using nuclear weapons against its perceived enemies is far greater than the use of such weapons by the superpowers against each other. "Israeli spokesmen [thus] argued that their action constituted a legitimate, albeit novel, application of the doctrine of anticipatory self-defence,"[26] although even Israel's allies disagreed publicly with this stance. Ironically, in the U.N. debate following the Israeli strike, "Iran complained that its nuclear facilities had been destroyed by the Iraqi Air Force, and insisted that this be explicitly stated" in any declaration adopted by the General Assembly.[27] Iraq rejected Iran's allegation.

Israeli Nuclear Bomb Exposé (1986–1988) (222)

The kidnapping and trial of a man who claimed to have worked at a secret Israeli atomic bomb factory. On September 30, 1986, Mordechai Vanunu, a former technician for Israel's atomic energy program, was kidnapped by Israeli intelligence agents from his London hotel room. Vanunu had just completed a widely publicized story for the London *Sunday Times*, in which he claimed that Israel had built "at least 100 A-bombs at a factory hidden beneath the Dimona nuclear research plant in the Negev Desert. Israel was also thought to have the ability and components to build advanced neutron and hydrogen weapons."[28] Israel denied the story, but many observers felt that Vanunu's abduction proved his allegations. Vanunu was prosecuted in 1987—and convicted in 1988—for disclosing state secrets; no outside observers or reporters were allowed at the trial. *See also* IRAQI NUCLEAR POWER PLANT RAID, 221; NONPROLIFERATION, 225; NON-PROLIFERATION TREATY (NPT), 226; NUCLEAR PROLIFERATION, 231.

Significance   Israel's nuclear spy scandal confirmed for many what the Central Intelligence Agency of the United States had already concluded in its 1974 document, "Prospects for Further Proliferation of Nuclear Weapons": that Israel had developed an atomic bomb. Its conclusions were based on "Israeli acquisition of large quantities of uranium, partly by clandestine means; the ambiguous nature of Israeli efforts in the field of uranium enrichment; and Israel's large investment in a costly missile system [the Jericho I] designed to accommodate nuclear warheads."[29] On July 21, 1987, the *International Defense Review* reported that Israel had tested a new intermediate-range missile, the Jericho II, with a range of 900 miles; U.S. specialists reported that "the new missile was designed specifically to carry a nuclear warhead."[30] The Soviet Union accused Israel of "trying to acquire a nuclear capability for intimidating its Arab neighbors."[31] Iraq and Libya, Israel's implacable enemies, both have been reported as actively seeking materials for construction of nuclear weapons.

Latin American Nuclear-Free Zone Treaty (1967)   (223)

An agreement to ban nuclear weapons in Latin America. The Treaty for the Prohibition of Nuclear Weapons in Latin America, also called the Treaty of Tlatelolco, was the first agreement to prohibit nuclear weapons in an inhabited area of the Earth. Following the 1962 Cuban missile crisis, the presidents of Brazil, Bolivia, Chile, Ecuador, and Mexico proposed a multilateral treaty to make Latin America (including Central America, South America, and the Caribbean) a nuclear weapons-free zone. Negotiations commenced at the Mexico City Conference (November 1965), and the treaty was signed on February 14, 1967. The signatories agreed to use nuclear material for peaceful purposes only, and to ban "the testing, use, manufacture, production or acquisition by any means whatsoever of nuclear weapons, by the Parties themselves, directly or indirectly, on behalf of anyone else or in any other way, and the receipt, storage, installation, deployment, and any form of possession of any nuclear weapons" (Article I).[32] Compliance would be verified by the "Agency for the Prohibition of Nuclear Weapons in Latin America," whose principal organs consist of a biennial general conference, a council of five members, and a secretariat. The signatories also agreed to negotiate agreements with the International Atomic Energy Agency to monitor safeguards in the handling of nuclear materials. *See also* INTERNATIONAL ATOMIC ENERGY AGENCY (IAEA), 219; NONPROLIFERATION, 225; NON-PROLIFERATION TREATY (NPT), 226; NUCLEAR-FREE ZONES (NFZ), 228; NUCLEAR PROLIFERATION, 231; SOUTH PACIFIC NUCLEAR-FREE ZONE TREATY, 235.

Significance　　The Latin American Nuclear-Free Zone Treaty contains a number of ambiguities, chief among them being the allowance of nuclear explosions for peaceful purposes and the inherent difficulty of determining when a nuclear device is being developed for peaceful or military purposes. Several protocols have extended the agreement's provisions to territories owned by outside states, including the United States, and to the nuclear weapon states, who by their signatures agree not to violate the treaty. Cuba refused to ratify the pact, while Argentina, Brazil, and Chile signed the treaty, but have failed technically to meet its requirements; the three latter states all have large nuclear power industries. Argentina and Brazil have also reserved the right to carry out nuclear explosions for peaceful purposes. The United States, Britain, and the Soviet Union have entered reservations "in the event of any act of aggression with the support of, or together with, a nuclear weapon state."[33] Still, even with these exceptions, the Latin American Nuclear-Free Zone Treaty remains a landmark agreement, one that was used as a pattern for the South Pacific Nuclear-Free Zone Treaty in 1985.

New Zealand's ANZUS Withdrawal (1985)　　　　(224)

The breakdown of a mutual defense treaty between Australia, New Zealand, and the United States (ANZUS) over New Zealand's refusal to allow ships carrying nuclear weapons to dock at its ports. In 1980 a grass-roots campaign to make New Zealand a nuclear-free zone began, and had attained such success by 1984 that it forced the ruling Conservative Party into premature elections. The Labour Party of David Lange contested the vote primarily on the nuclear issue, and won a large majority. The new prime minister immediately announced (July 1984) a ban "on nuclear weapons on New Zealand soil and in our harbours";[34] he then refused permission (February 4, 1985) for a U.S. warship to dock in New Zealand, after the Americans declined to certify that the ship was nuclear-free. The U.S. government "announced it would no longer share intelligence and surveillance information with its ANZUS partner."[35] On June 27, 1986, U.S. Secretary of State George Shultz stated that the United States would no longer promise to defend New Zealand, and on August 11, the United States officially suspended its treaty obligations under ANZUS. In 1987, the United States indicated that New Zealand's military forces no longer had priority access to U.S. arms or munitions, forcing the latter to raise its military budget by 18 percent in one year. *See also* BRITISH LABOUR PARTY MANIFESTOS ON NUCLEAR WEAPONS, 215; GREEN PARTY MOVEMENT, 217; NONPROLIFERATION, 225; NON-PROLIFERATION TREATY (NPT), 226; NUCLEAR FREEZE MOVEMENT, 227; NUCLEAR-FREE ZONES (NFZ), 228; SOUTH PACIFIC NUCLEAR-FREE ZONE TREATY, 235.

Significance   New Zealand's withdrawal from ANZUS represents the first instance where one of the Western allies of the United States has voluntarily withdrawn itself from the nuclear arms race. The United States immediately sought to punish New Zealand, first by abandoning joint military exercises, then by suspending treaty obligations, and, finally, by refusing to allow New Zealand to resupply its conventional forces from U.S. stocks, thus forcing that country to purchase its supplies in the more inflated world market. Lange responded by introducing a bill into the New Zealand parliament giving internal effect to the South Pacific Nuclear-Free Zone Treaty, specifically prohibiting future prime ministers from approving entry of foreign warships or aircraft into New Zealand territory unless they have been certified nuclear free.[36] The United States fears that the New Zealand example may prompt other states, particularly in Europe, to follow suit, thereby disrupting the strategic basis for the Western alliance. It may well be right.

Nonproliferation (225)

The limitation of nuclear weapons to those states that already have them. Efforts to halt the spread of the atomic bomb began shortly after World War II, with the 1946 proposal of Bernard Baruch to limit the spread of nuclear technology and destroy the remaining weapons in the U.S. nuclear arsenal. Baruch's proposal failed in 1948. The 1953 Atoms for Peace proposal of U.S. President Dwight D. Eisenhower led to the formation of the International Atomic Energy Agency (IAEA) in 1956. "The realization that the possession of nuclear weapons by many countries would increase the threat to world security led to the unanimous adoption, in 1961, of a U.N. General Assembly resolution calling on all states to conclude an international agreement to refrain from the transfer or acquisition of these weapons. This resolution formed the basis for the Non-Proliferation Treaty signed in 1968."[37] *See also* ATOMIC ENERGY ACT OF 1946, 210; ATOMS FOR PEACE PROPOSAL, 212; BARUCH PLAN, 213; INTERNATIONAL ATOMIC ENERGY AGENCY (IAEA), 219; NON-PROLIFERATION TREATY (NPT), 226; NUCLEAR FREEZE MOVEMENT, 227; NUCLEAR-FREE ZONES (NFZ), 228; NUCLEAR NON-PROLIFERATION ACT OF 1978 (NNPA), 229; NUCLEAR PROLIFERATION, 231; NUCLEAR SUPPLIERS GROUP (NSG), 233; THRESHOLD NUCLEAR POWERS, 236.

Significance   The nonproliferation of nuclear weapons is something virtually every country agrees with, but on which very little agreement was reached until the mid-1960s. By then "the two superpowers, while unable to agree on measures to curb the nuclear arms race, were united in their concern that nuclear weapons might spread beyond the five [now six] states with a proven nuclear weapons capability. The ability to pursue, whether overtly or covertly, an indigenous or other unsafeguarded route to the acquisition of nuclear weapons was now within the reach of a growing number of states."[38] The spread of commercial nuclear power plant technology has given many of these nations the ability to produce or acquire the enriched uranium necessary to construct an atomic bomb, making them threshold nuclear powers. As India demonstrated so convincingly in 1974, it is then a very small step actually to produce a working nuclear device.

Non-Proliferation Treaty (NPT) (1968)   (226)
An agreement to limit the spread of nuclear weapons. The Treaty on the Non-Proliferation of Nuclear Weapons, its official title, arose from a 1961 proposal in the U.N. General Assembly that established the Eighteen-Nation Disarmament Committee (ENDC) to begin negotiations on a nonproliferation pact. The talks proceeded slowly until the U.S. and Soviet representatives began private consultations in 1966. On August 24, 1967, both superpowers were able to submit identical texts to the ENDC; the General Assembly approved the treaty on June 12, 1968, and the major powers signed it on July 1. Signatories who already possess nuclear weapons agree "not to transfer to any other recipient whatsoever nuclear weapons or other nuclear explosive devices or control over such weapons, . . . and not to in any way assist . . . any non-nuclear-weapon state to manufacture or otherwise acquire nuclear weapons" (Article I); non-nuclear weapon states (NNWS) agree "not to receive the transfer . . . of nuclear

weapons or explosive devices directly or indirectly . . . [and] not to manufacture or otherwise acquire" such weapons (Article II).[39] The treaty further provides that the International Atomic Energy Agency shall establish and monitor a series of safeguards in the transportation and use of nuclear materials, and that NNW states must conclude separate implementation agreements with IAEA. *See also* ATOMIC ENERGY ACT OF 1946, 210; ATOMS FOR PEACE PROPOSAL, 212; BARUCH PLAN, 213; INTERNATIONAL ATOMIC ENERGY AGENCY (IAEA), 219; NONPROLIFERATION, 225; NUCLEAR PROLIFERATION, 231; NUCLEAR SUPPLIERS GROUP (NSG), 233; THRESHOLD NUCLEAR POWERS, 236.

Significance   The Non-Proliferation Treaty immediately created controversy when France, one of the Western nuclear powers, refused to sign it, although the French government has said it will abide by its terms. Other major states have also refused to sign, including India, which exploded a test device in 1974, its rival Pakistan, the People's Republic of China, Israel, and South Africa. Another controversial issue was created by Article VI of the agreement, which provides that "each of the Parties to the Treaty undertakes to pursue negotiations in good faith on effective measures relating to the cessation of the nuclear arms race at an early date and to nuclear disarmament, and on a treaty on general and complete disarmament under strict and international controls."[40] Both superpowers have pointed to the SALT, INF, and START negotiations as signs of their good faith; other nations, however, have questioned their sincerity. Critics have also noted that the treaty favors the status quo: "In renouncing the nuclear weapon option, the NNW states have assumed the main burden of obligation; the nuclear weapon states, in undertaking not to disseminate the weapons, have sacrificed little if anything: it would not be [in] their interests to encourage or permit the spread of nuclear weapons."[41] They also are not required to have their commercial nuclear activities regulated by the IAEA. With all these defects, however, the NPT still remains one theoretically limiting factor in the spread of nuclear weapons, surely a good thing in this most dangerous of ages.

Nuclear Freeze Movement   (227)
A grass-roots campaign to freeze the nuclear arsenals of the superpowers at their current levels, as an initial step toward arms control. The nuclear freeze movement arose spontaneously in the mid-1970s, in reaction to the continuous buildup of missiles and warheads in both the East and the West, and to the slow progress of arms-control and disarmament talks. The movement is composed of a wide variety of

unaffiliated groups, including religious bodies (the Roman Catholic Council of Bishops), environmental groups, political organizations (the Greens in Europe, the Committee for National Security and the Committee on the Present Danger in the United States), social, educational, and professional societies (Physicians for Social Responsibility, the Nuclear Freeze Campaign), and prominent individuals (e.g., Carl Sagan). These groups often do not share exactly the same programs or agenda, but all desire to freeze the production and deployment of nuclear arms, as a first step toward serious East-West negotiations on their reduction and ultimate eradication. *See also* BRITISH LABOUR PARTY MANIFESTOS ON NUCLEAR WEAPONS, 215; GREEN PARTY MOVEMENT, 217; NEW ZEALAND'S ANZUS WITHDRAWAL, 224; NONPROLIFERATION, 225; NON-PROLIFERATION TREATY (NPT), 226; NUCLEAR-FREE ZONES (NFZ), 228; NUCLEAR PROLIFERATION, 231.

Significance   The nuclear freeze movement is one aspect of a growing nongovernmental organization (NGO) campaign that is slowly but progressively affecting the thinking of political leaders and citizens alike, particularly in the West. The influence of the movement increased in the early 1980s, when new computer projections indicated that a nuclear war waged at even the most minimum levels of exchange would create a nuclear winter, thereby dooming survivors to starvation, ozone-layer depletion, ultraviolet radiation, disease, and probable extinction. The impact of the nuclear winter scenario, combined with the 1986 Soviet nuclear power plant disaster at Chernobyl, and growing scientific evidence that even very small levels of radiation can be harmful to human physiology, bolstered the movement's support, particularly at the local level. Beginning in 1981, local governmental authorities throughout the West began legislating "nuclear-free zones," banning the use, construction, or siting of nuclear weapons and power plants within their legal jurisdictions. Should the nuclear freeze movement continue to grow at its present rate, spontaneously, in slow but measurable increments, it will gradually exert almost unbearable pressure on the governments of the nuclear powers, forcing them to find some middle ground that will reduce the possibility of accidental or purposeful nuclear war to zero.

Nuclear-Free Zones (NFZ)   (228)

Regions where nuclear weapons are banned from use, storage, or assembly. The concept of nuclear-free areas first appeared in the 1959 Antarctic Treaty, which forbade atomic bombs anywhere on the continent. Other treaties, dealing with Latin America (1967), outer space (1967), and the South Pacific (1985), extended the nuclear-free concept further, and similar agreements have been proposed for Europe and other areas of the world. In the late 1970s, a number of environmental movements with antinuclear views moved into the political arena, forming the Green parties of Western Europe, and seeking to enlarge the NFZs on a piecemeal basis. In 1981, Hawaii County, Hawaii, became the first U.S. governmental body to declare itself a "nuclear-free zone," and by 1986 more than a hundred other cities and counties in the United States had followed suit.[42] Elsewhere in the world, many other cities and states have adopted NFZ ordinances, including the entire country of New Zealand in 1986. *See also* ANTARCTIC TREATY, 237; BARUCH PLAN, 213; BRITISH LABOUR PARTY MANIFESTOS ON NUCLEAR WEAPONS, 215; GREEN PARTY MOVEMENT, 217; LATIN AMERICAN NUCLEAR-FREE ZONE TREATY, 223; NEW ZEALAND'S ANZUS WITHDRAWAL, 224; NONPROLIFERATION, 225; NON-PROLIFERATION TREATY (NPT), 226; NUCLEAR FREEZE MOVEMENT, 227; NUCLEAR PROLIFERATION, 231; SOUTH PACIFIC NUCLEAR-FREE ZONE TREATY, 235.

Significance   Nuclear-free [weapons] zones (NFZ or NFWZ) have three main characteristics: "non-possession, non-deployment, and non-use of nuclear weapons";[43] to these may be added a fourth element, nonconstruction. NFZs have become an increasingly attractive option to those opposing the dangers of atomic weapons, as one means of slowing the arms race and raising individual consciousness about the dangers of nuclear war. In New Zealand, the antinuclear weapons forces started slowly, with cities and local regional governments, until 65 percent of the country had been declared "nuclear free"; the Labour Party then embraced the movement, was itself elected in 1984 over the nuclear visitation issue, and two years later declared the entire country an NFZ. The NFZ movement is strong in Western Europe, particularly in Greece, Spain, the Federal Republic of Germany, the Benelux countries, and Scandinavia; it is also growing rapidly in the United States. Not only have more than 100 cities and counties in the United States forbidden the use, storage, or transit of nuclear devices in their jurisdictions, but several have also banned investments by local governments in businesses producing nuclear weapons. Should the NFZ movement continue to spread throughout the industrialized Western states, the U.S. government will be forced to reevaluate its long-term military and political strategies.

Nuclear Non-Proliferation Act of 1978 (NNPA)   (229)

An act of the U.S. Congress to restrict U.S. exports of plutonium and enriched uranium. The Nuclear Non-Proliferation Act of 1978 arose from President Jimmy Carter's efforts to halt the proliferation of nuclear weapons and the technology to make them. The United States "would curb proliferation by renouncing the use of plutonium and steadily pressuring other nuclear supplier nations for tougher export restrictions and safeguards."[44] Congress followed the president's lead by passing almost unanimously the NNPA, following intense administration lobbying to water down the provisions prohibiting U.S. nuclear exports to nations engaged in uranium enrichment. The amended act "required foreign countries wishing to buy U.S. nuclear materials to accept marginally tougher safeguards on their nuclear facilities and to agree not to re-export purchased materials or to use them to make nuclear weapons."[45] Exports of plutonium and enriched uranium and enriched uranium-generating facilities were largely prohibited. The NNPA also encouraged the Nuclear Regulatory Commission to expedite licenses for the export of nuclear power plants constructed by U.S. firms. *See also* ATOMIC ENERGY ACT OF 1946, 210; ATOMS FOR PEACE PROPOSAL, 212; NONPROLIFERATION, 225; NUCLEAR POWER PLANTS, 230; NUCLEAR PROLIFERATION, 231; NUCLEAR REGULATORY COMMISSION (NRC), 232; THRESHOLD NUCLEAR POWERS, 236.

Significance The contradictions inherent in the Nuclear Non-Proliferation Act of 1978 were obvious from its onset. On the one hand, the law was intended to restrict the availability of enriched uranium and plutonium, materials useful in the construction of atomic bombs, to those who already had them; simultaneously, however, it authorized the NRC "to provide export licenses quickly to prove that the United States was a reliable nuclear supplier."[46] The Arms Control and Disarmament Agency was also given a role in nuclear export decisions, and was authorized to make periodic "nuclear proliferation assessment statements," the first of which (on Iran) being issued in 1978. The administration of President Ronald W. Reagan tended to downplay the nonproliferation aspects of the law, particularly in his second term.

Nuclear Power Plants (230)

Commercial electrical-generating facilities powered by atomic fuel. Nuclear power plants are fueled by uranium ore, the disintegration of which produces heat. The heat converts water into steam, which in turn is used to turn large, electrical-generating turbines. There are several different kinds of reactors: most commercial power plants (80 percent) employ light-water reactors (LWR), "of which there are two kinds: the pressurized-water reactor (PWR) and the boiling-water reactor (BWR)";[47] the remaining plants use heavy-water reactors (HWR). Other types of reactors used for experimental and military purposes include: high temperature gas-cooled reactors (HTGCR), liquid metal fast breeder reactors (LMFBR), gas-cooled fast breeder reactors (GCFBR), light-water breeder reactors (LWBR), steam-generated heavy-water reactors (SGHWR), and molten salt breeder reactors (MSBR). Breeder reactors generate more nuclear fuel than they consume, changing the uranium into plutonium; most commercial "burner" reactors generate as by-products an isotope of plutonium that cannot easily be reused, either commercially or militarily. *See also* ATOMS FOR PEACE PROPOSAL, 212; BREEDER REACTORS, 214; INTERNATIONAL ATOMIC ENERGY AGENCY (IAEA), 219; NONPROLIFERATION, 225; NON-PROLIFERATION TREATY (NPT), 226; NUCLEAR NON-PROLIFERATION ACT OF 1978 (NNPA), 229; NUCLEAR PROLIFERATION, 231.

Significance   The spread of nuclear power plants throughout the world has caused great concern to leaders in both the East and West, particularly in the last two decades. Old-style burner reactors use a kind of uranium, and produce a type of plutonium that cannot be converted to weapons-grade material without very sophisticated processing facilities that can enrich the fuel. Such plants are located only in the handful of states that now have nuclear-weapons capability, and in several other Western countries that have renounced such weapons. The possibility of such technology being exported to terrorist states, such as Libya or Iran, has caused nightmares for military planners and civilian leaders alike. Of equal concern are breeder reactors that generate weapons-grade plutonium as one of their by-products; should reactors of this type become commonplace, a real potential exists for the theft of their nuclear fuel, and its use in the creation of homemade atomic bombs.

Nuclear Proliferation   (231)

The spreading of atomic weapons or weapons technology to parts of the world that do not have them. "Horizontal proliferation refers to the transfer of weapons or weapons technologies to other states; vertical proliferation refers to an increase in numbers or diversities of nuclear weapons within a given state."[48] Some observers would include the spreading of commercial atomic power plant technology as part of nuclear proliferation. *See also* ATOMIC ENERGY ACT OF 1946, 210; ATOMS FOR PEACE PROPOSAL, 212; BARUCH PLAN, 213; EUROPEAN ATOMIC ENERGY COMMUNITY (EURATOM), 216; INTERNATIONAL ATOMIC ENERGY AGENCY (IAEA), 219; NONPROLIFERATION, 225; NON-PROLIFERATION TREATY (NPT), 226; NUCLEAR NON-PROLIFERATION ACT OF 1978 (NNPA), 229; THRESHOLD NUCLEAR POWERS, 236.

Significance   Nuclear proliferation has been an issue since 1946, when Bernard Baruch proposed that atomic weapons be outlawed, that countries without such arms not develop them, that the United States destroy its own nuclear arsenal, and that an international agency be created to monitor the denuclearization of the world. In 1953, U.S. President Dwight D. Eisenhower proposed the Atoms for Peace plan, by which the United States would assist other countries in developing a commercial nuclear industry. The United States insisted that countries participating in this program be open to inspection by the International Atomic Energy Agency, to prevent them from using the plants to acquire nuclear weapons. In more recent decades, both the Soviets and the Americans have realized that they share a common interest in not allowing proliferation of nuclear weapons to take place, although the question of commercial power plant technology has been treated much more ambiguously; in 1975, for example, West Germany sold Brazil a uranium enrichment plant.[49] Thus, despite the best efforts of the superpowers, a number of states, including Israel, Pakistan, South Africa, Brazil, and others, must now be considered threshold nuclear powers.

Nuclear Regulatory Commission (NRC)   (232)

An agency of the U.S. government that regulates the commercial atomic power plant industry. The NRC was created by the 1974 Energy Reorganization Act as a partial successor to the Atomic Energy Commission (the AEC's promotional activities were assigned to the new Energy Research and Development Administration [ERDA], later the Department of Energy), after questions were raised about the conflicts of interest inherent in AEC's many promotional and regulatory functions. Both the NRC and ERDA came into being on January 1, 1975. The NRC inherited the AEC's licensing and regulatory responsibilities, including the issuance of export licenses to allow U.S. firms to construct nuclear plants overseas. *See also* ATOMIC ENERGY ACT OF 1946, 210; ATOMIC ENERGY COMMISSION (AEC), 211; BREEDER REACTORS, 214; NUCLEAR POWER PLANTS, 230.

Significance   The Nuclear Regulatory Commission was constituted from the regulatory section of the Atomic Energy Commission, carrying over much of the same personnel, administrative structure, and philosophy. It has also been subject to much the same criticism for its alleged lack of effective supervision of the nuclear power industry. As K. S. Shrader-Frechette states: "The failure of the US Atomic Energy Commission and the US Nuclear Regulatory Commission to conduct wide-ranging assessments of fission technology is well-known. In fact, one of the top federal commissioners charged with evaluating and regulating atomic power said recently that he wanted 'to eliminate . . . from the public debate over nuclear energy' the 'extraneous' and 'irrelevant' ethical, social, and political issues 'which cloud . . . meaningful dialogue.'" [50] NRC safety reviewers have also been accused of sacrificing speed for safety; one staff member stated that "reviewers come under attack when they raise a safety issue, even though that is their job. Just as amazing is the fact that, if the reviewer does not raise a safety issue, everyone just accepts it, even though it may mean that the reviewer was not doing his job."[51] The NRC has been reported as catering heavily to the depressed U.S. nuclear power industry, which has attempted to increase its share of the overseas licensing of enriched uranium facilities, partly to offset the inroads of the French and Germans into the world market. The spread of such plants increases the risk of nuclear proliferation.

Nuclear Suppliers Group (NSG) (233) [The London Club]

A 15-member cartel comprising the major providers of commercial atomic power plant technology to the rest of the world. The Nuclear Suppliers Group, also called the London Club, began meeting in London in 1975 as a direct response to India's 1974 explosion of an atomic device, to regularize their nuclear export policies. The group eventually comprised fifteen nations: the United States, the Soviet Union, the United Kingdom, France, Belgium, Canada, Czechoslovakia, East Germany, West Germany, Italy, Japan, Netherlands, Poland, Sweden, and Switzerland. In 1977 the group completed its Guidelines for Nuclear Transfers, which restricted the types of equipment transfers that could be made to nonsignatories of the Non-Proliferation Treaty, and cataloged those items "which, when provided to any non-nuclear weapon state, would 'trigger' IAEA safeguards."[52] *See also* INDIAN NUCLEAR TEST, 218; INTERNATIONAL ATOMIC ENERGY AGENCY (IAEA), 219; NONPROLIFERATION, 225; NONPROLIFERATION TREATY (NPT), 226; NUCLEAR PROLIFERATION, 231.

Significance   The London [Club] Guidelines extended the 1974 list of the Zangger Committee, which had similarly attempted to provide the International Atomic Energy Agency with a catalog of nuclear materials and equipment that would trigger IAEA intervention if exported to non-NPT members, but which had failed to include a major supplier, France, as one of its members. "Under the London Guidelines, the recipients of the trigger-list items must pledge not to use them for the manufacture of nuclear explosions and to provide effective physical protection of the imported materials."[53] The safeguards also apply to other, similar facilities constructed by the recipient state during the same period, and to retransfers of trigger-list materials. "However well-intentioned may have been the motives of the NSG, the guidelines have prompted a hostile response from NNWS [nonnuclear weapon states] who view them as a *demarche* that runs counter to the letter and spirit of Article IV of the NPT"; John Woodliffe also believes that "in the long term, the 'policy of denial' embodied in the NSG guidelines may prove counterproductive by encouraging states to achieve a nuclear fuel cycle that is wholly independent of outside assistance, thereby weakening non-proliferation objectives."[54]

South African Nuclear Test Incident (1979)   (234)

A potential atomic explosion reported by satellite observation in the ocean south of South Africa. On September 22, 1979, a U.S. Vela reconnaissance satellite detected two flashes of intense light separated by a second of elapsed time some 1,500 miles south of the Cape of Good Hope. According to the U.S. State Department, which reported the blast on October 25, the flashes could not have been caused by natural phenomena except under the most unusual circumstances, and were most likely the result of a low-yield (three megaton) nuclear device. No further corroboration could be found by U.S. vessels dispatched to the site, but U.S. Defense Department spokesmen indicated little was expected, given the location and size of the explosion.[55] South Africa announced on August 13, 1988, that it had the capability of constructing an atom bomb, but neither confirmed nor denied actually building one. *See also* ISRAELI NUCLEAR BOMB EXPOSÉ, 222; LIMITED TEST BAN TREATY (LTBT), 251; NONPROLIFERATION, 225; NONPROLIFERATION TREATY (NPT), 226; NUCLEAR PROLIFERATION, 231; THRESHOLD NUCLEAR POWERS, 236.

Significance   The phenomenon reported by the Vela satellite in 1979 was very probably a small atomic test by one of the threshold nuclear powers, exploded in a remote site to minimize the possibility of detection, and designed to camouflage the perpetrator if detection occurred. Speculation has centered on South Africa and Israel as the two most likely culprits. Both states are signatories to the Limited Test Ban Treaty, and such a test would have been a violation of the agreement's provisions; neither state has signed the Non-Proliferation Treaty. Both have denied any participation in the 1979 event. In 1980, "CBS News" reported that the blast was "the test of a nuclear bomb by Israel with the 'help and cooperation' of the South Africans."[56] Whatever the truth, the mysterious flash is simply one more indication of how easy it would be for any of the threshold nuclear powers to slip over the line into acquiring and building an atomic arsenal, with or without actually testing such weapons.

South Pacific Nuclear-Free Zone Treaty (1985) (235)

An agreement to ban nuclear weapons in the South Pacific region. The South Pacific Nuclear-Free Zone Treaty, also called the Treaty of Rarotonga, was signed on August 6, 1985, after two years of negotiations among the South Pacific governments. The initial proposal was made by the Australian government in 1983, and received a boost the following year after one of the severest critics of the treaty, New Zealand Prime Minister Robert Muldoon, was defeated for reelection. The new prime minister, David Lange, strongly favored the agreement. In the end, only Vanuatu among the island states refused to sign. The signatories agree "not to manufacture or otherwise acquire, possess or have control over any nuclear explosive device by any means anywhere inside or outside the South Pacific Nuclear Free Zone," and not to assist in the construction or acquisition of such devices (Article 3).[57] The stationing of nuclear devices by other powers in the South Pacific is also prohibited, as is the testing of atomic weapons by outsiders, and the dumping of radioactive nuclear waste anywhere at sea within the zone. The zone includes Australia, New Zealand, Papua New Guinea, and all of the islands east of these states, bounded by Nauru and Kiribati in the north, and Pitcairn in the east. *See also* BRITISH LABOUR PARTY MANIFESTOS ON NUCLEAR WEAPONS, 215; GREEN PARTY MOVEMENT, 217; LATIN AMERICAN NUCLEAR-FREE ZONE TREATY, 223; NEW ZEALAND'S ANZUS WITHDRAWAL, 224; NONPROLIFERATION, 225; NON-PROLIFERATION TREATY (NPT), 226; NUCLEAR FREEZE MOVEMENT, 227; NUCLEAR-FREE ZONES (NFZ), 228.

Significance   The South Pacific Nuclear-Free Zone Treaty contains several curious anomalies. Although the agreement prevents both the stationing and testing of nuclear devices within the zone, signatory states are free to allow transit of the region (and visits) by foreign ships and aircraft carrying atomic bombs (New Zealand has separately declared itself a nuclear-free zone, however, and has banned such visits from its territory). Atomic power plants are permitted, but not the dumping of radioactive wastes. The testing of missile delivery systems is allowed, but peaceful nuclear explosions are banned. Two protocols attached to the treaty provide for the nuclear weapons powers to add their signatures, thereby accepting the provisions of the agreement for their territories within the zone. France, which conducts all of its atomic tests in its Pacific departments, has already indicated it will not sign the document.

Threshold Nuclear Powers (236)
Those states believed to have the capability of quickly developing nuclear weapons, if they so choose. These include East and West Germany, Canada, Australia, India (which claims only to have exploded a "peaceful" nuclear device), Pakistan, New Zealand, Switzerland, Brazil, Argentina, Israel, South Africa, Italy, Japan, Sweden, Czechoslovakia, Belgium, Netherlands, and Poland, among others. Some observers would limit the definition only to countries such as Brazil, Argentina, Pakistan, Israel, South Africa, and India, which have nuclear weapons potential and have never signed the Non-Proliferation Treaty. *See also* INDIAN NUCLEAR TEST, 218; IRAQI NUCLEAR POWER PLANT RAID, 221; ISRAELI NUCLEAR BOMB EXPOSÉ, 222; NONPROLIFERATION, 225; NON-PROLIFERATION TREATY (NPT), 226; NUCLEAR PROLIFERATION, 231; SOUTH AFRICAN NUCLEAR TEST INCIDENT, 234.

Significance The nuclear threshold states pose long-term security problems for both East and West, particularly in the four countries (India, Pakistan, South Africa, and Israel) where "at least one significant nuclear activity [remains] non-safeguarded and capable of producing nuclear weapons-grade material. . . . The adamant refusal of these states to accede to the Non-Proliferation Treaty must, therefore, 'raise questions about the plans of the country concerned.' Suspicion is fueled further when these same states are observed to have opted for advanced forms of nuclear technology which, given the absence of any civil nuclear power programme in those states, can serve no immediate commercial purpose."[58] Concerns have also been raised about two other states, Iraq and Libya, both parties to the NPT, which have also been accused of attempting to build a nuclear arsenal. The fact remains that many of the threshold nuclear powers may have already built such weapons, without having tested them, effectively rendering obsolete the article in the Non-Proliferation Treaty that bases its definition of proliferation on the actual detonation of an atomic bomb. If this is indeed true, ending the arms race between the East and the West will be insufficient to control the proliferation of nuclear weapons and nuclear-weapons technology; a truly multinational effort will be required.

9. Arms Control and Disarmament

Antarctic Treaty (1959) (237)

An arms control agreement banning all weapons and military activities on the continent of Antarctica. The 1959 Antarctic Treaty declared that the area south of 60 degrees south latitute "shall be used for peaceful purposes only. There shall be prohibited, *inter alia,* any measures of a military nature, such as the establishment of military bases and fortifications, the carrying out of military maneuvers, as well as the testing of any type of weapons" (Article I).[1] Further, "Any nuclear explosions in Antarctica and the disposal thereof of radioactive waste material shall be prohibited" (Article V).[2] Unresolved disputes under the treaty shall "be referred to the International Court of Justice for settlement" (Article XI).[3] The initial parties to the treaty were Argentina, Australia, Belgium, Chile, France, Japan, New Zealand, Norway, South Africa, the Soviet Union, Great Britain, and the United States. It was signed at Washington on December 1, 1959. *See also* NONPROLIFERATION, 225; NON-PROLIFERATION TREATY (NPT), 226; NUCLEAR-FREE ZONES (NFZ), 228.

Significance   The Antarctic Treaty was the first arms control agreement to be signed by the major world powers following World War II, serving as a model for later accords. According to Jozef Goldblat, the arms control provisions of the treaty derived from its three main objectives: "to establish a foundation for international cooperation in scientific investigation in Antarctica, successfully initiated during the 1957/58 International Geophysical Year; to protect the unique Antarctic environment; and to avert discord over territorial claims."[4] The agreement allows on-site inspection of all Antarctic installations by each signatory, with complete freedom of access by national

observers, a particularly noteworthy precedent in light of the verification provisions of the 1987 INF treaty. Americans have actually
inspected Soviet bases in Antarctica numerous times since the treaty
went into effect; no evidence of military activity has ever been found.
The treaty is subject to review and possible revision in 1991.

Arms Control and Disarmament (238)

The reduction or eradication of specific classes of weapons. The terms
are often used synonymously, but "arms control" actually refers to
limitations in the quantity or quality of certain types of weapons, while
"disarmament" seeks to eradicate arms, either in their entirety or by
specific group. According to Thomas C. Schelling and Morton H.
Halperin, the objectives of arms control are: (1) to reduce the risk of
war; (2) to reduce destructiveness when war occurs; and (3) to reduce
the cost of providing an adequate military defense.[5] The objective of
disarmament is the complete elimination of war and the weapons of
war as one option in the settlement of disputes between nations. Disarmament may be either mutual or unilateral. *See also* BARUCH PLAN,
213; NONPROLIFERATION, 225; NON-PROLIFERATION TREATY (NPT), 226;
NUCLEAR-FREE ZONES (NFZ), 238; the specific treaties included in this
chapter.

Significance　　The history of arms control agreements can be traced
as early as 1139, when Pope Innocent II attempted to ban use of the
crossbow. Early twentieth-century efforts include the Washington Naval Treaty (1921), which limited growth in capital vessels, the 1925
Geneva Protocol on bacteriological and chemical weapons, the League
of Nations Disarmament Conference of 1932, and the second London
Naval Agreement of 1935. All failed except the Geneva Protocol.
Following World War II, the Baruch and Gromyko plans (1946) proposed the elimination of nuclear weapons, but fell victim to the cold
war. In 1952, the United Nations established the U.N. Disarmament
Commission, and in 1954 the Subcommittee on Disarmament, which
collapsed in 1957. Following the 1962 Cuban missile crisis, U.S. and
Soviet negotiators successfully concluded the Limited Nuclear Test
Ban Treaty and the first of several Hot Line Agreements (1963), the
first serious attempts by the superpowers to reduce the risk of a nu-
clear holocaust. Under the leadership of President Richard M. Nixon,
U.S.-Soviet relations improved, resulting in the Seabed Arms Control
Treaty (1971), the Agreement on the Prevention of Nuclear War
(1973), the Threshold Test Ban Treaty (1974), the Peaceful Nuclear
Explosions Treaty (1976), and the two SALT treaties. However, the
Soviet invasion of Afghanistan in 1979 killed the second SALT treaty,

and the inauguration of President Ronald W. Reagan in 1981, and his subsequent buildup of U.S. armed forces, greatly increased tensions between the superpowers. The Geneva Summit (1985) between President Reagan and Soviet leader Mikhail Gorbachev opened the door to new talks, resulting in the INF treaty of 1987, and the promise of additional negotiations to reduce or eliminate entire classes of nuclear and conventional weapons. Many observers believe that the ultimate survival of the human race depends on the ability of the superpowers to limit the spread of nuclear weapons to other countries (and to terrorist groups); to reduce the numbers of nuclear, biological, and chemical weapons in their own arsenals; to limit the possibility of accidental nuclear war; to reduce military forces in Europe and the Middle East; and generally to regularize relations on all levels between the large states. Arms control is clearly a major part of this process.

Arms Control and Disarmament Agency (ACDA)   (239)

A semi-independent agency of the United States government established to provide an official bureaucratic voice for arms control. The Arms Control and Disarmament Agency was proposed by President John F. Kennedy and enacted into law in 1961; the new agency, he said, should have "exceptionally broad competence, functions, and resources . . . to bring its point of view and recommendations promptly to the highest level of Government."[6] Further, ACDA would coordinate research into arms control, and participate in future arms negotiations. The Arms Control and Disarmament Act (ACD) made the agency's director "the principal advisor to the Secretary of State and the President on arms control and disarmament matters,"[7] but left the coordination of foreign policy to the State Department. A 1975 amendment to the ACD act required the agency to issue arms control impact statements (ACIS) to Congress "for any strategic weapons program whose estimated annual cost exceeded $50 million, or when the Director determined that any government agency had taken an action that would substantially impact upon strategic arms or arms control policies."[8] *See also* ARMS CONTROL AND DISARMAMENT, 238; NONPROLIFERATION, 225; STRATEGIC ARMS LIMITATION TALKS I (SALT I), 264; STRATEGIC ARMS LIMITATION TALKS II (SALT II), 265.

Significance   The Arms Control and Disarmament Agency arose from President John F. Kennedy's concern over the lack of balance on arms control issues at the center of the U.S. government. Creation of the agency was opposed both by the Defense Department and by congressional hawks, and it has remained an uncertain stepchild of the U.S. government from its inception, its influence rising or falling depending on the personal interest of each president. Its greatest results were achieved in the period 1963–1974, with numerous treaties and agreements successfully concluded, culminating in SALT I. Perhaps the agency's "most important contribution was its very existence: it provided both a focal point for arms control work and a vested interest in showing results."[9] The 1975 amendment requiring executive departments and the ACDA to file arms control impact statements was an attempt by Congress to insert itself into the decision-making process for major weapons systems; it has generally been unsuccessful. Under the Reagan administration, the ACDA was largely "excluded from the weapons acquisitions process and many key defense program decisions, even when they bear directly upon arms control."[10]

Biological Weapons Convention (BWC) (1972) (240)

A treaty that prohibits the development of biological weapons. The Convention on the Prohibition of the Development, Production, and Stockpiling of Bacteriological (Biological) and Toxin Weapons and on Their Destruction, its official title, supplements the Geneva Protocol of 1925, which bans the use of bacteriological agents in war. The agreement derived from discussions held in 1962 by the Eighteen-Nation Disarmament Committee (ENDC), and from 1969 drafts proposed by Britain and the Soviet Union. The convention was signed in 1972, and ratified in 1975; over 100 nations had acceded by the 1980s. Under terms of the agreement, each state undertook never "to develop, produce, stockpile, or otherwise acquire or retain: (1) microbial or other biological agents or toxins, whatever their origin or method of production, of types and in quantities that have no justification for prophylactic, protective, or other peaceful purposes; (2) weapons, equipment, or means of delivery designed to use such agents or toxins for hostile purposes or in armed conflict" (Article I).[11] *See also* BIOLOGICAL (BACTERIOLOGICAL) WARFARE, 117; CHEMICAL WARFARE, 119; GENEVA PROTOCOL, 247.

Significance The Biological Weapons Convention was the first attempt by the major powers in the post–World War II era to eliminate an entire class of weapons. An attempt to link the convention with a chemical warfare agreement failed, due to stockpiles of such weapons already held by the major powers. The treaty required signatories to destroy any existing biological agents, in addition to prohibiting development of new weapons of this type. The United States announced after the convention went into effect that it had converted its biological warfare facilities to peaceful uses; both the Soviet Union and the United Kingdom denied having any such weapons. In 1984, President Ronald W. Reagan accused the Soviets of violating the convention by maintaining an offensive biological warfare program. Curiously, the treaty does not actually ban the *use* of biological agents in war, only their production, development, and stockpiling.

Catholic Conference Pastoral Letter (1983)   (241)

An officially sanctioned document of the Roman Catholic Church urging the complete ban of nuclear weapons. *The Challenge to Peace,* the pastoral letter of the National Conference of Catholic Bishops, was the first official position paper by a major U.S. church to state that nuclear war in any form could not be justified morally, and that the production, development, deployment, and stockpiling of nuclear weapons should immediately be halted. *See also* ARMS CONTROL AND DISARMAMENT, 238; CONFERENCES AND COMMITTEES ON DISARMAMENT, 244; NONPROLIFERATION, 225; NUCLEAR-FREE ZONES (NFZ), 228.

Significance   The publication of the pastoral letter, on May 3, 1983, resulted in an immediate storm of protest from U.S. conservatives (including some Catholics), who argued that the unilateral nuclear disarmament implied by the document would inevitably result in the subjugation of the United States by atheistic communism, thereby leading ultimately to the destruction of the Catholic Church itself. The bishops refused to withdraw their controversial statement, however, stating that their remarks were based on moral issues; several other major U.S. religious groups have since followed suit.

Comprehensive Test Ban Treaty (CTBT)   (242)

A proposed agreement between the major powers, never finalized or ratified, that would have banned all tests of nuclear weapons. The 1963 Limited Test Ban Treaty, the 1974 Threshold Test Ban Treaty, and the 1976 Peaceful Nuclear Explosions Treaty led to additional talks between the United States, Great Britain, and the Soviet Union, beginning in 1977. Agreement was reached on the following points: (1) all nuclear weapons tests in any environment would be prohibited; (2) amendments to the treaty would require the approval of a majority of the signatories, plus all five permanent members of the U.N. Security Council; (3) the parties would use national technical means (NTM) to verify compliance, and no signatory could interfere with such checks; (4) any party would have the right to request on-site inspection to determine whether a particular seismic event was, in fact, a nuclear explosion.[12] The treaty would have had a duration initially of three years. Talks were suspended in 1980 following the Soviet invasion of Afghanistan and the election of Ronald W. Reagan as U.S. president. *See also* LIMITED TEST BAN TREATY (LTBT), 251; NATIONAL TECHNICAL MEANS (NTM), 253; PEACEFUL NUCLEAR EXPLOSIONS TREATY (PNET), 258; THRESHOLD TEST BAN TREATY (TTBT), 267.

Significance   The problem of verification lies at the heart of any test ban treaty, and it was the major difficulty with the proposed CTBT. Without constant on-site verification, laboratory tests of low-yield explosions could conceivably be conducted without external detection; also, while improvements in warheads ultimately require field testing, some of these embellishments can be tested in other, nondetectable ways. Nevertheless, as Jozef Goldblat states, the proposed treaty "would have an arms limitation impact in that it would make it difficult, if not impossible, for the nuclear weapons parties to develop new designs of nuclear warheads, and would also place constraints on the modification of existing weapon designs. It would narrow, thereby, one channel of arms competition among the major powers."[13] The administration of President Ronald W. Reagan opposed this kind of treaty because it would directly interfere with development of the Strategic Defense Initiative ("Star Wars"), and because the Soviets have refused to allow massive on-site inspections.

Conference on Security and Cooperation in Europe (CSCE)   (243)

A meeting of European states that produced the Helsinki Accords in 1975. The Conference on Security and Cooperation in Europe was proposed in 1972 by the Soviet Union, and was convened in 1973. After two years of meetings, the 35 participants signed (on August 1, 1975) the "Document on Confidence-Building Measures and Certain Aspects of Security and Disarmament" as part of the Helsinki Final Act (popularly called the "Helsinki Accords"; other provisions of the act guaranteed the political rights of the signatory states' citizens). The document states that the signatories shall notify all other participating states of major military maneuvers exceeding 25,000 troops within 250 kilometers of a frontier shared with any other European state (Article I).[14] Review conferences at Belgrade (1978) and Madrid (1983) produced much rhetoric, but few additional developments. *See also* CONFERENCES AND COMMITTEES ON DISARMAMENT, 244; CONFIDENCE-BUILDING MEASURES (CBM), 245; NONPROLIFERATION, 225; MUTUAL AND BALANCED FORCE REDUCTIONS (MBFR), 252.

Significance   The Conference on Security and Cooperation in Europe was the first to adopt CBMs as part of its agenda. Such "confidence-building measures" are based on the assumption that the East-West conflict "reflects real incompatibilities of interest . . . but also assumes that anxieties and fears are often exaggerated."[15] Unfortunately, as devised in the Helsinki Final Act, they lack any real military significance, both because the major powers tend to ignore the reporting procedures whenever it suits them, and because the "CSCE negotiations on CBMs eschew MBFR's stratified, bloc-to-bloc format,"[16] including among its 35 participants such neutral ministates as Liechtenstein and Vatican City, neither of which possesses an army. President Ronald W. Reagan and many outside observers have accused the Soviet Union of wholesale violations of the Helsinki Final Act, both in the military sphere and in the human rights arena.

Conferences and Committees on Disarmament (244)

A series of international forums on arms control beginning in the post–World War I era. The use of chemical weapons in World War I prompted the 1925 Geneva Convention, the first of the roughly 30 conferences and committees on disarmament that have been organized since. The League of Nations sponsored the World Disarmament Conference from 1932–1935, but it produced few results, finally collapsing in the face of German and Italian belligerency. In the post–World War II era, major groups and meetings include: the 1958 Conference on Safeguards Against Surprise Attack, sponsored by the ten-nation Disarmament Committee; the meetings of the Eighteen-Nation Disarmament Committee (ENDC) in the 1960s (later expanded to forty nations in the 1970s); the Mutual and Balanced Force Reductions Talks; the International Arms Control Symposia; the All-European Conference on Security and Cooperation in Europe (CSCE); the Ettore Majorana Centre's International Seminar on Nuclear War (1983); the 35-nation Conference on Disarmament in Europe (CDE), which began in 1984; and many others. *See also* CONFERENCE ON SECURITY AND COOPERATION IN EUROPE (CSCE), 243; CONFIDENCE-BUILDING MEASURES (CBM), 245; GENEVA PROTOCOL, 247; MUTUAL AND BALANCED FORCE REDUCTIONS (MBFR), 252.

Significance The many conferences and committees on disarmament in the post–World War II era share a number of common characteristics: a heavy emphasis on European security questions, participation by the United States, Britain, the Soviet Union, and many of the European states, the use of these forums for propaganda purposes by both the United States and the Soviet Union, publication of proceedings, and the adoption of various resolutions to support world peace efforts, without the means of enforcing them. According to the assistant director of the ACDA, they have all also "failed to live up to their promise."[17] Their main contribution to the advancement of arms control and disarmament has been the introduction of confidence-building measures, small verifications and counterbalances that have added in minor ways to European security. Unfortunately, as long as the United States and the Soviet Union reserve real discussion on arms control to themselves, without including affected third parties, conferences of this type are doomed to produce little more than meaningless rhetoric.

Confidence-Building Measures (CBMs) (245)

Measures designed "to contribute to reducing the dangers of armed conflict and of misunderstanding or miscalculation of military activities which could give rise to apprehension, particularly in a situation when the participating states lack clear and timely information about the nature of such activities."[18] The Conference on Security and Cooperation in Europe (CSCE) produced, as part of its Final Act (popularly called the Helsinki Accords), the idea of CBMs (also called confidence- and security-building measures [CSBMs]), voluntary actions on the part of the signatories to notify each other of scheduled military maneuvers, thereby reducing tensions between East and West. Under the agreement, only movements of ground troops exceeding 25,000 had to be reported; naval and air force operations were not affected. NATO observers of Soviet-bloc military exercises have reported a long series of minor violations by the Soviets, including restrictions on travel, harassment, and lack of facilities, but the agreement continued to operate even during the renewed cold war of the early 1980s. There are two kinds of CBMs: information measures and constraint measures. *See also* CONFERENCE ON SECURITY AND COOPERATION IN EUROPE (CSCE), 243; CONFERENCES AND COMMITTEES ON DISARMAMENT, 244; MUTUAL AND BALANCED FORCE REDUCTIONS (MBFR), 252.

Significance The theory behind confidence-building measures is that they "lead to increased openness, . . . which is necessary . . . to enhance predictability; predictability is essential for the development of mutual confidence; and mutual confidence is needed to curb the dynamics of the arms buildup and to embark on arms restraint and disarmament,"[19] and to avoid nuclear war by accident or misunderstanding. They also give "effect and expression to the duty of States to refrain from the threat or use of force in their mutual relations."[20] In reality, however, they have failed to produce any real easing of tensions between the two superpowers, who have historically preferred to negotiate such measures directly; on the contrary, relations between the United States and the Soviet Union were decidedly chilly during the early Reagan years. As Jonathan Alford states: "To the extent that states genuinely desire a reduction in tension, CBMs of graduated and increasing severity can probably be negotiated, as long as each believes its own security to be augmented thereby."[21]

Environmental Modification Convention (ENMOD) (246) (1977)

An agreement to ban the use of weather-modification techniques as a weapon of war. One of a series of treaties that derived from the Nixon administration's efforts to reduce tensions between the superpowers, the ENMOD convention prohibits each party from engaging in "military or any other hostile use of environmental modification techniques having widespread, long-lasting, or severe effects as the means of destruction, damage, or injury to any other State party" (Article I); such modifications are defined as: "any technique for changing, through the deliberate manipulation of natural processes, the dynamics, composition, or structure of the Earth, including its biota, lithosphere, hydrosphere, and atmosphere, or of outer space" (Article II).[22] *See also* ARMS CONTROL AND DISARMAMENT, 238.

Significance Although environmental weapons remain in the realm of science fiction, the ENMOD convention reflects genuine concern on the part of military strategists and politicians that they could be developed at some future date, and that their use could have widespread (and largely unforeseen) impacts on Earth's fragile ecosphere—or, at the very least, could affect the territories of states other than those at whom they are directed. That such effects would surely result from a nuclear holocaust has been ignored by the agreement; there are also no restrictions on the *development* of such techniques for military purposes. The ambiguities inherent in the convention, and the difficulties of enforcing (or even judging) a violation of its provisions, have left it a well-meaning but largely ineffectual piece of paper.

Geneva Protocol (1925) (247)

An international agreement banning the use of chemical and bacteriological weapons in war. The Protocol for the Prohibition of the Use in War of Asphyxiating, Poisonous, or Other Gases, and of Bacteriological Methods of Warfare, its official name, was a direct reaction to the German use of mustard gas in World War I, which so horrified the world that the major nations determined to eliminate this class of weapons altogether. The agreement grew out of the 1925

Geneva Conference for the Supervision of the International Traffic in Arms, where the United States took the initiative in proposing a prohibition on the export of gases for use in war. It was then extended by amendment to prohibit the "use in war of asphyxiating, poisonous, or other gases, and of all analogous liquids, materials, or devices," as well as "the use of bacteriological methods of warfare."[23] *See also* BIOLOGICAL (BACTERIOLOGICAL) WARFARE, 117; BIOLOGICAL WEAPONS CONVENTION (BWC), 240; CHEMICAL WARFARE, 119; IRAN-IRAQ WAR, 126.

Significance The Geneva Protocol is the only arms control treaty from the interwar period to survive to modern times as a working agreement. Ironically, the United States Senate failed to ratify the treaty upon its original submission, and it was not until 1975 that the U.S. government formally acceded. Several of the major powers, including the Soviet Union, have declared on various occasions that they regard the protocol as nonbinding under certain circumstances, particularly if they are themselves attacked with chemical weapons, or if the enemy state in question is a nonsignatory. Both superpowers have accused the other of violating the protocol in Southeast Asia; the Reagan administration further claimed that the Soviets used chemical weapons in Afghanistan. The large stockpiles of chemical arms held by both the United States and the Soviet Union have prevented the realization of a comprehensive chemical warfare treaty. The treaty has not prevented Iran or Iraq from making the first widespread use of chemical weapons in modern times, despite the fact that both countries are signatories to the agreement.

Geneva Summit (1985) (248)

A meeting between Soviet General Secretary Mikhail Gorbachev and U.S. President Ronald W. Reagan that reopened U.S.-Soviet arms discussions. Within a month of Gorbachev's succession to power in March of 1985, he announced postponement of the planned deployment of Soviet intermediate-range missiles in Europe until November, and further suspended unilaterally all Soviet nuclear tests in July. His willingness to negotiate with the United States led to the 1985 Geneva Summit, breaking the period of cold war that had resumed with the Soviet invasion of Afghanistan in 1979, and setting the stage for further meetings between the superpowers. On November 21, the two leaders issued a joint statement, declaring that "nuclear war cannot be won and must never be fought," and announcing new negotiations on nuclear and space arms, including intensive bilateral discussions on a chemical weapons ban.[24] *See also*

INTERMEDIATE-RANGE NUCLEAR FORCES TREATY (INFT), 250; REYKJAVIK SUMMIT, 260.

Significance   The Geneva Summit was the first meeting between President Reagan and the new Soviet leader, following a period of icy relations that had been marked by harsh rhetoric and a large arms buildup on both sides. Although nothing tangible came from the meeting, the Geneva Summit set the stage for the Reykjavik Summit the following year, and the Washington Summit in 1987, the latter resulting in the INF treaty, which eliminated intermediate-range missiles in Europe. By demonstrating that some common middle ground could be found between two such incompatible political systems, the Geneva Summit may well be regarded by future generations as a major turning point in history, one that led to a world where war is no longer an alternative to settle disagreements between states.

Hot Line Agreements (249)

Four agreements between the superpowers designed to improve communications and avoid the possibility of accidental nuclear war. The Hot Line Agreements derived from the 1962 Cuban missile crisis, and the difficulties experienced by President John F. Kennedy in contacting Premier Nikita Khrushchev. On December 12, 1962, the United States submitted a proposal to the Eighteen-Nation Disarmament Committee urging the adoption of reliable communication links between Moscow and Washington; the superpowers signed on June 20, 1963, the "Memorandum of Understanding Between the United States of America and the Union of Soviet Socialist Republics Regarding the Establishment of a Direct Communication Link, . . . including continuous functioning of the link and prompt delivery of communications to its head of government."[25] In 1971, the two states signed the "Agreement Between the United States of America and the Union of Soviet Socialist Republics on Measures to Improve the USA-USSR Direct Communications Link," which expanded communications via satellite channels; a second modernization agreement was signed in July 1984, adding facsimile transmission capability; a further upgrade was added in 1988. *See also* HOT LINE, 17; LIMITED TEST BAN TREATY (LTBT), 251; PREVENTION OF NUCLEAR WAR AGREEMENT, 259.

Significance   The near disaster of October 1962 was exacerbated by breakdowns in communications between the Soviet Union and the United States, prompting both states to seek adoption of Hot Line Agreements. The possibility of accidental or unauthorized nuclear war became for the first time a real threat in the minds of world leaders; the direct communications link was seen by both countries as one way of reducing tensions in time of crisis. The link is generally believed to have been used seriously for the first time during the 1967 Six-Day War between Israel and its neighbors, and again in the Yom Kippur War of 1973.[26] The original agreement also represents the first real effort by the superpowers to reduce tensions spawned by the cold war, and must therefore be regarded as the precursor to the arms control treaties reached during the Johnson and Nixon administrations.

Intermediate-Range Nuclear Forces Treaty (INFT)   (250) (1987)

An agreement between the United States and the Soviet Union to eliminate medium-range nuclear missiles in Europe. The INF treaty, its popular name, was signed during the December 1987 summit between President Ronald W. Reagan and General Secretary Mikhail Gorbachev (the third such meeting in as many years), being the culmination of negotiations that started shortly after Ronald Reagan took office, in November 1981. Its provisions include: the destruction of all ground-launched, intermediate-range nuclear missiles in Europe with a range of 300–3,400 miles (approximately 2,300 missiles), including ground transportation vehicles, the missiles themselves, and the warhead casings, but not the fissionable materials; plus on-site inspections at the manufacturing plants in both countries for a period of 15 years, with the foreign inspectors actually residing near the facilities on a year-round basis. Under the agreement, the Soviet Union would actually destroy about four times as many missiles as the United States. Not affected by the treaty are some 4,000 nuclear warheads on aircraft, submarines or other naval vessels, in artillery shells, or on short-range missiles. The treaty was ratified by the U.S. Senate and the U.S.S.R. Supreme Soviet in the Spring of 1988, and proclaimed in force at the May 1988 Moscow Summit between Reagan and Gorbachev; actual destruction of the missiles began in July 1988, in full view of both the national inspectors and the world press. *See also* GENEVA SUMMIT, 248; MUTUAL AND BALANCED FORCE REDUCTIONS (MBFR), 252; REYKJAVIK SUMMIT, 260.

Significance   The INF treaty represents a breakthrough in arms control discussions between the two superpowers. It was the first agreement actually to cut the numbers of nuclear missiles available to either side, the first to eliminate an entire class of nuclear weapons outright, and the first to allow extensive on-site verification measures. Although criticized by U.S. conservatives as destroying the balance of power in Europe (the Soviets maintain a large superiority there in conventional forces), most U.S. politicians and the vast majority of overseas observers hailed the treaty as a giant step forward in reducing tensions worldwide. While acknowledging that "the Soviet record of compliance with treaties is far from perfect," Secretary of State George Shultz declared that the INFT "has the most stringent and comprehensive scheme of verification in the history of arms control."[27] These provisions, unprecedented in modern arms control pacts, include: on-site inspections, verification of missile destruction, short-notice calls by monitors of missile-construction and missile-repair facilities, as well as the usual satellite surveillance. It seems certain that the success or failure of the INF treaty will determine the course of arms control negotiations for decades to come.

Limited Test Ban Treaty (LTBT) (1963)   (251)

An agreement to ban atmospheric nuclear tests. The Treaty Banning Nuclear Weapon Tests in the Atmosphere, in Outer Space, and Under Water, its official name, prohibits "any nuclear test explosion, or any other nuclear explosion, at any place under its jurisdiction or control: (a) in the atmosphere; beyond its limits, including outer space; or under water . . . ; or (b) in any other environment if such explosion causes radioactive debris to be present outside the territorial limits of the State under whose jurisdiction or control such explosion is conducted" (Article I).[28] According to then Acting Secretary of State George W. Ball, in a report to President John F. Kennedy, "The phrase 'any other nuclear explosion' includes explosions for peaceful purposes."[29] The United States has accused the Soviet Union of violating the treaty on numerous occasions by allowing atmospheric venting of underground nuclear tests (which are permitted under the agreement). *See also* COMPREHENSIVE TEST BAN TREATY (CTBT), 242; NATIONAL TECHNICAL MEANS (NTM); PEACEFUL NUCLEAR EXPLOSIONS TREATY (PNET), 258; THRESHOLD TEST BAN TREATY (TTBT), 267.

Significance   The Limited Test Ban Treaty grew out of a 1955 Soviet proposal to ban all nuclear tests, but failed to draw much support until the dangers of atmospheric contamination became obvious in the early 1960s. By then the "national technical means" (NTM) existed in both countries to verify the treaty without on-site inspections, always a sore point with the Soviets. Since underground explosions could not be so verified, they were permitted. In addition, according to Werner Kaltefleiter, "The essential motivation of the two signatories was a mutual interest in preventing other countries from becoming nuclear powers. It seemed unlikely they could do so without atmospheric testing. Consequently, neither the People's Republic of

China nor France signed the treaty"[30]—and have not done so to this day. The LTBT was the first agreement between the superpowers to limit in any way their nuclear arsenals, and as such, it set the tone for the future. As President Kennedy noted, the treaty was an important step in "man's efforts to escape from the darkening prospects of more destruction."[31]

Mutual and Balanced Force Reductions (MBFRs)   (252)

The joint reduction of conventional army and air force units in Europe. Negotiations between NATO and Warsaw Pact representatives on MBF reductions began in October 1973, and have continued to the present day. The goal of these talks is "to establish a balance in conventional manpower forces between East and West in Central Europe at lower and equal levels."[32] By stabilizing conventional forces at some lower parity level, MBFRs would presumably lessen military tensions in Europe, eliminate the possibility of a surprise attack by either side, and reduce the potential for a nuclear holocaust. Soviet General Secretary Mikhail Gorbachev, in his December 1987 Washington summit meeting with President Ronald W. Reagan, seemed to commit the Soviet bloc for the first time to MBFRs in Europe. Both the Soviets and the Americans seem to prefer the MBFR approach to that of confidence-building measures. *See also* CONFERENCE ON SECURITY AND CO-OPERATION IN EUROPE (CSCE), 243; CONFIDENCE-BUILDING MEASURES (CBM), 245; GENEVA SUMMIT, 248; INTERMEDIATE-RANGE NUCLEAR FORCES TREATY (INFT), 250; REYKJAVIK SUMMIT, 260.

Significance   Although talks on Mutual and Balanced Force Reductions have continued intermittently at Vienna since the administration of President Richard M. Nixon, with few tangible results, they remain the only arms control negotiations being conducted on an alliance-to-alliance basis, with all members of NATO and the Warsaw Pact participating except for France and Romania. The West has used the talks to highlight disparities in conventional military strength in Europe, but also to maintain contact between the principal military officers on both sides. The Soviets, on the other hand, have consistently claimed to have fewer forces in Eastern Europe than those cited in NATO estimates; thus, they have sought equal reductions in the military forces of both blocs, rather than reductions to specific levels. They have historically opposed any agreement that would leave vast stretches of Soviet territory open for constant inspection by the West.[33] Conservatives in the United States attempted to link adoption of a NATO-sponsored MBFR agreement with ratification of the INF treaty, ignoring the fact that troop reductions might not enhance the security of either side. The INF treaty was ratified by the U.S. Senate in May 1988, without such provisions.

National Technical Means (NTM) (253)

The verification of arms control agreements through external methods. The term "National Technical Means" first appears in the 1963 Limited Test Ban Treaty, having been proposed by the Soviets as one way of concluding arms control agreements without the need for on-site inspections. NTM may include monitoring by spy satellites and planes, radios, electronic devices, seismometers, geiger counters, and other methods. Agreements relying on NTM verification invariably include clauses forbidding interference by signatory states with efforts by the other parties to collect such data externally. *See also* COM-PREHENSIVE TEST BAN TREATY (CTBT), 242; INTERMEDIATE-RANGE NUCLEAR FORCES TREATY (INFT), 250; LIMITED TEST BAN TREATY (LTBT), 251; "OPEN SKIES" PROPOSAL, 256; PEACEFUL NUCLEAR EXPLOSIONS TREATY (PNET), 258; THRESHOLD TEST BAN TREATY (TTBT), 267.

Significance Throughout the history of disarmament negotiations between the United States and the Soviet Union, the Americans have insisted on the need for on-site verification, while the Soviets have denounced such proposals as providing an excuse for espionage or interference in Soviet affairs. As the network of spy satellites grew in the 1960s and 1970s, and as electronic monitoring devices became more sophisticated, U.S. negotiators gradually accepted the premise that certain treaties could be verified externally through National Technical Means. In 1967, "Assistant Secretary of Defense Paul Warnke publicly suggested that the United States could avoid the issue of on-site inspection by agreeing to rely on 'our own unilateral capability' for verifying Soviet compliance, and after July 1968 the U.S. was unofficially prepared to accept arms-control agreements on that basis."[34] The ABM treaty, the Interim Agreement, and the TTB treaty all specified NTM verification. Under President Reagan, the United States again insisted on direct, on-site verification of arms control agreements, and it is noteworthy that the 1987 INF treaty provides such verification for the first time.

Nuclear Accidents Agreement (NAA) (1971) (254)

An agreement to limit the dangers of accidental nuclear war. The Agreement on Measures to Reduce the Risk of Outbreak of Nuclear War Between the United States of America and the Union of Soviet Socialist Republics was one of the measures produced by the SALT I talks. The possibility of a nuclear conflict being triggered by equipment malfunctions, insanity, terrorism, or other accidents has become an increasing concern to responsible leaders in both the Soviet Union and the United States. The NA agreement provides that each party will "immediately notify the other in the event of an accidental, unauthorized, or any other unexplained incident involving a possible detonation of a nuclear weapon which could create a risk of outbreak of nuclear war" (Article 2).[35] The party whose nuclear weapon is involved must then make every effort to render it harmless. Advance notification is required for any planned missile launches extending beyond each state's own territory. *See also* HOT LINE AGREEMENTS, 249; LAUNCH-ON-WARNING (LOW), 198; NUCLEAR MATERIAL CONVENTION (NMC), 255; PEACEFUL NUCLEAR EXPLOSIONS TREATY (PNET), 258; PREVENTION OF NUCLEAR WAR AGREEMENT, 259; STRATEGIC ARMS LIMITATION TALKS I (SALT I), 264.

Significance   The Nuclear Accidents Agreement is an attempt to counter the launch-on-warning philosophy that now pervades the military establishments on both sides of the Iron Curtain. The possibility of a terrorist or madman starting an unwanted war, or the potential that such a conflict might arise from false instrument readings (for example, the many false alarms experienced by NORAD) has haunted the dreams of military planners for decades. The leaders of the two superpowers now have less than a 30-minute window (perhaps as little as 5–10 minutes) to decide whether a nuclear attack has been started by the other side, and respond accordingly. The NAA was conceived as one possible solution to this dilemma, and it led directly to improved hot-line links between the two capitals. Whether the system would work in a real crisis can only be determined with an actual field test.

Nuclear Material Convention (NMC) (1981)   (255)

An agreement to safeguard nuclear fuel during shipments overseas. The Convention on the Physical Protection of Nuclear Material, its official title, was originally proposed by the United States in 1974, and endorsed at the 1975 Non-Proliferation Treaty review conference. Two provisions of the Nuclear Non-Proliferation Act of 1978 call for negotiation of such an agreement.[36] The convention provides for specific levels of safeguards on international shipments of nuclear materials, including storage in areas under constant surveillance. Theft or robbery of nuclear fuel is made an international crime, subject to extradition and prosecution between the signatory states. *See also* NONPROLIFERATION, 225; NON-PROLIFERATION TREATY (NPT), 226;

NUCLEAR ACCIDENTS AGREEMENT (NAA), 254; NUCLEAR NON-PROLIFERATION ACT OF 1978 (NNPA), 229.

Significance   The danger of terrorists or the agents of nonnuclear countries acquiring sufficient nuclear fuel to build atomic weapons led to the Nuclear Material Convention. The major nuclear powers, particularly the United States and the Soviet Union, share a common interest in keeping the number of states with nuclear arsenals to a minimum. The possibility of an Ayatollah Khomeini-like figure or some radical group acquiring an atomic bomb has fueled the night-mares of politicians in both the East and West. This convention rep-resents one small positive step toward safeguarding uranium and plutonium stockpiles throughout the industrialized world.

"Open Skies" Proposal (1955)   (256)

A U.S. plan for arms control that relied heavily on unrestricted aerial surveillance. At the 1955 Geneva Summit, the U.S. delegation, under orders from President Dwight D. Eisenhower, offered the "Open Skies" Proposal to counter British and Soviet plans for disarmament. Under the U.S. program, East and West would exchange detailed information ("blueprints") about "the strength, command structure, and disposition of personnel, units, and equipment of all major land, sea, and air forces, as well as a complete list of military plants, facili-ties, and installations. Verification of information was to be accompa-nied by ground observation and by mutual, unrestricted aerial reconnaissance."[37] *See also* INTERMEDIATE-RANGE NUCLEAR FORCES TREATY (INFT), 250; LIMITED TEST BAN TREATY (LTBT), 251; NATIONAL TECHNICAL MEANS (NTM), 253.

Significance   The "Open Skies" Proposal set the tone for arms con-trol negotiations for decades to come. The Soviets immediately re-jected the plan as "control without disarmament," while the U.S. delegation stressed that "an effective method of inspection and con-trol was the first requirement of an agreement."[38] Both countries would return to the same themes in summit after summit during the 1960s through 1980s. Ironically, many of the U.S. proposals were actually put into effect by both sides with the development of sophis-ticated spy satellites, which enabled any state with sufficient technol-ogy to examine all parts of the globe in great detail. Such surveillance became an integral part of the "national technical means" (NTM) cited in later agreements. The original "Open Skies" Proposal died when negotiations fell apart in 1957.

Outer Space Treaty (1967) (257)

An agreement to limit the use of weapons in outer space. The Treaty on Principles Governing the Activities of States in the Exploration and Use of Outer Space, Including the Moon and Other Celestial Bodies, its formal name, was first proposed in part by President Dwight D. Eisenhower in 1959, and was successfully concluded and ratified in 1967. The treaty states: "Outer space . . . is not subject to national appropriation by claim of sovereignty, by means or use of occupation, or by any other means" (Article II); further, the parties "undertake not to place in orbit around the Earth any objects carrying nuclear weapons or any other kinds of weapons of mass destruction, install such weapons on celestial bodies, or station such weapons in outer space in any manner" (Article IV).[39] The agreement also states that signatories must render aid to astronauts in distress, that nations are liable for damage caused by their satellites and rockets, and that all vehicles and installations in outer space must be open to visits by other parties, on a basis of reciprocity. The 1984 Moon Treaty (Agreement Governing the Activities of States on the Moon and Other Celestial Bodies) similarly prohibits hostile acts on or around the Moon, including the use of nuclear or destructive weapons. *See also* SEABED ARMS CONTROL TREATY, 261; STRATEGIC ARMS LIMITATION TALKS I (SALT I), 264; STRATEGIC DEFENSE INITIATIVE (SDI), 141.

Significance The Outer Space Treaty does not specifically prohibit military activities in space, and the two major superpowers have, in fact, continued to send their astronauts on military-related missions, to orbit spy satellites, and to test (and deploy) ASAT (antisatellite) weapons. President Ronald W. Reagan's Strategic Defense Initiative ("Star Wars"), major components of which would be placed in permanent orbit around the Earth, is just the latest of a series of weapons systems which are technically permitted by the agreement, but which many nations (including the Soviets) regard as a violation in spirit. As William A. Hill, Jr., states, "The practice by nations of making some military use of space seems virtually compelled by the circumstances of earthly political and ideological tensions and suspicions, despite the sincere longing of all well-motivated people for peace."[40] Thus, while well-meaning, this agreement has had little practical effect on disarmament efforts.

Peaceful Nuclear Explosions Treaty (PNET) (258)
(1976)

An agreement to regulate nuclear explosions outside of established test sites. The Treaty Between the United States of America and the

Union of Soviet Socialist Republics on Underground Nuclear Explosions for Peaceful Purposes, its official title, derived from negotiations for the Threshold Test Ban Treaty (TTBT) in 1974, and is linked to it both in duration (five years), and the fact that withdrawal from one negates the other. The treaty bans peaceful nuclear tests exceeding 150 kilotons, unless they are carried out under the terms of the TTBT. Group explosions exceeding this kilotonnage must be observed to determine that no individual explosion exceeds the limit. Each party must provide the other with information concerning such tests, and access to test sites for verification purposes. *See also* COMPREHENSIVE TEST BAN TREATY (CTBT), 242; LIMITED TEST BAN TREATY (LTBT), 251; THRESHOLD TEST BAN TREATY (TTBT), 267.

Significance   The PNE treaty was designed to supplement the TTBT so that nuclear tests conducted for "peaceful" purposes could not be used for weapons development, thereby bypassing the provisions of the TTBT agreement. Both treaties were established with five-year terms, automatically renewable unless one of the parties gave notice to the other six months prior to the expiration date. Neither treaty has entered into force, since they have never been ratified by the U.S. Senate; however, "both countries . . . have said they would abide by the general prohibition; but, in the absence of ratification, there has been no exchange of data."[41] Both agreements proved victims of the slide toward cold war in the later years of the Carter administration, eventually being killed by the Soviet invasion of Afghanistan in 1979. The Comprehensive Test Ban Treaty, which would have replaced these interim agreements, died a lonely death in 1980, as negotiations fell apart.

Prevention of Nuclear War Agreement (1973)   (259)

A treaty to regulate relations between the United States and the Soviet Union and minimize the risk of nuclear war. The Agreement Between the United States of America and the Union of Soviet Socialist Republics on the Prevention of Nuclear War, its official name, was one of the documents to come out of the SALT I negotiations. National Security Adviser Henry A. Kissinger described it as "an agreement which is designed to regulate the relations of the two nuclear powers to each other and to other countries in time of peace. It is an attempt to prevent the outbreak of nuclear war."[42] Article IV states: "If at any time relations between the Parties or between either party and other countries appear to involve the risk of a nuclear conflict, or if relations between countries not parties to this Agreement appear to involve the risk of nuclear war . . . [the parties] shall immediately enter into urgent consultations with each other and make every effort to avert this risk."[43] *See also* HOT LINE AGREEMENTS, 249; NUCLEAR ACCIDENTS AGREEMENT (NAA), 254; STRATEGIC ARMS LIMITATION TALKS I (SALT I), 264; STRATEGIC ARMS LIMITATION TALKS II (SALT II), 265.

Significance   The Prevention of Nuclear War Agreement was never submitted to the U.S. Senate to be ratified as a treaty, perhaps because it is largely meaningless as a document. After promising to discuss potential nuclear conflicts, the two powers then unequivocally reiterate their right to self-defense, and to take whatever steps may be necessary to defend themselves, including, apparently, the use of atomic bombs against nonnuclear states. By implication, the agreement gives rise to the suspicion "that the two powers accord absolute priority to their bilateral relations over their multilateral commitments, and that they arrogate to themselves the role of referee in matters relating to the security of others,"[44] so long as they can both agree on a course of action. Surely this must be the ultimate nightmare of both the Europeans and the Third World states, that the United States and the Soviet Union will eventually reach some accommodation that allows their national interests to converge on a wide variety of issues. In the meantime, this kind of document, while very high-sounding, represents no real advance in arms control.

Reykjavik Summit (1986)   (260)

The second summit between Soviet General Secretary Mikhail Gorbachev and U.S. President Ronald W. Reagan. The two leaders met at Reykjavik, Iceland, on October 11–12, 1986. What was initially intended to be a brief meeting to set an agenda for a third summit in the United States was turned by the Soviet leader into a wide-ranging discussion on arms control and other issues. Agreement was reached on the following points: a 50 percent reduction in long-range nuclear weapons, with a combined limit of 1,600 bombers and a total limit of 6,000 warheads on each side; the elimination of all strategic missiles within ten years; the removal of all medium-range missiles from Europe; a gradual reduction in weapons testing, with on-site verification; the nonproliferation of chemical weapons. Despite these broad understandings, the meeting was abruptly terminated by President Reagan when the Soviets insisted that the agreements were conditioned upon U.S. adherence to an interpretation of the ABM treaty that would have prohibited any further work on the Strategic Defense Initiative ("Star Wars") other than basic laboratory research.[45] *See also* GENEVA PROTOCOL, 247; GENEVA SUMMIT, 248; INTERMEDIATE-RANGE NUCLEAR FORCES TREATY (INFT), 250; STRATEGIC DEFENSE INITIATIVE (SDI), 141.

Significance   The Reykjavik Summit appeared to many outside observers a significant propaganda victory for the Soviets. President Reagan was clearly caught by surprise when General Secretary Gorbachev seized control of the agenda on the first day of the talks, bringing to the table a wide range of new proposals on arms control issues. Although the president and his advisers quickly recovered their poise, it was Reagan who was continually put on the defensive by Gorbachev, and it was an obviously angry Reagan who ultimately was forced to cancel the summit over the SDI issue. Many Europeans in particular blamed the Americans for wasting the first "real" opportunity for serious arms control in a decade; both East and West accused each other publicly of killing agreements already reached. In reality, however, the Reykjavik meeting set the stage for two additional summits, in Washington (December 1987) and Moscow (May 1988), at the latter of which the Soviets finally dropped their demand for an SDI linkage, and where a successful INF treaty was finally concluded and promulgated.

Seabed Arms Control Treaty (1971)   (261)

A convention to prohibit permanent placement of weapons of mass destruction on the ocean floor. The Treaty on the Prohibition of the Emplacement of Nuclear Weapons and Other Weapons of Mass Destruction on the Sea-Bed and the Ocean Floor and in the Subsoil Thereof, its complete title, forbids the establishment of nuclear launch, testing, or storage facilities on the ocean floor beyond the 12-mile territorial limits of each state, and also within that zone for any country not actually having sovereignty there. Submarines are regarded as ships, and thus are not affected by the treaty, even when resting on the seabed. *See also* NONPROLIFERATION, 225; NON-PROLIFERATION TREATY (NPT), 226; NUCLEAR-FREE ZONES (NFZ), 228; OUTER SPACE TREATY, 256.

Significance   The main intent of the Seabed Arms Control Treaty was to prevent intrusion of nuclear weapons into an area presumably still free of them. Once again, objections raised by both the Soviet Union and the United States resulted in a watered-down version of the original text that contained major ambiguities and loopholes. For example, although nuclear emplacements are forbidden, permanent structures to service missile-carrying submarines are not; neither are nuclear facilities placed in the territorial waters of client states who give their permission for such structures.[46] In addition, the entire issue of territorial limits remains unclear under international law; this has caused some signatories to add clauses reserving the right to remove any military facilities they discover within 200 miles of their coasts, or on the continental shelves adjoining their coasts, however far they may extend. The issue of enforcement is also a problem; only the major powers have the technology to produce (or even detect) such facilities, and they are not apt to be forthcoming with hard data about their own underwater military capabilities.

Standing Consultative Commission (SCC)   **(262)**
A joint U.S.-Soviet commission established by SALT I and II to implement the agreements produced by those talks. The Standing Consultative Commission was established by Article XIII of the ABM treaty, which stated that the SCC would "(a) consider questions concerning compliance with the [treaty] and related situations which may be considered ambiguous; (b) provide . . . such information as either party considers necessary to assure . . . compliance; (c) consider questions involving unintended interference with . . . verification; (d) consider possible changes in the strategic situation . . . ; (e) agree upon procedures and dates for destruction . . . of ABM systems . . . ; (f) consider . . . possible proposals for further increasing the viability of this Treaty . . . ; (g) consider . . . proposals for further measures aimed at limiting strategic arms."[47] In December 1972, the "Memorandum of Understanding Between the USA and USSR Regarding the Establishment of a Standing Consultative Commission" provided that each government would be represented by a commissioner and deputy commissioner (plus appropriate staff), and that the SCC would meet at least twice annually at Geneva. A May 1973 "Protocol, with Regulations, Regarding the US-Soviet Standing Consultative Commission on Arms Limitation" further elaborated on this framework. The unratified SALT II treaty also provided for implementation by the SCC, assigning it much greater responsibilities than did SALT I. *See also* STRATEGIC ARMS LIMITATION TALKS I (SALT I), 264; STRATEGIC ARMS LIMITATION TALKS II (SALT II), 265.

Significance   The Standing Consultative Commission was established by SALT I both to implement the dismantling of ABM sites, and to provide a permanent forum for discussions on arms control matters between the superpowers; SALT II merely expanded upon these responsibilities. Located at Geneva, Switzerland (a neutral site), "the essence of the SCC implementation task is to head off potential gross dislocations or irretrievable circumstances by acting early enough and finding mutually acceptable clarifications and implementing understandings, as well as inducing unilateral changes in troublesome activities, to sustain intact the agreements."[48] In these tasks the SCC has generally been successful at reducing tensions and stopping potential violations of the ABM treaty and the Interim Agreement, even during the early years of President Ronald W. Reagan. As Robert W. Buchheim and Dan Caldwell state, it "serves as a proven prototype to be used as a model in devising consultative mechanisms for implementations of agreements" on other subjects;[49] it also provides an ongoing structure of permanent consultation between East and West on arms control matters, which could itself be easily expanded upon.

Stockholm International Peace Research Institute (263) (SIPRI)

An organization which sponsors research into peace, conflict, the arms trade, and arms control. Established in 1966 by the Swedish parliament to commemorate 150 years of unbroken peace in Sweden, SIPRI is financed by the Swedish government, but operates as an independent institute, its staff, governing board, and Scientific Council being drawn from experts around the world (including Eastern Europe). Its stated aim is "to produce a factual and balanced account of a controversial subject—on the arms race and how to stop it."[50] SIPRI promotes such research by sponsoring conferences and publishing books, particularly its yearbook (beginning in 1968–69), which provides voluminous statistics on the world arms trade, plus ongoing monitoring of arms control agreements and their implementation. *See also* ARMS CONTROL AND DISARMAMENT, 238; ARMS CONTROL AND DISARMAMENT AGENCY (ACDA), 239; CONFERENCES AND COMMITTEES ON DISARMAMENT, 244; NONPROLIFERATION, 225; UNITED NATIONS DISARMAMENT COMMISSION (UNDC), 268.

Significance　The effectiveness of organizations such as SIPRI is difficult to judge. Although its stated purpose is providing hard information on arms transactions and arms control issues, which it does very effectively, the rationale behind the compilation of this data is the "reversal of increasingly militarized international political relations through arms control and disarmament agreements."[51] SIPRI's effect on this process is unknown and probably unknowable, although probably more limited than SIPRI members believe, since the two superpowers have tended to reserve any real arms control negotiations to themselves. Still, the publication of accurate information on arms sales and disarmament agreements clearly serves a useful purpose, as does the education of the populace at large. The world would probably be better served if SIPRI had more influence on events, but that is unlikely, given the realities of superpower politics.

Strategic Arms Limitation Talks I (SALT I)   (264)
(1969–1972)

A series of arms control talks between the United States and the Soviet Union that resulted in the ABM treaty and the Interim Agreement. Negotiations began in November 1969, not long after President Richard M. Nixon's inauguration, and were concluded in May 1972. The first agreement reached, the Treaty Between the United States of America and the Union of Soviet Socialist Republics on the Limitation of Anti-Ballistic Missile Systems (popularly known as the ABM treaty), limits such systems to two emplacements each in the United States and Soviet Union (one covering each national capital, one an ICBM site); these facilities cannot be made the basis of a nationwide ABM system. Both states also agree not "to develop, test, or deploy ABM systems or components" (Article V).[52] Certain types of radar installations beneficial to ABM systems are prohibited. The treaty was ratified on September 30, 1972. A second document, the Interim Agreement Between the United States of America and the Union of Soviet Socialist Republics on Certain Measures with Respect to the Limitation of Strategic Offensive Arms (popularly called the Interim Agreement), was intended to last for five years, until a SALT II treaty could be negotiated. The document froze ICBM launchers at then-existing levels, and submarine-based systems at agreed-upon ceilings; mobile launchers were not affected by the agreement. Post–SALT I agreements include the Prevention of Nuclear War Agreement, the Threshold Test Ban Treaty, and the Peaceful Nuclear Explosions Treaty. The ABM treaty also established the Standing Consultative Commission (SCC) at Geneva to provide a continuing forum for both states to resolve differences under the agreements. *See also* PEACEFUL NUCLEAR EXPLOSIONS TREATY (PNET), 258; PREVENTION OF NUCLEAR WAR AGREEMENT, 259; STANDING CONSULTATIVE COMMISSION (SCC), 262; STRATEGIC ARMS LIMITATION TALKS II (SALT II), 265; THRESHOLD TEST BAN TREATY (TTBT), 267.

Significance   SALT I represented the culmination of President Richard M. Nixon and Henry A. Kissinger's efforts to reduce superpower tensions by slowing or stopping the arms race, thereby inaugurating a decade of euphoria in superpower relations. The administration of President Ronald W. Reagan, however, accused the Soviets of violating the ABM treaty by constructing unauthorized radar installations in Siberia; the Soviets raised similar questions about U.S. radar installations in Greenland and England. The Russians have also labelled President Reagan's Strategic Defense Initiative ("Star Wars") a violation of the spirit, if not the letter, of the ABM treaty, since its main effect would be to provide an umbrella against nuclear attack, clearly prohibited by the agreement. The United States has responded by pointing to the supplemental Agreed Statements, Common Understandings, and Unilateral Statements to the ABM treaty, Paragraph D, which states: " . . . in the event ABM systems based on other physical principles and including components capable of substituting for ABM interceptor missiles, ABM launchers, or ABM radars are created in the future, specific limitations on such systems and their components would be subject to discussion in accordance with . . . the Treaty."[53] Since they have not been so discussed or agreed upon separately, they are, according to the United States, permitted. SIPRI and many outside observers, particularly West Europeans, disagree with this view. Nonetheless, despite Soviet objections to SDI, the ABM treaty remains in effect, and its SCC operational, providing an ongoing forum for arms control discussions between the superpowers, and fueling the hope that true arms control or disarmament may yet be achieved.

Strategic Arms Limitation Talks II (SALT II) (265) (1972–1979)

A series of discussions that led to an arms control treaty that was never ratified. Negotiations for SALT II began in November 1972, immediately following ratification of the SALT I agreements. President Richard M. Nixon's exit from office in 1974 marked the beginning of a long decline in U.S.-Soviet relations that culminated with the Soviet invasion of Afghanistan in December of 1979. However, a SALT II treaty, formally called the Treaty Between the United States of America and the Union of Soviet Socialist Republics on the Limitation of Strategic Offensive Arms, was signed on June 19, 1979, but never ratified. It provided for an equalization of delivery vehicles on both sides, a ban on construction of new land-based missile launchers, and limits on the number of warheads that could be carried by specific kinds of missiles or bombers. The treaty would be verified through national technical means (NTM), including spy satellites, intelligence reports, etc., with which each country pledged not to interfere.[54] *See also* AFGHAN WAR, 109; NATIONAL TECHNICAL MEANS (NTM), 253; STANDING CONSULTATIVE COMMISSION (SCC), 262; STRATEGIC ARMS LIMITATION TALKS I (SALT I), 264; STRATEGIC ARMS REDUCTION TALKS (START) AND INTERMEDIATE-RANGE NUCLEAR FORCES (INF) TALKS, 266.

Significance The ink was scarcely dry on the SALT II treaty before it was attacked in the United States by both the left and right. The latter claimed the Soviets would use loopholes in the treaty to expand its military superiority over the United States, while the former said the agreement provided little more than superficial readjustments of existing nuclear weaponry. As W. K. H. Panofsky states: "One has to conclude that the enactment of these treaties [SALT I and SALT II] has only a relatively small technical impact on the evolution of the strategic arms race between the United States and Soviet Union. . . . SALT has done . . . little to reduce the risks . . . from possible nuclear war."[55] The 1979 Soviet invasion of Afghanistan, combined with President Ronald W. Reagan's efforts to restore U.S. military forces to parity levels, spelled an end to chances for ratification in the U.S. Senate. However, both sides did agree to abide by the treaty so long as their opposites followed suit. This tacit compliance ended in 1986, when President Reagan deliberately allowed the limit on submarine-based missile launchers to be exceeded. Arms control discussions resumed in 1981 and 1982 with the INF talks and START, but real progress on disarmament remained crippled until the Reagan-Gorbachev summits began in 1985.

Strategic Arms Reduction Talks (START) and Intermediate-Range Nuclear Forces (INF) Talks (1981–1983) (266)

A series of arms control discussions held by the United States and the Soviet Union between November 1981 and December 1983 that achieved few results in themselves, but set the stage for later negotiations. After the Soviet invasion of Afghanistan had effectively killed the SALT II treaty, the new U.S. president, Ronald W. Reagan, criticized the SALT negotiations as "freezing" in place artificial limits on U.S. forces that, he said, had given the Soviets a strategic advantage while offering superficial arms control benefits to the United States. In October 1981, Reagan proposed his "zero option" plan, which would have eliminated all intermediate-range nuclear missiles. Negotiations with the Soviets began in Geneva the following month. In 1982, President Reagan similarly proposed deep cuts in missile launchers, particularly the land-based systems favored by the Soviets, with a ceiling of 5,000 total warheads available to each side (and a subceiling of 2,500 for land-based systems);[56] the START negotiations began in June 1982. In March 1983, Reagan proposed his "Star Wars" (Strategic Defense Initiative) program, and later that year NATO announced deployment of U.S. INF missiles in Europe. The Soviets then walked out of the Geneva talks in December. *See also* AFGHAN WAR, 109; GENEVA SUMMIT, 248; INTERMEDIATE-RANGE NUCLEAR FORCES TREATY (INFT), 250; STRATEGIC ARMS LIMITATION TALKS II (SALT II), 265.

Significance   The START and INF negotiations were the Reagan administration's first arms control proposals, and reflected President Reagan's particular view of the world: the Soviets were an "evil empire," the Americans the force for good in the world. U.S. military strength had been allowed to diminish during the SALT years, Reagan stated, so freezing military forces at their current levels, which the Soviets offered, was unacceptable. The U.S. proposals were made on a take-it-or-leave-it basis, using the threat of a new arms race and subsequent U.S. military buildup to counter Soviet objections. Not surprisingly, with both sides unwilling to compromise, the talks failed. They were not to resume again until Soviet General Secretary Mikhail Gorbachev acceded to power in March of 1985. By then President Reagan's original INF proposals had assumed new life, and were largely incorporated into the INF treaty signed at Washington in December 1987, and ratified and promulgated in May 1988.

Threshold Test Ban Treaty (TTBT) (1974) (267)

An agreement to limit the testing of nuclear weapons. The Treaty Between the United States of America and the Union of Soviet Socialist Republics on the Limitation of Underground Nuclear Weapons Tests, its official title, derived from follow-up negotiations to the original SALT talks, and was designed to complement the Limited Test Ban Treaty (which banned all nuclear tests except those underground). Article I states: "Each Party undertakes to prohibit, to prevent, and not to carry out any underground nuclear weapon test having a yield exceeding 150 kilotons at any place under its jurisdiction or control."[57] The treaty further provides for an exchange of data on permitted tests in order to calibrate instruments, and states that verification shall be through national technical means (NTM). The agreement was linked with the Peaceful Nuclear Explosions Treaty, with an initial duration of five years; neither was ratified by the U.S. Senate, but both sides have agreed to observe the limits so long as the other follows suit. *See also* COMPREHENSIVE TEST BAN TREATY (CTBT), 242; LIMITED TEST BAN TREATY (LTBT), 251; NATIONAL TECHNICAL MEANS (NTM), 253; PEACEFUL NUCLEAR EXPLOSIONS TREATY (PNET), 258; STANDING CONSULTATIVE COMMISSION (SCC), 262; STRATEGIC ARMS LIMITATION TALKS I (SALT I), 264.

Significance   The Threshold Test Ban Treaty was intended to prevent tests of large nuclear weapons without on-site verification. Negotiators felt that tests over 150 kilotons could be detected with the means then available, and so set that level as the threshold. The

Soviets insisted upon a clause that allowed one or two "accidental" tests over this limit annually. Senate critics were concerned over the relatively high level of the threshold (most underground tests are in the 10–20 kiloton range) and the difficulty of verification. President Jimmy Carter hoped to replace the TTBT with a Comprehensive Test Ban Treaty, but was unsuccessful. In 1983, President Ronald W. Reagan stated: "We have reason to believe that there have been numerous violations. And, yet, because of the lack of verification capability, we could not make such a charge and sustain it."[58] Subsequently, revisions were proposed to the Soviets—these were rejected. With the increasing multiplication of missile warheads and the increasing accuracy of their delivery systems, the need to test large weapons has declined greatly, leaving the TTBT as an example of an arms control agreement that has largely been eclipsed by subsequent events.

United Nations Disarmament Commission (UNDC)   (268)
An agency of the United Nations promoting arms control and disarmament. The United Nations Disarmament Commission was founded in 1952 from the merging of two previous commissions on atomic energy and conventional armaments. It accomplished little until 1954, when a five-nation subcommittee (the United States, the Soviet Union, Canada, the United Kingdom, and France) was formed. Several nations then put forward arms control proposals, eventually leading to the 1955 Geneva Summit and the "Open Skies" Proposal from the United States. The subcommittee dissolved in acrimony in 1957. In 1961, the Eighteen-Nation Committee on Disarmament (ENDC) was formed, with membership increasing to 26 nations in 1969, and to 31 nations in 1974. The 1978 Special Session on Disarmament (SSOD) reactivated the UNDC in 1979 as a successor to the Conference of the Committee on Disarmament (CD), with a membership of 40 nations, including all the nuclear powers. *See also* ANTARCTIC TREATY, 237; ARMS CONTROL AND DISARMAMENT, 238; LIMITED TEST BAN TREATY (LTBT), 251; "OPEN SKIES" PROPOSAL, 256.

Significance   The original U.N. Disarmament Commission led to the first serious negotiations between the atomic powers on the restriction of nuclear weapons, and while the talks were ultimately unsuccessful, they did set the stage for the Antarctic Treaty and the Limited Test Ban Treaty. The new UNDC has been controlled by Third World countries, who have focused "most of its attention on comprehensive disarmament strategies and programs, including the 'Declaration of the 1980s as the Second Disarmament Decade,'"[59] and have used the commission to recommend items for consideration by the Geneva-based Committee on Disarmament (CD). Both bodies have been criticized by outside observers, particularly the major powers, as being interested primarily in making political points rather than striving for any real arms control.

NOTES

1. War and Peace

1. David W. Ziegler, *War, Peace, and International Politics* (Boston: Little, Brown, 1987), 460.

2. James Lee Ray, *Global Politics* (Boston: Houghton Mifflin, 1987), 323.

3. Randolph M. Siverson and Michael R. Tennefoss, "Power, Alliance, and the Escalation of International Peace, 1815–1965," *American Political Science Review* 78 (December 1984): 1062.

4. Ibid., 1063.

5. Ziegler, *War, Peace, and International Politics*, 34.

6. John Spanier, *Games Nations Play* (Washington, D.C.: Congressional Quarterly Press, 1987), 34.

7. Karl Deutsch, *The Analysis of International Relations* (Englewood Cliffs, N.J.: Prentice-Hall, 1968), 21–39.

8. James Dull, *The Politics of American Foreign Policy* (Englewood Cliffs, N.J.: Prentice-Hall, 1985), 159.

9. Henry A. Kissinger, *White House Years* (Boston: Little, Brown, 1979), 67–68.

10. Ziegler, *War, Peace, and International Politics*, 221.

11. Spanier, *Games Nations Play*, 142–150.

12. Kenneth N. Waltz, "The Stability of a Bipolar World," *Daedalus* 12 (Summer 1964): 881–909.

13. Richard N. Rosecrance, "Bipolarity, Multipolarity, and the Future," *Journal of Conflict Resolution* 10 (September 1966): 314–337.

14. Richard Ned Lebow, *Between Peace and War: The Nature of International Crisis* (Baltimore: Johns Hopkins University Press, 1981): 62–71.

15. Forest L. Grieves, *Conflict and Order: An Introduction to International Relations* (Boston: Houghton Mifflin, 1977), 101.

16. Spanier, *Games Nations Play*, 128–130.

17. Ziegler, *War, Peace, and International Politics*, 113.

18. Ibid., 114.

19. Theodore Abel, "The Element of Decision in the Pattern of War," *American Sociological Review* 6 (December 1941): 853–859.

20. Grieves, *Conflict and Order,* 92–95.

21. Charles W. Kegley, Jr., and Eugene R. Wittkopf, *World Politics: Trend and Transformation* (New York: St. Martin's, 1981), 353.

22. Ibid.

23. Spanier, *Games Nations Play,* 568.

24. Claude E. Welch, Jr., "Civilian Control of the Military: Myth and Reality," in *Civilian Control of the Military: Theory and Cases from Developing Countries* (Albany: State University of New York Press, 1976), 26.

25. J. William Fulbright, *The Crippled Giant* (New York: Vintage Books, 1972), 193.

26. Ibid.

27. Ziegler, *War, Peace, and International Politics,* 294.

28. Gilbert R. Winham, "Practitioners' Views of International Negotiation," *World Politics* 32 (October 1979): 111–135.

29. Grieves, *Conflict and Order,* 344.

30. Jeffrey M. Elliot and Mervyn M. Dymally, *Fidel Castro: Nothing Can Stop the Course of History* (New York: Pathfinder Press, 1986), 8–9.

31. Paul Warnke, "The Need for Arms Control," in *Defense Sense: The Search for a Rational Military Policy,* ed. by Ronald V. Dellums (Cambridge, Mass.: Ballinger, 1983), 34.

32. Jeremy J. Stone, "Reagan's Policy Can't Work," in *Defense Sense: The Search for a Rational Military Policy,* ed. by Ronald V. Dellums (Cambridge, Mass.: Ballinger, 1983), 132.

33. Ibid.

34. Donald M. Snow, *National Security: Enduring Problems of U.S. Defense Policy* (New York: St. Martin's, 1987), 143.

35. Henry A. Kissinger, *Nuclear Weapons and Foreign Policy* (New York: Harper & Row, 1957), 425.

36. Jack C. Plano and Roy Olton, *The International Relations Dictionary* (Santa Barbara, Calif.: ABC-CLIO, 1982), 179–180.

37. Bernard Brodie, *Strategy in the Missile Age* (Princeton, N.J.: Princeton University Press, 1959), 311.

38. Doris A. Graber, *Mass Media and American Politics* (Washington, D.C.: Congressional Quarterly Press, 1984), 325.

39. Dan Nimmo and James E. Combs, *Mediated Political Realities* (New York: Longman, 1983), 34.

40. Edward H. Carr, *The Twenty Years' Crisis, 1919–1939* (London: Macmillan, 1951), 8.

41. Kenneth W. Thompson, "Paths Toward Peace," in *The Theory and Practice of International Relations,* ed. by David S. McLellan, William C. Olson, and Fred A. Sonderman (Englewood Cliffs, N.J.: Prentice-Hall, 1974), 484.

42. National Academy of Peace and Conflict Resolution, *To Establish the United States Academy of Peace* (Washington, D.C.: U.S. Government Printing Office, 1981), 146.

43. Grieves, *Conflict and Order*, 186.

44. Richard H. Foster and Robert V. Edington, *Viewing International Relations and World Politics* (Englewood Cliffs, N.J.: Prentice-Hall, 1985), 124.

45. Spanier, *Games Nations Play*, 164–166.

46. Lloyd Jensen, *Explaining Foreign Policy* (Englewood Cliffs, N.J.: Prentice-Hall, 1982), 200–202.

47. Kegley and Wittkopf, *World Politics*, 97.

48. Spanier, *Games Nations Play*, 371.

49. Ibid.

50. Ibid., 213.

51. Ibid., 3.

52. Thomas F. Eagleton, *War and Presidential Power: A Chronicle of Congressional Surrender* (New York: Liveright, 1974), 11.

53. Ibid., 207.

54. Ibid., 218–219.

2. Military Security

1. Donald M. Snow, *National Security: Enduring Problems of U.S. Defense Policy* (New York: St. Martin's, 1987), 163.

2. Ibid., 164.

3. Ibid.

4. Bob Burton, *Top Secret: A Clandestine Operator's Glossary of Terms* (New York: Berkley Books, 1987), 101–102.

5. Robert J. Art and Robert Jervis, *International Politics: Anarchy, Force, Political Economy, and Decision Making* (Boston: Little, Brown, 1985), 147–148.

6. Burton, *Top Secret*, 165–167.

7. Ibid., 174.

8. Martin Binkin, "Manpower Procurement: The Influence of Demography, Technology, and Budgets," in *The Strategic Dimension of Military Manpower*, ed. by Gregory D. Foster, Alan Ned Sabrosky, and William J. Taylor, Jr. (Cambridge, Mass.: Ballinger, 1987), 91.

9. Ibid.

10. Ibid., 92.

11. James Fallows, *National Defense* (New York: Vintage Books, 1981), 108–109.

12. Ibid., 107.

13. Ibid., 108.

14. David P. Barash, *The Arms Race and Nuclear War* (Belmont, Calif.: Wadsworth, 1987), 203.

15. John Spanier, *Games Nations Play* (Washington, D.C.: Congressional Quarterly Press, 1987), 506.

16. Harry Kaufmann, *Social Psychology: The Study of Human Interaction* (New York: Holt, Rinehart and Winston, 1973), 432.

17. Jay Luvass, "Napoleon on the Art of Command," in *The Parameters of War: Military History from the Journal of the U.S. Army War College,* ed. by Lloyd J. Matthews and Dale E. Brown (Washington, D.C.: Pergamon-Brassey's, 1987), 79.

18. Ibid.

19. Ibid., 80.

20. Ibid.

21. Kaufmann, *Social Psychology,* 434.

22. Gregory D. Foster, "Manpower as an Element of Military Power," in *The Strategic Dimension of Military Manpower,* ed. by Gregory D. Foster, Alan Ned Sabrosky, and William J. Taylor, Jr. (Cambridge, Mass.: Ballinger, 1987), 13.

23. Ibid., 14–15.

24. Snow, *National Security,* 160.

25. Michael I. Handel, "Numbers Do Count: The Question of Quality versus Quantity," in *The Strategic Imperative: New Policies for American Security,* ed. by Samuel P. Huntington (Cambridge, Mass.: Ballinger, 1982), 194.

26. Ibid., 195.

27. Ibid.

28. Karl von Clausewitz, *On War,* ed. by Anatol Rapoport (Baltimore: Penguin Books, 1968), 241.

29. Bruce Palmer, Jr., "Strategic Guidelines for the United States in the 1980s," in *Grand Strategy for the 1980s,* ed. by Bruce Palmer, Jr. (Washington, D.C.: American Enterprise Institute, 1978), 73.

30. Michael Howard, *The Causes of War and Other Essays* (Cambridge, Mass.: Harvard University Press, 1984), 112.

31. Organization of the Joints Chiefs of Staff, *Military Posture FY 1985* (Washington, D.C.: U.S. Government Printing Office, 1984), 8.

32. Snow, *National Security,* 32.

33. Harold Brown, *Thinking about National Security: Defense and Foreign Policy in a Dangerous World* (Boulder, Colo.: Westview Press, 1983), 9.

34. Barash, *The Arms Race and Nuclear War,* 323.

35. Ibid.

36. Ibid.

37. Ibid.

38. James Paul Wesley, "Frequency of Wars and Geographical Opportunity," *Journal of Conflict Resolution* 6 (December 1962): 387–389.

39. Walter S. Jones, *The Logic of International Relations* (Glenview, Ill.: Scott, Foresman, 1988), 273.

40. Patrick Robert Reid and Maurice Michael, *Prisoners of War* (New York: Beaufort Books, 1984), 30.

41. Ibid., 14.

42. Ibid., 51.

43. Ibid.

44. Snow, *National Security*, 168.

45. *The National Observer*, April 12, 1975, 4.

46. Forest L. Grieves, *Conflict and Order: An Introduction to International Relations* (Boston: Houghton Mifflin, 1977), 176.

3. The Arms Race

1. Jacques S. Gansler, *The Defense Industry* (Cambridge, Mass.: MIT Press, 1980), 1.

2. J. M. Blair, *Economic Concentration: Structure, Behavior, and Public Policy* (New York: Harcourt Brace Jovanovich, 1972), 380.

3. Jack C. Plano and Roy Olton, *The International Relations Dictionary* (Santa Barbara, Calif.: ABC-CLIO, 1982), 120.

4. Coit D. Blacker, *Reluctant Warriors: The United States, the Soviet Union, and Arms Control* (New York: W. H. Freeman, 1987), 79.

5. Arthur Macy Cox, *Russian Roulette: The Superpower Game* (New York: Times Books, 1982), 94.

6. Ibid., 95.

7. Blacker, *Reluctant Warriors*, 96.

8. Gansler, *The Defense Industry*, 205.

9. Michael Moodie, "Arms Transfers and Future Conflict," in *The Future of Conflict in the 1980s*, ed. by William J. Taylor, Jr., and Steven A. Maaranen (Lexington, Mass.: Lexington Books, 1982), 65.

10. Richard K. Betts, "Elusive Equivalence: The Political and Military Meaning of the Nuclear Balance," in *The Strategic Imperative: New Policies for American Security*, ed. by Samuel P. Huntington (Cambridge, Mass.: Ballinger, 1982), 122.

11. Morris Janowitz, *Military Conflict: Essays in the Institutional Analysis of War and Peace* (Beverly Hills, Calif.: SAGE Publications, 1975), 58.

12. Henry E. Eccles, *Military Power in a Free Society* (Newport, R.I.: Naval War College Press, 1979), 126.

13. John Finnis, Joseph M. Boyle, Jr., and Germain Grisez, *Nuclear Deterrence, Morality and Realism* (Oxford: Clarendon Press, 1987), 116.

14. President's Commission on Strategic Forces, "Final Report," in *The Race for Security: Arms and Arms Control in the Reagan Years*, ed. by Robert Travis Scott (Lexington, Mass.: Lexington Books, 1987), 111.

15. Ibid.

16. Ronald L. Tammen, "The Reagan Strategic Program," in *The Race*

for Security: Arms and Arms Control in the Reagan Years, ed. by Robert Travis Scott (Lexington, Mass.: Lexington Books, 1987), 10.

17. President's Commission on Strategic Forces, "Final Report," 111.

18. Plano and Olton, *The International Relations Dictionary,* 379–380.

19. Gansler, *The Defense Industry,* 13.

20. Cox, *Russian Roulette,* 62.

21. Ibid., quoting Jimmy Carter, 83.

22. Finnis, Boyle, and Grisez, *Nuclear Deterrence, Morality and Realism,* 170.

23. Ibid.

24. Ibid., 148.

25. Aaron L. Friedberg, "The Evolution of U.S. Strategic 'Doctrine'— 1945 to 1981," in *The Strategic Imperative: New Policies for American Security,* ed. by Samuel P. Huntington (Cambridge, Mass.: Ballinger, 1982), 78.

26. Ibid., 79.

27. Lincoln P. Bloomfield, "Nuclear Crisis and Human Frailty," in *Prospects for Peacemaking: A Citizen's Guide to Safer Nuclear Strategy,* ed. by Harlan Cleveland and Lincoln P. Bloomfield (Cambridge, Mass.: MIT Press, 1987), 105–106.

28. Cox, *Russian Roulette,* 167.

29. Ibid., 76–77.

30. Barry M. Blechman, *U.S. Security in the Twenty-First Century* (Boulder, Colo.: Westview Press, 1987), 61.

31. Blacker, *Reluctant Warriors,* 154–155.

32. Samuel P. Huntington, "The Renewal of Strategy," in *The Strategic Imperative: New Policies for American Security,* ed. by Samuel P. Huntington (Cambridge, Mass.: Ballinger, 1982), 2, 22.

33. Edgar G. Kleckley, "The Political Prerequisites of Alliance Strategy," in *Conventional Deterrence: Alternatives for European Defense,* ed. by James R. Golden, Asa A. Clark, and Bruce E. Arlinghaus (Lexington, Mass.: Lexington Books, 1984), 59, 61.

34. Raymond Gartoff, *Perspectives on the Strategic Balance* (Washington, D.C.: Brookings Institution, 1983), 5.

35. George H. Quester, *The Future of Nuclear Deterrence* (Lexington, Mass.: Lexington Books, 1986), 69–70.

36. Bernard J. Firestone, *The Quest for Nuclear Stability: John F. Kennedy and the Soviet Union* (Westport, Conn.: Greenwood Press, 1982), 80–81.

37. Blacker, *Reluctant Warriors,* 20.

38. Plano and Olton, *The International Relations Dictionary,* 10–11.

39. James R. Golden, Asa A. Clark, and Bruce E. Arlinghaus, eds., *Conventional Deterrence: Alternatives for European Defense* (Lexington, Mass.: Lexington Books, 1984), 186, 228.

40. Brian Beckett, *Weapons of Tomorrow* (New York: Plenum Press, 1983), 148.

4. Collective Security

1. Lawrence Ziring, *The Middle East Political Dictionary* (Santa Barbara, Calif.: ABC-CLIO, 1984), 309.

2. Roy Godson, "Special Supplement: U.S. Intelligence Policy," in *American Defense Annual, 1986–1987*, ed. by Joseph Kruzel (Lexington, Mass.: D. C. Heath, 1986), 197.

3. David W. Ziegler, *War, Peace, and International Politics* (Boston: Little, Brown, 1987), 185.

4. Ibid., 193.

5. Forest L. Grieves, *Conflict and Order: An Introduction to International Relations* (Boston: Houghton Mifflin, 1977), 207–211.

6. Leon P. Baradat, *Political Ideologies* (Englewood Cliffs, N.J.: Prentice-Hall, 1979), 291.

7. Ibid.

8. Larry Berman, *Planning a Tragedy: The Americanization of the War in Vietnam* (New York: W. W. Norton, 1982), 9.

9. Ibid., 9–10.

10. Richard H. Foster and Robert V. Edington, *Viewing International Relations and World Politics* (Englewood Cliffs, N.J.: Prentice-Hall, 1985), 147.

11. Walter S. Jones and Steven J. Rosen, *The Logic of International Relations* (Boston: Little, Brown, 1982), 476–477.

12. Grieves, *Conflict and Order*, 153–154.

13. Ernest E. Rossi and Jack C. Plano, *The Latin American Political Dictionary* (Santa Barbara, Calif.: ABC-CLIO, 1980), 231.

14. Ibid., 234.

15. Ibid., 233.

16. Ibid., 235.

17. Ibid., 232.

18. John Spanier, *American Foreign Policy Since World War II* (New York: Holt, Rinehart and Winston, 1985), 153.

19. Ibid.

20. Ziegler, *War, Peace, and International Politics*, 202–203.

21. Rossi and Plano, *The Latin American Political Dictionary*, 211.

22. Richard M. Nixon, *U.S. Foreign Policy for the 1970's: Building for Peace: A Report to the Congress* (Washington, D.C.: U.S. Government Printing Office, February 25, 1971), 14.

23. Melvin Gurtov, *The United States Against the Third World: Antinationalism and Intervention* (New York: Praeger, 1974), 86–87.

24. Ibid., 87.

25. Spanier, *American Foreign Policy Since World War II*, 78–79.

26. Grieves, *Conflict and Order*, 246.

27. Ziegler, *War, Peace, and International Politics*, 158.

28. Jones and Rosen, *The Logic of International Relations*, 59.

29. James A. Nathan and James K. Oliver, *Foreign Policy Making and the American Political System* (Boston: Little, Brown, 1987), 64.

30. Jones and Rosen, *The Logic of International Relations*, 60.

31. Ibid.

32. Ibid., 60–61.

33. Ibid., 61.

34. Ibid.

35. Nathan and Oliver, *Foreign Policy Making and the American Political System*, 66.

36. Grieves, *Conflict and Order*, 280.

37. Ibid.

38. James L. Ray, *Global Politics* (Boston: Houghton Mifflin, 1987), 361.

39. Grieves, *Conflict and Order*, 307.

40. United Nations, "Report on the Work of the Organization," *UN Chronicle* 19 (October 1982): 2.

41. Robert E. Riggs and Jack C. Plano, *The United Nations: International Organization and World Politics* (Chicago: Dorsey Press, 1988), 36–37.

42. Ibid., 40.

43. Ibid., 134.

44. Ray, *Global Politics*, 365–366.

45. Jack C. Plano and Roy Olton, *The International Relations Dictionary* (Santa Barbara, Calif.: ABC-CLIO, 1982), 362.

46. Ibid.

47. Ziegler, *War, Peace, and International Politics*, 139–140.

5. Conventional Wars and Weapons

1. Anthony Arnold, *Afghanistan: The Soviet Invasion in Perspective* (Stanford, Calif.: Hoover Institution Press, 1985), 90.

2. Ibid., xii.

3. John I. Alger, *Definitions and Doctrine of the Military Art: Past and Present* (Wayne, N.J.: Avery Publishing Group, 1985), 187.

4. Michael Skinner, *USN: Naval Operations in the Eighties* (Novato, Calif.: Presidio Press, 1986), 46.

5. William W. Kaufmann, *A Thoroughly Efficient Navy* (Washington, D.C.: Brookings Institution, 1987), 7.

6. Harlan K. Ullman and R. James Woolsey, "Seapower and Projection Forces," in *American Defense Annual: 1985–1986*, ed. by George E. Hudson and Joseph Kruzel (Lexington, Mass.: Lexington Books, 1985), 124.

7. Paul L. Pierce, "Aircraft Carriers and Large Surface Combatants,"

in *The Soviet Navy: Strengths and Liabilities,* ed. by Bruce W. Watson and Susan M. Watson (Boulder, Colo.: Westview Press, 1986), 72–73.

8. James N. Constant, *Fundamentals of Strategic Weapons: Offense and Defense Systems* (The Hague: Martinus Nijhoff, 1981), 15.

9. Michael Krepon and Alton Frye, "Arms Control," in *American Defense Annual: 1985–1986,* ed. by George E. Hudson and Joseph Kruzel (Lexington, Mass.: Lexington Books, 1985), 174.

10. Constant, *Fundamentals of Strategic Weapons,* 356–357.

11. Ibid., 356.

12. Ibid., 372.

13. J. A. English, "Thoughts on Close-Quarter Anti-Tank Combat," in *Jane's Military Review,* ed. by Ian V. Hogg (London: Jane's, 1985), 126.

14. Michael C. Brown and Thomas J. Leney, "Battlefield Nuclear Weapons and NATO Defense Doctrines and Technologies," in *Conventional Deterrence: Alternatives for European Defense,* ed. by James R. Golden, Asa A. Clark, and Bruce E. Arlinghaus (Lexington, Mass.: Lexington Books, 1984), 166–167.

15. Thomas Davis, "Another Decade of Confrontation in the Middle East," in *The Future of Conflict in the 1980s,* ed. by William J. Taylor, Jr., and Steven A. Maaranen (Lexington, Mass.: Lexington Books, 1982), 240–241.

16. Michael I. Handel, "Numbers Do Count: The Question of Quality versus Quantity," in *The Strategic Imperative: New Policies for American Security,* ed. by Samuel P. Huntington (Cambridge, Mass.: Ballinger, 1982), 194.

17. Brown and Leney, "Battlefield Nuclear Weapons and NATO Defense Doctrines and Technologies," 170.

18. Eliot A. Cohen, "Guessing Game: A Reappraisal of Systems Analysis," in *The Strategic Imperative: New Policies for American Security,* ed. by Samuel P. Huntington (Cambridge, Mass.: Ballinger, 1982), 185.

19. Ibid., 182.

20. Jorma K. Miettinen, "The Effect of New Military Technology on Future Battlefield Tactics and the Structure of the Armed Forces," in *The Dangers of New Weapons Systems,* ed. by William Gutteridge and Trevor Taylor (London: Macmillan, 1983), 69.

21. English, "Thoughts on Close-Quarter Anti-Tank Combat," 134.

22. Norman Polmar, *The Ships and Aircraft of the U.S. Fleet* (Annapolis, Md.: Naval Institute Press, 1984), 102.

23. Skinner, *USN: Naval Operations in the Eighties,* 61.

24. Ibid., 62.

25. Constant, *Fundamentals of Strategic Weapons,* 238.

26. Ibid.

27. Alger, *Definitions and Doctrine of the Military Art,* 181–182.

28. *Jane's All the World's Aircraft: 1985–1986.* (London: Jane's, 1985), 495.

29. Brian Beckett, *Weapons of Tomorrow* (New York: Plenum Press, 1983), 28–29.

30. Constant, *Fundamentals of Strategic Weapons,* 240–244.

31. Owen Carrow, "Chemical Warfare," in *Jane's Military Review,* ed. by Ian V. Hogg (London: Jane's, 1985), 171.

32. Alger, *Definitions and Doctrine of the Military Art,* 169.

33. Kosta Tsipis, "Directed Energy Weapons—Feasibility and Effectiveness," in *The Dangers of New Weapons Systems,* ed. by William Gutteridge and Trevor Taylor (London: Macmillan, 1983), 31–32.

34. Beckett, *Weapons of Tommorow,* 92.

35. R. Reginald and Jeffrey M. Elliot, *Tempest in a Teapot: The Falkland Islands War* (San Bernardino, Calif.: Borgo Press, 1983), 129–139.

36. Alger, *Definitions and Doctrine of the Military Art,* 137.

37. Ibid., 179–180.

38. P. D. L. Glover, "Air Supremacy—The Enduring Principle," in *War in the Third Dimension: Essays in Contemporary Air Power,* ed. by R. A. Mason (London: Brassey's Defence Publishers, 1986), 74.

39. Mary Kaldor, "Introduction," in *Mad Dogs: The US Raids on Libya,* ed. by Mary Kaldor and Paul Anderson (London: Pluto Press, 1986), 1.

40. Richard A. Melanson, "The Grenada Intervention and U.S. Foreign Policy," in *Revolution and Intervention in Grenada: The New Jewel Movement, the United States, and the Caribbean,* ed. by Kai P. Schoenhals and Richard A. Melanson (Boulder, Colo.: Westview Press, 1985), 161.

41. Ibid., 154.

42. Ibid., 156.

43. Ibid., 160.

44. Ibid., 175–176.

45. *Jane's All the World's Aircraft: 1985–1986,* 240, 247, 310, 509.

46. Alger, *Definitions and Doctrine of the Military Art,* 183.

47. Brown and Leney, "Battlefield Nuclear Weapons and NATO Defense Doctrines and Technologies," 170.

48. Anthony Robinson, "Air Forces in Vietnam," in *The Vietnam War: An Almanac,* ed. by John S. Bowman (New York: World Almanac, 1985), 416.

49. Richard Cottam, "Iran and Soviet-American Relations," in *The Iranian Revolution and the Islamic Republic,* ed. by Nikki R. Keddie and Eric Hooglund (Syracuse, N.Y.: Syracuse University Press, 1986), 235.

50. Muriel Atkin, "The Islamic Republic and the Soviet Union," in *The Iranian Revolution and the Islamic Republic,* ed. by Nikki R. Keddie and Eric Hooglund (Syracuse, N.Y.: Syracuse University Press, 1986), 200.

51. Rodney W. Jones, "Regional Conflict and Strategic Challenge in Southwest Asia," in *The Future of Conflict in the 1980s,* ed. by William J. Taylor, Jr., and Steven A. Maaranen (Lexington, Mass.: Lexington Books, 1982), 263.

52. Michael T. Klare, "The Interventionist Impulse: U.S. Military Doctrine for Low-Intensity Warfare," in *Proinsurgency and Antiterrorism in the Eighties,* ed. by Michael T. Klare and Peter Kornbluth (New York: Pantheon Books, 1988), 67–68.

53. Malcolm Spaven, "A Piece of the Action: The Use of US Bases in Britain," in *Mad Dogs: The US Raids on Libya,* ed. by Mary Kaldor and Paul Anderson (London: Pluto Press, 1986), 22, 24.

54. Robert H. Kupperman and William J. Taylor, Jr., "Special Supplement: Low Intensity Conflict: The Strategic Challenge," in *American Defense Annual: 1985–1986,* ed. by George E. Hudson and Joseph Kruzel (Lexington, Mass.: Lexington Books, 1985), 211.

55. Ullman and Woolsey, "Seapower and Projection Forces," 120–121.

56. Caspar W. Weinberger, *Report of the Secretary of Defense* (Washington, D.C.: U.S. Government Printing Office, 1985), 139.

57. Alger, *Definitions and Doctrine of the Military Art,* 108, 113, 156, 178.

58. *Jane's Weapons Systems, 1986–1987,* ed. by Ronald T. Pretty (London: Jane's, 1986), 241–242.

59. Alger, *Definitions and Doctrine of the Military Art,* 187.

60. *Jane's Weapons Systems, 1986–1987,* 160.

61. Ibid., 166.

62. Ibid., 156.

63. Weinberger, *Report of the Secretary of Defense,* 144–145.

64. Christy Campbell, *Weapons of War* (New York: Peter Bedrick Books, 1983), 211–212.

65. Ibid., 228–229.

66. Gary Hart, "Arms Control: Toward a Redefinition," in *The Race for Security: Arms and Arms Control in the Reagan Years,* ed. by Robert Travis Scott (Lexington, Mass.: Lexington Books, 1987), 250.

67. "New Military Technologies," in *Arms Control and Military Force,* ed. by Christoph Bertram (Westmead, England: Gower & Allanheld, for the International Institute for Strategic Studies, 1980), 232.

68. Ibid., 234.

69. Ibid., 235.

70. Michael Moodie, "Arms Transfers and Future Conflict," in *The Future of Conflict in the 1980s,* ed. by William J. Taylor, Jr., and Steven A. Maaranen (Lexington, Mass.: Lexington Books, 1982), 67.

71. Christopher Lamb, "The Nature of Proxy Warfare," in *The Future of Conflict in the 1980s,* ed. by William J. Taylor, Jr., and Steven A. Maaranen (Lexington, Mass.: Lexington Books, 1982), 171.

72. Ibid., 175, 191.

73. Polmar, *The Ships and Aircraft of the U.S. Fleet,* 22.

74. Samuel P. Huntington, "The Renewal of Strategy," in *The Strategic Imperative: New Policies for American Security*, ed. by Samuel P. Huntington (Cambridge, Mass.: Ballinger, 1982), 27.

75. Kaufmann, *A Thoroughly Efficient Navy*, 97.

76. John Marriot, *International Weapons Developments: A Survey of Current Developments in Weapons Systems* (London: Brassey's Defence Publishers, 1979), 108.

77. Michael Armitage, "Manned and Unmanned Aircraft," in *War in the Third Dimension: Essays in Contemporary Air Power*, ed. by R. A. Mason (London: Brassey's Defence Publishers, 1986), 194–195.

78. "New Military Technologies," 232.

79. David Hobbs, *An Illustrated Guide to Space Warfare* (New York: Salamander Books, 1986), 85–86.

80. George E. Brown, Jr., *Newsletter to Constituents* (March 25, 1988): 1–4.

81. "Military Competition in Space," in *Arms Control and Military Force*, ed. by Christoph Bertram (Westmead, England: Gower & Allanheld, for the International Institute for Strategic Studies, 1980), 245.

82. Kupperman and Taylor, "Special Supplement," 212.

83. Weinberger, *Report of the Secretary of Defense*, 276.

84. Hobbs, *An Illustrated Guide to Space Warfare*, 50.

85. Ibid., 54–57.

86. "Military Competition in Space," 245.

87. Campbell, *Weapons of War*, 216.

88. Walter B. Slocombe, "Strategic Forces," in *American Defense Annual: 1985–1986*, ed. by George E. Hudson and Joseph Kruzel (Lexington, Mass.: Lexington Books, 1985), 84.

89. Alger, *Definitions and Doctrine of the Military Art*, 170.

90. David MacIsaac, "The Evolution of Air Power Since 1945: The American Experience," in *War in the Third Dimension: Essays in Contemporary Air Power*, ed. by R. A. Mason (London: Brassey's Defence Publishers, 1986), 13.

91. Bernard J. Firestone, *The Quest for Nuclear Stability: John F. Kennedy and the Soviet Union* (Westport, Conn.: Greenwood Press, 1982), 48–49.

92. Henry A. Kissinger, *Nuclear Weapons and Foreign Policy* (New York: W. W. Norton, 1969), 131–132, 233.

93. Albert Carnesale, "Special Supplement: The Strategic Defense Initiative," in *American Defense Annual: 1985–1986*, ed. by George E. Hudson and Joseph Kruzel (Lexington, Mass.: Lexington Books, 1985), 187–191.

94. Robert Travis Scott, "Star Wars and the Race in Space," in *The Race for Security: Arms and Arms Control in the Reagan Years*, ed. by Robert Travis Scott (Lexington, Mass.: Lexington Books, 1987), 39.

95. McGeorge Bundy, "The Real Relationship Between Star Wars and

Arms Control," in *The Race for Security: Arms and Arms Control in the Reagan Years,* ed. by Robert Travis Scott (Lexington, Mass.: Lexington Books, 1987), 46.

96. Edward M. Kennedy, "Star Wars vs. the ABM Treaty: Which Path Offers More Security," in *The Race for Security: Arms and Arms Control in the Reagan Years,* ed. by Robert Travis Scott (Lexington, Mass.: Lexington Books, 1987), 58.

97. Alger, *Definitions and Doctrine of the Military Art,* 113, 187.

98. Polmar, *The Ships and Aircraft of the U.S. Fleet,* 52.

99. Ibid., 42.

100. Skinner, *USN: Naval Operations in the Eighties,* 75.

101. Fox Butterfield, "Introduction," in *The Vietnam War: An Almanac,* ed. by John S. Bowman (New York: World Almanac, 1985), 8.

102. Alger, *Definitions and Doctrine of the Military Art,* 167.

6. Nuclear Weapons

1. Donald M. Snow, *National Security: Enduring Problems of U.S. Defense Policy* (New York: St. Martin's, 1987), 179.

2. Jennifer Leaning, "An Ill Wind: Radiation Consequences of Nuclear War," in *The Counterfeit Ark: Crisis Relocation for Nuclear War,* ed. by Jennifer Leaning and Langley Keyes (Cambridge, Mass.: Ballinger, 1984), 198.

3. Hanson W. Baldwin, "The Strategic Need for the Bomb Questioned," in *The Atomic Bomb: The Great Decision,* ed. by Paul R. Baker (New York: Holt, Rinehart and Winston, 1968), 33.

4. Paul R. Baker, *The Atomic Bomb: The Great Decision* (New York: Holt, Rinehart and Winston, 1968), 6.

5. Ibid.

6. Ibid., 7.

7. Henry L. Stimson, "The Decision to Use the Bomb," in *The Atomic Bomb: The Great Decision,* ed. by Paul R. Baker (New York: Holt, Rinehart and Winston, 1968), 21.

8. Baker, *The Atomic Bomb,* 7.

9. Thomas B. Cochran, William M. Arkin, and Milton M. Hoenig, *Nuclear Weapons Databook: Vol. I: U.S. Nuclear Forces and Capabilities* (Cambridge, Mass.: Ballinger, 1984), 100.

10. Snow, *National Security,* 208.

11. Ibid.

12. Charles W. Kegley, Jr., and Eugene R. Wittkopf, *American Foreign Policy: Pattern and Process* (New York: St. Martin's, 1987), 82.

13. Baker, *The Atomic Bomb,* 2.

14. Ibid., 3.

15. Ibid., 3–4.

16. Snow, *National Security,* 183–184.

17. Ibid., 185.

18. James Fallows, *National Defense* (New York: Vintage Books, 1981), 142.

19. David W. Ziegler, *War, Peace, and International Politics* (Boston: Little, Brown, 1987), 229.

20. Seyom Brown, *The Causes and Prevention of War* (New York: St. Martin's, 1987), 93.

21. Cochran, Arkin, and Hoenig, *Nuclear Weapons Databook: Vol. I*, 100.

22. Ibid.

23. William M. Arkin and Richard W. Fieldhouse, *Nuclear Battlefields: Global Links in the Arms Race* (Cambridge, Mass.: Ballinger, 1985), 84.

24. Richard K. Betts, "Elusive Equivalence: The Political and Military Meaning of the Nuclear Balance," in *The Strategic Imperative: New Policies for American Security,* ed. by Samuel P. Huntington (Cambridge, Mass.: Ballinger, 1982), 120.

25. Morton H. Halperin, *Nuclear Fallacy: Dispelling the Myth of Nuclear Strategy* (Cambridge, Mass.: Ballinger, 1987), 49.

26. Ibid., 50.

27. Ibid., 53.

28. Ibid., 57.

29. William W. Jeffries, *Geography and National Power* (Annapolis, Md.: U.S. Naval Institute, 1967), 1.

30. Arkin and Fieldhouse, *Nuclear Battlefields,* 6.

31. Ibid., 7.

32. Ibid., 65.

33. Ibid., 65–66.

34. Ibid., 14.

35. Betts, "Elusive Equivalence," 119.

36. Arthur M. Katz, *Life After Nuclear War: The Economic and Social Impacts of Nuclear Attacks on the United States* (Cambridge, Mass.: Ballinger, 1982), 4.

37. Ibid.

38. International Task Force on Prevention of Nuclear Terrorism, *Report of the International Task Force on Prevention of Nuclear Terrorism* (Washington, D.C.: Nuclear Control Institute, June 25, 1986), 1.

39. Edward J. Markey and Douglas Walker, *Nuclear Peril: The Politics of Proliferation* (Cambridge, Mass.: Ballinger, 1982), 17.

40. Halperin, *Nuclear Fallacy,* 24.

41. Ibid., 25.

42. Cochran, Arkin, and Hoenig, *Nuclear Weapons Databook: Vol. I*, 17.

43. Ibid., 15–16.

44. Ibid., 16.

45. Brown, *The Causes and Prevention of War,* 218.

46. Ibid.

47. Paul Chilton, "Nukespeak: Nuclear Language, Culture, and Propaganda," in *The Nuclear Predicament: A Sourcebook*, ed. by Donna Gregory (New York: St. Martin's, 1986), 128.

48. Ibid.

49. Ibid.

50. Ibid., 128–129.

51. Ibid., 138.

52. Ibid., 135.

53. Thomas B. Cochran, William M. Arkin, Robert S. Norris, and Milton M. Hoenig, *Nuclear Weapons Databook: Vol. II: U.S. Nuclear Warhead Production* (Cambridge, Mass.: Ballinger, 1987), 47.

54. Ibid., 48.

55. Snow, *National Security*, 213.

56. Arkin and Fieldhouse, *Nuclear Battlefields*, 87.

57. Ibid.

58. Ibid.

59. Ibid.

60. Ibid.

61. Ibid., 88.

62. Ibid.

63. Cochran, Arkin, and Hoenig, *Nuclear Weapons Databook: Vol. I*, 5.

64. Gwynne Dyer, *War* (New York: Crown Publishers, 1985), 215.

65. Ibid.

66. Cochran, Arkin, Norris, and Hoenig, *Nuclear Weapons Databook: Vol. II*, 52.

67. Ibid., 54.

68. Ibid.

69. Fallows, *National Defense*, 146–147.

70. Snow, *National Security*, 206–207.

71. Herbert Scoville, Jr., "Assumptions Behind U.S. Strategic Policy," in *Defense Sense: The Search for a Rational Military Policy*, ed. by Ronald V. Dellums (Cambridge, Mass.: Ballinger, 1983), 20–21.

7. Nuclear Strategy

1. James A. Blackwell, Jr., "Conventional Doctrine: Integrating Alliance Forces," in *Conventional Deterrence: Alternatives for European Defense*, ed. by James R. Golden, Asa A. Clark, and Bruce E. Arlinghaus (Lexington, Mass.: Lexington Books, 1984), 141.

2. Ibid., 145.

3. Wallace Earl Walker and Andrew F. Krepinevich, "Domestic Coalitions and Defence Policymaking in the United States," in *Conventional Deterrence: Alternatives for European Defense*, ed. by James R.

Golden, Asa A. Clark, and Bruce E. Arlinghaus (Lexington, Mass.: Lexington Books, l984), 97.

4. James N. Constant, *Fundamentals of Strategic Weapons: Offense and Defense Systems* (The Hague: Martinus Nijhoff, 1981), 200.

5. Ibid., 202

6. Brian Beckett, *Weapons of Tomorrow* (New York: Plenum Press, 1983), 61.

7. John Finnis, Joseph M. Boyle, Jr., and Germain Grisez, *Nuclear Deterrence, Morality and Realism* (Oxford: Clarendon Press, 1987), 38.

8. Desmond Ball, "Counterforce Targeting: How New? How Viable?" in *The Race for Security: Arms and Arms Control in the Reagan Years,* ed. by Robert Travis Scott (Lexington, Mass.: Lexington Books, 1987), 128.

9. Beckett, *Weapons of Tomorrow,* 55.

10. Reginald Bretnor, *Decisive Warfare: A Study in Military Theory* (San Bernardino, Calif.: Borgo Press, 1986), 40–41.

11. George H. Quester, *The Future of Nuclear Deterrence* (Lexington, Mass.: Lexington Books, 1986), 130.

12. Arthur Macy Cox, *Russian Roulette: The Superpower Game* (New York: Times Books, 1982), 103.

13. Beckett, *Weapons of Tomorrow,* 55–56.

14. Quester, *The Future of Nuclear Deterrence,* 108.

15. Finnis, Boyle, and Grisez, *Nuclear Deterrence,* 48.

16. Constant, *Fundamentals of Strategic Weapons,* 108.

17. Lincoln P. Bloomfield, "Nuclear Crisis and Human Frailty," in *Prospects for Peacemaking: A Citizen's Guide to Safer Nuclear Strategy,* ed. by Harlan Cleveland and Lincoln P. Bloomfield (Cambridge, Mass.: MIT Press, 1987), 113, 115.

18. Samuel P. Huntington, "The Renewal of Strategy," in *The Strategic Imperative: New Policies for American Security,* ed. by Samuel P. Huntington (Cambridge, Mass.: Ballinger, 1982), 37.

19. Office of Technology Assessment, *Strategic Defense* (Princeton, N.J.: Princeton University Press, 1986), 67.

20. Samuel P. Huntington, "Conventional Deterrence and Conventional Retaliation in Europe," in *Conventional Forces and American Defense Policy,* ed. by Steven E. Miller (Princeton, N.J.: Princeton University Press, 1986), 254–255.

21. Finnis, Boyle, and Grisez, *Nuclear Deterrence,* 132.

22. Christy Campbell, *Weapons of War* (New York: Peter Bedrick Books, 1983), 271.

23. Constant, *Fundamentals of Strategic Weapons,* 160–161.

24. Ibid., 161.

25. James A. Thompson and Nanette C. Brown, "Theater Forces: U.S. Defense Policy in NATO," in *American Defense Annual: 1985–1986,*

ed. by George E. Hudson and Joseph Kruzel (Lexington, Mass.: Lexington Books, 1985), 102.

26. Ronald L. Tammen, "The Reagan Strategic Program," in *The Race for Security: Arms and Arms Control in the Reagan Years,* ed. by Robert Travis Scott (Lexington, Mass.: Lexington Books, 1987), 22.

27. Les AuCoin, "What Good Is a Freeze? Nailing Shut the 'Window of Vulnerability,'" in *The Race for Security: Arms and Arms Control in the Reagan Years,* ed. by Robert Travis Scott (Lexington, Mass.: Lexington Books, 1987), 272–273.

28. "New Military Technologies," in *Arms Control and Military Force,* ed. by Christoph Bertram (Westmead, England: Gower & Allanheld, for the International Institute for Strategic Studies, 1980), 238–239.

29. Finnis, Boyle, and Grisez, *Nuclear Deterrence,* 49.

30. Lincoln P. Bloomfield, "The Fourth 'C' in C3: Crisis," in *Prospects for Peacemaking: A Citizen's Guide to Safer Nuclear Strategy,* ed. by Harlan Cleveland and Lincoln P. Bloomfield (Cambridge, Mass.: MIT Press, 1987), 114.

31. Cox, *Russian Roulette,* 5.

32. Thompson and Brown, "Theater Forces," 102.

33. Gary Hart, "Arms Control: Toward a Redefinition," in *The Race for Security: Arms and Arms Control in the Reagan Years,* ed. by Robert Travis Scott (Lexington, Mass.: Lexington Books, 1987), 250.

34. Quester, *The Future of Nuclear Deterrence,* 20.

35. Thompson and Brown, "Theater Forces," 102.

36. Albert Gore, Jr., "Midgetman: Our Best Hope for Stability and Arms Control," in *The Race for Security: Arms and Arms Control in the Reagan Years,* ed. by Robert Travis Scott (Lexington, Mass.: Lexington Books, 1987), 147.

37. Quester, *The Future of Nuclear Deterrence,* 76.

38. Harlan K. Ullman and R. James Woolsey, "Seapower and Projection Forces," in *American Defense Annual: 1985–1986,* ed. by George E. Hudson and Joseph Kruzel (Lexington, Mass.: Lexington Books, 1985), 116.

39. *IISS Yearbook 1985–1986* (London: IISS, 1986), back cover copy.

40. Ibid.

41. Jack Plano and Roy Olton, *The International Relations Dictionary* (Santa Barbara, Calif.: ABC-CLIO, 1982), 391.

42. "New Technology and Deterrence," in *Arms Control and Military Force,* ed. by Christoph Bertram (Westmead, England: Gower & Allanheld, for the International Institute for Strategic Studies, 1980), 241.

43. Cox, *Russian Roulette,* 26.

44. Coit D. Blacker, *Reluctant Warriors: The United States, the Soviet Union, and Arms Control* (New York: W. H. Freeman, 1987), 31.

45. Scott, *The Race for Security,* 273.

46. Ibid.

47. Campbell, *Weapons of War*, 158.

48. Plano and Olton, *The International Relations Dictionary*, 214.

49. Robert Perry, "Verifying SALT in the 1980s," in *Arms Control and Military Force*, ed. by Christoph Bertram (Westmead, England: Gower & Allanheld, for the International Institute for Strategic Studies, 1980), 129.

50. Campbell, *Weapons of War*, 31.

51. Caspar W. Weinberger, *Report of the Secretary of Defense* (Washington, D.C.: U.S. Government Printing Office, 1985), 197.

52. Campbell, *Weapons of War*, 51.

53. Ibid.

54. Golden, *Conventional Deterrence*, 39.

55. Campbell, *Weapons of War*, 51.

56. Beckett, *Weapons of Tomorrow*, 61.

57. Constant, *Fundamentals of Strategic Weapons*, 34.

58. Campbell, *Weapons of War*, 63.

59. Quester, *The Future of Nuclear Deterrence*, 73.

60. Constant, *Fundamentals of Strategic Weapons*, 77.

61. Huntington, "The Renewal of Strategy," 37.

62. Leonard Sullivan, Jr., "The Defense Budget," in *American Defense Annual: 1985–1986*, ed. by George E. Hudson and Joseph Kruzel (Lexington, Mass.: Lexington Books, 1985), 79.

63. Constant, *Fundamentals of Strategic Weapons*, 25.

64. Keith A. Dunn, "The Missing Link in Conflict Termination Thought: Strategy," in *Conflict Termination and Military Strategy: Coercion, Persuasion, and War*, ed. by Stephen J. Cimbala and Keith A. Dunn (Boulder, Colo.: Westview Press, 1987), 186.

65. Quester, *The Future of Nuclear Deterrence*, 30.

66. Edward N. Luttwak, "The Operational Level of War," in *Conventional Forces and American Defense Policy*, ed. by Steven E. Miller (Princeton, N.J.: Princeton University Press, 1986), 210.

67. John J. Mearsheimer, "Maneuver, Mobile Defense, and the NATO Central Front," in *Conventional Forces and American Defense Policy*, ed. by Steven E. Miller (Princeton, N.J.: Princeton University Press, 1986), 231.

68. Luttwak, "The Operational Level of War," 230.

69. Bloomfield, "Nuclear Crisis and Human Frailty," 114.

8. Nuclear Proliferation

1. John Woodliffe, "Nuclear Weapons and Non-Proliferation: The Legal Aspects," in *Nuclear Weapons and International Law*, ed. by Istvan Pogany (New York: St. Martin's, 1987), 84–85.

2. Fritz F. Heimann, "How Can We Get the Nuclear Job Done?" in *The*

Nuclear Power Controversy (Englewood Cliffs, N.J.: Prentice-Hall, 1976), 90–92.

3. Daniel Ford, quoting Harold Green, former AEC attorney, in *The Cult of the Atom: The Secret Papers of the Atomic Energy Commission* (New York: Simon & Schuster, 1984), 42.

4. Woodliffe, "Nuclear Weapons and Non-Proliferation," 86.

5. B. Goldschmidt and M. Kratzer, *Peaceful Nuclear Relations: A Study of the Creation and Erosion of Confidence* (New York: Rockefeller Foundation/The Royal Institute of International Affairs, 1978), 9.

6. Ibid., 117–118.

7. Joseph Kruzel, "Arms Control: What's Wrong with the Traditional Approach?" in *Conflict and Arms Control: An Uncertain Agenda*, ed. by Paul R. Viotti (Boulder, Colo.: Westview Press, 1986), 235.

8. Austin Mitchell, *Four Years in the Death of the Labour Party* (London: Methuen, 1983), 120–121.

9. Mark Hertsgaard, *Nuclear, Inc.: The Men and Money Behind Nuclear Energy* (New York: Pantheon Books, 1983), 36–37.

10. Ibid., 38.

11. Werner Kaltefleiter, "Structural Problems in Negotiations: A View from Europe," in *Arms Control: Myth versus Reality*, ed. by Richard F. Staar (Stanford, Calif.: Hoover Institution Press, 1984), 63.

12. Charlene Spretnak and Fritjof Capra, *Green Politics* (Santa Fe, N.M.: Bear & Co., 1986), 17.

13. Ibid., 18.

14. Richard F. Nyrop, ed., *India: A Country Study* (Washington, D.C.: U.S. Government Printing Office, 1985), 517.

15. Ibid., 517–518.

16. Jozef Goldblat, "The Nuclear Non-Proliferation Imperative," in *Arms and Disarmament: SIPRI Findings*, ed. by Marek Thee (Oxford: Oxford University Press, 1986), 336.

17. Jozef Goldblat, *Agreements for Arms Control: A Critical Survey* (London: Taylor & Francis: 1982), 149.

18. Woodliffe, "Nuclear Weapons and Non-Proliferation," 86–87.

19. Jozef Goldblat, "Arms Control Agreements and the Humanitarian Laws of War," in *Arms and Disarmament: SIPRI Findings*, ed. by Marek Thee (Oxford: Oxford University Press, 1986), 303.

20. Benjamin N. Schiff, "The 1985 Non-Proliferation Treaty Review Conference: Positive Steps or Damage Limitation?" in *Conflict and Arms Control: An Uncertain Agenda*, ed. by Paul R. Viotti (Boulder, Colo.: Westview Press, 1986), 84.

21. Goldblat, *Agreements for Arms Control*, 41.

22. Hertsgaard, *Nuclear, Inc.*, 88.

23. Goldblat, *Agreements for Arms Control*, 43.

24. *Facts on File* 41 (June 12, 1981): 385.

25. Hertsgaard, *Nuclear, Inc.*, 227.

26. Istvan Pogany, "Nuclear Weapons and Self-Defence in International Law," in *Nuclear Weapons and International Law*, ed. by Istvan Pogany (New York: St. Martin's, 1987), 67.

27. Jozef Goldblat, "The Third Review of the Non-Proliferation Treaty," in *World Armaments and Disarmament: SIPRI Yearbook 1986* (Oxford: Oxford University Press, 1986), 472.

28. *Facts on File* 46 (November 21, 1986): 877.

29. *Facts on File* 38 (February 4, 1978): 61.

30. *Facts on File* 47 (August 28, 1987): 625.

31. Ibid.

32. *Arms Control and Disarmament Agreements* (New Brunswick, N.J.: Transaction Books, 1984), 65.

33. Goldblat, "Arms Control Agreements and the Humanitarian Laws of War," 312.

34. David Freestone and Scott Davidson, "Nuclear Weapon-Free Zones," in *Nuclear Weapons and International Law*, ed. by Istvan Pogany (New York: St. Martin's, 1987), 208.

35. Gordon C. Bennett, *The New Abolitionists: The Story of Nuclear Free Zones* (Elgin, Ill.: Brethren Press, 1987), 146.

36. Freestone and Davidson, "Nuclear Weapon-Free Zones," 209.

37. Goldblat, *Agreements for Arms Control*, 38–39.

38. Woodliffe, "Nuclear Weapons and Non-Proliferation," 87.

39. *Arms Control and Disarmament Agreements*, 92.

40. Ibid., 93.

41. Goldblat, *Agreements for Arms Control*, 39.

42. Bennett, *The New Abolitionists*, 254–256. Specifically, 119 American governmental agencies had declared themselves NFZs between February 4, 1981, and November 5, 1986, including New York City and Chicago.

43. Sverre Lodgaard, "Nuclear Disengagement in Europe," in *Arms and Disarmament: SIPRI Findings*, ed. by Marek Thee (Oxford: Oxford University Press, 1986), 224.

44. Hertsgaard, *Nuclear, Inc.*, 88.

45. Ibid.

46. Ibid., 89.

47. Nuclear Energy Policy Study Group, *Nuclear Power Issues and Choices* (Cambridge, Mass.: Ballinger, 1977), 392.

48. Schiff, "The 1985 Non-Proliferation Treaty Review Conference," 95.

49. Hertsgaard, *Nuclear, Inc.*, 82–83.

50. K. S. Shrader-Frechette, *Nuclear Power and Public Policy: The Social and Ethical Problems of Fission Technology* (Dordrecht, Netherlands: D. Reidel Publishing Co., 1980), 2.

51. Ford, quoting José Calvo, in *The Cult of the Atom*, 214.

52. Goldblat, *Agreements for Arms Control*, 40.

53. Ibid., 41.

54. Woodliffe, "Nuclear Weapons and Non-Proliferation," 96.

55. *Facts on File* 39 (November 2, 1979): 824.

56. *Facts on File* 40 (February 29, 1980): 141–142.

57. Greg E. Fry, "The South Pacific Nuclear-Free Zone," in *World Armaments and Disarmament: SIPRI Yearbook 1986* (Oxford: Oxford University Press, 1986), 510.

58. Woodliffe, "Nuclear Weapons and Non-Proliferation," 100.

9. Arms Control and Disarmament

1. *Arms Control and Disarmaments Agreements: Texts and Histories of Negotiations* (Washington, D.C.: United States Arms Control and Disarmament Agency, 1982), 22.

2. Ibid., 23.

3. Ibid., 25.

4. Jozef Goldblat, *Agreements for Arms Control: A Critical Survey* (London: Taylor & Francis, 1982), 61.

5. Thomas C. Schelling and Morton H. Halperin, *Strategy and Arms Control* (New York: Twentieth Century Fund, 1961), 171–172.

6. Duncan L. Clarke, *Politics of Arms Control: The Role and Effectiveness of the U.S. Arms Control and Disarmament Agency* (New York: Free Press, 1979), 20.

7. Ibid., 23.

8. Ibid., 190.

9. William Epstein, "The Role of the Public in the Decisionmaking Process for Arms Limitation: Past Impact and Future Requirements," in *Decisionmaking for Arms Limitation: Assessments and Prospects*, ed. by Hans Guenther Brauch and Duncan L. Clarke (Cambridge, Mass.: Ballinger, 1983), 283.

10. Duncan L. Clarke, "Conclusion: Giving Arms Control Greater Salience in Policy Processes," in *Decisionmaking for Arms Limitation: Assessments and Prospects*, ed. by Hans Guenther Brauch and Duncan L. Clarke (Cambridge, Mass.: Ballinger, 1983), 302.

11. *Arms Control and Disarmament Agreements* (New Brunswick, N.J.: Transaction Books, 1984), 125.

12. Goldblat, *Agreements for Arms Control*, 28.

13. Ibid., 29.

14. Ibid., 216.

15. Sverre Lodgaard, "The Building of Confidence and Security at the Negotiations in Stockholm and Vienna," in *World Armaments and Disarmament: SIPRI Yearbook 1986* (Oxford: Oxford University Press, 1986), 423.

16. Richard E. Darilek, "Separate Processes, Converging Interests: MBRF and CBMs," in *Decisionmaking for Arms Limitation: Assessments and Prospects*, ed. by Hans Guenther Brauch and Duncan L. Clarke (Cambridge, Mass.: Ballinger, 1983), 241.

17. James L. George, "Discussion" [a forum], in *Arms Control: Myth versus Reality,* ed. by Richard F. Staar (Stanford, Calif.: Hoover Institution Press, 1984), 45.

18. "Document on Confidence-Building Measures and Certain Aspects of Security and Disarmament, Included in the Final Act of the Conference on Security and Co-operation in Europe" [Preamble], in Goldblat, *Agreements for Arms Control,* 216.

19. Lodgaard, "The Building of Confidence and Security at the Negotiations in Stockholm and Vienna," 435–436.

20. Ibid., 423.

21. Jonathan Alford, "Confidence-Building Measures in Europe: The Military Aspects," in *Arms Control and Military Force,* ed. by Christoph Bertram (Westmead, England: Gower & Allanheld, for the International Institute for Strategic Studies, 1980), 196.

22. *Arms Control and Disarmament Agreements,* 194.

23. Ibid., 14.

24. Jozef Goldblat and Ragnhild Ferm, "Chronology," in *World Armaments and Disarmament: SIPRI Yearbook 1986* (Oxford: Oxford University Press, 1986), 593.

25. *Arms Control and Disarmament Agreements,* 29.

26. Jozef Goldblat, "Arms Control Agreements and the Humanitarian Laws of War," in *Arms and Disarmament: SIPRI Findings,* ed. by Marek Thee (Oxford: Oxford University Press, 1986), 313.

27. Rudy Abramson and John Broder, "Shultz Opens Drive for Arms Pact Approval," in *Los Angeles Times* 107 (January 26, 1988): I, 11.

28. *Arms Control and Disarmament Agreements,* 41.

29. Ibid., 40.

30. Werner Kaltefleiter, "Structural Problems in Negotiations: A View from Europe," in *Arms Control: Myth versus Reality,* ed. by Richard F. Staar (Stanford, Calif.: Hoover Institution Press, 1984), 62.

31. Joseph Kruzel, "Arms Control: What's Wrong with the Traditional Approach?" in *Conflict and Arms Control: An Uncertain Agenda,* ed. by Paul R. Viotti (Boulder, Colo.: Westview Press, 1986), 240.

32. Richard F. Staar, "The MBRF Process and Its Prospects," in *Arms Control: Myth versus Reality,* ed. by Richard F. Staar (Stanford, Calif.: Hoover Institution Press, 1984), 48.

33. Gerald Segal, *The Simon & Schuster Guide to the World Today* (London: Simon & Schuster, 1987), 150.

34. Robert Perry, "Verifying SALT in the 1980s," in *Arms Control and Military Force,* ed. by Christoph Bertram (Westmead, England: Gower & Allanheld, for the International Institute for Strategic Studies, 1980), 125.

35. *Arms Control and Disarmament Agreements,* 111.

36. Ibid., 278.

37. Goldblat, *Agreements for Arms Control,* 18.

38. Ibid., 18–19.

39. *Arms Control and Disarmament Agreements*, 52.

40. William A. Hill, Jr., "Permissible Scope of Military Activity in Outer Space," in *Conflict and Arms Control: An Uncertain Agenda*, ed. by Paul R. Viotti (Boulder, Colo.: Westview Press, 1986), 182.

41. *World Armaments and Disarmament: SIPRI Yearbook 1986* (Oxford: Oxford University Press, 1986), 116.

42. Henry A. Kissinger, "Kissinger Explains the Agreements on Prevention of Nuclear War, 22 June 1973," in *SALT Handbook: Key Documents and Issues, 1972–1979*, ed. by Roger P. Labrie (Washington, D.C.: American Enterprise Institute for Public Policy Research, 1979), 188.

43. *Arms Control and Disarmament Agreements*, 160.

44. Goldblat, *Agreements for Arms Control*, 80.

45. *Facts on File* 46 (October 17, 1986): 761–62.

46. Goldblat, *Agreements for Arms Control*, 59.

47. *Arms Control and Disarmament Agreements*, 142.

48. Robert W. Buchheim and Dan Caldwell, "The U.S.-U.S.S.R. Standing Consultative Commission: Description and Appraisal," in *Conflict and Arms Control: An Uncertain Agenda*, ed. by Paul R. Viotti (Boulder, Colo.: Westview Press, 1986), 137.

49. Ibid., 143.

50. Frank Blackaby, "On the Nature of SIPRI's Peace Research Studies," in *Arms and Disarmament: SIPRI Findings*, ed. by Marek Thee (Oxford: Oxford University Press, 1986), 1.

51. *Arms and Disarmament: SIPRI Findings*, ed. by Marek Thee (Oxford: Oxford University Press, 1986), back cover copy.

52. *SALT Handbook: Key Documents and Issues, 1972–1979*, ed. by Roger P. Labrie (Washington, D.C.: American Enterprise Institute for Public Policy Research, 1979), 17.

53. *Arms Control and Disarmament Agreements*, 143.

54. *SALT Handbook*, 621–653.

55. W. K. H. Panofsky, *Arms Control and SALT II* (Seattle: University of Washington Press, 1979), 50.

56. Edward A. Kolodziej, "Nuclear Weapons in Search of a Role: Evolution of Recent American Strategic Nuclear and Arms Control Policy," in *Conflict and Arms Control: An Uncertain Agenda*, ed. by Paul R. Viotti (Boulder, Colo.: Westview Press, 1986), 16.

57. Goldblat, *Agreements for Arms Control*, 211.

58. Mark B. Schneider, "The Future: Can the Issues Be Resolved?" in *Arms Control: Myth versus Reality*, ed. by Richard F. Staar (Stanford, Calif.: Hoover Institution Press, 1984), 121.

59. L. M. Ross and John R. Redick, "National Arms Control Mechanisms: A Global Survey," in *Decisionmaking for Arms Limitation: Assessments and Prospects*, ed. by Hans Guenther Brauch and Duncan L. Clarke (Cambridge, Mass.: Ballinger, 1983), 208.

INDEX

In this index, a reference in **bold** type indicates the entry number where a particular term is defined within the text. Numbers in roman type refer to entries the reader may wish to consult for further information about a term.

Index

Index

Nuclear superiority, **162**
Nuclear supplier nations, 229
Nuclear Suppliers Group (NSG), 218, **233**
Nuclear technology, **163**, 166, 211, 219, 236
Nuclear terrorism, **164**, 214. *See also* Terrorism
Nuclear testing, 30
Nuclear threat myth, **165**, 178
Nuclear war, 10, **23**, 70, 120, 138, 158, 167, 168, 172, 198, 201, 227, 241, 259
Nuclear warhead, 5, 53, **166**, 169
Nuclear weapons, 23, 24, 41, 56, 65, 74, 84, 117, 120, 133, 144, 148, 149, 153, 156–158, 161, 163, 166, 177, 225
Nuclear Weapon Effects Program, 177
Nuclear weapons industry, 228
Nuclear weapons material, 236, 255. *See also* Fission material
Nuclear winter, 65, **167**, 183, 184, 194, 204–207, 227
Nukespeak, **168**

Oak Ridge, Tennessee, 149
OAS. *See* Organization of American States
OAU. *See* Organization of African Unity
Oceanographic research, 38
Ocean surveillance, 112
Office of Emergency Planning, 44
Office of International Security, 170
Office of Naval Intelligence (ONI) 42
Office of Technical Assessment, 186
Officer Candidate School, 37
Officers Training School (OTS), 35
Offutt Air Force Base, 172
Oil supply, 126, 134
Olney, Richard, 92
Olton, Roy, 200
OMG. *See* Operational Maneuver Group
ONI. *See* Office of Naval Intelligence
On-site inspection, 200, 212, 213, 216, 237, 242, 250, 253, 260, 267. *See also* National Technical Means
"Open Skies" Proposal, **256**, 268
Operational Maneuver Group (OMG), 115, 208
Oppenheimer, J. Robert, 149
Order, The, 206
Organization of African Unity (OAU), **94**, 96
Organization of American States (OAS), **95**, 96, 97
Organization of Eastern Caribbean States, 124

Ortega, Daniel, 80
Osirak reactor, 221
Osnabrück Conference, 101
OTS. *See* Officers Training School
Outer Space Treaty, **257**
Oversight, 182, 211
Overt activities, 86. *See also* Covert activities

Pacific Northwest, 206
Pahlavi, Mohammad Reza, 126
Pakistan, 87, 98, 164, 219, 226, 231, 236
PAL. *See* Permissive Action Links
Palestine, 113
Palestine Liberation Organization (PLO), 31, 85, 114
Palmer, Bruce, Jr., 54
Pan African Congress, 94
Panama, 46, 95
Panofsky, W. K. H., 265
Papua New Guinea, 235
Parity, 5, 154, 162, 178, 252, 265. *See also* Military parity
Parliamentarianism, 103
Partial Test Ban Treaty, 30
Particle beams, 121, 141, 136
Particular international law. *See* International law
Passive policy, 100
Pax Britannica, 92
Pax Romana, 108
Payload, 150, 171
PCIJ. *See* Permanent Court of International Justice
Peace, 1, 3, 13, **24**, 32, 102, 221. *See also* Peace studies; Peaceful coexistence
Peace of Westphalia, 101
Peaceful coexistence, **26**, 73
Peaceful Nuclear Explosions Treaty (PNET), 238, 242, **258**, 264, 267. *See also* Threshold Test Ban Treaty
Peacekeeper missile, 148
Peacekeeping operations, 96, 101, 105, 106, 127
Peace studies, **25**
Pearl Harbor, 39
Penetration, 171, 176, 189
Pentagon, 130, 209
People's Republic of China, 26, 29, 59, 63, 88, 90, 98, 101, 105, 107, 126, 143, 153, 161, 164, 179, 183, 218, 226, 251. *See also* China; Taiwan
Perception theory, **59**
Pérez de Cuéllar, Javier, 102
Permanent Court of International Justice (PCIJ), 104
Permissive Action Links (PAL), 191, 193
Pershing missile, 175

339

San Marino, 104
Sarin. *See* GB (Sarin)
Satellite intelligence, 122, 234, 250
Satellite interceptor program (SAINT), 111, 136
Satellite killer, 136
Satellites, communication, 17
Saturation attack, 130
Saudi Arabia, 85
Savimbi, Jonas, 133
Scandinavia, 160, 228
SCC. *See* Standing Consultative Commission
Scenario, 158, 190, 194. *See also* Nuclear winter; War games
Schelling, Thomas C., 238
Schiff, Benjamin N., 219
Schlesinger, Arthur M., 74
Schweitzer, Albert, 24
Scientific Council, 263
Scoon, Paul, 124
Scope Light, 153
Scott, Robert Travis, 199
Scowcroft, Brent, 70
Scowcroft Commission, 58, 70, 190
SDI. *See* Strategic Defense Initiative
Sea-based ICBM, 173
Sea-based mines, 129
Seabed Arms Control Treaty, 30, 238, **261**
SEAL. *See* Navy SEAL forces
Sea Palm 2000, 110
SEATO *See* Southeast Asia Treaty Organization
Second-echelon forces, 189
Second strike, 154, 171, 172, 204. *See also* Retaliatory strike
Secondary targets, 184
Secretary of Defense, 39, 72, 79, 197
Secretary of State, 79
Secretary of the Army, 37
Secretary of the Navy, 46, 57
Security, 197
Security Council. *See* United Nations, Security Council
Seismometers, 200, 253
Selective Draft Law Cases, 61
Selective Service System, 53, **61**
Semipalatinsk, Soviet Union, 161
Senate. *See* United States Senate
Sensing devices, 112, 135
SENTRY, 166
Seoul Summer Olympics, 137
Sergeant (atom bomb), 168
Sergeant York gun, 72

SHAPE. *See* Supreme Headquarters, Allied Power Europe
Shatt-al-Arab waterway, 126
Shawnee, 125
Ship-to-air missiles, 130
Ship-to-ship missiles, 116, 130
Shock waves, 190
Short-range ballistics missiles, 175
Shrader-Frachette, K. S., 232
Shultz, George, 76, 224, 250
Siberia, Soviet Union, 161
SICBM. *See* Midgetman
Sidewinder missile, 57
Signature, 139
Sikhs, 31
Silk Purse, 154
Silkworm missile, 63
Silo, fixed, 142, 178
Silo-basing, 190
Simulations, 177
Sinai, Egypt, 114
Single Integrated Operations Plan (SIOP), 172
Single shot kill probabilities, 132, 203
Sino-Indian border dispute, 7
Sino-Soviet relations, 26
SIOP. *See* Single Integrated Operational Plan
SIPRI. *See* Stockholm International Peace Research Institute
Situation assessment, 192
Siverson, Randolph M., 2
Six-Day War, 114, 120
SLBM. *See* Submarine-launched Ballistic Missile
SLCM. *See* Tomahawk sea-launched cruise missile
Sleepers, 40
Small war. *See* Limited war
Smart bombs, 127
Snow, Donald M., 16, 36, 51, 56, 61, 144, 148, 150, 171
Soldiers of the sea, 46
Somalia, 95, 96
Somoza, Anastasio, 80
South Africa, 63, 66, 94, 164, 226, 231, 236, 237
nuclear test incident, **234**
Southeast Asia, 89, 142, 246
Southeast Asia Collective Defense Treaty, **98**
Southeast Asia Treaty Organization (SEATO), 87, 96–98, 175
South Korea, 76, 98, 137. *See also* Seoul Summer Olympics